# THE HUMAN SERVICES DELIVERY SYSTEM

# THE HUMAN SERVICES DELIVERY SYSTEM

MENTAL HEALTH · CRIMINAL JUSTICE · SOCIAL WELFARE
EDUCATION · HEALTH SERVICES

## S. RICHARD SAUBER

WITH CONTRIBUTIONS BY

HAROLD J. VETTER
HAROLD H. WEISSMAN
MARIO D. FANTINI
F. DOUGLAS SCUTCHFIELD

COLUMBIA UNIVERSITY PRESS
NEW YORK   1983

Library of Congress Cataloging in Publication Data

Sauber, S. Richard.
The human services delivery system.

Bibliography: p.
Includes index.
1. Social service—United States—Addresses, essays,
lectures.  I. Vetter, Harold J., 1926–
II. Title.
HV91.S27   1983      361'.973      82-23645
ISBN 0-231-04314-7


Columbia University Press
New York   Guildford, Surrey

Copyright © 1983 Columbia University Press
All rights reserved
Printed in the United States of America

*I am pleased to dedicate this book to my parents, Gladys and Henry Sauber, for their continuous support of my education and their encouraging the development of my sensitiveness to the complexity of human needs that has led to my interest concerning the provision of comprehensive human services.*

# CONTENTS

# FOREWORD

The bleak funding picture facing human services has occurred through design, not chance. The priorities of this nation have changed. Decision makers have decided that human services have received their share of the pie and are not going to get much more. The public clearly appears to support this position. The challenge for us will be to meet the increasing demand for services with decreasing resources in an environment of austerity. Theoretically the block grant mechanism will allow states to consolidate services where appropriate, to improve coordination across categorical services (e.g., linking general health to mental health services), and to be more responsive to variations in local need. In each state and local agency, the human services environment is shaped by a variety of unique concerns and forces. Each has a different philosophical approach, political climate, and value system. But each agency and system of service delivery is also facing strikingly similar issues and problems in the management of its human service programs. This is why this book is timely, needed, and an essential statement that in an age of resource scarcity and increasing service demands, the human service professional must remember that there are systems of service delivery other than their own self-serving interests. Complementing systems are trying to reach the same population of people in need and each caregiver must be aware, informed, and respectful of the other human services delivery systems and, when possible, facilitate efforts toward co-ordination, integration, and compromise in order to adapt, survive, and provide a viable service within one's own organization and interdependent system of human services.

During the last decade, there have been many specialized books published in the human services field. Yet, no text was available until now which describes human services from a broad perspective, endorsing a systemic conceptualization of the diverse components in the field while at the same time capturing the specific elements and intricacies involved in each of the complex systems of human services delivery. Dr. Sauber, advocates coordination and integration with the conviction that not one specialist or one discipline or one system alone can accomplish the challenge of providing human services.

Sauber achieves this message in his organization of the book as he sets a model for us to follow in delivering comprehensive, coordinated services. As a human services generalist and mental health specialist, he called upon experts from the other service systems of criminal justice, health, education, and social welfare to collaborate in writing an integrative approach to understanding the vast array of human services. Specialists in these systems present essays to illustrate Dr. Sauber's objective that the student and practitioner of human services today need a conceptual foundation as presented in general systems theory, an understanding of ecology and the level of intervention in reaching distressed individuals and populations-at-risk, a knowledge of each of the systems—mental health, corrections, education, social welfare, and health, and the expertise to coordinate and integrate services within and between these systems. The human services professional also needs to appreciate the impact and benefits of the mutual-help movement as well as the skill requirements of planning, designing, and evaluating to effectively work in and be held accountable for one's endeavors in the demanding field. This book may be considered a handbook in the profession since it offers an introduction in advanced language to attract the serious-minded beginning student and stimulate the specialist who usually lacks a comprehensive recognition of the other systems in which he relates to but often operates independently of.

Sauber suggests how programs can be designed to serve a wide range of clients with different problems and needs. The future of human services is linked to economic and political circumstances. A creative response to community needs will require a recognition of the role of the private sector as well as greater sensitivity to systemic approaches involving coordination between each of the human services delivery subsystems. However coordination is not always a natural tendency, despite the fact that coordinated activities may be more economical and in the community's best interests. Cooperation often means that some of the parties must give up something they have and are familiar with in return for "yet-to-be realized gains" and an uncertain future. The major payoffs of cooperation are increased service availability, accessibility, comprehensiveness and continuity of care, effectiveness, efficiency, and accountability. We are in the midst of rapid social change and inconsistent government mandates and intersystemic human services planning will become increasingly critical, offering a sense of program coherence and direction, an orderly process for setting goals and solving complex difficulties.

The book is directed toward the health, mental health, criminal justice, education, and social welfare professionals who are learning about or caught up in the bureaucratic craziness of the current system and who sense the need for a fundamental understanding of how to relate to the system in which they are a part.

Daniel R. Panitz

# PREFACE

Delivering human services in one help-giving system requires knowledge and understanding of the other systems and how to conceptualize, coordinate, and integrate comprehensive services to people in need. Within a general systems theory framework, five national experts provide insight into each of the five systems according to their specialty and how to relate to the other systems of care. Additional chapters cover the mutual-help approach and methods of coordinating and integrating services within the complexity of the established systems of care-giving, diversity of human needs, and the ever-changing sociopolitical climate of the turbulent environment in which we live.

The primary purpose of this book is to provide human service professionals and students with a theoretical approach and practical guide to a broad understanding and knowledge of each of the five areas of human services: mental health, criminal justice, health, education, social welfare.

During the 1960s, for example, mental health professionals expanded their perspective in activities from the isolated clinic to the more encompassing community mental health program. During the 1970s, mental health professionals were challenged to evolve the scope of their activities even further by designing integrated human services systems which are organized to provide *comprehensive* and *coordinated* assistance to clients. Features of comprehensiveness and coordination include: decentralization of services into areas of high need, concerting of resources from different programs, comprehensiveness of services, co-location of service components, and operational integration of services in proper sequence thereby eliminating present duplication and wasted time for clients and employees. Many states have already combined several services and many other states are seriously considering similar reorganizations. At the federal level, "service integration" legislation has been developed at HEW which has encouraged states and localities to unify the various programs and resources available to provide human services.

Although the population is defined differently by each human service system, the people—patients, students, clients, or criminals are one and the same whether they be labeled "sick" or "healthy" in the health system, "stupid" or "intelligent" in education, "indigent" or "middle class" in the social welfare field, "crazy" or "normal" in mental health, or "bad" or "good" in the criminal justice system. For instance, no matter what discipline, profession, or field the student or practitioner represents, the book is written to provide new information about related disciplines, professions, and fields that a human service worker is bound to be confronted in every day practice. The school social worker has to relate to the child's teacher for poor grades, his family welfare assistant for having insufficient clothing and money for school, his pediatrician for continual absenteeism due to recurring illness, his siblings for getting caught with drugs and having to go to juvenile court, his mother's psychotherapist for depression, and his father's alcoholism counselor. This appellation reflects the increasing recognition of the commonalities in problems as well as in services. A trend toward comprehensiveness and coordination of many of the services traditionally supplied by separate disciplines or agencies can be observed. Examples of comprehensiveness include such organizations as community mental health centers, multiservice centers, neighborhood health centers, youth opportunity centers, neighborhood health agencies, and health maintenance organizations.

The human service ideology is characterized by five general themes:

*Integration of Services.* Genuinely effective, comprehensive services can be provided only through the forging of systemic linkages which bring together the various caregiving agencies needed to provide a complex array of resources, technologies, and skills. Public health, mental health, and social welfare programs should be unified into an effective system of human services.

*Comprehensiveness and accessibility.* Effective community action for troubled individuals requires continuity of concern for the person in his involvements with society, regardless of awkward jurisdictional boundaries of agencies, institutions, and professions. Programs must be designed to reach the people who are hardly touched by our best current efforts, for it is actually those who present the major problems of mental health in America.

*Client troubles defined as problems in living.* Rather than attaching a diagnostic label, it is more useful to examine an individual's problems in living in order to be helpful to him. Instead of focusing on individual deficiencies, the deficiencies of social systems should be our principal target and the fit between a person and his environment.

*Generic characteristics of helping activities.* Responsibility in a comprehensive community service agency should depend upon competence in the jobs to be done. Distinctions between the client problems germane to a psychiatric service and an alcoholism clinic are largely artificial, and the quality that exists in the helping actions of care givers transcends disciplinary and professional barriers.

*Accountability of service providers to clients.* The provider of services has a responsibility of being accountable to the users of services. In order for an organization providing helping services to become an effective agency in the community, community control of agency policy is essential.

Local initiative toward the human service "network" and "comprehensive" program models in particular come about (in part) through a reaction to the inefficiency, compartmentalization, specialization, bureaucracy, program barriers, and service gaps which an increasing number of professionals, consumers, and citizens assert characterize the deficiencies of traditional patterns of organizing community resources and the shrinking human service dollar.

S. R. S.

**THE HUMAN SERVICES DELIVERY SYSTEM**

# INTRODUCTION TO HUMAN SERVICES

Human welfare today represents a central focus of society's concern. The human services "industry" has assumed a major role in addressing that concern and in utilizing the resources allocated to it.

The provision of human services has evolved into a great social undertaking. Measured by any of the usual economic yardsticks, human services might justifiably be considered a major industry. In the aggregate, expenditures for human services involve billions of dollars; consumers and providers number in the millions as these services seek to help troubled persons.

Human services, as defined in this book, encompass a variety of fields: mental health, social welfare, health, education, and criminal justice. For example, the national needs for education are to assist state and local governments in providing equal elementary and secondary educational opportunities for students of special concern to the federal government, particularly the disadvantaged, the handicapped, and those desiring higher education. Budget authority increases are proposed for the education of the Indian, education of the handicapped, bilingual education, and Head Start programs. The 1980 budget for higher education includes $2.4 billion in budget authority for the basic educational opportunity grant program, plus supplemental opportunity grants, state student incentive grants, and part-time jobs for students under the college work–study program (see figure 1.1).

The budget also emphasizes improved access to medical care and mental health services, expanded efforts to promote health and prevent illness, and continued attempts to reduce inflation in health care costs. Since 1965 federal outlays for health have risen at an annual rate of about 19 percent. Outlays for Medicare, whose beneficiaries are either aged or disabled, were approximately $29.1 billion in 1979 and $32.1 billion in 1980. Outlays for Medicaid, whose beneficiaries are low-income adults and children, were $11.8 billion in 1979 and $12.5 billion in 1980. The federal government funds more than 30 programs that support provision of health care directly or through grants and contracts such as maternal and child health, family planning, health maintenance organizations, public health service hospitals, emergency medical services, and alcohol and drug abuse services.

Increased support for health promotion activities in 1980 underscores a growing recognition that future improvements in health are more likely to

**Figure 1.1**
OUTLAYS FOR EDUCATION

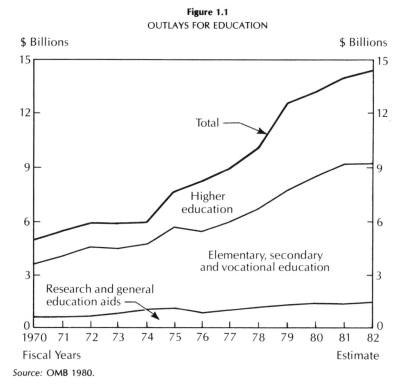

Source: OMB 1980.

**Figure 1.2**
OUTLAYS FOR HEALTH

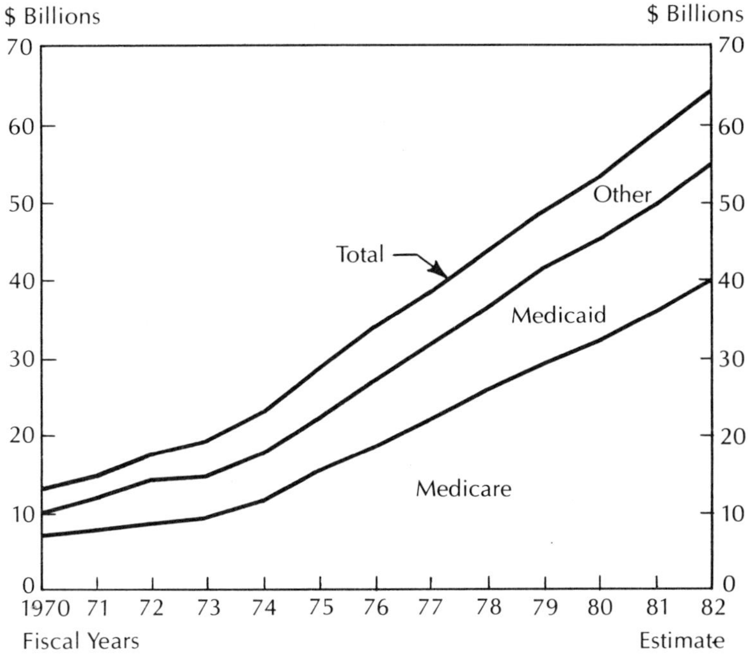

$ Billions                                    $ Billions

Fiscal Years                                  Estimate

*Source:* OMB 1980.

result from changes in individual life-styles than from an expansion of traditional medical services. New initiatives include expanded efforts in disease
prevention, in health information and promotion, and in health education. A
new prevention initiative for community water fluoridation is proposed in
this budget as well as new activities for the "antismoking" program and
alcohol abuse program with special emphasis on high-risk individuals (see
figure 1.2).

National needs for justice include the representation of the public in legal
matters, the provision of fair and prompt prosecution and trial procedures,
the maintenance of public order and enforcement of federal statutes, the
provision of detention and correctional facilities for those charged with or
convicted of violating federal laws, and provision of assistance to state and
local criminal justice systems. To serve these needs, the federal government
supports programs in four major areas: federal law enforcement, federal lit-
igative and judicial activities, correction, and criminal justice assistance.

Estimated outlays for these programs are \$4.4 billion in 1979 and in 1980 (see figure 1.3).

How has the human services industry grown to such mammoth proportions? Principally, as society has confirmed its approval of collective (as opposed to individual) solutions for an ever-increasing range of human problems. Otherwise expressed, existing human services have been made available on a universal basis to an increasing degree (Erikson 1977:60).

Society has traditionally established discrete programs to meet discrete needs. As an increasing number of needs have come to be recognized, and as those needs have been recognized to an increasing extent, the number of programs has grown proportionately. Each program, with its particular special interest or technology, has selected its clientele according to criteria such as geographic place of residence, economic ability, and attractiveness of the focal problem. The more narrowly a caregiving agency defined its services and clientele, the more specialized became the staffing pattern it utilized. A great number of publicly and voluntarily supported caregivers emerged as providers of expert help; by the early 1970s most communities were liberally dotted with health and social welfare service agencies. In urban areas it has become common to find human services offices or agencies in the ratio of 1 to 1,000 persons. The organizations, with few exceptions, have been sponsored and financed by varying combinations of federal, state, and local governments and by private associations.

## PRESENT STATUS AND PROBLEMS

The human service industry has thus grown as a result of a proliferation of agencies empowered to bring collective solutions to an increasing number of human problems. With increased allocations of resources for this purpose, a question has inevitably arisen: How well does the human service industry succeed in its mission? Recent evaluations have shown what many people have recognized for some time: that a large and growing gap lies between what we expect from government-supported human service systems and what these systems in fact deliver. This gap—better known as the "human services shortfall" (e.g. *Evaluation 2,* 1974—results from the fact that the federal government has undertaken far more programs than can possibly be financed adequately from available tax revenues.

As one example, Department of Health, Education, and Welfare estimates indicate what it would cost if the federal government were to provide the services of deaf–blind centers, specific learning disabilities projects, handi-

**Figure 1.3**
OUTLAYS FOR ADMINISTRATION OF JUSTICE

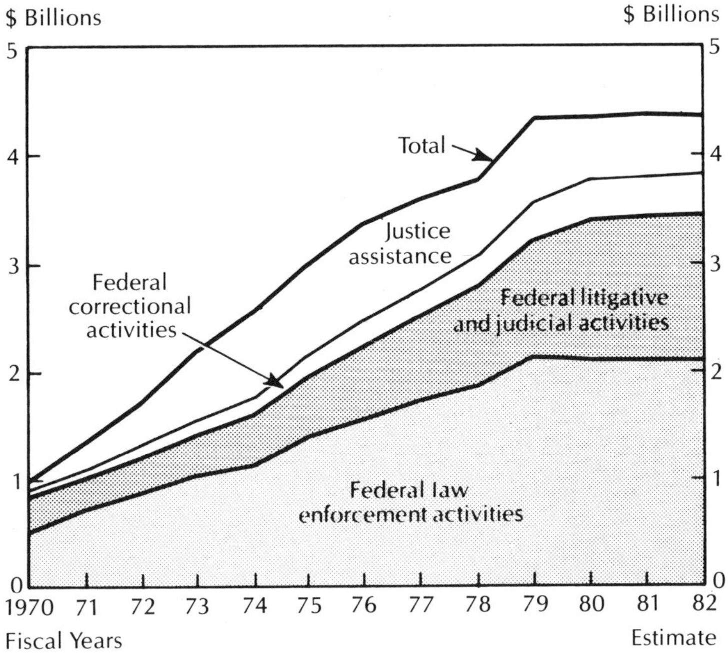

Source: OMB 1980.

capped early childhood projects, follow-through parent–child centers, and dropout prevention projects—now available on a limited demonstration basis—to all those needing them. According to these estimates, additional expenditures of about $10.5 billion and additional manpower of 2.8 million trained people would be required. In addition, the delivery on a national level of services now provided for bilingual education, nutrition projects for the elderly, health services delivery for the poor, and community mental health centers (CMHCs) would cost an additional $17.1 billion above what is currently being spent. In order to extend services to all of those eligible, DHEW programs could cost well over $200 billion more than is currently being spent on them; nearly 15 million more trained people would be needed.

A recent report of the President's Commission on Mental Health noted that CMHCs provide 30 percent of all instances of care for mentally impaired persons. The centers receive only 5 percent of the available funds (Long 1978:47). President Carter's introduction of a mental health bill in 1979 represents a first attempt to increase the number and scope of CMHCs since they were introduced by President Kennedy nearly two decades ago (1979:327). However, Reagan repealed it in 1981.

Serious as the situation has been, it is becoming even more serious. Angry citizens, eligible by law for services but unable to receive them because they are not available, have been taking their cases to court—and winning. Citizens have also won court judgments indicating that available services are of insufficient quality and therefore inequitable.

Why has this situation developed? According to a recent Brookings Institute study, federal intervention in supporting human services reflects the fact that, at least historically, concerns with alleviating poverty and its associated ills have been felt more strongly at the national level. States have not been uniform in the attention they have paid to these problems and the resources they have devoted to alleviating them. Consequently, federal grants have been necessary to improve the quantity and quality of these services and to equalize their distribution. Even with significant federal support and block grants to states, gaps and inequities are large and apparently still growing.

Alternative methods of dealing with this situation could be cited. Taxes could be raised nationally to provide full coverage for the various programs. Resources could be transferred to the states through such means as revenue sharing; the states could then make their own decisions regarding types and levels of services. The federal role could be limited to demonstration programs to show the efficacy of various types of services; afterward the states would be encouraged to find the resources to develop the service systems if they so desired. "New Deal" expectations about the role of the federal government in supporting human services could be dampened, thereby quelling the notion that government has the resources or the capability to solve complex human and social problems. Or, the government could continue to "muddle through," doing the best job possible, chipping away at the problems and hoping for the best.

These five alternatives are not necessarily mutually exclusive or exhaustive. National debate on these options indicates that none of them, as a solo strategy, seems to offer a solution satisfactory to many people.

Two recent developments in the field of human services have encouraged the use of new nonservice approaches to address human services. First, growing demands and sharply constrained budgets have prompted local governments to search for alternatives to traditional publicly financed service delivery. Second, many local governments have recognized that the direct provision of service in itself is often an inadequate or inappropriate response to basic human problems. Consequently, public officials and people outside of government are experimenting with approaches that use existing local governance powers in new ways.

Nonservice approaches include a wide variety of interventions: government regulation or deregulation, tax policy changes, administrative reform, involvement of the private sector, promotion of self-help, and public advocacy (see table 1.1). These approaches are distinguished from traditional direct service approaches by their emphasis on the power of local government to "govern" rather than simply to "spend" (Gollub, Henton, and Waldhorn 1980).

The new federal law (P.L. 97-35) effective October 1981 is an example of the impact of the Reagan administration upon human services. The major changes of the law affect welfare, food stamps, Medicaid, Medicare, public housing, public service jobs, and block grants.

First, welfare estimates indicated that 687,000 of the 3.9 million families receiving public assistance would be removed from the rolls or have their benefits reduced. Congress tightened eligibility for Aid to Families with Dependent Children, the basic public assistance program. The new law restricts eligibility to families with gross incomes at or below 150 percent of a state's "standard of need." Currently there is no gross income limit. (The standard of need is set by each state and is supposed to reflect the minimum income necessary for subsistence.) The new law also prescribes a "retrospective" system of accounting, which means that benefits must be computed on the basis of actual income in the previous month.

Second, food stamp administrators estimated that 875,000 of the 22.6 million food stamp recipients would be forced out of the program, mainly due to a provision of the new law stating that families whose gross income is more than 130 percent of the poverty level will become ineligible for food stamps. The new income limit for a family of four is about $11,000 a year. In the past, some families with incomes as high as $14,000 were eligible. Most other food stamp recipients will have their benefits reduced below what they would have received under the old law.

Third, Congress ordered a reduction in federal Medicaid payments to the states by 3 percent in the fiscal year 1982, 4 percent the next year, and 4.5 percent the following year. A state may partly offset its reduction if it has a formal program for reviewing hospital costs, experiences unemployment more than 1.5 times the national rate, or recovers substantial amounts of money misspent through fraud and abuse.

**TABLE 1.1.**

NONSERVICE APPROACHES TO SOCIAL WELFARE PROBLEMS

| Policy Approach | Consequences | |
|---|---|---|
| | *Intended* | *Unintended* |
| **Regulation and Deregulation** | | |
| Enforcement of federal building requirements to provide access for the handicapped | Remove access barriers to disabled and aged, thus increasing capacity for independent living | Can increase costs to both public and private sectors by requiring additional or retroactive enforcement of codes; may serve as a disincentive for construction |
| Ordinance requiring that private forms provide specific services to employees, such as day care, alcoholism and family crisis counseling, and transportation | Reduce government responsibility in providing special services; increase private sector role in meeting community needs; increase worker productivity | May increase cost of doing business, possibly driving firms to move out of city if services do not increase worker productivity |
| **Taxation** | | |
| State and local income property tax deductions for provision of child care facilities for working parents, or training and employment for a target group | Increase number of companies willing to provide child care, hire and train youth, disabled disadvantaged, etc., thus reducing alternative welfare costs | Deductions are not related to quality or quantity of child care; may be a windfall to employer who would have hired workers anyway |
| Deductions from state and local taxes for provision of long-term care to disabled family member | To reduce incentives to institutionalize disabled family member | Not related to quality of care provided; vulnerable to abuse; may provide disincentive for traditional care roles |
| **Administrative Reform** | | |
| Nontraditional locations for social welfare services, including sites like shoping centers, libraries, and schools; locating prosecuting attorney's office in neighborhood | Increase access, utilization, and effectiveness of services, like counseling, education, and legal services through better visibility and acceptability to user | Low service use through possible incompatibility with site; possible conflicts at site; increased need for security; reduced business because of image issue |

| Development of new work and volunteer roles in the public sector for special need groups, e.g., youths, elderly, disabled | Provide work opportunities; strengthen peer-help roles using youth to staff services for youth as paraprofessionals; using aged as analogous peer-counselor and paraprofessional roles (homemaker aides); new government apprentice roles for youth | Inexperience or heavy work load may detract from the quality of service or might interfere with the conduct of other professional activities; may displace existing workers |

## Collaboration with the Private Sector

| Private-sector provision of occupational training for target groups in school system or under their auspices at work site; provision of new forms of apprenticeships for youth by firms and unions | Improve job skills of disadvantaged, disabled, and youth; reduce consumption of welfare services and transfer payments | Private-sector training may be inappropriate to meet public need or too limited to help address basic issues of economic development or basic education |
| Use of private business groups or trade associations to aid public sector through in-kind or loaned manpower to help improve management of government | Offer private-sector expertise and resources (computers, facilities) to public to increase cost-effectiveness and increase needed resources not otherwise available | Private sector may not understand public sector problems or be willing to respond |

## Promotion of Self-Help

| Strengthening personal networks, mutual aid roles, and neighborhood supports:<br>—Facilitating friendly visiting among at-risk groups<br>—Supporting telephone check-up and information networks<br>—Coordinating food buying clubs<br>—Assistance in housing design for the disabled<br>—Roommate referral and shared housing brokerage<br>—Coordinated family-neighborhood childcare<br>—Organizing tenant inspection of housing<br>—Neighborhood crime watch and grievance board | Helping individuals and groups of neighborhood residents to meet needs that are either too extensive for government to meet within cost constraints, or are areas where individuals and groups can act as well or better than government, providing linkages, such as transportation, or use of telephones to promote contact between at-risk and isolated elderly and disabled; providing use of public space and technical assistance to aid cooperative ventures to increase food buying power, reduction of crime, identification of housing resources, and development of local day care | Not often reported. In many cases expectations of level or quality of performance are lower or more adjusted to the realities of the setting, e.g., to the willingness of local participants to act, share, or support activities such as cooperative food buying, house sharing, neighborhood watching, day care and work exchanging |

**TABLE 1.1.** (continued)

NONSERVICE APPROACHES TO SOCIAL WELFARE PROBLEMS

| | Consequences | |
| --- | --- | --- |
| Policy Approach | Intended | Unintended |
| **Promotion of Self-Help** | | |
| —Mutual work exchange | | |
| —Emergency support by volunteer care provider | | |
| **Public Advocacy** | | |
| General advocacy and follow-up by staff of various social welfare services used by clients | Increase appropriate access and utilization of social welfare services by clients | May increase use of services beyond level of local capacity to serve in some cases, or increase use of unneeded resources |
| Consumer advocacy, education, and investigation of complaints on issues such as credit, contracts, and service quality | Protect the economic and personal rights of citizens from fraud and abuse; encourage responsiveness of private sector to consumers | Increase levels of litigation. |

Source: SRI International 1980.

Congress, at the request of the administration, gave states greater flexibility in the operation of their programs, encouraging them to economize wherever possible. States, for example, no longer have to pay all the "reasonable costs" of hospitals treating Medicaid patients, but may choose methods of reimbursement resembling fixed-cost contracts. States could also direct Medicaid patients to use certain hospitals and physicians if, as expected, the federal government waives the traditional requirement for "freedom of choice." Federal officials expected states to take advantage of provisions in the new law permitting them to cut back coverage and services for the "medically needy." Approximately twenty-nine states extend Medicaid benefits to people who do not receive welfare but are deemed to be medically needy.

Fourth, with respect to Medicare, Congress made several changes that will require elderly and disabled people to pay more for medical care. Other changes limit reimbursement of hospitals. Starting in January of 1983, Medicare patients will have to pay the first $260 of their hospital bills. Under the old law, they would have had to pay $232. The annual deductible for a physician's services will rise by $15, to $75.

Fifth, federal officials said that rents for all 2.4 million families living in subsidized or public housing would rise. These families, whose incomes average less than $5,400 a year, are now charged a maximum of 25 percent of their adjusted income for rent. The new law raises the limit to 30 percent over the next five years; the increase is being made in increments of one percentage point a year. Congress also reduced the number of additional subsidized housing units being made available to low-income families. President Carter had proposed financing to provide 255,000 additional units in fiscal 1982. Congress provided funds for 153,000 additional units, or 22,000 fewer than President Reagan had requested. The supply of low-rent housing has dwindled in recent years because of inflation, condominium conversions, and abandonment of older units.

Sixth, the maximum duration of unemployment insurance benefits is being reduced from thirty-nine to twenty-six weeks in most of the country. Labor Department actuaries said that as many as 640,000 workers would lose some benefits that they would have received had the law not been changed.

Seventh, the Reagan administration is eliminating public service jobs subsidized under the Comprehensive Employment and Training Act. Funds ran out on September 30, 1982. There were 30,000 peole in the program in March of 1982, when the administration announced plans to end it. The

Labor Department has set aside $245 million to provide unemployment insurance benefits to those who cannot find other work. Many of the employees thrown out of work lack skills, education, and job experience.

Eighth, Congress consolidated fifty-six special-purpose programs into nine block grants. Total financing authorizations for the various programs were reduced 20 to 25 percent, but federal regulations and reporting requirements were also reduced. States were given wide latitude in how to spend the federal money, so some programs will be cut back more than others, and some may actually have their allotments increased.

State officials expressed most concern about the future of social services financed under Title XX of the Social Security Act. These include day care services, services for the elderly and disabled, and child protective services designed to halt child abuse and neglect. There is no longer a requirement that funds be used for welfare recipients or families with incomes below 115 percent of the state median.

The other block grants cover preventive health services, maternal and child health, treatment of alcohol and drug abuse, community health centers, programs to help low-income families pay energy costs, community development programs, antipoverty programs, and education.

## THE COMMUNITY

The human services delivery system operates at all levels—local, regional, state, and federal—but the emphasis of this book is upon the delivery of human services in the local community environment. But what is a "community," and how does one define and operationalize the concept of "community" in order to begin to plan and develop human services? In his book *Future Shock* (1970), Toffler aptly describes the great complexities of our urban technological society. These complexities seriously complicate the problem of both identifying and defining communities. The urban dweller, for instance, is typically dependent on many different social groups for the fulfillment of his daily needs. He may depend on one community for his financial income, another for his recreation, and a third for his residence.

A "good" community is often thought of as one that provides an environment that permits, makes possible, and encourages individual growth to full maturity. This community utilizes its citizenry for social betterment, and its residents set up standards to be achieved, select leaders to give direction, and initiate community action to discuss plans, collaborate, cooperate, and participate in its decision making. A "good" community is also one that provides human services to those who need them. The community thus functions as a context for the delivery of human services. The interaction between a service program and its clients represents the essence of human services delivery. The interaction between a service program and its clients represents the essence of human services delivery. The two major sectors of the system, one representing the service program, the other representing the client or client population, are linked together through services that are provided by the program in response to demand generated by the client (see figure 1.4).

**Figure 1.4**
THE CLIENT AND THE PROGRAM: THE ESSENCE OF HUMAN SERVICES SYSTEM

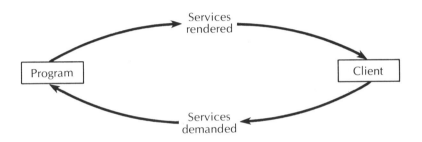

The need for service is itself dependent on the client's level and standard of functioning. When the level of functioning is low, the client's need for service tends to increase. However, this increase in need does not necessarily result in a visible demand for service. Demand for service increases only when the client's level of functioning is significantly at variance with his standard of functioning, that is, the level at which the client feels he should be functioning (see figure 1.5). This standard reflects not only the expectations of the individual client but also those of his family, friends, and others in his immediate social environment. The client's demand for service at any moment is based on the difference between his actual level of performance functioning or behavior and his standard of functioning or expectations others have of him (Levin and Roberts 1976).

Thus, a community is really a society in which the ideal life—level of functioning—of all members is promoted as efficiently and effectively as possible by means of human services as well as other resources. In this way

**Figure 1.5**
THE NEED FOR SERVICE AND THE CLIENT'S LEVEL AND STANDARD OF FUNCTIONING

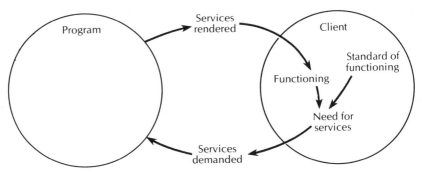

*Source:* Levin and Roberts, 1976.

of life a community is not merely houses, stores, and streets, but a group of people who share feelings of security, pride, self-respect, and hope.

The dimensions of community life are multifaceted and include the personal, spiritual, cultural, political, vocational, industrial, educational, and social. Social planning involves the provision of suitable ways to allocate and to marshall resources—territorial, fiscal, and human—within the community so that individual and group needs and aspirations for a high quality of life will be realized. Community structure attempts to provide possibilities for personal development; the certainty of a reliable environment with safety and a sense of security, free from anxiety and menace for its members; a support system making accessible formal agencies and institutions as well as an informal network of friends, family members, acquaintances, neighbors, and work associates; a method by which residents can participate effectively in community decisions while facilitating understanding across barriers of race, culture, age, and class; and an approach toward enhancing community life that affects its membership with feelings of significance ("others value me") and contributes to the individual's increased sense of self-esteem and social worth. Citizens also enjoy unlimited opportunities to extend the range of their experiences through cooperative community efforts directed toward broad objectives such as a better life.

Every community has its problems, be it inadequate housing, crime in the streets, drugs in the school, or high rates of unemployment. The efforts of citizens must be planned toward correcting these shortcomings through redevelopment, industrial expansion, rising standards of living, manpower training, racial harmony, and improved delivery of human services. Services may be directed at an individual level and aimed toward the generalized goal of improved "self-esteem" or, in contrast, may take an intervention approach at the collective or system level.

Community variables may affect the operation of human services delivery and therefore should be taken into account in the planning phase. Some variables to be considered include the settlement pattern, competition for space, and establishment of boundaries (Saunders 1958). *Settlement pattern* subsumes location, size, shape, surface features, climate, and natural resources—in short, physical environment. *Competition for space* refers to land use and to the ecological processes of concentration, centralization, segregation, and invasion. *Boundaries* involve such variables as degrees of isolation and the rural–urban continuum. These physical variables can be taken into account, for example, in considering the constraints of climate on client transportation, the concentration of types of clients and resources in particular neighborhoods, and degrees of isolation from resources in neighboring cities or the state.

In addition to these primarily physical variables the following social variables should be considered: the degree to which only special interest groups are served, for example, mothers of retarded children; the degree of prejudice in community representation; the basis for identification, for example, by shared attitudes, life-styles, beliefs, or economic and political similarities; feelings of belongingness, or ingroup–outgroup sentiment; degrees of elitism among human service personnel in serving clients; and the system of interaction (Regester 1974).

The social variables appear to be more directly related to the everyday delivery of human services. Human services in turn, are affected by a number of factors, including characteristics of the target population, characteristics of institutional personnel, awareness of community needs among staff, effects of services on the population, and variables roles of citizens, consumers, and professional staff in delivery of services. Similarity of characteristics in staff and target population, as an example, might make it more difficult for staff to develop elitist sentiments or to serve only special interest groups. Similarly, the variable roles of people in the community will affect not only interactions within the community but interactions between the community and the outside environment. If, for instance, families in a community take an active role in providing care for the mentally impaired, it is less likely that institutional arrangements within or outside the community will be made. Thus transactions have been classified as personal, caregiver, professional, and out-of-community (Adler 1972).

Planning for human services must take into account all physical and social arrangements that significantly affect the physical safety, personal security, problem-solving capabilities, and social significance of the residents of the community. Planning must also be accountable to the process by which the resources of an organizational system are adapted to the changing internal and environmental forces.

Two complementary, but not mutually exclusive, kinds of strategic planning approaches may be applied to the conduct of a community analysis: the intraorganizational approach (the inside-out method) and the extraorganizational approach (the outside-in method). The intraorganizational approach is exemplified, for example, when program directors of a community mental health center first assess their staff desires and abilities, distribution of resources, and the patient population and only then survey the community for opportunities to utilize the center's special strength, to satisfy its particular needs, and to achieve its organizational goals. The development of community-based psychiatric after-care services resulting from the need to discharge hospitalized patients serves as an illustration of this method.

The extraorganizational approach, by contrast, begins with a survey, forecast, and analysis of the external environment, focusing on immediate, intermediate, and future conditions. Such action is followed by an examination of the organization's resources to see how it can serve the population and adapt to external environmental demands. In problem solving, setting priorities and allocating resources becomes a matter of determining a starting point. The intraorganizational and extraorganizational methods constitute foci for such a starting point in an open-systems approach. One may proceed from either focus or from both. Nonetheless, the viewpoints of the people and facilities of the organization itself and the viewpoint of particular components of the environment must always be taken into consideration in any community analysis (Sauber 1977).

## THE CONCEPT OF HUMAN SERVICES

The term "human services" has proved confusing because it allows for multiple meanings and interpretations. For purposes of operational clarity, usefulness, and ideological congruence, though, human services can be defined as including service delivery systems for mental health, social welfare, health, education, and criminal justice (see figure 1.6). Other overlapping

**Figure 1.6**
HUMAN SERVICES SUBSYSTEMS

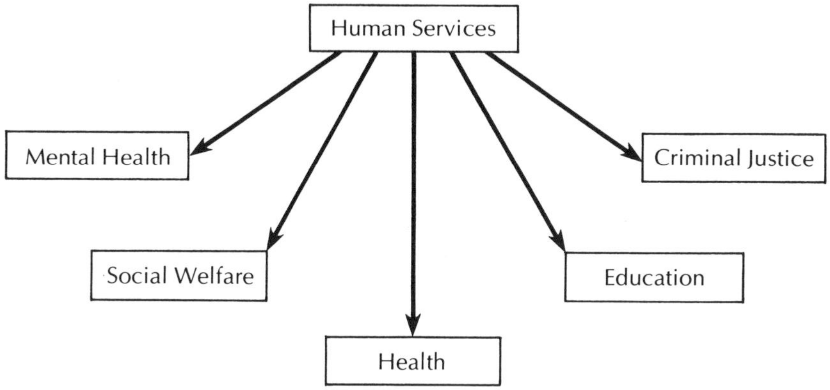

```
                    ┌──────────────────┐
                    │  Human Services  │
                    └──────────────────┘
       ┌──────────────┐              ┌──────────────────┐
       │ Mental Health│              │ Criminal Justice │
       └──────────────┘              └──────────────────┘

    ┌────────────────┐                 ┌─────────────┐
    │ Social Welfare │                 │  Education   │
    └────────────────┘                 └─────────────┘

              ┌──────────┐
              │  Health  │
              └──────────┘
```

service areas frequently are classified under the human services rubric. These include family planning, recreation, parole and probation, advocacy and legal services, industrial relations, protective and foster care services for children and the aged, employment counseling, vocational rehabilitation, youth services, and education programs for formal training, alternative learning schools, and continuing education.

Rossi (1978) has defined human services simply as those services that depend on direct interpersonal contact between deliverer and client. Although some services involve interpersonal contact in the rendering of a service—for example, in sales—it is in the contact itself that the service inheres.

Human service may be qualified still further. Harshbarger has described human services in terms of basic systemic properties:

> Human service organizations are dependent upon public resources, relatively structured, normatively based and morally involving, social or socio-technical service oriented, and aimed at clients, residents, or members as primary beneficiaries and staff members as secondary beneficiaries. Organizationally, the nature of their efforts is to deal with those bio-social problems that arise from the vagaries and complexities of being human. (1974a:25)

Service recipients are defined and labeled differently according to the kinds of behaviors they exhibit. They are labeled a "problem" by significant segments of the community, including certain societal groups, caregivers in the public and private sectors, and the service recipients themselves—largely through indoctrination. The diagnostic, or labeling, process is a function of the person or group making the determining judgment, of the particular method by which such a judgment is reached, and of the situation and context within which such a determination is made. Ignoring the complex and variable character of the human services identification process tends to limit the understanding of such behavior, the etiology, and the helping process and also the design of service delivery systems to assist the individual in need.

Service users may be perceived as patients, students, clients, deviants, or law violators. A given client or problem may be addressed by more than one system. Nevertheless, each individual within the identified population experiences or suffers from very similar and basic problems in everyday living (whether they are labeled as "sick" or "healthy" in the health system, "crazy" or "normal" in the mental health area, "stupid" or "intelligent" in education, "indigent" or "middle-class" in the social welfare field, or "good" or "bad" in the criminal justice system). An adolescent who has a drinking problem, for example, is likely to come to the attention of the traffic court for driving while intoxicated; to the school counselor for truancy and inability to concentrate; to his family physician for disturbed sugar metabolism with symptoms of dizziness, weakness, and blackouts; to the welfare worker for episodes of fighting and abuse at home; and to the mental health center for alcoholism. Such an example is an indication of increasingly recognized commonalities in problems as well as in professional services. This point is illustrated more specifically in table 1.2 which shows various levels of preventive intervention in each of the human services delivery fields.

Unfortunately, the awareness of overlap in client problems and services is frequently manifested by caregivers as competition, distrust, prejudice, and professional chauvinism; boundary maintenance and domain protection are the result, rather than the collaboration and cooperation so desperately needed.

The boundaries of the systems of mental health and other human services have, over time, undergone alteration under the influence of a number of factors. These include historical events, the fluctuating power of vested interests, value changes in the larger society, changing public perceptions of the appropriate role of government, technological developments in the production and distribution of services, newly emerging professional ideologies, economic growth or deficit in available resources, and myriad other unplanned social and political forces. Periodically, all of these interacting

**TABLE 1.2.**

HUMAN SERVICES PROGRAMMATIC STRUCTURE

| Prevention Program | Health | Mental Health | Education | Welfare | Correction |
|---|---|---|---|---|---|
| **Primary** | Education<br>Screening programs<br>Nutrition program<br>Ecological<br>Environmental<br>Well-baby clinic | Education<br>Consultation<br>Screening<br>  Retardation<br>  Lead ingestion<br>Well-baby clinic | Curriculum development<br>Teacher training<br>Educational support system<br>— | Family program<br>Advocacy program<br>— | Education<br>— |
| **Secondary** | Primary level<br>Interaction<br>  Acute<br>  Ambulatory<br>Secondary level of care<br>  Clinic<br>  Hospital<br>— | Early case-finding<br>Outreach program<br>Consultation<br>Collaboration in non-mental systems<br>Programs for alcohol, drugs, emotional disturbance, severe mental illness, retardation | Early identification of learning and behavior deviance<br>Tailoring program to children's needs<br>Vocational educational<br>— | Early identification of family problems<br>Monitoring programs<br>Funding<br>— | Education<br>Drugs<br>Alcohol<br>Programs against delinquency<br>Limit-setting programs<br>Parole<br>Probation<br>— |
| **Tertiary** | Rehabilitation of chronic diseases<br>Public health for tuberculosis victims, crippled children | Rehabilitation<br>Retardation<br>Severe and chronic mental illness<br>— | Rehabilitation of chronic educational disorders<br>— | Rehabilitation and funding of rehabilitation programs<br>— | Rehabilitation programs<br>— |

Source: Sauber 1977:125.

factors have resulted in a readiness to reassess the boundaries of the service networks and to reconceptualize a systemic pattern of service.

Boundary changes for system transformation have been of two major types: first, boundary spanning, in which emphasis is on the coordination across existing boundaries of the activities of separate professional caregivers and human service agencies; and, second, boundary expansion, in which the emphasis is upon incorporating a wider variety of functions within a single organization or, at the professional, individual level, upon developing generalist activities that cut across traditional disciplinary lines (Baker 1973).

Human service organizations may adopt alternative patterns of response. One takes the form of "system maintenance" and focuses primarily on existing agencies and on maintaining levels of service. A second pattern is to develop standards of "system change," redistributing resources to meet financial and human needs better. In each of these two response patterns, attention must be directed to the interrelated variables listed above that determine the appropriate system activity. For example, a pro-active rather than "re-active" organization is more apt to lean toward system change than toward system maintenance.

The problems and benefits resulting from contemporary categorical programs offering specialized services have led to a reaction and countertrend that has been most observable during the 1970s. For example, in the mental health system there has been a tendency to separate treatment for drug addiction from treatment for alcohol addiction and to separate both of these areas from the general mainstream of mental health care. In another case, child specialists have not treated adults and adolescents in child guidance clinics because of the cut-off age of sixteen. Because adult mental health clinics did not offer services to children there arose service fragmentation and severe difficulties in family problem solving.

In reaction to such specialization and professionalization, society and its caregivers have emphasized the common rather than the unique needs that motivate persons along with the common measures necessary to help them. Thus we are witnessing an increasing tendency to designate a given community's variety of educational, health, and social welfare interventions as "human services," a tendency that reflects both discontent with existing practice and recognition of the common elements that underlie the helping actions of diverse professional and nonprofessional caregivers.

It remains to be seen, however, whether lumping all these services together conceptually as "human services" will result in practice in an identification or a coordination among respective professionals. One can make the useful distinction between human services as an overarching care discipline and as a new discipline somehow separate from the traditional care professions. Although both may be seen as "core" helping disciplines, the specific model adopted may make a practical difference. If it is the latter, McKenzie (1978) warns, we may inherit political and territorial battles among existing disciplines, tightening of disciplinary boundaries, increasing gaps in care between disciplines, less comprehensiveness rather than more, and, in the end, another discipline to be given credentials. This process would aggravate existing gaps in human services, for example, the almost total lack of rapprochement between physical and mental health care, as noted by the President's Commission on Mental Health (Long 1978:46).

McKenzie suggests possible avenues for systems change in human services. First, we can seek the comprehensiveness that existed before professional specialization and fragmentation occurred. The traditional family can provide clues here. Second, we can explore the process by which we ask questions, that is, understand our own thinking in order to change it. Third, we can concentrate on the "human" as well as the "service." To this end we might well emulate such traditional and comprehensive disciplines as history, philosophy, anthropology, and communications. Finally, we can stress continuing education as a kind of ongoing corrective experience to the existing fragmentation (McKenzie 1978:41–43). Whatever the outcome, the ideologies of care disciplines are certain to be affected in one way or another. Considerable comprehensiveness already exists in ideologies. These and related aspects of human service disciplines are discussed below.

## IDEOLOGY AND PROGRAM VARIABLES

Traditional service patterns, technological improvements, and changing social, political, and economic movements have played an important role in the development and succession of human service ideologies during the nineteenth and twentieth centuries. A number of commonly adhered-to systems of ideas and beliefs that serve to justify one's position and act as a behavior rationale for human service administrators, educators, and practitioners have been identified by Baker (1974) and Baker and Schulberg (1967). Profound changes in the social environment have led, for example, to the development of disparate constellations of theory and technology that are associated with each of the three ideological subsystems of mental health—

**TABLE 1.3.**

ORGANIZATIONAL MODELS AND PROGRAM VARIABLES

| Program Variables | Mental Health Organizational Models | | |
|---|---|---|---|
| | Clinical Variables | Public Mental Health | Human Services |
| Etiology | Psychopathology (intrapsychic, personality system) | Populations at risk (environmental forces) | 1. Psychosocial-developmental 2. Organizational-ecological (social pathology, social system) |
| Caregiving networks | Medical organizations (state and general hospitals, out-patient clinics) | Hospitals, clinics, agencies and associations | Transitional, decentralized, deinstitutionalized facilities (services: comprehensive, integrated, accessible, continuous, accountable) |
| Roles and leadership | Hierarchical structure, medical-legal framework, mental health specialist | Hierarchical structure, medical and nonmedical leadership, mental health professional (generalist and specialist) | Role diffusion (ambiguous lines of authority), administrator (principles of management), mental health generalist |
| Goals | Ameliorate or alleviate psychiatric illness of individuals | Prevention and rehabilitation at the environmental level | 1. Problem solving for individuals and families 2. Interventions—intra- and interorganizational structures and environment |

clinical psychiatry, public mental health, and human services, as shown in table 1.3.

The clinical psychiatry model is the most traditional approach and has much in common with the medical model of illness. In the latter, the cause is thought to be an environmental agent—such as a virus or an experience of deprivation—that initiates the process that culminates in individual illness.

During the 1960s, however, mental health professionals expanded their areas of responsibility and the designs of their services from the relatively insular mental hospital or clinic practice to the more inclusive programs of public mental health. During the 1970s, mental health providers have further

| Program Variables | Mental Health Organizational Models | | |
|---|---|---|---|
| | Clinical Variables | Public Mental Health | Human Services |
| Sponsorship | Private or public local funds (funding formula "fee for medical service") | Public funds—local, regional, state, or federal (control and regulations) | Mix of private and public funds at all levels of government (regulations are a function of the sponsor) |
| Manpower | Classic disciplines (psychiatry, psychology, social work, and nursing), paraprofessionals | Multidisciplinary (epidemiology, environmental health, population sciences, etc.) | Interdisciplinary (health, education, and welfare), pro-, para-, and non-professionals (generic characteristics of helping activities) |
| Services | Direct care, patient-oriented (psychotherapy—short-term and time limited, crisis intervention; other therapies: behavior, chemo, activity, group and family) | Indirect methods, population-centered (planning, consultation, collaboration, epidemiological studies, education, information dissemination) | Interpersonal and social action (counseling, advice, advocacy, community control, community organization, and community development) |
| Consumers | Individual patients | Caregivers, community leaders, patient populations (ex-alcoholics) | Clients with "problems-in-living" (mostly from low socioeconomic classes) |

*Source:* Sauber 1973:18.

enlarged the scope of their activities and perspectives by designing extensive human service systems. These bring together a wide variety of human resources that provide comprehensive, integrated assistance to clients.

Baker and Schulberg (1967) have described the ideology of the community mental health movement as one concerned with various issues. These include the professional assumption of responsibility for an entire bounded population, rather than only an individual patient; the primary prevention of mental illness through the amelioration of harmful environmental conditions; the treatment of patients with the goal of social rehabilitation rather than personality reorganization; comprehensive, continuous care and concern for the mentally ill; and total involvement with both professional and nonprofessional helpers in caring for the mentally ill. A human service orientation is not considered incompatible with acceptance of public mental health concepts, but is viewed rather as natural extension of these ideas.

Human service orientation is characterized by a trend toward comprehensiveness and coordination of the many services traditionally supplied by separate disciplines or agencies. A population orientation now incorporates the following features: comprehensiveness of services; decentralization of services into areas of high needs; concerting of resources from different programs; co-location of service components; and operational integration of services in proper sequence, thereby eliminating present duplication and wasted time for clients and employees (March 1968). This orientation toward human service ideology and delivery system at the community level is also apparent in the actions of many state governments (Demone 1974; O'Donnell 1969; Sauber 1976), at the federal level (Demone and Schulberg 1975; *Washington Reports on Medicine and Health* 1972), and at the local level as well (Evans 1978).

Basic concepts in the programming of human services described by Baker (1974) include the following categories:

1. *Systematic integration of services.* Genuinely effective, comprehensive services can only be provided through forging systemic linkages that bring together the various caregiving agencies needed to provide a complex array of resources, technologies, and skills. Public health, mental health, education, criminal justice, and social welfare programs need to be unified into an effective system of human services.

2. *Comprehensiveness and accessibility.* Effective community action for troubled individuals requires continuity of concern for the person in his involvements with society, regardless of awkward jurisdictional boundaries of agencies, institutions, and professions. Programs must be designed to reach the people who are hardly touched by the best of the current efforts, for it is actually those individuals who present the major problems in America.

3. *Client troubles defined as problems-in-living.* Rather than attach a diagnostic label, it is more useful to examine an individual's problems-in-living and ability to cope with his environment in order to be most helpful to him. Thus, instead of individual deficiencies, the shortcomings of the social system become the principal target for intervention.

4. *Generic characteristics of helping activities.* Responsibility in a comprehensive community service agency should be assigned according to demonstrated competence in ability and task achievement as opposed to professional degrees and discipline-specified education. Further, distinctions such as that between the client problem germane to a psychiatric clinic and that of an alcoholism service are largely artificial and serve more as a conve-

nience for the professional than as factors related to the specific services provided to the client.

5. *Accountability of service providers to clients.* The provider of services has a responsibility to the users of services. In order for an organization providing helping services to become an effective agency in the community, community control of agency policy is essential.

Although ideologies and social values are neither universal nor external, several contemporary belief trends described by Demone and Schulberg (1975) have had a major contributing influence on the molding of the human services delivery system for the latter part of the 1970s and may set policy and program direction for the early 1980s. Most of these trends had their genesis at the community and state level, where people express personal concern and where responsive action must be taken. Although such trends may be quickly promoted to the national level and then adopted throughout the country, they become even more powerful influences on local programs. Demone and Schulberg (1975) noted seven trends:

1. *Equity of care.* It has always been argued that there are two systems of care. One for the "have's" and one for the "have-not's." It is now believed that human services should be provided as a "right" rather than a "privilege." Most politicians and citizens now agree that such equity of care is essential, and, in terms of its availability, accessibility, continuity, and quality, it must be delivered as a fundamental service in a democratic society. The national health insurance proposals now being considered by Congress, for example, are intended to provide low-income persons with fiscal equity when they seek necessary health care.

2. *Personal choice.* Closely related to the idea of equity of care is the growing belief that the individual is entitled to participate in the choice of a clinically and psychologically relevant human services treatment plan. No longer are professional judgments considered sacrosanct. The rights of clients and patients and the laws regarding informed consent obligate the caregiver to explain the nature of the presenting problems so that the person seeking assistance may participate in the choice of suggested remediations. A pregnant woman's decision as to whether or not to have an abortion and the terminally ill person's desire for an earlier rather than a later death provide examples of personal choice more commonly exercised today than a decade ago.

3. *Citizen participation.* Not only is the personal choice of the client indicated on the consumer level; citizen input at the program and policy level

is now being dictated. Traditional distinctions between professional expertise and lay contributions are becoming increasingly blurred, and citizen participation in the establishment and operation of human services is now widespread. A dynamic tension always arises between citizen control and professional domination; a mix of the two usually results after the "pushing and pulling" process settles down.

*4. Deinstitutionalization.* Deviant and clinically ill persons have for years been sent off to large impersonal institutions, often cynically referred to as "human warehouses." The current trend is to increase community responsibility and involvement at the level of the family unit and the surrounding neighborhood. A more compassionate set of values has modified society's impulse to exclude such individuals as the tubercular, the chronically and mentally ill, the developmentally disabled, and the juvenile and adult offender. Alternatives to institutional care are planned as a means of decreasing new admissions and discharging existing clients in various kinds of traditionally respected facilities.

*5. Decriminalization.* Closely associated with society's changing belief about the exclusion of deviant individuals from their local community is the fact that localism permits a greater willingness to acknowledge that therapeutic rather than punitive measures may be more beneficial for both society and the offending person. There is an increasing trend toward accepting behavior patterns once labeled objectionable and including a variety of human problems and symptoms of distress within the community's human services network for rehabilitation and remediation.

Many examples could be cited. More than twenty states, for instance, have eliminated the crime of public drunkenness within the past four years. In these states alcoholic citizens are treated in health facilities rather than in jails. The personal possession or use of minor drugs has been similarly decriminalized in many states, and the treatment of drug addiction has shifted into the arena of human services.

*6. Profit making.* The helping professions and the services they provide have traditionally been understood as disciplines within the realm of socially conscious academicians, social workers, physicians, and others whose fundamental value systems revolved around the alleviation of human suffering rather than the achievement of personal fiscal gain. However, because of the geometric rates of growth experienced by the human services in the recent years, their operations have increasingly come to resemble those of a socioindustrial complex. Profitmaking has been legitimized by local and national policy setters as an inevitable corollary to such rapid growth and expansion. Examples include such proprietary organizations as nursing homes, homemaker organizations, and day care centers; these facilities are providing formidable competition to well-established nonprofit and voluntary human service organizations.

7. *Civil rights.* Another major force affecting the contemporary human services delivery system, following the changes that have resulted from ideologies and social values, is that of civil rights decisions. Five particular areas that have been shaped by judicial decisions, legislation, and rules and regulations have been identified.

The notion of equal protection under the law represents an initial area of civil rights significance. A growing number of court cases have applied the due process clauses of the Fourteenth Amendment to human services. The 1967 *Hobson v. Hansen* decision in Washington, D.C., for example, abolished educational tracking in the District of Columbia's public school system. A 1970 California decision, *Diana v. The State Department of Education,* established new procedures for utilizing IQ tests with racial and ethnic minorities.

Other decisions have dealt with the basic right to education. Some state legislatures have responded by passing enabling legislation to implement contemporary interpretations of equal protection. In Massachusetts, Chapter 766, effective in 1974, mandated local educational responsibility for all children between the ages of three and twenty-one. This programmatic approach—another argument against specialization of services and compartmentalization of people—redirects handicapped children from special schools into the mainstream of education and implies that all children will ultimately be returned from institutions of their local school systems. In 1975, P.L. 94-192 extended this mandate to the entire nation. It is reasonable to anticipate that court decisions, combined with legislative actions, will eventually eliminate from our public schools such segregatory practices as tracking, special placement, and ability groupings.

The second issue, that of privacy and confidentiality, is replete with hidden depths and complexities. In most situations where claims to privacy are urged there are two sides to the issue. If the matter is decided in favor of privacy, some other societal value may suffer. Supreme Court Justice William Rehnquist has spoken of privacy as "a concept going to the roots of our citizens' independence, dignity, and integrity."

The advent of computer technology has, in some respects, highlighted public awareness of the potentially negative effects of our data-gathering and information-dissemination capabilities. Even prior to computers, social welfare professionals had for many years tried to protect the rights of their clients. Many of these professionals held that the inherent dangers to individual dignity and autonomy are of the utmost importance. Miller (1975) warns that we are potentially endangered by computer monitoring of the physiological status of hospital-based patients, by a checkless cashless economy, by automated multiphasic health testing, by multistate mental health information systems, by computer-based credit and consumer reporting services, and by job applicant and welfare data banks.

Compensatory modes to preserve privacy have been the subject of recent court decisions. Many have found expression in various laws and regulations that protect the individual, whether he is a student, client, patient, or inmate. Such protective procedures include permitting the individual to see his file and correct errors therein, controlling the exchange of information between organizations, limiting staff access to data within organizations, increasing emphasis on professional confidentiality, not recording some data, deleting purging data, and establishing standards for all data handlers.

A third area of civic rights concern refers to those experiments, often federally financed, that seek to control antisocial behavior with brain surgery, drugs, computers, radio transmitters implanted in the head, and other questionable means. Senator Sam Ervin, chairman of the Senate Subcommittee on Constitutional Rights, states, ''There is a real question whether the government should be involved at all in programs that potentially pose substantial threats to our basic freedoms.'' The committee suggested specific regulatory and administrative procedures to prevent such potentially gross abuses.

A fourth issue is the right to treatment, starting with the 1966 decision by the U.S. Court of Appeals that criminally committed patients have a right to treatment, and a series of judicial decisions has reaffirmed and expanded this concept. The 1972 *Wyatt v. Stickney* decision in Alabama has established statewide standards of care for the mentally ill and retarded. More recently, a Florida court ruled in *Donaldson v. O'Connor* that a state superintendant and a staff psychiatrist were personally liable for fines of $38,000 because they failed to treat a patient and would not discharge him. The scarcity of psychiatrists in state institutions will give further impetus to litigation against state governments for failing to provide minimal resources, and the inevitable closing of state hospitals and state schools will surely be accelerated.

A final issue relates to the protection of human research subjects. The American Public Health Association notes that health research actually involves seven major interest groups: the researchers and those responsible for evaluation of the research; the sponsors of the research, including the funding agency and the institutions employing the researchers; the agency or institution providing the research setting; the providers of health care services involved in the research; the recipients of care, individually and collectively; the community (geographic, ethnic, professional, and so on) in which the research is done or that is affected by it; and the levels of government whose policies and programs will need to respond to the results. The conflict between ethical issues and the importance of research in the field of human services, between the interests of the caregiver and society on the one hand and the client on the other, must be resolved. In contrast to earlier times, when the clients needs would most likely have been bypassed in favor of society's and the caregiver's, the balance is increasingly on the side of the client.

## THE ORGANIZATIONS

"Do-gooding," as Demone and Harshbarger (1974) write, is a major industry in the United States. It has become a tough and variable business—large, complex, and diverse and involving millions of consumers and employees and billions of dollars. Universally, effort is directed toward remaining viable and constructive in an increasingly complex, turbulent, technological, and depersonalized society. These factors, and the beliefs and value systems of professional disciplines, provide difficult problems in the effective development and operation of human service organizations.

An especially noteworthy example becomes apparent when physicians and organized medicine are contrasted to other human service professionals. The following organizational characteristics of medicine illustrated this contrast: working under a policy-making board, receiving an annual salary, assigning high status to administration, attending to the importance of governmental influence, and believing that all recipients are equally entitled to the same services regardless of other factors. On the other hand, the various human service professional disciplines, including medicine, generally agree on the following organizational criteria: services provided to clients are direct rather than indirect; treatment and rehabilitation, rather than prevention, are the prime objectives; design of service delivery is individual oriented rather than systemic, population, or environment oriented; and recognition of the value of planning is given a low status. Thus, the ideology and program variables of organized medicine, in particular, and of human service agencies to some extent, are antithetical to the rational basis of operation of complex organizations (Demone and Harshbarger 1974).

Gaps in intersystem relations among health and medical, criminal justice, welfare and rehabilitation, education, and mental health organizations have long been considered to be a major problem as well as a deterrent to effective service delivery. Human service leaders have continued to emphasize the importance of interagency cooperation in planning efforts relating to service delivery. Broadened participation and consumer representation have also been urged. Despite this, there has tended to persist, with some exceptions, a lack of awareness and even disinterest on the part of caregivers in the essential symbiosis that overlays the entire human services network.

A shift of focus from the single organization to the complex network of agencies has led to renewed interest in the latter. More and more, planning has taken place in terms of a community of interorganizational systems in which individual organizations constitute components or subsystems. Applying the term "system" to an organization implies interdependence in the sense of necessary input and output linkages; but this also means independence in the sense of maintenance of the integrity of system elements through boundary control processes. Human service organizations find themselves entering into relationships and decisions that are aimed at multilevel outcomes. These transactions and resource exchanges must be approached in terms of their relevance to community needs, interorganizational relationships, and intraorganizational requirements for system survival.

The defender of the status quo needs only to follow a few clients through the present system in order to realize the limitations of the complex inter- and intraorganizational and policy arrangements that reflect the artificial boundaries currently under attack. These arrangements can be described by such terms as "fragmentation," "overlap," "professionalism," "bureaucratization," "duplication," "service gaps," and "lack of coordination." A major strategy for facility access to a comprehensive range of coordinated human services is to change the structure through which services are provided. Demone (1974) has identified four prominent models at the local level that provide comprehensive neighborhood or community human services.

First, the *advice service* (or information and referral) is a simple concept based upon more than forty years of experience. A small group of generalists receive inquiries regarding any type of problem from the defined community and make appropriate referrals and followup cases based upon their knowledge of available local services (see Demone and Long 1969).

Second, the *diagnostic center* is based on a medical orientation, and thus its services are generated from the premise that a careful analysis of the patient's problems will lead to a more accurate intervention and treatment plan geared to the person's unique needs.

Third, the *multiservice center* offers an arrangement of services containing all of the program elements found in the two preceding models. Additionally, it offers the internal capacity to follow through on selected problems. The rationale for this kind of service reflects the orientation that human problems are multifaceted in nature and require multiple caregiving responses rather than a single-category service. Many multiservice facilities now in existence, and a rapidly increasing number of new centers throughout the country, provide such diverse services as employment counseling, psychiatric consultation, legal assistance, and information on public welfare benefits to clients in a single physical location. Community mental health centers, health maintenance organizations, neighborhood service operations, multiservice facilities, neighborhood health clinics, and youth opportunity centers provide examples of emerging organizations designed to accommodate integrated human services of a multiorganizational approach (i.e., a union of parts of a number of organizations that come together with the performance of a common task).

Each kind of multiservice facility offers its own unique complexities. For example, consider the community mental health center in terms of its organizational patterns (Levenson 1969) and administrative practices (Pusic 1969). The organizational patterns may be listed as follows: a center in a general hospital; a multiple-agency center—the affiliation of two or more independent agencies in a single center program, the most common arrangement involving a general hospital and a psychiatric clinic; a center in a state hospital; an independent, free-standing center; and a center in a private practice setting, for example, where private practitioners provide psychiatric services on a fee-for-service basis. A hospital is characteristically the employer of the center's nonmedical personnel, and the hospital is the fiscal agent of the center's operation.

Within each of these organizational patterns one encounters two basic approaches to administration—territorial and functional. The two represent end points on a continuum, and most multiservice centers incorporate some elements of both approaches. The term "territorial" refers to the generalist approach that is organized around a geographic, political base; the term "functional" refers to the specialist approach, organized around single service functions based on social needs. Specifically, a territorial administration has the following distinguishing characteristics: it is organized around a geographic, political base; it is composed of technically unrelated multifunctional units; it accomplishes its objective through the division of labor, with tasks divided into smaller units; it distributes power through a hierarchical chain of command whereby "domination based on power" resolves conflict; and it services the interests of political power groups, the providers of the funds. The dominating interest and hierarchical rank determine the distribution of rewards and the satisfaction of interests.

Functional administration may be described as having four main dimensions: organizational units have a single function based on a social need; the knowledge and skills of several disciplines are integrated into technically determined, complex combinations of functions; a nonhierarchical distribution of power prevails throughout the system; and interests are more common and overlapping because of interdisciplinary relationships and because of reduced potential for conflict resulting from the structural differences.

Fourth, *human services networks* focus on building linkages between existing and planned organizations so as to facilitate client services rather than to incorporate all relevant services within a single agency. The funds formerly used to stimulate the development of "new" nonreplicable organizations are instead used to facilitate availability, access, continuity of care, and organizational responsiveness to client needs. After determining the basic needs of the various population groups, the environmental conditions and demands, and the necessary essential services, a consortium of agencies may divide responsibilities according to their particular kinds of expertise. For example, the network approach is often utilized to meet the needs of such diverse high-risk populations as runaway youth and the elderly.

## ISSUES IN PLANNING

Regardless of the service delivery model, organizational pattern, or administrative approach, a fundamental set of organizational issues arises in the field of human services. These issues may be identified and responses developed, but only after there has been an analysis of the community and a study of the variables of its geography, population density, political jurisdictions, economic and marketing areas, population trends and composition, existing and predicted service needs among clients requiring assistance, transportation, and utilization and planning of financial considerations (Sauber 1976). Our society has not, until recently, begun to deal consciously with the problems of program outcomes and community social indicators; nor have we reached a level in the analysis of organizational impact that goes beyond simple health indicators, welfare case loads, and educational test scores.

The manner in which key issues are considered and the consequences of the choices made are critical determinants of the possibilities for the human service organization. Among these issues are: program auspices (public versus private-for-profit and private-not-for-profit); program control—designed in terms of the human service professional, the active upper middle-class volunteers who have been long invested in the voluntary health and welfare system, resident participation and neighborhood direction, and/or consumer control; source of authority, including sanctions and resources derived from a single source or multiple sources for its financial base and determining its limitations, constraints, sanctions, objectives, and boundary maintenance; a center with the emphasis upon the building as the central focus for all resources in a given catchment area versus an organizational plan with emphasis upon the programmatic activities related to a network approach; core services, which require a functional determination based on organizational objectives, (e.g. intake, outreach, diagnosis, referral, followup, client advocacy and/or case coordination); manpower patterns—such as nonprofessionals, indigenous community workers, paraprofessionals or second careerists, volunteer resources, related professionals who by the addition of pertinent behavioral skills can more effectively practice their primary tasks, and students at all level (associate degree to doctoral degree and postgraduate academic placements); and alternatives to direct services, such as social action, mutual-help groups, community organization, client advocacy, consultation and education, and collaborative planning (Demone and Harshbarger 1974).

## ADMINISTRATIVE PRACTICES

An additional factor affects current and future human service delivery systems: the new administrative procedures and practices developing within, or being imposed upon, the organizations providing these programs. *Generally speaking, administrative considerations rank second to clinical predilections in determining the directions and policies of service delivery.* Even though clinicians may deny their influence in determining organizational priorities, the wishes and policies of service personnel have held greater sway than those of managers, who have often resorted to negativism and recalcitrance in order to exert their influence. Currently, however, a number of new administrative practices, which include such procedures as accountability and evaluation techniques, management control, program elimination, planning procedures, and unionization of personnel, are emerging.

Over the years human service workers have failed to formulate goals and objectives that might lead to an adequate evaluation of their achievements. The intangible nature of most human services is certainly an intrinsic factor in this situation; but the lack of goal clarification and evaluation has also been maintained because of society's deferral to professionals in areas where most laymen consider themselves ignorant. Thus for many years the human services system has operated beyond the pale of public scrutiny.

Another major set of forces affecting contemporary human services is our society's level of technological sophistication. For the most part the field of human services, and particularly health care, has in recent years benefited enormously from scientific breakthroughs and the resulting technological advances. Some of these innovations are relatively inexpensive and can be widely utilized; others are extremely costly and can be used only in selected instances. Nevertheless, new standards for human services care are established by the most advanced technological methods, since they inevitably become the yardstick against which all other relevant programs and techniques are assessed.

Effective service for the alleviation of human distress generally leads to more equitable care. Instances in which technological advances conflict with contemporary ideologies and values, however, create difficult situations requiring complex and controversial solutions. For example, recent refinements in behavioral therapy techniques and psychopharmacological agents have made it possible to rehabilitate many persons previously deemed chronically maladjusted. These efforts have on occasion violated the social values of personal choice and civil rights, as when negative reinforcement procedures and tranquilizing drugs are used on inmates of correctional facilities.

Psychiatric projects supported by Federal Law Enforcement Assistance Administration funds intended to reduce violent behavior among inmates have provoked the wrath of civil libertarians. Under these circumstances, the conflicting needs of the caregiver and society, on the one hand, and the client, on the other, must be resolved. At one time the professional control and social circumstances surrounding decision making had the greatest influence; today the balance is being altered to enhance the client's and citizen's position and preference.

Evaluation research in human services is extremely difficult because the objectives of the programs are rarely explicit and the conceptual and methodological issues encountered in the evaluation process are always difficult and complex. The pressures under which evaluators are compelled to work, the ambiguity and lack of agreement with respect to program goals, and the theoretical and methodological complexity of the subject matter all seem to underlie the paucity of research on program evaluation. The goal of data gathering is to provide an immediate feedback that will permit continual adjustment to program objectives. The notion of accountability involves reference to the community, including citizens, legislators, recipients of services, and fellow professionals. However, ours is a day and age in which citizens exhibit discontent with professional assurances and want the facts to back up their assurances. This is especially true today because the availability of resources for programs and the survival of services depends on tightly constructed proprietoring or prioritizing techniques.

For some years, federally funded contracts and grants have required that evaluative procedures be incorporated as integral elements of the total program. At the operational level, this mandate is moving increasingly from lip service to actual practice. In the past, the amount of funds provided was frequently inadequate to carry out any real evaluative endeavor; because of funding shortages for programs, dollars earmarked for evaluation were often used to provide services for needy clients.

It is now necessary, however, for human service administrators and clinicians to function with an eye toward accountability. Consequently, the use of relevant managerial goals has grown. Simple cost-accounting procedures and line item budgets have been changed into more sophisticated accrual accounting, program budgets, and management information systems. Human services practitioners are identifying the discrete caregiving elements that comprise their total effort and are generating appropriate data about the clients, personnel, and costs associated with each component. Sophisticated indexes are being developed for measuring success with clients (Miley, Lively, and McDonald 1978). Thus operations research, systems analysis, and other sophisticated management control mechanisms well established in business and industry are now being applied to the field of human services.

The results are becoming apparent. The term "reorganization" has become a functional word in the field of human services. Administrative changes leading to centralization, decentralization, and recentralization are frequent, as responsibilities, roles, and functions are assessed and new organizational structures are proposed and implemented to enhance managerial effectiveness. Problems in reorganization will continue well into the 1980s.

Short- and long-term planning procedures have assumed a new legitimacy within the human services arena. Client, program, and fiscal projections have become more firmly grounded in hard information instead of resting primarily on theoretical predictions. Along with the expanded use of technological decision-making apparatus such as computers, the planning of human services at all program levels is beginning also to utilize the input of key citizens who reflect their community's humanistic concerns. Planners and administrators are challenged to maintain a balance between these impersonal and personalized contributions—since overreliance on either may produce misleading projections.

Because their employers were most often nonprofit corporations, human service personnel have traditionally relied on national and local professional bodies to speak for their needs and rights. This pattern of pseudoamicability, however, has been plagued with shortcomings. Unions have been increasingly successful in rallying the support of nonprofessional and, in many cases, professional human service workers to improve personnel–management relations. Grossly underpaid lower-level employees are now demanding dramatically improved salary schedules; to them, the fact that human service agencies are nonprofit in nature as irrelevant to their demands. Unions are increasingly recognized as the spokesmen for employee groups, a phenomenon that has already become reality in many general hospital facilities. Interestingly, the unionization of publicly employed personnel is occurring simultaneously with efforts by program administrators to reduce the near stranglehold over public human services exercised by civil service and merit system controls. Because these two trends are in many ways antithetical, heightened management–union friction can be expected. The continued reduction of institutionally based human services and the expansion of community-centered ones may well depend on a successful resolution of this knotty personnel problem.

**Program Patterns**   Community human services agencies have long shared service goals and clients. However, their interactions and cooperative ventures to ensure comprehensive care have often proven minimal; organizational concerns rather than client benefits were paramount. The pressing problem that now faces planners, clinicians, and administrators is that of linking the many caregiving elements in the broad field of human services.

Because no single agency, discipline, or service system can provide the total range of helping services required to meet the diverse problems of troubled or distressed people, organizational administrative barriers to service delivery must be minimized. The program model should create integrative mechanisms that ease the flow of clients, resources, and information service subsystems. Toward this end, some emerging trends include: purchase of service, decentralization, caregiving networks, and self-help groups.

**Purchase of Services**    The frequent lack of personal resources with which the troubled individual might purchase human services in the private sector produced, during the Roosevelt era of the 1930s, a geometric expansion of publicly supported and operated programs. The New Deal philosophy viewed direct governmental involvement and administration as necessary and appropriate. These precepts guided the funding and operation of human service programs during the subsequent three decades. This approach and philosophy is now being questioned as federal, state, and local governments begin to remove themselves from the direct delivery of personal services and concentrate on developmental, standard-setting, regulatory, and monitoring roles.

Governments now subsidize human services in the voluntary and private sectors through grants-in-aid and purchase-of-service contracts. In some cases, clients are provided with vouchers that permit them to negotiate arrangements directly with personally selected caregivers. Under the Medicare and Medicaid programs, public welfare clients and the medically indigent are no longer focused to use municipal health services; they can turn instead to private practitioners and voluntary hospitals. This trend toward purchase of services can also be expected to extend to dental care and legal assistance as prepayment and third-party fiscal arrangements become more common in these areas.

Voluntary organizations will probably experience new growth as they assume responsibilities in areas where their previous involvement was either limited or constrained. The donated-funds programs authorized by the 1967 amendment to the Social Security Act has significantly expanded several programs of voluntary agencies, including day care, protective services, and camping. Departments of public welfare write purchase-of-service contracts for low-income clients unable to afford these benefits. These developments were extended by the 1975 Title XX amendment to the Social Security Act to establish a consolidated program of federal financial assistance to encourage provision of services by the states. One result of such arrangements will be a reduction in the government's inherent conflict of interest in both operating and monitoring its own human services. By purchasing services, public agencies will move simultaneously into a position to play a more sophisticated standard-setting and regulatory role and to operate within a more flexible organizational structure.

**Decentralization** A major trend that became apparent under the Nixon administration was the shift of responsibility for human services from the national level to the local level of government. General revenue sharing marked noteworthy achievement in this regard. Many federally supported categorical grant programs have been eliminated, and state and local governments have themselves begun to assign priorities for human services. Decentralization, in consequence, arrived some time ago; but the service delivery implications of this trend are contradictory. On the one hand, more appropriate decisions about local needs for human services can be made and bureaucratic rigidities can be reduced as the locus of power is moved closer to the client. The personal element can be reasserted and impersonal administrative vagaries minimized. On the other hand, local politics and traditional community prejudices against many of those persons needing human services may assume renewed significance as decision making is decentralized. A recognition of this danger is evident in the federal government's decision to centralize welfare payments to the aged, blind, and disabled under the Supplemental Security Income program, which became effective in January 1974.

**Caregiving Networks** The movement toward caregiving networks, first evidenced in the 1960s, had become even more significant in the 1970s. Human service administrators have focused on building linkages between existing and planned organizations rather than on attempting to incorporate all relevant services within a single agency. In most communities it is not fiscally, politically, or practically feasible for an individual facility to provide, by itself, all the elements of a comprehensive human services program. In fact, most demonstration projects of this kind have failed to survive (Evans 1978).

Some services are likely to exist and operate elsewhere. After determining the basic needs of the community and the essential services for meeting them, a consortium of agencies divides responsibilities according to the particular expertise of each. The use of "interfaced" teams, which include the staffs of general agencies to review specific cases, has been particularly helpful in resolving the remaining problems and in fostering cooperative activities. The network approach to human services implicitly accepts the pluralistic nature of American society and attempts to maximize the assets and minimize the deficits of contemporary community patterns.

**Self-Help Groups**  A final influence on the delivery of human services is the rapidly growing self-help movement. Countless small, aggressive, non-profit groups have been created in recent years by persons who are distressed by a variety of problems. Their organizations are based on the principle that people with similar needs can reach out and help one another as much as, and in some cases more than, professionals. The mutual-help movement has expanded into all areas of human services. Because such groups are now an alternative to professionally dominated support systems, ways must be devised for them to be linked when necessary.

Despite the growth of the system of mutual-help providers, there remains general hostility and suspicion among human service professionals and establishment agencies. Since clients frequently use a variety of helping systems, professionals must facilitate movement across organizational boundaries in the client's quest for needed services. Professionals have even to consider the problem of continued funding, a factor that varies in severity depending on the program format. As one example, Alcoholics Anonymous groups, which use the program design and strategy of AA founders, are fiscally viable. However, if AA members wish individually or collectively to extend their efforts to the operation of a detoxification center or a halfway house, they must compete for limited funds and risk the same fiscal crises that plague all other human service agencies.

These introductory remarks, which are based upon the concepts and trends observed by Demone and Schulberg (1975), pinpoint the major aspects of current human services delivery, including ideology, social values, emerging technologies, changing administrative practices, and modified programs and patterns. An analysis of these various interwoven factors leads to the conclusion that, after several decades of geometric growth and expansion, the human services field is contracting in the face of adverse economic conditions. In contrast to the wide-ranging war on poverty of the 1960s, the more focused human services interventions of the 1970s, the 1980s is a time of program elimination and diversification of the affordable in an expanding but less inflationary economy.

## ECOLOGY AND INTERVENTION STRATEGIES

The concept of ecology has particular relevance to the human services field. Its concern is "the nature of the interaction of organisms and populations with the embedding environment, which supports, influences, and determines the limits of structure and function for the life that exists within it" (Sells 1969:15). An ecological viewpoint of human services should take into consideration at least three different types of ecological analyses (Kelly 1966).

**Ecological Approaches** The first type of analysis considers the community, the social system, or the organizational network and studies the interrelationships among the various kinds of human services provided within a defined geographic and population density area. The rationale for study according to this method is the belief that any change in operation of one service unit will affect the operation of all other service units. For example, an increase in admissions to one local human service agency is likely to be attributed either to a decrease in service opportunities at another facility or to a change in the patterns of social stress and tolerance that may produce more clients.

Second, an ecological analysis must consider the relationship between the physical environment, or the setting's physical characteristics, and individual behavior. Research on population density, the response of local community action groups to public housing, or the effects of urban renewal upon life-styles is an example of evaluation of the effects of nonpersonal structures upon behavior.

A third consideration is the interrelationship between individual behavior and the immediate social environment. Here attention is directed toward the study of individuals in specific behavioral settings and a redefinition of the concept of pathology:

> . . . sickness or wellness is defined as transactional, an outcome of reciprocal interactions between specific social situations and the individual. Adaptive behavior then can be expressed by any individual in a restricted number of social settings or in a variety of environments, and can vary from time to time as well as from place to place. The basic premise is reciprocity between the social structure and one's own behavior. (Kelly 1966:538)

Each of these three approaches takes into account the specific social environment, the discrete psychological activities within that social unit, and the behavior of the individuals who are members of that environment. The ecological thesis is that there are predictable patterns of individual behavior that are characteristic of a given social situation and that the expressive behavior of the individual changes in a newly defined social setting.

Examples of basic principles for human service delivery that are consistent with an ecological viewpoint and that can be applied to the unemployment problem include: a population orientation in which the community is the client; community programming of services to high-risk groups in their natural settings to reduce unnecessary utilization of community services; strengthening community resources through such methods as coordination of current services, better collaboration, community organization, and development; planning for change, including short- and medium-range planning, a technique that often results in improved anticipatory problem solving for clients as well as caregiving agencies and professionals. Such planning dictates the rearrangement of interrelationships between the social system structure and the individual. Kelly (1968) has identified four variables that are relevant to the individual–system relationships: individual coping styles, adaptive role functions, social setting structure, and environmental (population) characteristics.

**Intervention strategies**  Murrell (1973) described six levels of intervention. Based on the definition of ''intervention'' as a systematic effort to introduce change in individuals, social systems, populations, or networks of systems, the desired end becomes the improvement of the fit between individual and environment. The ''intervenor'' is defined as the person or group assuming the greatest responsibility for initiating the change.

*Level 1: Individual Intervention.* A basic strategy is to change or add to the individual's resources so that he may remain in, better accept, adapt to, and achieve within his present human network and environmental relations. Examples of this method include education, job training, psychotherapy, remedial reading, behavior modification, medication, crisis intervention, and physical exercise.

*Level 2: Individual Relocation.* When the relationship between the individual and his environment is incompatible—to the degree where improvement is beyond the capability of one or both sides—the individual should be relocated into a system more compatible with his problem management. Examples of such a strategy would be relocating a mentally retarded child from a regular classroom to a special education class, relocating a child to a foster home from his natural parents when they are incapable of caring for him, and relocating a man into an employment training program and then into a new job situation, thus removing him from a previous work situation where his personal abilities were incompatible with his vocational demands. Thus the strategy is to relocate the individual into a different system that can be more facilitative, primarily for the individual and secondarily for the organization.

*Level 3: Population Intervention.* The focus at this level is to change, prepare, or provide added resources for a population that is, or will be, in an inharmonious relationship with its social systems. Prevention programs in mental health are good illustrations of this kind of intervention, as are attempts to prepare a population for future crises. Examples include preparation of older middle-aged people for retirement, preparation of parents and children for the initial entry of a child into school, premarital counseling, and enrichment programs for infants. A major difficulty in implementing population-oriented programs, however, is mobilizing the voluntary participation of target and high-risk groups, whose understanding and motivation are not based upon visible problems or experienced pain.

*Level 4: Social Systems Intervention.* For extended improvement, changes in the social system's structure may be advantageous. An intervention of this kind is more enduring and effective when it influences the structure of the social system (e.g., rearranging the power hierarchy or changing the behavior of key systems personnel), rather than simply adding new tasks or activities within the existing structure.

*Level 5: Intersystem Intervention.* Methods at this level require the examination of the complex array of health, education, social welfare, mental health, and criminal justice organizations as an intersystem field. Interventions include: (1) intersystem assistance programs, such as involving mothers with their children in the early stages of separation (i.e., when entering school or at the time of admission to a hospital); (2) intersystem coordination programs, such as suicide prevention centers, or the collaboration of adult education officials, juvenile court probation workers, mental health professionals, religious leaders, and employment agency representatives to increase employment opportunities for adolescents as a deterrrent to juvenile delinquency; and (3) community action programs involving citizen and consumer participation.

*Level 6: Network Interventions.* Efforts at this level are communitywide, aimed at designing a new environment that will enhance the community's psychosocial responsiveness to its individual residents (Klein 1975; Murrell 1971). For example, immigrants from Vietnam have required special re-

HUMAN SERVICES FOR CHILDREN

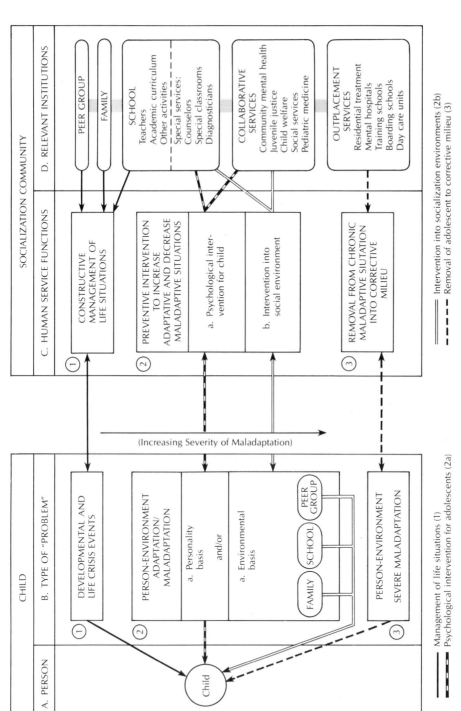

Source: Adapted from Tricklett, Kelly, and Todd 1972; Sauber 1977.

ceiver systems to help them adapt to their new habitat. Many opportunities or early input into this process exist with urban and regional planning commissions.

Figure 1.7 illustrates behavior as a function of the capabilities of the child, for example, and the demands of his environment when "goodness of fit" is lacking; therefore, the careful choice of the level of intervention is essential to restore the incongruence and maladaptation.

## CONCLUSION

Planning is the vital process that links needs to solutions. The interorganizational field of human services constitutes a "turbulent environment" in a state of rapid change. It is essential that there be greater receptivity to comprehensive and coordinated planning on the part of local agencies and state departments. The increased overlap of various welfare, mental health, and educational services, advances in scientific knowledge, and shifts in general attitudes and social philosophy have led to demands for new and different types of service and require changes in approach and methodology.

A broad knowledge and understanding of the human services delivery system is essential in contemporary society. Each of its elements—the community, human services, ideology and program variables, organizations, and intervention strategies—must be considered in an open-systems formulation and must be directed toward the interacting components in an input–output commerce with an external environment in the processing of material objects, information, and people.

The human services pattern is a sequential process: identification of a biosocial problem, followed by public and professional concern, and concluding with the development of a categorical delivery subsystem that is integrated within its suprasystem and coordinated intersystemically while also remaining responsive to the dynamic properties of a rapidly changing social environment. Responsiveness is a crucial element. For example, anthropology has long emphasized the mutual adaptation of the individual and his culture; those who survive well or fit in one society may well be considered deviant or maladjusted in another. Thus prevention of disturbance, or development of adequate adaptation in any setting, is relative to the demands of the system and the capabilities of individuals to meet those demands.

Unemployment and its consequences offer an illustration of what can occur. In an economic crisis millions of Americans worry about jobs, bills, taxes, and the cost of meat. Congressmen, columnists, and economists worry publicly about economic trend indicators on unemployment and inflation.

But very few seem to worry about the effect of all the worrying except for people like M. H. Harvery Brenner of Johns Hopkins University, who fears that if the current recession persists it will bring on a dramatic increase in mental illness, alcoholism, suicide, and many other health difficulties. Brenner's study of economic change in mental hospitalization over the last half-century shows that recessions lead to increases in mental disorders.

Traditional mental health theory considers mental illness the result of childhood trauma or psychosocial problems that predispose an individual to neurotic or psychotic behavior. In recent years, psychiatric epidemiology has begun to concentrate instead on the kinds of short-term environmental stresses that may precipitate mental disorders—factors in the immediate social or physical environment that trigger neurotic, psychotic, and other pathological reactions. An early finding of psychiatric epidemiology was a definite inverse relationship between socioeconomic status and mental illness: the lower the economic level of a population, the greater the incidence of mental illness.

In the model epidemiologists use, the distribution of any disease varies over time among different populations. Increases and decreases in the incidence and prevalence of a particular disease can usually be traced to some change in the ecology of the susceptible organism. Partly because of their traditional concern for the individual, psychiatric and medical researchers have all ignored such large-scale phenomena as economics, which changes the ecology of the population as a whole. The great majority of people have no control over economic changes and must simply endure and adapt to them as well as possible.

To test the relationship between economic conditions and mental illness, Brenner (1977) compared employment figures in the United States from 1922 to 1968 with first admissions in state hospitals during the same period. The results show a clear inverse relationship that holds up even for minor declines in all regions of the country: as employment drops, mental hospital admissions rise. This relationship holds true whether we use employment or per capita income as the economic indicator. The admission rates tend to lag somewhat behind the economic swings, but they generally respond within a year. The connection between rises in hospital admissions and a falling economy is most noticeable among people in their middle years. Men in the age groups 34–45 and 45–54 show the greatest sensitivity to economic change. Women 25–34 and 35–44 feel the impact most strongly. The reason is simple: These people are at the peak years of their employment and are most likely to be main providers for families.

Brenner uses unemployment as an economic indicator, not because it is the principal cause of mental illness but because it most accurately reflects the different indicators. These indicators (such as per capita income and the price index) together govern the economic changes that affect our daily lives. Since the trend of the country's economy has been toward long-term growth of real income, any slowing of this continuous growth creates a conflict between expectations and reality.

An informal survey of suicide prevention centers across the country indicates that the current recession has already begun to fulfill Brenner's fears. One suicide prevention center in the vicinity of the auto industry's production center, which has truly been hard hit by industrial layoffs, has received an increasing number of calls from people experiencing depression because of job layoffs and rising prices. Some of the threats are serious; psychiatrist-director Dr. Danto has reported, "A decided increase in suicidal deaths due to financial pressure and unemployment has resulted" (Rice 1975).

The Gainesville Center in Florida reported that beginning in 1973 the Gainesville area has experienced a sharp increase in suicidal acts:

> We are getting a lot more self-injury and suicide behavior based on economic crises. The callers are often people who are not able to meet their monthly bills, who are losing their jobs for the first time, and are panicked because for the first time economic failure is staring them in the face. Not all those who attempt suicide really want to die: they are really crying, "Help me!" (Rice 1975)

There is much talk (and intuitive belief) regarding "social costs" of unemployment, but little has been done to measure the costs quantitatively.

**TABLE 1.4.**

CUMULTATIVE IMPACT OF THE 1.4 PERCENT RISE IN UNEMPLOYMENT

| Social Stress Indicator | Stress Incidence 1975 | Change in Stress Indicator for 1.4 Percent Rise | Increase in Stress Incidence Due to 1.4 Percent Rise |
|---|---|---|---|
| Suicide | 26,960 | 5.7% | 1,540 |
| State mental hospital admission | 117,480 | 4.7 | 5,520 |
| State prison admission | 136,875 | 5.6 | 7,660 |
| Homicide | 21,730 | 8.0 | 1,740 |
| Cirrhosis of the liver mortality | 32,080 | 2.7 | 870 |
| Cardiovascular-renal disease mortality | 979,180 | 2.7 | 26,440 |
| Total mortality | 1,910,000 | 2.7 | 51,570 |

Source: Brenner 1977.

**TABLE 1.5.**

ECONOMIC LOSS RESULTING FROM THE SUSTAINED RISE IN UNEMPLOYMENT

| Social Stress Indicator | Classification of Economic Cost | Economic Loss Due to the 1.4 Percent Rise in Unemployment Sustained from 1970–1975 ($ million) |
|---|---|---|
| Suicide | Suicide | $ 63 |
| State mental hospital admission | Hospitalization for mental illness in state and county mental hospitals | 82 |
| State prison admission | Imprisonment in state institutions | 210 |
| Homicide | Homicide | 434 |
| Cirrhosis of liver mortality | | |
| Cardiovascular-renal disease mortality | Disease of the circulatory system | 1,372 |
| Total Mortality: | Total Illness | $6,615 |

*Source:* Brenner 1977.

One of the few efforts in this regard has been the work of Harvey Brenner in a recent report by the Joint Economic Committee, "Estimating the Social Costs of National Economic Policy: Implications for Mental and Physical Health and Criminal Aggression" (Brenner 1977).

Brenner has calculated the effect of the 1.4 percent rise in unemployment in 1970 according to figures for the fifth year thereafter, 1975. This 1.4 percent increase, which has been sustained ever since, has resulted, for example, as noted in table 1.4 in an additional 26,440 cardiovascular-renal deaths in 1975.

Finally, Brenner calculated the direct economic loss in 1975 resulting from the illnesses, deaths, and institutional admissions that occurred from 1970 to 1975 as a result of the sustained 1970 increase in unemployment (see table 1.5). To the $6.6 billion in lost income due to illness, mortality, and institutional outlays must be added public outlays of $2.8 billion annually over the 1970–1975 period for unemployment insurance and welfare costs associated with the sustained 1.4 percent rise in unemployment. Thus, in those five years the costs of unemployment were some $21 billion. All this excludes the costs of further increases in unemployment since 1970. The 1.4 percent increase in 1970 that Brenner noted lifted the unemployment rate to 4.9 percent. As of today, it is about 8 percent: Projecting Brenner's data into the future, the costs yet to come will run to hundreds of thousands of lives and tens of billions of dollars.

As the late Hubert Humphrey stated in his introduction to Brenner's report: "These dollars represent resources lost or diverted from productive use. They represent wealth never to be realized, lost forever to our economy and society. They measure, in part, the human tragedy of unemployment. But significantly, their loss could have been avoided."

There is a need for intervention at all levels, starting at the social system and intrasystem levels at which economists and businessmen must consider the effects of their decisions on human problems. After all, if the actions of the government, beyond the average citizen's control, lead to economic conditions that precipitate mental and physical illness, it becomes the government's responsibility to take some preventive measures. At the population level, existing community mental health services and clinics should be expanded, particularly if they could be geared to high-risk populations and regions or industries suffering from economic decline and recession. In cases of decline in specific industries or recessions in particular regions, the speedy establishment of manpower or retraining programs would have to cushion the economic income. Where alternative job markets do not exist, minimum income maintenance programs would have substantial mental health and general human benefits.

Although all these proposals for alleviating damaging effects of economic problems have been used or at least considered, they have not received high priority in government circles. Besides, they all represent "bandaids" applied to already existing wounds. It is time our government officials and human service professionals practiced some preventive interventions according to the levels previously described. If they would begin giving consideration to the potential mental health consequences of events—for example, the impact of economic policy—they could probably reduce greatly the severity and dislocation caused by recessions.

## REFERENCES

Adler, P. 1972. Conceptual approach to the function of a community mental health center with particular emphasis on consultation and education services. *Mental Hygiene,* 56(4):28–32.

Baker, F. 1973. Comparative systems analysis of human service programs. Manuscript. Boston: Harvard Laboratory of Community Psychiatry.

Baker, F. 1974. From community mental health to human services ideology. *American Journal of Public Health,* 64(6)(576–581).

Baker, F., A. Broskowski, and R. Brandwein. 1973. System dilemmas of a health and welfare council. *Social Service Review,* 47(1):63–80.

Baker, F. and H. C. Schulberg. 1967. The development of a community mental health ideology scale. *Community Mental Health Journal,* 3:216–225.

Brenner, H. 1977. Estimating the social costs of national economic policy: Implications for mental and physical health and criminal aggression. Summarized in "The consequences of unemployment," *New Human Services Review,* 3(31):2–51.

Brown, B. S. and J. D. Isbister. 1974. U.S. governmental organizations for human services: Implications for mental health planning. In G. Caplan, ed., *American Handbook of Psychiatry.* 2d ed. New York: Basic Books.

Campbell, Lenore A. 1979. Consumer participation in planning social service programs. *Social Work,* 24(2):159–162.

Cohen, R. E. 1973. Models in search of community mental health programs. Paper presented at the 126th Annual Meeting of the American Psychiatric Association, Honolulu, Hawaii.

Cohen, R. E. 1974. Conceptual human services model for children. Paper presented at the Workshop on Human Services for Children, Middletown, Rhode Island.

Demone, H. 1974. Human services at state and local levels and the integration of mental health. In G. Caplan, ed., *American Handbook of Psychiatry.* 2d ed. New York: Basic Books.

Demone, H. W. and D. Harshbarger. 1974. *A Handbook of Human Service Organizations.* New York: Behavioral.

Demone, H. W. and D. Long. 1969. Information referral: The nucleus of a human-needs program. *Community,* 44:9–11.

Demone, H. W. and H. S. Schulberg. 1975. Human services trends in the mid 1970s. *Social Casework,* May:268–279.

Erikson, Karin. 1977. *Human Services Today.* Reston, Va.: Reston Publishing.

Ethical issues in health services research and development. 1973. *American Journal of Public Health,* 63:552.

Evans, Eunice B. 1979. An integrated social service delivery system. In *The Social Welfare Forum, 1978.* New York: Columbia University Press.

Gollub, S. O., D. C. Henton, and S. A. Waldhorn. 1980. Nonservice approaches to social welfare problems. *New England Journal of Human Services.* October:29–38.

Harshbarger, D. 1974a. The human service organization. In H. W. Demone and D. Harshbarger, eds., *A Handbook of Human Service Organizations.* New York: Behavioral.

Harshbarger, D. 1974b. Turbulence and resources: The basic for a predictive model of interorganizational communication in the human services. In H. W. Demone and D. Harshbarger, eds., *A Handbook of Human Service Organizations.* New York: Behavioral.

Kelly, J. G. 1966. Ecological constraints on mental health services. *American Psychologist,* 21:535–539.

Kelly, J. G. 1968. Toward an ecological conception of preventive interventions. In J. Carter, Jr., ed., *Research Contributions from Psychology to Community Mental Health.* New York: Behavioral.

Kennedy, J. F. 1979. "Mental Health Bill Introduced." *Science News* (May 19), p. 327.

Klein, D. C. 1975. Developing human services in new communities. In H. C. Schulberg and F. Baker, eds., *Developments in Human Services.* New York: Behavioral.

Levenson, A. I. 1969. Organizational patterns of community mental health centers. In L. Bellak and H. Barten, eds., *Progress in Community Mental Health.* New York: Grune and Stratton.

Levin, G. and E. B. Roberts. 1976. *The Dynamics of Human Service Delivery.* Cambridge: Ballinger.

Long, B. B. 1979. Report from the President's Commission on Mental Health. In *The Social Welfare Forum, 1978.* New York: Columbia University Press.

Lynn, L. E. Jr. and N. S. Salasi. 1974. Human services: Should we, can we, make them available to everyone, everytime. Spring:4–45.

March, N. 1968. The neighborhood center concept. *Public Welfare,* 26:97–111.

McKenzie, R. H. 1978. The fragmented search for the whole in human services. In Joann Chenault and Fran Burnford, eds., *Human Services Professional Education: Future Directions.* New York: McGraw-Hill.

Miley, A. D., B. L. Lively, and Robert D. McDonald. 1978. An index of mental health system performance. *Evaluation Quarterly,* 2(1):119–126.

Miller, A. R. 1975. The assault of privacy. *Psychiatric Opinion,* 12:6–14.

Murrell, S. A. 1975. *Community Psychology and Social Systems.* New York: Behavioral.

Murrell, S., ed. The psychosocial environment for the new communities family mobility system. OEO Grant 8002 Report, vol. 2. Louisville: Urban Studies Center, 1971.

O'Donnell, E. 1969. Organization for state-administered human resource programs in Rhode Island. Report to the General Assembly by the Special Legislative Commission to Study Social Services, June.

OMB. 1980. *The U.S. Budget in Brief: Fiscal Year 1980.* HJ 2005 U.S. Washington, D.C.: Office of Management and Budget, Executive Office of the President.

Pustic, E. 1969. Territorial and functional administration in Yugoslavia. *Administrative Science Quarterly,* 14:62–64.

Regester, D. C. 1974. Community mental health—for whose community? *American Journal of Public Health,* 64(9):886–893.

Rice, B. 1975. The worry epidemic. *Psychology Today,* August:74, 76.

Rossi, Peter H. 1978. Issues in the evaluation of human services delivery. *Evaluation Quarterly.* 2(4):573–599.

Sauber, S. R. 1973. *Preventive Educational Intervention for Mental Health.* Cambridge: Ballinger.

Sauber, S. R. 1976. State planning of mental health services. *American Journal of Community Psychology,* 4(1):35–45.

Sauber, S. R. 1977. The human services delivery system. *International Journal of Mental Health,* 5(4):121–140.

Sauber, S. R. 1978. Community analysis and program planning. *International Journal of Social Psychiatry,* 24(4):263–271.

Saunders, I. T. 1958. *The Community: An Introduction to a Social System*. New York: Ronald Press.

Sells, S. B. 1969. Ecology and the Science of psychology. In E. P. Williams and H. L. Raush, eds., *Naturalistic Viewpoints in Psychological Research*. New York: Holt, Rinehart, and Winston.

Special Analyses: Budget of the U.S. Government, Fiscal Year 1978. 1978. Washington, D.C.

SRI International. 1980. Rediscovering governance: Using nonservice approaches to address social welfare problems. Interim report.

Toffler, A. 1970. *Future Shock*. New York: Bantam Books.

Trickett, E. J., J. G. Kell, and D. M. Todd. 1972. The social environment of the high school student: Guidelines for individual change and organizational redevelopments. In S. E. Golann and C. Eisdorfer, eds., *Handbook of Community Mental Health*. New York: Appleton-Century-Crofts.

Washington Reports on Medicine and Health. Washington, D.C.: GPO, 1972.

# 2

# HUMAN SERVICES AND
# GENERAL SYSTEMS THEORY

General systems theory (GST) and its principal concepts represent a heuristic approach to understanding the human services. The various services—mental health, education, health, social welfare, and criminal justice—have already been noted as subsystems of the human service system. This chapter outlines the main concepts and propositions of GST as they may be applied to human services and suggests directions for future research and development.

## DEFINITIONS OF SYSTEMS THEORY

The term "systems" is currently very much in fashion. A rapidly growing body of "systems" literature reflects the variety of professional disciplines that have increasingly focused attention on systems theory, systems analysis, systems design, systems engineering, and the like. Boguslaw (1965) has labeled the enthusiastic new practitioners who seek to apply systems concepts toward the solution of a broad range of world problems the "new Utopians." The concept of systems, however, is not new and, in fact, has been the subject of study for centuries. Today, because of increased specialization, the appeal of a "general theory" has drawn together individuals from widely ranging fields who seek to bridge the gaps among disciplines and who feel the need for a "general systems theory": a body of organized theoretical constructs that can be used to discuss the general relationships of the empirical world.

Boulding (1956) has identified two objectives of general systems theory:

> At a low level of ambition but with a high degree of confidence, GST aims to point out similarities in the theoretical constructions of different disciplines, where these exist, and to develop theoretical models of study. At a higher level of ambition, but with perhaps a lower degree of confidence, GST hopes to develop something like a "spectrum" of theories—a system of systems which may perform the function of a "gestalt" in theoretical construction. (p. 198)

The purpose of this text is not to present a total and systematic orientation of general systems theory to human services, but rather to present each of the fields from a descriptive vantage point. It will acquaint the reader with the advantages of approaching human services from a general systems theoretical point of view and will suggest some specific ways in which GST can be used to illuminate our understanding of human services.

Ludwig Von Bertalanffy, a theoretical biologist, is generally recognized as the founder of general systems theory. Although the theory originated in the field of biology, its wide acceptance has resulted in the application of open-systems approaches to the study of all living systems, including such large social systems as complex organizations. The major concept of the approach—that living systems are essentially "open" as opposed to "closed" systems—comes from an article by Bertalanffy published in *Science* in 1950. Two closely related conceptual systems, Shannon and Weaver's information theory (1949) and Wiener's cybernetics (1948), emerged during the same period demonstrating that creative minds often reverberate in parallel ways within a particular historical time frame.

Some basic concepts of general systems theory should be reviewed before discussion of the application of the systems framework to the field of human services. Bertalanffy (1956) defined systems as "the totality of elements in interaction with each other." Other definitions follow similar lines, such as the totality of objects together with their mutual interactions (Hall and Fagen 1956); unity consisting in mutually interacting parts (Ackoff 1960); a recognizably delimited aggregate of dynamic elements that are in some way interconnected and interdependent and that continue to operate together according to certain laws and in such a way as to produce some characteristic total effect (Boguslaw 1965). General systems theory is, in brief, primarily concerned with the problems of relationships, of structure, and of interdependence rather than with the constant attributes of objects. Earlier formulations of systems constructs had dealt with the closed systems of the physical sciences, in which relatively self-contained structures could be treated successfully as if they were independent of external forces.

Recently more attention has been focused on "living systems," which are open to, and acutely dependent upon, an external environment. These systems are also in a sense self-contained. Man in this view is an active system, capable of self-regulation, goal seeking, growth, development, and learning; man is not only externally responsible but also internally active. The human system, like all living systems, is an open one. Its boundaries are permeable, permitting energy and information to pass from the inside out and from the outside in. This open-systems capacity to incorporate energy and information makes *negative entropy,* or growth, possible; that is, it enables man, like other living things, to grow, learn, and reproduce over time. Personality develops out of the interaction of the biological substrate of the human system, along with its various subsystems, with matter, energy, and information from outside the biological system. Thus from the physical environment, the nuclear family, the school system, peer groups, the community, the nation, and the culture at large the personality receives inputs for its change and growth.

## LINEAR CAUSATION VERSUS SYSTEMIC COMPLEXITY

The systems approach focuses on relationships between elements rather than on the elements themselves. Furthermore, the approach allows for complex relationships among elements as opposed to mere cause-and-effect relationships. A systems model subsumes a causal model by specifying the possibility that an effect usually produces *feedback,* which then "loops" back to modify the cause. In a set of interacting elements with such cause–effect feedback loops–in GST terms, input–output feedback loops—a causal model is too simplistic to account for the complexity of interactions. The behavioral sciences have already undergone the transition from causal to systems models, and the applied behavioral sciences—the human services—are now undergoing a similar transition.

The "medical model" of mental illness has shortcomings that may well go deeper than was once believed, and to appreciate the ecological factors that contribute to the phenomena that we call "mental illness" we may have to reconsider totally our traditional explanations for all disease, including those considered to be biological illnesses. Cassel (1970), reviewing a considerable body of research on both animal and human illness, suggests that a germ theory of disease is inadequate to explain the epidemiological facts. Germ theory was nevertheless a tremendous improvement over the previous philosophical conceptions of illness, for example, Hippocrates' hormonal theory and the theory of Miasma. The widespread acceptance and utility of the germ theory concept of disease has unfortunately reinforced our simplistic linear cause-and-effect model of all illnesses.

Cassel argued convincingly that all disease, both mental and biological, may be due to a complex interaction between environmental agents such as germs or toxins, on the one hand, and the "general susceptibility" of the organism on the other. Accordingly, he argued that being placed within an environment where one's behavior no longer leads to formerly predictable outcomes and has no impact on that environment raises one's general susceptibility to all types of illness, both biological and mental. The probability of contracting a disease will also depend on the extent of the social assets or social support systems that the individual can use as a "buffer" when placed in this turbulent and unpredictable environment.

In general, Cassel suggests, a high rate of change, unpredictability in one's social environment,. lack of any "turf control," and lack of social supports or assets will lead to an increased susceptibility to disease, "mental" or biological. Consequently, the "germ" is conceptualized as simply the trigger for a disease and is not necessarily viewed as its "cause." Kelly (1966) has presented data supporting this view of disease, specifically on the role of change in the adjustment of school children, including the incidence of illness and accidents.

If Cassel's analysis is correct, one can no longer focus primary efforts simply on the control and treatment of germs. Rather, one must concentrate on environmental factors that are unpredictable or unresponsive to the behavior of persons. For purposes of prevention, therefore, one ought to work on developing in people the ability to respond to rapid change and to carry within themselves, as internalized values or reference group norms (i.e., culture), what Cassel refers to as social assets.

If epidemiological research is beginning to document the importance of general environmental change and unpredictability for physical illnesses, psychosocial factors in the environment may play an even more crucial role in psychological illness. In the latter case, nothing like "germs" has been isolated with anything approaching the precision with which germs have been identified in physical illness. Because precipitating factors as exclusive explanations for psychological illness are rather tenuous, it makes more sense to use a systems approach in which internal and external factors interact.

As alternatives to a simple linear cause–effect model, one needs to develop models, or ways of thinking, that take into account the complex network of forces and feedback loops that influence the quality of our lives— and, consequently, the occurrence of personal and social problems. A general open-systems model (Bertalanffy 1968; Miller 1965, 1971) may be precisely such a mode of thought. It can readily be seen that changes in one subsystem—changes designed to improve a given situation—may cause change in other subsystems. Equally clearly, the result may be a state of affairs more negative than before the change. As Forrester (1971a, 1971b) has demonstrated, most social systems are so complex that myriad unanticipated consequences follow intuitive interventions. In fact, the nature of social systems is such that they attract our attention to precisely those problems that are, in reality, only coincidental occurrences of a much larger set of critical factors. Most of our intuitive solutions, therefore, tend to be counterproductive; moreover, most effective solutions turn out to be counterintuitive.

Some of the responses to the urban ills of housing, crime, and drug use are examples of intuitive solutions that have caused greater problems than those they set out to correct. Approaches to primary prevention must thus take into account the total ecological system in which the population resides. Research by Kelly (1966, 1968, 1971) has demonstrated the necessity of considering ecological complexitites in the planning of preventive intervention at the level of broad social institutions, such as the schools. Sanford's (1970) work on the prevention of alcoholism has led to a view of the problem as a multidetermined phenomenon rather than one amenable to narrow diagnosis. In this view, the etiology of alcoholism was promoted by specialty disciplines that failed to collaborate and coordinate efforts in theory and practice. Here, "system" refers to all factors—internal and external— that inhibit, interact with, and contribute to the incidence of alcoholism. Ignoring some of these factors or how they interact hinders preventive efforts.

A more complicated example of the difficulties arising out of one state government as a case in point, this researcher demonstrated that a reimbursement of the local school system for every child diagnosed as requiring special education rewards the financially burdened system with a substantial sum of money every time a child is so labeled. No similar financial reward or incentive follows the successful treatment or solution of the child's problem. An early identification program for prevention tends to lead to labeling and, consequently, adversely affects children's behavior since peers, parents, and teachers develop negative expectations that they would not otherwise have.

Programs based on the strategy of early identification of problems, particularly in young children, demonstrate how problems have arisen as a result of failure to account for systemic complexity. Such programs, for example, seldom take into account the social implications of labeling. Only limited evidence suggests that early detection necessarily leads to a more favorable outcome (Whittington 1966). Early detection also requires effective treatment. The effectiveness of the treatment may, in turn, be mitigated or compromised if the persons are labeled prior to treatment.

Some outstanding programs devoted to the early detection and treatment of problem children (e.g., Zax and Cowen 1967) demonstrated their effectiveness on a sample of urban children and parents that was likely to validate the early detection and treatment hypothesis. If one were to attempt the same program, however, on an inner city population sample—one characterized by rapid turnover, unresponsive and unpredictable environments, and a different set of attitudes toward "mental health"—it might be found that early detection, labeling, and treatment were dysfunctional. Furthermore, labeling probably affects adversely many related issues, such as the definition of appropriate and adequate manpower, the relationship of "mental health" to other disciplines, and the degree of responsibility that society assigns to the individual for his problem (Lennard and Bernstein 1971).

In brief, early case finding, with or without effective treatment, has systemic implications throughout the entire mental health network. As a preventive strategy, therefore, we must seriously question approaches that depend on early "detection and treatment" even though such tactics have been found useful for biologically based illnesses.

Problems, conflicts, and tensions within any interacting system can produce ripple effects in any or all of the other systems. Thus changing cultural mores, the result of many complex forces within other systems, can produce changes in governmental legislation, community reactions, judicial decisions, family patterns, and individual psychodynamics. Examples may be found in the movement for the right to health care and in the women's liberation movement.

In the right-to-health movement, for example, sheer demand has underscored the nation's inadequate supply of health services, with the result that a thorough reassessment of the situation was undertaken. The ramifications included legislation, judicial decisions, new administrative structures and concepts such as the Professional Services Review Organization (PSRO), and altered expectations at the individual, family, and community levels.

Similarly, the actions of individuals who are influenced by complex systemic interactions can also have implications that profoundly alter each of those interacting systems from the level of the individual to the culture itself. Examples are marijuana use and the utilization of birth control and abortion in family planning.

The development of human services as a conceptual system reflects the influence of systems thinking over the years since World War II. It has gradually become obvious that the concept of single causation in human services is no longer viable and that the areas of concern in the human services field must extend beyond the borders of the individual client, and indeed beyond family dynamics into the community itself. The initial question, then, must be: What is the basic unit of study? Is it the individual, or is it the system that constitutes what has been called "the organized complexity"?

Earlier approaches, as well as those in common practice today, identify the individual as the problem for outreach and resolution. One must, however, remain constantly alert to the dangers inherent in using an individual as a starting point from which to investigate human services and community problems. If one is to use the symptom as a starting point, one immediately confronts a problem: the use of traditional nosology, in which the classification system for labeling deviance is almost exclusively individual oriented and not well suited to consideration of the interpersonal contacts in which the client's behavior takes place. As a theoretical system, human services conceives of human problems and suffering as a result of a concentric network of interconnected determinants with the individual at the core of the network but in a constant state of dynamic interaction with elements related to the family, peers, social class, and the larger community as well as ethnic, racial, economic, and cultural subsystems. Human services see the roots of most problems-in-living not only within the individual but also in disturbances within the dynamic network of interacting systems.

Significant implications for human services practice inevitably follow from this theoretical formulation. For example, in terms of prevention, human services take cognizance of the fact that the relief of stress in another part of the network can have important positive effects on the well-being of individuals within the system. If an intervention has a positive influence on the housing, employment, nutrition, or general health of an individual, it can also have a constructive effect on the emotional and physical well-being of people in need. On the other hand, inadequate schooling and racial, religious, or sexual prejudice and discrimination leave scars on the human spirit and intellect just as do the effects of poor parenting or a broken home and an unhappy family life.

It is fallacious to conclude from this that human services professionals have to bring about such changes in society. Indeed, one has neither the power nor the ability to do so. One can and should, however, function in this area somewhat as do public health officials, who call attention to the existence of a health hazard that threatens the well-being of the community, through appropriate political pressure on its governmental institutions. They can thus bring about the necessary steps to remove the hazard. As citizens, of course, we have a responsibility to participate in this political process; but as human service professionals our skills are needed, and should be used, to help both to relieve and to prevent the broad range of human problems that result from these systemic disturbances.

## MAJOR CONCEPTS

It is beyond the scope of this paper to attempt even to outline the complexities and ramifications of general systems theory. Applied to human personality, behavior, and service delivery, at least in part, general systems theory encompasses the following major principles:

**Open Systems**   These are systems in which there is a continuous flow of component materials from the environment and a continuous output of products of the system's action back to the environment. This concept rejects the notion of a closed system, which describes cases with impermeable boundaries through which no matter, energy, or information transmissions of any sort can occur. No actual system found in nature is ever in fact completely closed; systems are, therefore, only relatively closed.

**Entropy, Negentropy**   A central concept in systems theory is entropy—the tendency for a system to lose energy or information to the environment. When entropy occurs unimpeded, maximum disorganization or disorder is the result. In order for open systems to survive, therefore, they must acquire a steady state of negentropy, or negative entropy; this counterbalances the process of entropy, which is a constant occurrence and therefore needs to be checked constantly. Organization represents the presence of information, and disorganization the absence of information. Thus the way to balance entropy is to introduce more organization. In this way, open systems restore their own energy and repair breakdowns in their own organization. There is then a general trend in an open system, as long as it is alive, to maximize this ratio of imported to expended energy. Open systems typically seek to improve their survival position and to acquire in their reserves a comfortable margin and operation.

**Input, Transformation, Output**   The pattern of activities of the energy exchange in an open system has a cyclic character. Open systems receive input—they import some form of energy from the external environment—and then transform or reorganize it through the application of throughput processes. The outputs of one system become available for use as inputs for another system. The basic conception of an open system as a cycle of input–conversion–output facilitates the analysis of living systems at a variety of levels from the cell to the society.

**Boundaries and Interface**   As a distinct systemic entity, a human service facility must maintain some discontinuity with its external environment in order to continue to exist as a separate system. Boundaries may be rigid and closed, not permitting any interaction between the elements inside and outside the system; or they may be flexible and open, permitting interaction with elements belonging to the system. In the case of the human services, a boundary may be difficult to detect in terms of physical factors, but may be more readily observed in terms of the discontinuity in *pattern clusterings* of human interactions. Katz and Kahn (1966) offer a succinct definition of boundaries as "the demarcation lines or regions for the definition of appropriate system activity, for admission of members into the system, and for other imports into the 'system' " (pp. 60–61).

A related term that is useful in understanding boundary relationships is the concept of *interface,* which may be defined as the area of contact between one system and another. An organizational system engages in numerous transactions at the interface—including those involving the transfer of matter, energy, information, and people. Drawing the boundaries of a system is the first step in defining the structure; the next step usually entails defining the relationship of the elements to each other. Most frequently the elements are grouped together in a hierachical arrangement so as to be either subordinate or superordinate to each other. Accordingly, groups of related elements may be classified as subsystems or suprasystems. Even face-to-face interaction by individuals across the system interface can be conceptualized as interaction between the system and its environment (Jette and Montanino 1978).

**Subsystems**  In every system it is possible to identify an element or functional component of the larger system that fulfills the conditions of a system in itself but that also plays a specialized role in the operation of a larger system. Taking a particular living system as the focus, one may define as a subsystem as the totality of all structures in the focal system that carry out a particular process. Thus at least three types of subsystems can be identified for an open system: an input subsystem, a conversion or operating subsystem, and an output system.

Figure 2.1 shows an open system interacting with its environment through inputs, outputs, and feedback. Part of the output is entropy, and part of the input is negentropy. The boundary between the system and the environment is semipermeable, allowing passage of inputs and outputs. The system consists of subsystems specialized for handling and converting inputs and outputs. Table 2.1 lists a clustering of elements that help to delineate a particular system apart from its environment. An additional element—throughput structures—represent the processing subsystems of figure 2.1, which produce output and are modified by feedback through further input.

**Suprasystem and Environment**  Just as a living system may be analyzed in terms of its components or subsystems, so may it also be viewed as part of a higher-level system, a suprasystem, in which the system then plays a subsystem role. The suprasystem of an individual is the group of which he is a member. For example, justice is a subsystem of the suprasystem of human services; and criminal justice is the suprasystem of the subsystem of juvenile justice.

**Differentiation and Integration**  A movement occurs in open systems in the direction of differentiation and elaboration, within which specialized functions replace diffuse global patterns. Human service organizations move in the direction of multiplication and elaboration of roles with greater specialization of functions. In this way, some parts of an open system come to cope with different parts of the external environment; other parts perform specialized tasks related to input, throughput, output, and other critical system processes. In order to maintain the unity of parts as components of the

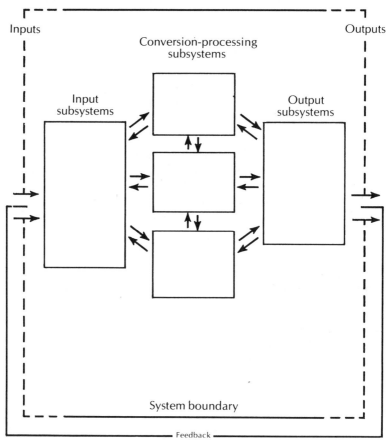

**Figure 2.1**
OPERATING PROCESS FLOW OF A SIMPLE FORMAL ORGANIZATIONAL SYSTEM

Inputs

Outputs

Conversion-processing
subsystems

Input
subsystems

Output
subsystems

System boundary

Feedback

**Environment**

This is a simplified and highly stylized diagram of the input-throughput-output-feedback flow through a formal organizational system. It is not intended to represent the full complexity of most organizations, and for the sake of simplicity does not show managerial subsystems of informal communication structures.

Although shown as a single line, the feedback loop represents numerous feedback channels. Internal feedback is represented by reversed arrows ($\rightleftarrows$).

*Source:* Schulberg and Baker 1976:70.

**TABLE 2.1.**

MODEL OF THE MENTAL HOSPITAL AS AN OPEN ORGANIZATIONAL SYSTEM

| | | |
|---|---|---|
| Patients | Patient Care Subsystems | Discharged Patients |
|   Demographic characteristics |   Patient admissions | Trained or Educated Personnel |
|   Personal histories |   Therapy provision | Research: information distributed |
| Staff and Students |     Verbal | Change in Level of Health of Population |
|   Professionals, students, and other personnel: |     Somatic | Patient Maintenance Programs |
|   professional skills, personality, attitudes, in- |     Activity | Community Education |
|   terests, goals, ideologies, habits, values, ref- |   Custodial care provision | |
|   erence groups |   Community Placement | |
| Legitimation | Training Subsystems | |
| Political |   Education of professionals | |
| Legal |     Residents | |
| Financial |     Nurses | |
| Technology |     Social workers | |
| Material |     Other nonprofessionals | |
| Money | Research Subsystems | |
| Supplies | Boundary-Spanning Subsystems | |
| Facilities |   Aftercare | |
| |   Primary prevention programs | |
| |   Community relations | |
| | Managerial and Administrative Subsystems | |
| |   Receiving and processing information | |
| |   Planning | |
| |   Decision making | |
| |   Integrating | |
| |   Controlling and direction | |
| |   Personnel functions | |
| |   Physical plant maintenance | |

*Source:* Baker 1976:98.

FEEDBACK: Patients, other people, and information returned to the hospital from other systems in the environment.

whole, a reciprocal process of integration must occur. Without a sufficient degree of integration, a system breaks down into several elements. A personality, for example, grows from crude, rather primitive organizations of mental functions into hierarchically structured and well-differentiated systems of beliefs and feelings. In another example, in this country today there are more medical specialists than general practitioners. Yet a new trend toward family practice or family medicine marks a revival of the generalist's attempt to integrate the parts into a whole.

**Feedback**  The system continually receives information from the environment that helps it to adjust and to take corrective actions on deviations from a prescribed course. In feedback, a portion of the output (e.g., behavior) is returned to the system as input, which functions to modify succeeding outputs of the system. A living system may be viewed as self-regulating because, within it, input affects output and output often adjusts input. Negative feedback is informational input looping back to the system in such a way as to decrease the deviation of output from a steady state. Positive feedback occurs when signals are fedback over a feedback channel in such a way that they increase the deviation of the output from a steady state.

**Equifinality**  In any closed system the final state is unequivocally determined by initial conditions, but an open system may reach the same final state in different ways from different starting conditions. Finality as a concept is the reverse of causality: the process and structure of a system depend on future rather than past circumstances. The amount of equifinality in an open system may be reduced as the system moves toward the regulatory mechanisms to control its operations. System performance can be predicted by its goals and objectives as well as by its past behavior.

**Areas of Interdependency**  The basic areas of interdependency include the exchanges between the system and its environment, the processes within the system, and the processes through which parts of the environment are related to each other. Each of these three sets of interdependencies—transactional, internal, and interdependencies within the environment itself—should be considered.

**Monitoring and Boundary Control Activities**  Monitoring is an intrasystem regulatory activity that involves checking an operating activity or taking action to institute a new or modified operating activity. Boundary control is a regulatory activity external to the operating activity of the system; it consists of activities that relate a system to its environment by controlling the input and output transitions across the system's boundary.

**Morphostasis and Morphogenesis**  The term "morphostasis" describes the processes that tend to preserve or maintain a given system's form, structure, or state. Homeostatic processes in organisms and rituals in sociocultural systems are examples of morphostasis. Morphogenesis describes those processes in complex system–environment exchanges that tend to elaborate or change the system's organization, state, or form (for example, biological evolution, learning, and societal development).

The major processes of a system, as defined by Kuhn (1962) are communication, transaction, organization, and change. Communication involves the exchange of information; transaction is the exchange of matter and energy between any two elements of a system. Organization is a process in which any two systems engage in joint behavior. Change involves the modification of and/or within any system; one kind of change, *growth,* entails an increase in the quality or quantity of the elements within a system; and *decay* is a decrease in the opposite direction, eventually to the state of entropy. The criteria of open systems are as follows: there is intake and output of both matter and energy; there is the achievement and maintenance of steady (homeostatic) states, so that the intrusion of outer energy will not seriously disrupt internal form and order due to an increase in complexity and differentiation of parts; finally, at least at the human level, there is not merely intake and output of matter and energy but extensive transactional commerce with the environment.

Society, or the sociocultural system, is not principally an equilibrium system or a homeostatic system but rather a complex adaptive system. Complex adaptive systems (biological species, psychological and sociocultural systems) are open "internally" as well as externally, in that the interchanges are among their components themselves, with important consequences for the system as a whole. The energy level that may be mobilized by the system is subject to relatively wide fluctuation. Internal as well as external interchanges are mediated characteristically by information flows, that is, cultural encoding and decoding. True feedback loops make possible not only self-regulation but self-direction, or at least adaptation to such a change in environment that the system may change or elaborate its structure as a condition of survival. Some of the more important differences among various complex adaptive systems include the following: the substantive nature of the components; the types of linkage of the components; the kinds and levels of feedback between the system and environment; the degree of internal feedback of a system's own state (for example, "self-awareness"); the method of transmission of information between subsystems; the length of generation; the degree of refinement and finality of mapping (e.g., encoding, decoding, correlating, understanding) and information transfer; and the degree and rapidity with which the system can restructure itself in adapting to variations and changes in the environment.

In order to survive and maintain some degree of autonomy of action in a "turbulent" environment, a human services organization must fulfill a number of important functions. It must deal with the external environment in such a way that it can acquire and maintain sufficient levels of necessary resources as well as adapt to the environment itself.

An organizational system must perform four general systems functions in order to maintain autonomy and ensure continued survival. It must acquire inputs and deliver outputs, develop system goals, achieve integration and coordination subsystems in the face of differentiating environmental influence, and adapt to both the environment and its internal requirements and to some degree try to control or adapt the environment itself.

An open-systems conceptual framework for analyzing human services program development grows out of an elaboration and consideration of each of these four key functions.

## THE MENTAL HEALTH SYSTEM: AN ILLUSTRATION

According to the basic definition of a system, the mental health system (MHS), as currently structured, involves every person in the United States in a variety of ways. Figure 2.2 attempts to delineate the major structural elements of the MHS. Obviously, any such two-dimensional illustration must be greatly simplified for presentation on a single page.

All of the structural elements in this figure are represented as open systems because literally very level of the MHS is constantly bombarded with environmental stimuli. The major linkages, presented as directed lines, run between the major elements in each level and between the administrations of each level. Important, each of the elements has some interaction with, and impact on, every other element; the extent of that impact tends to be greater as one proceeds downward from the top of the hierarchy, however.

Within the federal government it is, therefore, theoretically possible to define all the structural elements and levels of interaction. But operationally

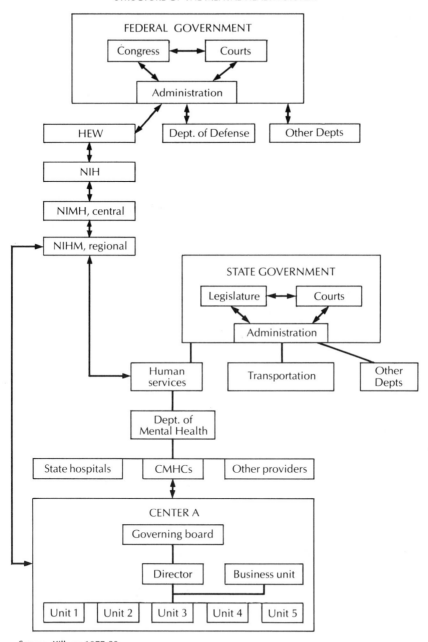

**Figure 2.2**
STRUCTURE OF THE MENTAL HEALTH SYSTEM

*Source:* Kilburg 1977:83.

this is impossible, not only because of the size of the system but also because many of the interactions are unknown for national security or other political reasons. This is not as true for the mental health components of the federal government, however, as for some others. It would be possible, for example, to detail the interactions in Congress, the federal court system, and the administration that concern the MHS. Most important would be the passage of the various pieces of legislation affecting mental health, most recently P.L. 94-63 (1975); the court's role in interpreting and enforcing such laws; and the administration's role in implementing the laws and regulating compliance through the Department of Health, Education, and Welfare and the National Institute of Mental Health in the Department of Health. It might be added that the interface between health and mental health has been all but ignored (Long 1979: 46). The processes of communication, transaction, and change and the goal structure for each of these subsystems could be examined. Such analysis, however is outside the scope of this chapter.

Following the principle of structual isomorphism, the second level of figure 2.2 is labeled state government. The major elements are defined as the legislature, the courts, and the administration. At this level there also tends to be isomorphism between the administration's agency for human services and the Department of Mental Health, on the other hand, and the comparable subsystems at the federal level.

The third level in figure 2.2 is "Center A." Its major structural elements are identified as governing board, a director, and a series of clinical and business units relating to thedirector. Center A is shown as being linked to the state government through the Department of Mental Health, and to the federal government via its regional office of NIMH. Obviously these are not the only possible or existing linkages between Center A and the two supersystems shown in the figure. On the contrary, for the average center the linkages are much richer, especially to the state government via local congressmen and other departments of state government with which centers interact on a regular basis.

Broadly speaking, the goals of a typical community mental health center (CMHC) are defined by the mandates of the supersystems of federal and state governments in the form of laws, rules, and regulations. The mandates govern everything from the types of services to be delivered to the organizational structure, population(s) to be served, processes of financial management, and types of homeostatic feedback loops to be employed. It is, therefore, a well-controlled system; much of the control is, in fact, located in the supersystems of the state and federal government.

**Figure 2.3**
MIS AND PROGRAM ENVIRONMENT, STRUCTURE, EVALUATION, AND PLANNING

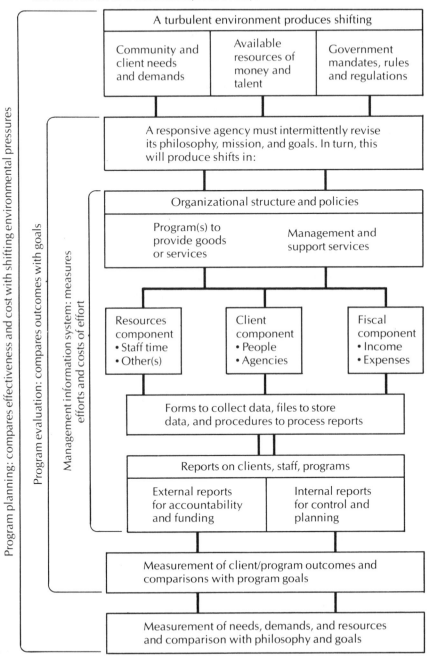

Source: Broskowski 1976.

Figure 2.3 illustrates the various levels and aspects of program planning and evaluation. Without an organized way of establishing measurable goals and monitoring the performance of the center against these goals, there can be no truly accurate feedback loops, and thus no true homeostasis in a CMHC. Moreover, there can be no organized change.

Figure 2.4 demonstrates how Center A might look after full implementation of the CMHC act. Although different centers will start from different stages, finality predicts that similar structures and processes will result.

## INTERSYSTEM RELATIONSHIPS

Gaps in coordination among health, criminal justice, welfare, mental health, and educational systems have long been considered a major problem for community organizers, local planners, and other human service practitioners attempting to understand and improve the human services delivery system.

The relative absence of coordination in the activities and programs of these systems may be explained at least partly by inadequate knowledge and insufficient utilization of the essential factors and procedures involved in organizational coordination. Effective action in dealing with difficulties in intersystem coordination requires conceptual and empirical knowledge about interorganizational systems relations. As a distinct systemic entity having input–output interactions with the environments, an organization must maintain some discontinuity (boundaries) with its environment to continue to exist. This ''boundary'' of a system may be a territorial line; however, in social systems such as human service organizations it exists more importantly as a boundary in ''social space,'' representing discontinuity in patterns and clusterings of human interactions. An example would be a state department of social and rehabilitative services with its ''independent–dependent'' regional and local offices and mandates.

Applying the term ''systems'' to an organization implies both interdependence—in the sense of necessary input and output linkages—and independence—in the sense of maintenance of the integrity of system elements through boundary control processes. One is persuaded to shift one's focus from the single agency to the complex network of organizations, speaking of a community interorganizational system in which individual organizations constitute components or subsystems. It is incorrect to assume that there is one coherent system of human service caregivers whose boundaries are well defined, whether conceptually or empirically.

An intersystem model tries to ascertain empirical relationships. Thus it focuses on determining the degree and nature of interchanges between sys-

**Figure 2.4**

STRUCTURE OF A COMMUNITY MENTAL HEALTH CENTER (CENTER A) ALTERED TO MEET THE REQUIREMENTS OF P.L. 94-63

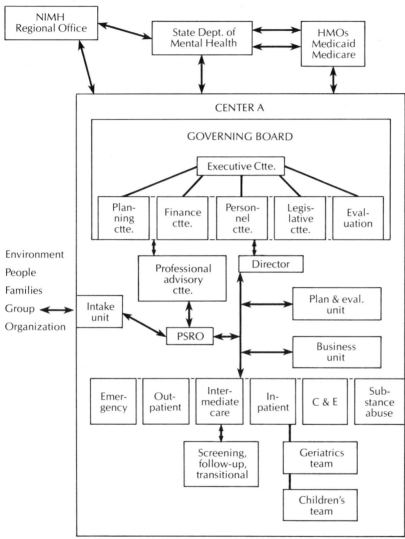

*Source:* Kilburg 1977:87.

tems, rather than assuming the operation and organization of a single large suprasystem. A general intersystem approach emphasizes the relative autonomy of interactive systems, rather than assuming interdependencies that may or may not exist—for example, three state departments of education, mental health, and corrections, one with a division of special education, another with one of child mental health, and another with one of juvenile justice. Further, a general intersystem theory states that relationships between systems in an interorganizational field may differ qualitatively as well as quantitatively as a function of the differing types of interaction that are being used to assess interdependence. As an example, two systems may be highly interdependent in terms of information flow but mutually autonomous with regard to financial exhange.

Baker (1969) and Chin and O'Brien (1970) point out that the relative amount of interchange between organizational systems is a function of the permeability of the boundaries between the two related, but partially autonomous, systems. Boundaries will be differentially permeable to different media of exchange; they may be permeable in one direction for one type of exchange and in the opposite direction for another type of exchange. Coordination may be seen as the most important intervening variable between human and material resource allocation and "effective" or "comprehensive" human service delivery. Thus coordination affects both the boundaries between organizations and the interval functioning of those organizations.

## SYSTEM INTEGRATION AND DIFFERENTIATION

Human service organizational systems differ from industrial production systems—within which much of the organizational systems theory and research has been developed—because the former are primarily people-processing systems. Unlike business and industrial organizations, human service agencies usually have an extremely close relationship to their consumers, the clients.

Human service organizations are multi-unit, multi-goal systems. Although one can define the primary task of a human service facility as service in the public interest, there are within them many public interests, which must relate to a number of different constituencies. In its relationships with these various constituencies, the human service agency must become highly differentiated. As its different parts pursue different goals, and as it performs heterogeneous functions simultaneously, the organization will experience major problems of integration.

Integration is one of the major defining characteristics of a system. System, in turn, can be defined as a group or combination of component parts arranged in such a way as to constitute a unified, interrelated whole. Without some degree of integration among its parts, there is no unification, and instead of a system one has a collection of individual, isolated elements. A human service organization is comprised of distinctive internal components, including the specific operating service program in managerial subsystems. The internal operating subsystems of a complex human service organizational system are differentiated according to the requirements of their respective service technologies, the beliefs of the professionals who constitute the major components of the system, and the relationship of these components to external parts of the environment.

Integration is defined as the degree to which these service structures exist in a state of mutual independence and interconnectedness. Operationally, subsystem integration is determined by the levels of collaboration, exchange, and mutual understanding that have been achieved within the boundaries of the organizational system. Administrative management subsystems have major responsibilities for accomplishing the vital organizational functions of integrating operating service subsystems with each other and with maintenance subsystems. As an open system, human services are dependent upon their environments. Thus, when considering an agency's effectiveness in offering integrated services in the processing of its clients, one must also consider the expectations imposed by its environment.

The human service organizational system engages in transactions with a number of input–output constituencies, including the following major sectors: clients and consumer groups (both potential and current users); suppliers of staff, finances, materials, technology, and information; other individual, group, and agency service providers who may compete or cooperate with regard to clients and resources; and regulatory organizations, including governmental agencies and professional associations.

There are two basic criteria by which one may assess levels of integration: the extent to which service components actively interact in a coordinated fashion; and the nature of the services provided to the clients.

In examining the interrelatedness of organizational subunits with one another, one must examine the effort devoted to integration, as well as the degree of integration achieved. In terms of the degree of integration achieved, it is important to examine both collaboration and the achievement of mutual understanding among units. Collaboration can be assessed by examining participants in organizational decision making, particularly as it relates to the distribution of scarce resources and the disposition of clients. Another measure of collaboration is the degree of self-containment of various units in terms of activity patterns and the extent to which the unit exclusively depends on its own staff to accomplish its functions. It is also important to assess types of interunit communication, as well as the use of specific information exchange not only of staff and information but also of material resources and, of course, clients. The number of joint projects (including planning, training, and experimental treatment programs) is also relevant.

The degree of cross-unit identification, the use of unitary identifying labels for multiple units and a high level of agreement about the respective roles of units are also indicative of a high degree of mutual understanding. Bass and Windle (1972) have defined continuity of care operationally:

1. client movement or the absence of it in appropriate response to treatment needs;
2. stability of the client–caretaker relationship;
3. both verbal and written communication among staff members;
4. efforts made to retrieve clients who appear to be dropping out of treatment prematurely.

At the level of individual care patterns, it is important to examine typical patterns of care relative to the types of service units used by clients and the actual number of sources of care that a client must employ. It is expected that service by a comprehensive, integrated human service center requires a client to use fewer organizational sources in seeking the care that he needs.

Schumaker (1972) has developed measures of two major dimensions of individual care patterns: compactness and cohesiveness. Compactness of an individual care pattern is ascertained by observing the range of sources or types of sources of care used by a client or consumer. The smaller the range, the more compact the pattern. The range of this dimension exists on a continuum from a single source of care to multiple sources of care. Schumaker defines "single type of multiple sources" as a situation in which a consumer uses a number of sources of care that are of the same type—such as several emergency rooms or several outpatient departments. The category of "multiple type of sources" refers to situations in which a consumer makes use of a number of different types of health and social caregivers. Such a pattern would involve the use of services at an outpatient department, a community mental health center, the emergency room of a general hospital, a private physician, a welfare agency, and so on.

Schumaker defines an index of the "cohesiveness of a care pattern" as the "the degree of integration of sources of care into an organized pattern" (p. 933). The cohesiveness of a human service care pattern is related to the number of sources of care in the pattern, to the number of sources of a particular type in the pattern, and to the number of types of sources in the pattern. This index considers such dimensions as duplication, supplementation, completeness, and dispersion and deals with the question of whether the patient or client is using more services than appear to be necessary. Other questions of concern are whether there are sufficient sources to meet the patient's needs and those of his family and whether there are obvious gaps and discontinuities.

A concept closely associated with the degree of effective integration at the level of the patient or client is continuity of service over time. The degree of concert achieved among organizational components and the extent to which there are adequate subsystem linkages will affect the degree to which services become discontinuous and a client fails to receive necessary simultaneous or sequential services.

Integration may be illustrated by the case of a social service delivery system designed for the Wilkes-Barre, Pennsylvania, area. Continuity of care is assured by single-entry service centers established in convenient population areas. Case managers serve as a single point of intake for all services, with continuing services also provided by generic caseworkers retrained for specific services. A system of fiscal management and program accountability was established. In addition to these integrative features, acceptance by the community, county commissioners, and the voluntary sector helped to assure the survival of the program (Evans 1979).

## ORGANIZATIONAL SURVIVAL

Organizational survival depends on how an organization handles both its internal and its external relationships. Drucker (1973) outlined eight areas in which an organization needs to establish objectives: marketing, innovation, human organization, financial resources, physical resources, productivity, social responsibility, and profit requirements. Without measureable objectives in these areas, enterprises are doomed to lower levels of efficiency and effectiveness than they might otherwise attain.

As noted, the human service agency is part of a larger system and is also a system in itself. Whether it will function effectively or ineffectively depends not only on its internal relationships but also on the nature of the relationships with various external systems. One may use an example of a health clinic, a community mental health center, or any other human service multipurpose facility to illustrate four major interfacing variables affecting the organization's ability to survive and function.

The first variable is the agency's institutional base: the nature of the sponsoring institution, whether it is a university, a general hospital, a community organization, a governmental agency, or a group of the human service facility. Certain tensions, such as those between intake and outreach orientations, between research and service preferences, between an individual-centered approach and a community-centered one, or between a behavioral approach and a psychodynamic one, can often be traced to the orientation of the sponsoring institution. Also relevant is the degree of the sponsoring system's commitment to the agency's program and its willingness and ability to allocate resources that will enable the agency to survive declining staff–grant balances and inflationary pressures. The capacity of the institution to mobilize governmental and community support and the nature of its relationship to the community all have important effects on the agency's capacity to function.

A second major interface is with local, state, and federal governmental agencies, whether or not they are supportive of the agency's program. This variable relates, in many aspects, to the broader political scene. For example, in the mental health system, as a result of passage of the 1963 Community Mental Health Center Act by Congress, a very favorable national political climate regarding mental health support continued over the next five years. With the election of a new administration in 1968, however, the climate altered drastically. Construction of new centers all but ceased, and existing centers had great difficulty in obtaining or extending vitally needed staffing grants. As a result of the congressional override of the presidential veto of the Revenue Sharing and Health Services bill, however, many CMHCs have revived once-ailing programs, and other areas of the country without mental health services may not be able to initiate them.

State and local configurations are also important. Governors, state legislators, and county or city governments may be supportive of or antagonistic toward mental health programming. This may be crucial, because an agency needs the supplementary local financial support built into the community human services agencies' system.

On a still broader societal scale, the twin economic stresses of recession and inflation, prevalent in recent years, represent still another social factor that can seriously affect an agency's ability to survive and function. During periods of economic stringency, sources of private support, as well as public funds, tend to decrease. Ironically, operating costs continue to rise at the same time, and the need for human services tends to multiply, thus putting agencies in an impossible bind. Given the scarcity of resources, competing power bases and interests within the human services field itself can also significantly affect an agency's capacity to serve. Some of the potential pressure points include the interfaces between the state department (be it health, corrections, education, or another) and the local community-based program; among research, training, and service programs; between the private sector and public sector; and between national or state human service administrators who feel that their power bases are threatened by one of the components of the human services system. It is probably one of Parkinson's laws (and if not, it should be) that programs follow the availability of funds. Thus, when major funds become available for alcohol and drug programs, rather than, say, for child or geriatric programs, many agencies will modify their programs to take advantage of the new funding sources. Such was the case in the early 1970s, when various job development agencies were created and other existing structures redefined their missions to deal with high unemployment.

A third major variable in the agency's ability to survive and to function is the nature and quality of the professional and paraprofessional providers of the human services. The following subfactors are of paramount importance: the degree of such providers understanding and skill; their commitment to the agency's program; and their ability to work collaboratively and to develop a base of mutual trust, not only with the sponsoring institution's representatives and government regulators but also with representative leaders in organizations in the community itself. Related to this factor is the need for an understanding of the interrelational aspects of the various systems and subsystems within a catchment area that are necessary to meet the needs of the residents of a community.

Consider a city with a population of approximately one million of which 60 percent is of Portuguese extraction. The local family service agency is recognized and funded as a major provider of child and family programs and serves approximately 10 percent of the Portuguese community. When the agency's director was asked why such a small percentage of that ethnic group had been reached, he commented that, although it would be easy to develop services to meet broader needs, he was already overwhelmed with the large number of clients that the facility was servicing. If, however, the staff had included members of the Portuguese community, new kinds of programs might have emerged and eventually attracted an increasing number of clients from the large ethnic population.

This example also relates to a fourth major variable: the nature of the community that the agency attempts to serve. Actually the use of the term "community" is misleading. A community is not a monolithic structure but usually consists of multiple subsystems, which are often in conflict with each other and represent different interests, different power bases, and different needs (Sauber 1977). The agency's administration may have to balance, reconcile, and mediate between conflicting groups and to attempt to evolve programs that meet the needs of each. This requires a considerable level of political skill, which, as the history of many agencies has unhappily shown, may not always be possible to develop.

The agency with a responsive, cooperative, and highly motivated group of community leaders is fortunate indeed. It is doubly fortunate if, in addition, the community has or can mobilize resources that enable the agency to survive both fiscally and programatically.

## INDIVIDUAL BEHAVIOR IN A SYSTEM

We stand on the threshold of a new era in human services and in the related disciplines of psychology, social work, anthropology, sociology, criminology, education, and health. Today we view human nature in a much more complex way than ever before. From this perspective, the view is not of the individual in vivo but instead of the small or larger groups within which any particular individual's behavior is adaptive. Theoretical trends are shifting from the assessment at the individual level to an analysis of the context— or, more precisely, of the system from which individual conduct is inseparable. What, then, is the basic unit of study: the individual, or the system, constituting what L. K. Frank called an "organized complexity"? It is important not to impose the elements of individual theory onto the systems because there is no evidence of isomorphism (equivalence of exchange ability). The shift in focus from the individual to the interactional or systemic approach may be discontinuous in many fields, and we must scrupulously examine the basic premises and methods of the former model before applying it to the latter.

It is likely, for example, that what we mean by the term "individual" when we take the family system into account may be quite different from what this term presently describes. Equally, we cannot classify families as systems, using individual nosology. Specifically, we must not permit our wish to understand and to ameliorate individual pathology carry us into family processes with individual-oriented theories. This error has two forms: one might try to treat a family as merely an additive component of its individual members and neglect the transactions of the group; or, out of habit, one might apply to this group the theoretical models of the individual.

A psychiatrist interviewing a couple who complain of marital difficulty provides a case in point. The psychiatrist might describe the wife as hypochondriacal, ineffectual, and dependent, with hysterical tendencies, and the husband as cold, efficient, passive-aggressive, and so forth. Short of sending them immediately to an attorney, his recommendation is apt to be based on the notion that each of these individuals is disturbed and will require a good deal of therapy if they are to live with each other. However, there is another way of looking at this couple. They can be viewed as a mutual causative system whose complementary communication reinforces the nature of their interaction. Rather than focusing on individual pathology, he might notice that this couple behaves in a remarkably consistent manner, the paradigm of which might be: The wife demands, in any of dozens of ways, that the husband love her (paradoxically, since "love" has to be spontaneous). The husband replies tangentially, or perfunctorily, that he does love his wife. She becomes enraged and refuses his message, saying she doesn't need it anyway. The husband is hurt and withdraws (paradoxical in the framework of marriage). The wife responds by demanding that he love her, and the game begins again.

## SERVICE DELIVERY

The interaction between a service program and its clients comprises the essence of human service delivery (Rossi 1978). Two of the major sectors of the system—one representing the service program and the other representing the client or client population—are linked together through services rendered by the program in response to the demands generated by the client. Each component contains many variables that operate through time and may cause the client to demand services and the program to respond by rendering services in varying quantity.

The delivery of human services is a dynamic process taking place in a changing environment. Traditional attempts to describe human service delivery are, however, overwhelmingly static, describing how things look rather than how they function, and a static view leads to emphasis upon discrete symptoms. For example, the cost of providing service is high and increasing too rapidly. Facilities are overcrowded and otherwise inadequate. Too few trained workers exist, and they are rarely distributed geographically. Services are bureaucratic. Those who need services most often get them least. Services are not relevant to the needs of the people. Specific techniques do not work. Politicalization interferes with service efficacy. Research and development priorities are influenced too little by the needs of the people. Too often simplistic cause-and-effect explanations are offered rather than an exploration of the underlying dynamic system structures that have generated the symptoms and offer remedies or action-oriented solutions. Too often, existing knowledge about service delivery systems is so highly compartmentalized that, for practical purposes, the suprasystem is hidden from view. Such compartmentalization reflects artificial demands of knowledge, with little cross-fertilization or integration. Evaluation of service delivery might be achieved, for example, by the criterion of participant satisfaction (Keeley 1978).

Integrative thinking about human service situations is important, more difficult to achieve than is usually supposed, and often neglected in favor of naive intuition. The intuitive solution of social problems often causes another, even more serious, concern. For example, federal assistance for the construction of single-family homes alleviated the postwar housing shortage but inadvertently contributed to today's problem by providing incentives for the middle class to leave the city, thus weakening its tax base. Likewise, the use of certain pesticides improves farm productivity but kills wildlife and birds and poisons waterways, ultimately decreasing the food supply. Highway construction eases traffic congestion but destroys neighborhoods and necessitates more cars. And a federal crackdown on the smuggling of marijuana from Mexico may have expanded the market for a more dangerous drug, heroin.

Why does the usual analysis fail to provide an adequate understanding of the human services delivery process? The major reason is that the cause-and-effect approach is perceived as a straight line moving through time, but experience from every discipline and service delivery system teaches that life situations do not follow such familiar forms of causation. Instead, the elements of such a change themselves interact in loops and circles so that, along with producing an outcome, the components affect each other. The outcome, in turn, then affects the initial conditions, blurring any absolute sense of beginning and end. Such interaction-oriented analysis is necessary in considering social systems that are necessarily complex, in which feedback loops and causal circles connect the interacting element.

Although most human services may be said to function well in the sense that some benefit results from contact between an individual provider and an individual consumer, human service agencies are often less effective than might be desired. The life cycle of many human service programs can be described as a process of growth and decay—similar to the behavior of a bacterial colony on a Petri dish or the rise and decline of an epidemic of influenza. Initially there is a short startup period during which the service efficacy grows slowly as the staff are hired and trained and various operating procedures are established. This is followed by a longer period of exponential growth, which then shifts gradually into a period of stable mature function. The primary cause of this shift is a scarcity of resources relative to demand or service. At this point in its development, the agency is forced either to increase its capacity or to reduce the demand for services. In privately financed practice, further expansion may be accomplished, as when a physician hires an additional nurse or takes in a younger physician associate. Raising his fee or referring new patients to another physician or agency are effective tactics for reducing the market. Other practices are employed by public agencies; they include waiting lists, strict standards of eligibility, complicated registration procedures, unattractive waiting spaces, and inhospitable behavior on the part of receptionists and other public contact personnel. These result in a reduction in the number of requests for service. A discouraged client hesitates to return unless motivated by greater needs; he may also discourage others from seeking help.

Consider the following scenario: A new public hospital is constructed to fill a gap in service, and it actually does so for a period of time. The capacity grows quickly and, in the process, stimulates a latent demand for service. The hospital responds by increasing its effective capacity to the limit, but eventually capacity is overtaken by demand. This stage is reached sooner if the hospital serves an urban population whose alternative service resources (such as private physicians) are leaving the area faster than they are being replaced. Ironically, an ever-widening gap between demand and capacity has classically been viewed as an opportunity for a profit-making company, yet this same gap is necessarily viewed as a problem by most municipal governments.

## SYSTEMIC LEVELS OF INTERVENTION

There are five basic levels of intervention from a systems perspective: (1) the individual, (2) the group and the family, (3) organizations, (4) communities, neighborhoods, catchment areas, and so on; and (5) society and its social structure (Reiff 1975). These levels are operational. For example, a CMHC may operate at the individual level (such as providing individual psychotherapy) or at the group level (providing family services or group therapy). At the organizational level it may be working with a school or welfare agency. At the community level it may be doing neighborhood work or community organizing with the city planner or with the council of community services. At the society level it may be attempting to influence legislators to change the abortion laws or some other social program or policy.

It is not sufficient simply to identify the operational level; what we need to know is what we are trying to change. The level of operation does not automatically define the unit of study or the nature and locus of change. One can work with individuals to change society and one can work with society to change individuals. There is no automatic relationship—once the decision is made to work at any operational level—between the locus of change and the unit of study.

In the first unit of study, that of the individual, we concentrate on dispositional or person-centered factors; these include the genetic, physiological, and psychological. In the field of mental health the psychological dispositional factors are generally attributed to intrapsychic phenomena; they are considered remediable by a number of different techniques primarily aimed at changing the individual. Thus the locus of change is within the individual.

The second level or unit of study is the situational. This is a class of phenomena that emerges out of the interaction of the self with its immediate milieu. It has to do with the social settings that are directly open to the individual's personal experience and to some extent subject to his willful activities.

The third level, the social, involves matters that transcend the immediate milieu or social situation of the individual in the range of his inner life. It has to do with many milieus and with the organization of cultural norms, values, and customs into substantive areas. These substantive areas are the institutional orders that make up the social structure of society. For example, a man and woman may be experiencing personal problems in their marriage; but when the divorce rate escalates to 50 percent, we are faced with an issue of social structure that relates to the norms, values, and customs of marriage, the institutional order of the family, and other institutional factors that bear on them.

Another distinction is that between problems of living and social issues. Problems of living occur within the individual and his immediate milieu. These involve self or disposition and those limited areas of social life that we are accustomed to call a social situation. A problem of living is a personal, private matter. Social issues have to do with the organization of many milieus into the institutional orders of society as a whole, with the ways in which various milieus overlap and penetrate to form the structure of social and historical life.

A social issue is a public matter, and the nature of social issues is such that they cannot be defined very well in terms of the everyday immediate environments of people. For example, a single man may be unemployed, and his unemployment may be attributable to his dispositional factors within his particular social situation. But when 50,000 people are unemployed, we have a totally different kind of situation. We are now talking about the institutional order: in this case, the economy, the availability of work for large segments of the population. Both the correct statement of the problem and the range of possible solutions require us to consider, in cases like unemployment, the economic and political institutions of society and not the personal situations and dispositions of a particular group of individuals.

## CONCLUSION

The major concepts of an open-systems approach have been reviewed in this chapter. Illustrations of how these concepts can be applied to human services delivery were presented. A series of hypotheses was presented for empirical testing; the hypotheses could guide the development of systems theory in human services.

GST, it was noted, is viewed as a heuristic way of understanding the phenomena of human services. Thus it is not implied that there are no limitations to the GST approach. Some limitations have in fact been pointed out—for example, not dealing directly with the relationship between educational problems and the school culture (Sarason 1977). On the whole, however, the systems approach has an advantage over the causal approach and promises to stimulate thinking in the human services area for some time.

## REFERENCES

Ackoff, R. L. 1960. Systems, organizations, and interdisciplinary research. *General Systems Yearbook* 5:1–8.

Baker, F. 1969. An open systems approach to the study of mental hospitals in transition. *Community Mental Health Journal* 5:403–412.

Baker, F. and G. O'Brien. 1971. Intersystems relations and coordination of human service organizations. *American Journal of Public Health* 61(1):130–137.

Baker, F. and C. H. Schulberg. 1967. The development of a community mental health ideology scale. *Community Mental Health Journal* 3:216–225.

Bass, R. S. and C. Windle. 1972. Continuity of care: Approaches to measurement. *American Journal of Psychiatry* 129, 196.

Bertalanffy, L. von. 1950. The theory of open systems in physics and biology. *Science* 3:23–29.

Bertalanffy, L. von. 1956. General systems theory. *General Systems Yearbook* 1:1–10.

Bertalanffy, L. von. 1968. *General Systems Theory.* New York: Brazillier.

Boguslaw, W. 1965. *The New Utopians.* Englewood Cliffs, N.J.: Prentice-Hall.

Boulding, K. E. 1956. General systems theory: The skeleton of science. *General Systems Yearbook* 1:11–17.

Broskowski, A. 1976. Management information systems for planning and evaluation. In C. Schulberg and F. Baker, eds., *Program Evaluation in the Health Fields,* vol. w. New York: Human Sciences.

Cassel, J. S. 1970. Physical illness in response to stress. In S. Levine and N. A. Scotch, eds., *Social Stress.* Baltimore: Johns Hopkins University Press.

Chin R. and G. O'Brien. 1970. General systems theory: The model and a case of practitioner application. In A. Sheldon, F. Baker, and C. McLaughlin, eds., *Systems in Medical Care.* Cambridge: MIT Press.

Drucker, P. F. 1973. *Management: Task, Responsibilities, Practices.* New York: Harper & Row.

Evans, Eunice B. 1979. An integrated social service delivery system. *The social welfare forum, 1978.* New York: Columbia University Press for National Conference on Social Welfare.

Forrester, J. W. 1971a. Counterintuitive behavior of social systems. *Technology Review* 73:1–16.

Forrester, J. W. 1971b. *World Dynamics.* Cambridge: Wright-Allen Press.

Guerney, B. G. 1969. *Psychotherapeutic Agents: New Roles for Nonprofessionals, Parents, and Teachers.* New York: Holt, Rinehart and Winston.

Hall, A. D. and R. E. Fagen. 1956. Definitions of a system. *General Systems Yearbook* 1:18–28.

Heck, E. T. 1970. Reinforcement of agency's system for the collection and utilization of behavioral data. Paper presented at the American Psychological Convention, Miami.

Jette, P. R. and F. Montanino. 1978. Face-to-face interaction in the criminal justice system: Differential leverage interaction strategies. *Criminology* 16(1):67–86.

Katz, D. and R. L. Kahn. 1966. *The Social Psychology of Organizations.* New York: Wiley.

Keeley, M. 1978. A social-justice approach to organizational evaluation. *Administrative Science Quarterly* 23(2):272–92.

Kelly, J. 1966. Ecological constraints on mental health services. *American Psychologist* 6:535–539.

Kelly, J. 1968. Toward an ecological conception of preventive interventions. In J. Carter, ed., *Research Contributions from Psychology to Community Mental Health.* New York: Behavioral.

Kelly, J. 1971. Qualities for the community psychologist. *American Psychologist* 26:897–903.

Kilburg, R. 1977. General systems theory and community mental health: A view from the boiler room. *International Journal of Mental Health,* 4:80–93.

Kuhn, T. S. 1962. *The Structure of Scientific Revolution.* Chicago: University of Chicago Press.

Lennard, H. L. and A. Bernstein. 1971. Dilemma in mental health program evaluation. *American Psychologist* 26:307–310.

Levin, G. and E. B. Roberts. 1976. *The Dynamics of Human Service Delivery.* Cambridge: Ballinger.

Long, B. B. 1979. Report from the President's Commission on Mental Health. In *The Social Welfare Forum, 1978.* New York: Columbia University Press for National Conference on Social Welfare.

Miller, J. G. 1965. Living systems: Structure and process. *Behavioral Sciences* 10:337–379.

Miller, J. G. 1971. The nature of living systems. *Behavioral Sciences* 16:277 301.

Reiff, R. 1975. Of cabbages and kings. *American Journal of Community Psychology* 3(3):187–196.

Rossi, Peter H. 1978. Issues in the evaluation of human services delivery. *Evaluation Quarterly* 2(4):573–599.

Sanford, N. 1970. Community actions and the prevention of alcoholism. In D. Adelson and B. L. Kalis, eds. *Community Psychology and Mental Health.* Scranton, Penn.: Chandler.

Sarason, S. B. 1977. A cultural limitation of systems approaches to educational reform. *American Journal of Community Psychology* 5(3):277–289.

Sauber, S. R. 1977. The human services delivery system. *International Journal Mental Health* 5(4):121–140.

Schulberg, C. H. and F. Baker. 1969. Community mental health: The belief system of the 1960s. *Psychiatric Opinion* 6:14–26.

Schulberg, C. H. and F. Baker. 1976. *The Mental Hospital and Human Services.* New York: Human Sciences Press.

Schumaker, C. J. 1972. Change in health sponsorship: II. Cohesiveness, compactness and family constellation of medical care patterns. *American Journal of Public Health* 62:931–935.

Sells, S. B. 1969. Ecology and the science of psychology. In E. P. Williams and H. L. Raush, eds., *Naturalistic Viewpoints in Psychological Research.* New York: Holt, Rinehart and Winston.

Shannon, C. E. and W. Weaver. 1949. *The mathematical Theory of Communication.* Urbana: University of Illinois Press.

Whittington, H. G. 1966. *Psychiatry in an American Community.* New York: International University Press.

Weiner, N. 1948. *Cybernetics.* New York: Wiley.

Zax, M. and E. L. Cowen. 1967. Early identification in prevention of emotional disturbance in a public school. In E. L. Cowen, E. A. Gardner, and M. Zax, eds., *Emergent Approaches to Mental Health Problems.* New York: Appleton-Century-Crofts.

# 3

## THE MENTAL HEALTH SYSTEM

Approaches to the care of the mentally ill have undergone historic changes over the centuries. Modern psychiatry has developed out of an evolutionary process that has brought the medical and helping professions to recognition of mental illness as curable.

### HISTORIC REVOLUTIONS IN ATTITUDES TOWARD MENTAL HEALTH

At one time the treatment of mental illness was the responsibility of priests, who functioned within the framework of popular beliefs in demonology. The priests employed ritualized, exorcistic practices for casting evil spirits out of the bodies of afflicted persons. Such practices were not universal (Neugebauer 1978); but in general the decision whether the "possession" was the work of good or evil spirits was usually dependent on the patient's symptoms. The belief in demoniacal possession eventually turned to beliefs about witchcraft. The mentally ill were labeled either witches or heretics. Only slowly did demonology give way to the view that the mentally ill were sick people.

Presaging later changes, the ancient Greek, Hippocrates, and other physicians of classical times denied the intervention of deities and demons in the development of disease. Hippocrates, the "father of medicine," and his copractitioners insisted that mental disorders had natural causes and required treatment like other diseases. The treatment of mental disorders, they argued, should be provided by physicians rather than priests.

Attitudes change slowly. Beginning in the sixteenth century, monasteries and prisons gradually relinquished the care of the mentally ill to the asylums, which were established in increasing numbers. By the late eighteenth century the spreading controversy over the question whether psychopathology related to disorders of the body or of the spirit was approaching a resolution. History's greatest revolution in mental health care had begun.

**Eighteenth- and Nineteenth-Century Reforms**  The belief in the curability of mental illness found expression in the theories of Phillipe Pinel in France, William Tuke in England, and Benjamin Rush, the "father of American psychiatry." These late eighteenth-century figures, along with Dorothea Dix in the mid-nineteenth century, strongly influenced the reformation of attitudes toward treatment of society's deviants in Europe and the United States.

Before the reformer's attitudes gained currency, however, the development of psychiatric hospitals was marked by a transitional period during which home care was provided, as it also was in medicine. Because few facilities existed for the humane treatment of the mentally ill during the first half of the nineteenth century, those hospitals that did exist were privately operated and tended to serve the few psychiatric patients who were able to pay for their treatment. Thus the majority of the mentally ill were "treated" in their home communities—grouped together with the physically sick, the poor, the aged, and the mentally retarded. Some people received care from paid individuals, while others suffering from emotional problems were lodged in prisons or poorhouses supported by the local community.

Kindness was the fundamental ingredient in Pinel's therapeutic approach. Seeking to gain the patient's confidence and instill in him a sense of hope, Pinel developed what became known as "moral treatment," which in contemporary psychiatry corresponds to milieu therapy. Moral treatment involved the creation of a total therapeutic environment—social, psychological, and physical; it assumed that insanity was a curable disease, given understanding, patience, kindness, and the proper care. The active participation of the patient in the therapeutic process was prescribed by the physician, and each individual was treated according to his unique needs. Advocates of moral treatment also placed great emphasis on providing mentally ill persons with a new physical environment in order to break the patterns associated with the patient's past history. Unfortunately, by the late nineteenth century, while the systems of state hospitals had grown in size and number, the quality of treatment they provided had begun to deteriorate to the extent that they were hardly better than the community programs that they had replaced. Shortages of funds, an influx of immigrants, and the use of the hospitals as dumping grounds for the poor and prisons for criminals resulted in overcrowding that made adequate care impossible.

**The Growth of Professionalism**   There were other influences on the growth of the custodial hospital. One major force was the growing sense of professionalism among psychiatrists. This involved the creation of a monopoly of special skills and of a subculture that gave its members a common pool of experience. The consequence was enhanced communication within the group and the power to exclude nonspecialists—including, of course, the layman. The establishment of a professional psychiatric subculture was marked by the founding in 1884 of the present-day American Psychiatric Association, whose major purpose was to define the standards that would govern treatment, administration, and management of services for the mentally ill.

The deterioration of state mental hospitals continued, in greater or lesser degree, until after World War II. Certain hospitals were unusually well staffed, but for the most part hospitals functioned with appropriations that averaged $2 to $3 per patient per day. Staffs were overworked, frequently untrained, and poorly paid; little could reasonably be expected in terms of "treatment." Between 1845 and 1945, 300 state mental hospitals were established in the United States. Founded with enthusiasm, these institutions had quickly lapsed into vast storehouses of disabled individuals. On an average day in 1955, nearly 600,000 persons occupied beds in mental hospitals supported by state and county funds. In 1957, of the 1,241,000 active patients in all psychiatric hospitals in the United States, including public, private, and Veterans Administration hospitals, nearly 840,000 (approximately two-thirds) were in state mental hospitals. In 1960, while general medical hospitals had daily patient cost of more than $27 and private psychiatric hospitals and psychiatric units and general hospitals expended about $17 per patient per day, the per patient daily cost in state mental institutions averaged less than $4.50 (Bloom 1973). As recently as 1971, court action was necessary to require a particular state to provide proper treatment for mental patients. The Department of Justice, in this court suit, noted that placement in this state mental hospital . . . means not only the absence of treatment but indeed is probably antitherapeutic and harmful to those unfortunate victims. . . . It has retrogressed since the nineteenth century when the institution was founded. It simply does not exist for those who were unfortunate enough to be old, mentally ill, or unwanted in the State of . . . and placed by the State in one of its human warehouses. (*APA Monitor* 1972)

The degree to which institutions actually help may, of course, be illusory. It has been documented that for some populations there may be deterioration, and this process is more pronounced the longer the term of institutionalization (Ohwaki and Stayton 1978; Zober 1978).

**Outcome of the First Revolution**   The first mental health revolution peaked around 1900. Following are some of its accomplishments up to 1915, when modern psychiatry began a new, more impressive growth phase. First, the early concepts of demonology had finally been destroyed, and the organic viewpoint of mental illness based on brain pathology was well established. Second, for general paresis and certain other mental disorders, definite underlying brain pathology had been discovered and appropriate methods of treatment developed. Third, on the basis of extensive research in such subjects as anatomy and biochemistry, mental illness had finally been recognized and had gained status equal to that of physical illness—at least within the medical profession. Also, for the first time, the mentally disturbed were receiving humane treatment based on emerging scientific theories and practices. Fourth, a workable, although not yet completely satisfactory, classification scheme had been established.

Fifth, and finally, emphasis had finally been placed upon the importance of public education for the understanding, early detection, and prevention of mental illness. The importance of public education regarding mental illness had been brought into focus by Clifford Beers, a former mental patient; his famous book describing his experiences, *A Mind That Found Itself,* was published in 1908. His energetic leadership brought him worldwide recognition and resulted in the formation of an International Committee for Mental Hygiene, which stimulated the interest and aid of many public-spirited citizens and scientists and fostered a public understanding of mental disorders while mitigating the prevalent attitudes of fear and horror. A great deal of research was underway in anatomy, physiology, biochemistry, and allied medical sciences in an attempt to study brain pathology and other types of mental illness and to clarify the role of organic processes in all behavior.

**The Second Revolution in Mental Health**   Sigmund Freud, alone, touched off the second great revolution in mental health. As a result of his growing dissatisfaction with the organic approach to mental illness, he went to study with Charcot in France and later returned to Vienna to work with Joseph Breuer, a physician who had been using hypnosis on his neurotic patients. Freud's work, mainly with neurotic patients, led to his comprehensive dynamic theory, which launched the movement away from the organic viewpoint. In a wider context, Freud is now considered as influential as Darwin, Marx, and Einstein in the shaping of our culture and our beliefs about man.

In Freud's view of man, the frustrations and conflicts common to everyday life can become so overwhelming that the individual may resort to unhealthy responses in an effort to adjust. For example, the individual who feels that he has failed miserably in life may become chronically discouraged and depressed, or he may project blame for his difficulties onto other people who he believes are "against" him. With emphasis on the unconscious, Freud placed the burden of influence on the family. He held that during the first five or six years of life the child develops an irrational, unconscious system that greatly influences him for the rest of his life. In establishing the theme of unconscious determinism, Freud again placed mental illness firmly within the context of the diseased person. In order to cure the mental patient, it was seen necessary to find a cause for the illness, which generally involved a long search into the early history of the individual. Freud evolved the diagnostic and therapeutic strategy of psychoanalysis for communicating with the unconscious; his techniques included free association, interpretation of dreams, interpretation of everyday pathology, projective techniques, and a detailed analysis of case histories.

Freud demonstrated that abnormal mental phenomena were simply exaggerations of normal phenomena and that the patient's symptoms represented the outcome of his attempts to meet his problems as best he could. With the recognition that the same fundamental principles are basic to both normal and abnormal development, much of the mystery and fear that had surrounded mental illness were dispelled; the mental patient was thus helped along the road to full human dignity.

**Other Movements**   Other movements current around the turn of the century included behaviorism, somatic treatment, self-theory, and the holistism. Pavlov's principle of conditioning was adopted by the American psychologist J. G. Watson as a procedure for studying human behavior more objectively and for avoiding the pitfalls of introspection implicit in psychoanalytic theory. This approach placed heavy emphasis on the role of the social environment in ''conditioning'' personality development and on learning and behavior.

At the same time, a number of somatic approaches were utilized in the search for more efficient cures. They included drug or electroconvulsive therapies; prefrontal lobotomy, which consisted of surgically severing the nerve fibers that connect the frontal lobe of the brain to the thalamus; and tranquilizers, which were introduced in 1952. Tranquilizing drugs did not come into general use in public institutions until the mid-1950s; but once utilized they provided a new method of restraint on deviant behavior. Their effectiveness in the reduction of extreme behavior has had a dramatic effect on the character of such institutions because they largely eliminated the necessity for physical restraint.

Self-theory as first described by William James had largely shaped conceptions up to the present. The self is seen both as an object—the individual's perception and evaluation of himself—and as a reference point and integrative center for evaluating new experiences and coordinating adjustive behavior. Both Jung and Adler emphasized the concept of a ''creative self'' striving toward wholeness and fulfillment, and the social psychologist George Mead elaborated on the social origin of the self and the importance of the self-concept to an understanding of human behavior. There are currently several mainstreams of self-theory, including existentialism, client-centered counseling, and humanistic psychology. Among them, the most clearly worked out system of self-theory is the client-centered approach of Carl Rogers, which is largely based on his pioneering research into the nature of the psychotherapeutic process (Sarason 1966).

**The Influence of Sociology**  It became apparent to social scientists that man is greatly influenced by—and that his personality development is largely a product of—the society in which he lives: its institutions, traditions, values, ideas, and technology, and the specific family and other interpersonal relationships to which he is exposed. Among the contributions of a sociological perspective are the uncovering of stereotypes, for example, of women as more prone to emotional disturbance (Stockburger and Davis 1978)—and the process by which people become labeled as mentally ill (Smith 1978). There also developed an understanding of the relationship between sociocultural factors in a given society and the incidence and types of mental illness that occur within it (Hollingshead and Redlich 1958; Turner and Gartrell 1978; Wheaton 1978). Among the psychiatrists who first recognized these findings and helped develop socially oriented personality theories were Alfred Adler, Karen Horney, Harry Stack Sullivan, and Erich Fromm.

Then Adolf Meyer promoted the holistic point of view, which asserts that the study of the determinants of the patient's behavior is pluralistic and interactional and that all the many relevant factors—biological, psychological, and sociological—must be investigated and coordinated to achieve an understanding of the development of the processes and patterns of mental illness. Despite the convergence of these various sciences on the problem of mental illness, there remains to this day a lack of confidence in psychiatric prediction (Cocozza and Steadman 1978).

**The Third Revolution in Mental Health**   The third revolution in mental health (see Hobbs 1964) is not ordinarily identified with an individual. Instead, it becomes evident in a common theme that runs through many seemingly disparate innovations of the years since 1960. The concepts of therapeutic community and the open hospital, the increased interest in children's problems, the growth in the field of social psychiatry, the broad base of professional responsibility for mental health programs, the search for new sources of manpower, the new concern for the mentally retarded, proposals for comprehensive community mental health centers—all these developments constitute evidence of a pervasive change. Indicative of the new revolution is that the basic principles of public health theory and practice have finally penetrated the field of mental health.

The term ''mental health'' at one time derived meaning mainly from its opposite, mental disease. Today it means not only health but human well-being as well. This contemporary revolution is therefore manifest both in changed practices and in new assumptions about the fundamental character of mental disorder and of mental health. If we consider that a great stride forward was made when aberrant behavior was recognized not as madness, lunacy, or possession by the devil but as an illness to be treated like other illnesses, it is conceivable that even greater advances may result from the growing recognition that mental illness is not merely the private organic misery of an individual but a social, ethical, and moral problem that confers responsibility on an entire community.

Seen in this light, the mission of the third mental health revolution is greatly enhanced service delivery: more specifically, the development of new ways to use manpower resources and knowledge to provide accessible, effective mental health services for the diagnosis, treatment, rehabilitation, and prevention of illness for all those in need. Two works that may serve as guidelines to such action are the report of the Joint Commission on Mental Illness and Health, *Action for Mental Health* (1961), and the report of the President's Panel on Mental Retardation, called *National Action to Combat Mental Retardation* (1962).

The second major innovation was the new philosophy of a "therapeutic community." This orientation to psychiatric treatment centers on the axiom that therapeutic potential resides in patients as well as in staff, and that by forming a democratic community within the hospital of both patients and staff the effectiveness of psychological treatment can be increased. A leading exponent of this approach was Maxwell Jones (1968), who first used it in England and Scotland; it was then adopted by many psychiatric hospitals in the United States.

The third development was the idea of geographic decentralization in large state mental hospitals. Whereas state hospitals were usually isolated—both geographically and functionally—from the community, today patients are placed and treated in institutions and agencies closer to their home communities.

In previous years, both acute and chronic treatment services were frequently organized around diagnosis and treatment modalities. Patients were classified according to diseases and labeled by age group and problem. For example, there were wards for elderly patients and wards for alcoholics. Today many chronic back wards have been abolished under the new concept of geographic decentralization, and chronic patients have been transferred to their respective geographical units. Manpower has also been equitably distributed among these treatment centers. Under such arrangements, hospital personnel commit part of their time to community work, first by providing after-care services and later by providing alternatives to hospitalization in collaboration with community-based agencies. It is also noteworthy that decision making has tended to democratize the former hierarchy of authority and power.

These three approaches—psychopharmacology, the therapeutic community, and geographic decentralization—have led to a lower hospital census, closer working relationships, collaborative responsibility between the community and hospital, and the democraticization of the clinical decision-making process.

**The Era of Deinstitutionalization**  The last quarter of the twentieth century has clearly become an era of deinstitutionalization. The large custodial hospitals, built in the late nineteenth and first half of the twentieth centuries, are beginning to reduce significantly their patient populations, if not to close outright. This recent trend has been perceptible since the late 1950s and continues on a nationwide basis. Witness the following statistics from the National Institute of Mental Health: In 1955, 49 percent of all psychiatric treatment was provided by in-patient services at state central hospitals; in 1971, the figure was only 19 percent. Out-patient services, other than community mental health centers, which accounted for 23 percent of the episodes in 1955, accounted for 42 percent of all psychiatric treatment by 1971. Whether in California—where many counties have few, if any, patients receiving services in state mental hospitals—or Massachusetts—where the state mental hospital census was declining at the rate of 19 percent a year in the 1970s—the trend is clear. Although the average daily census in state hospitals decreased from 559,000 in 1955 to well below 200,000 in 1980, admission rates have remained high (Schulberg and Killilea 1982). Deinstitutionalization has become a matter of public policy in many states.

The integration of mental health service in the community marks a resumption of an earlier approved plan, not an innovation, for historically that is where such services began. The large state mental health hospitals have existed for only the last one hundred years. In recent times, as the shortcomings of the state hospitals system have become more evident, the old idea of community-based help for the mentally disturbed person has found new expression and new structure in the community mental health center.

A number of alternatives to institutionalization have evolved. For example, retarded adults have at least twelve alternatives, including group homes, sheltered villages, workshop dormitories, and semi-individual units (Baker, Seltzer, and Seltzer 1977). The Veterans Administration has developed a day hospital program at thirty-four hospitals (Davis, Lorei, and Caffey 1978). Another approach is the use of after-care to shorten institutionalization (Hogan 1978; Byers, Cohen, and Harshbarger 1978). Alternatively, more effort is being exerted to prepare mental patients for deinstitutionalization (Siegel and Lasker 1978). Finally, the use of crisis intervention has the potential of averting institutionalization in the first place (Delaney, Seidman, and Grant 1978).

Institutionalization has carried with it the onus of the "total institution" life-style, which typically has deprived the chronic patient of skills and motivation to adjust to the community. While the rights of patients have improved, there still remain abuses (Cox 1978). Hence, there remain strong reasons for seeking alternatives to institutionalization.

**Manpower Development**  The concept of the mental health model has been established and transmitted mainly by the professionals within it. Over the years, their function has been fragmented through specialization into various roles that have evolved into "professions," each laying claim to a particular facet of the deviant individual. Mental health manpower now includes the following types of professionals: psychologists, social workers, psychiatrists, nurses, rehabilitation and school guidance counselors, activity therapists, and psychiatric aides.

During the last twenty years, the contribution of paraprofessionals has gained recognition and prompted an influx of funds to college and university training programs that offer associate degrees in mental health technology and related human services fields. Graduates of these associate of arts programs (which are highly practical in nature, with less emphasis on theory and liberal arts) usually find positions in new career ladders established by the mental health organizations.

Individuals with a bachelor's degree in psychology, sociology, or casework are also classified as paraprofessionals because they lack master's degree certification. While the role and functions of such paraprofessionals are often very similar to those of professionals, their salaries and formal responsibilities do not reflect their contribution. Because of successful contributions of the paraprofessional in the delivery system of mental health—as well as in health, corrections, and education (Gartner 1971)—mental health professionals and administrators of programs are increasingly receptive to inclusion of nonprofessionals and volunteers into its ranks of helpers. Many mental hospitals and mental health centers have established training programs for volunteers and attempted to identify community leaders and helpers, assigning them roles as nonprofessional caregivers. Examples are such programs as Big Brothers, college students working with emotionally disturbed children, peers as therapeutic agents, and parents as family life educators (Guerney 1969).

## RECENT DEVELOPMENTS: COMMUNITY MENTAL HEALTH

The third revolution in mental health, with all its innovations, has culminated in the community mental health movement. This movement has brought about a trend toward the standardization of services on a nationwide basis, on the one hand, while forging a firm local base for those services on the other.

**Community Mental Health**   The use of the terms "social psychiatry," "community psychology," "community psychiatry," and "community mental health" indicates that sociological thinking increasingly permeates the field of mental health. Moreover, mental illness is generally regarded by professionals and the general public as a national social problem as well as a health problem. Legislation to support mental health programs, involving massive amounts of public money, represents a major investment of our national resources. Another indication of the extent to which the public is now aware of mental health problems is that terms of mental disorder, such as anxiety, depression, compulsion, and schizophrenia, have become common household words.

When mental health is defined as a social problem, problems of behavior are seen to be signs of social disorder. The problem of the mentally ill represents socially intolerable deviance from patterns of normal or expected behavior. From this approach, treatment is organized to deal with the deviation—to make it conform to, or to separate it from, the rest of society.

Community mental health represents a unifying force between two rather different orientations toward mental illness: definition in terms of health and definition in terms of society. The health problem orientation focuses on the concern for individual well-being, on the prevention of recurring illness, and on establishing a state that has been called "high-level wellness" (Dunn 1961).

The social problem orientation has as its goal the efficient functioning of society. It is concerned with the social cost of deviant behavior, and its objective is stated in terms of deviance versus conformity. Struggles in society and social systems have always emphasized "getting rid of the bad." Marginal groups, such as the aged, crippled, retarded, and insane, have been expendable in many societies. Although industrially based affluence has allowed society to tolerate these identified groups, its philosophy, a carry-over from past traditions, is still to eliminate "undesirables."

**The Ecological Approach**   At their present stage of development, programs for dealing with mental health problems appear to have no overriding theory about the nature of mental health. When one examines the mental health movement, one finds various groups of people with differing training engaged in different activities with differing goals. They may be working toward mental health as a positive state variously defined; yet all can agree to be *against* mental illness.

One way of effecting a rapprochement between the health and the social orientations is to be found in a model based upon the concept of ecology. The concern of ecology is, by definition, "the nature of the interaction of organisms in populations with embedding environment, which supports, influences, and determines the limits of structure and function for the life that exists within" (Sells 1969:15). The ecological thesis in mental health is that there are predictable patterns of individual behavior that are characteristic of any given social situation and that the expressive behavior of the individual is subject to change within a new setting. Thus there exists a reciprocity between social structure and individual behavior.

One can begin to understand this approach by accepting the idea that each social system is unique and is organized in a particular way—much like the personality of a person—and that no other system is quite like it. Thus the psychology of individual differences may be applied as an analogy to understand social groups and social settings. Within this framework the regularities for which one searches are patterns of function and interrelationships rather than patterns of individual behavior.

In this context mental illness can be judged only in relationship to the context in which it occurs. The expression of mental illness—namely, its behavior, since it constitutes a deviation from expectations in a particular environment—tells us something about the nature of these expectations. Thus standards or norms for behavior are specific to the social group, and modes of deviance are expressions of these norms. The extent to which people outside the family, such as a physician or clergyman, are called to help in dealing with deviant behavior provides some indication of the variables of this phenomenon and of the extent to which a given culture approves of alcohol consumption and the points at which it distinguishes between a "social" drinker, a "problem" drinker, and an "alcoholic."

Similarly, as ecology in plant and animal biology has its origin in the study of the adaptation of organisms to their environment, so human ecology is derived from geography and sociology. Concepts and practices from many different disciplines provide the means for studying "man in his environment." One important reason for using the ecological approach in community mental health is that it allows one to begin with the assumption that virtually all problems of people are "specific" to themselves and their particular situation. From this theoretical position there is no "general" mental health problem. Communities must be seen as personalities, unique organizations of forces, needs, and resources. Services must then be custom tailored, with research helping to tell us how the tailoring might be done and training undertaken to provide skillful tailors.

The principles of community mental health may be viewed as providing a service beyond the illness concept and as including an environmental and ecological perspective. The operational form of the CMHC program is a center, locally based, and a broadly developed program serving a defined and manageable population. It is comprehensive in its range of services, is readily accessible to the people it serves, and provides an organizational framework that ensures continuity of care.

**The Community Mental Health Center**   President Kennedy, in his 1963 message to Congress, urged that the federal government provide financial assistance to mental hospitals during the transition to community-based centers so that hospitals might undertake demonstration and research programs, improve the quality of care, and provide in-service training for management personnel. As a result, Congress approved the Hospital Improvements program, one goal of which was the integration of the individual institution's activities into an overall statewide program.

In spite of this financial assistance to mental hospitals, however, it was made clear that the major thrust of future federal activity would be the support of community mental health centers. The need for such facilities was dramatically evidenced by the phenomenal costs of large mental institutions. To provide "inadequate" custodial care for mentally afflicted individuals in public institutions the total cost to the taxpayer was more than $2.4 billion a year in direct public outlay for services. Indirect public outlays, in welfare costs and in the waste of human recources, were even higher. It was, of course, impossible to measure the cost of personal anguish suffered in such institutions (Bindman 1959).

Congress therefore authorized the appropriation of $150 million to finance up to two-thirds of the cost of construction of CMHCs. These centers were to serve as the nucleus of a national mental health program in which the National Institute of Mental Health would be responsible for assisting states and communities to achieve the objectives outlined by President Kennedy. Fifty-three states and territories received planning grants for the preparation of comprehensive, long-range plans for the treatment of mental illness and improvement of the mental health of its residents. Staffing grants were authorized by an amendment passed in 1965, and the authorizations for both types of grants, construction and staffing, were extended and expanded by legislation passed in 1967, 1970, and 1975. Between 1965 and 1977, $1.85 billion was spent on CMHCs.

In 1955, Congress enacted a Mental Health Study Act, which established the Joint Commission on Mental Illness and Mental Health. This legislation mandated the commission to survey available resources and make recommendations for combating mental illness in the United States. After five years of analysis of the problems of mental illness in terms of manpower, facilities, and cost, the final report was published in 1961 under the title *Action for Mental Health*. The authors proposed that a full-time mental health clinic should be available to each 50,000 of population and that such clinics should serve both adults and children in short-term and long-term out-patient services.

Additionally, the commission recommended that community general hospitals of one hundred beds or more accpet mental patients for short-term hospitalization. The established set of locally available mental health services was to be supplemented by the development of a network of regional and statewide services for long-term and intermediate-term in-patient care. Community resources, on the other hand, were charged with offering in-patient care on an acute basis as well as out-patient and after-care services.

The guidelines for federal legislation rest on a number of principles. Thus they indicate that a community mental health center will offer a broad range of services to all citizens (principle of comprehensiveness), that such services will be interdependent (principle of coordination), and that there will be available, if needed, an easy succession of multiple services for each person (principles so important to the future of the community mental health movement).

The principle of comprehensiveness emphasizes the idea that effective mental health services should be inclusive rather than restrictive. Centers will offer services for discharged mental patients, including a variety of followup services, along with educative and consultative services that focus on early screening and detection.

The principle of coordination affirms that centers will provide services that are unduplicated and are integrated with other existing health and welfare services. Our mental health program in the United States has been criticized for not having offered optimal services to a maximum of the population. Instead, two population groups have received proportionally the majority of these services: the well-educated and the lower social class (Hollingshead and Redlich 1958; Miller and Mishler 1959). The latter group has largely been the recipient of public care, and the well-educated of private care. Each of these groups has received different types of services: psychotherapeutic benefits have been offered to the higher social classes; more medicinal and nonverbal treatment to the lower socioeconomic groups.

The principle of continuity of care relates to the coordination of several services made available by the center. This is in contrast to the above principle, which specifies coordination between or among community resources. Coordination, in the present context, constitutes an organizational and an administrative matter. Continuity of care, on the other hand, stresses the coordination that must exist or be developed in the realm of individual patient services. The principle of continuity of care means that the community mental health center does more than offer a range of services; it requires that these several services function as a unified program and that the center's staff maintain a concern for the patient in all phases of his difficulties. It is perhaps even more noteworthy that this principle requires the staff to pay particularly close attention to the patient's needs during transitional periods when he moves from one type of service to another.

The principle of continuity is closely related to the principle of comprehensiveness: if services are comprehensive, there is a greater likelihood that clients will receive effective service. If services are continuous, they are successive and administered with a minimum of delay. This principle, which deals directly with the quality control of therapeutic activities, affirms that decisions for treatment should be made with the intent of viewing the client as having available the therapeutic programs of the entire center rather than as receiving a specific service or a particular therapist. The concept also assumes that the provisions of mental health services in a community mental health center cannot be effective unless services are administered in a planned sequence. Services that are discrete, prolonged, or fragmented are contrary to the operating principles of a community mental health center program.

These three principles reflect an emerging consensus in the mental health profession; they also constitute a standard for the evaluation of programs that is independent of any particular philosophy of treatment. Even more significantly, these principles also give each community a new method for studying the development of changes in its own patterns of living (Miller and Mishler 1959).

**Characteristics of the Community Mental Health Center**   The establishment of a community mental health center means that services are made available on a local basis. The patient need not travel far from home, and treatment can take place without compounding the problem by placing the patient in unfamiliar surroundings. Moreover, the patient's family can be involved in the treatment process, and personal ties in normal living patterns can be maximally maintained.

To achieve accessibility, careful attention must be directed to the geographic location of the center. High fences and impenetrable walls were typical of nineteenth-century asylums, but they are hardly appropriate for today's mental health center. The design of a center must ensure an inviting appearance and must be harmonious with the community's other buildings.

To be truly accessible, the center must make its services available not only *where* they are needed but also *when* they are needed. Operationally, the center must function on a twenty-four hours a day, seven days a week. Services must be available at all times for new patients and for those clients who are already on the centers rolls.

A single patient facing emotional difficulties needs a variety of services. Likewise, patients with diverse problems must have different services available at any given time. At any time there may be patients of all ages, and they will come from a variety of social settings. It therefore follows that a variety of services must be made available to achieve comprehensiveness; the community mental health center must meet the needs for preventive, diagnostic, therapeutic, and rehabilitative services. In this sense, the comprehensiveness of the center enables it to offer help to the patient in all phases and sequences of the problematic behavior.

To achieve comprehensiveness, the community center must be able to serve the young as well as the old, must cooperate with other local service agencies, and must be available both to those who can pay for services and to those who cannot. Five essential services must be offered if the center is to qualify for federal funds under the Community Mental Health Centers Act of 1963 (Levenson 1972):

1. in-patient care for those who need intensive care or treatment around the clock;
2. out-patient care for adults, children, and families;
3. partial hospitalization; at least day care treatment for patients who are able to return home for evenings and weekends; and perhaps also night care for patients able to work but needing limited support or lacking suitable home arrangement;
4. emergency care on a twenty-four-hour basis by one of the three services listed in (3) above;
5. consultation and education to community agencies and professional personnel.

The regulations also specify additional services that, with the five essential ones, complete "the comprehensive community mental centers program":

6. diagnostic service, including both social and vocational rehabilitation;
7. precare and after-care, including screening of patients prior to hospitalization and home visiting or halfway houses after hospitalization;
8. training for all types of mental health personnel;
9. research and evaluation concerning the effectiveness of programs and addressing the problems of mental illness and its treatment.

The five "essential" services revolve around the traditional medical "in-patient–out-patient" model, which emphasizes the more traditional components of the comprehensive center idea—perhaps at the expense of new conceptualizations of what is crucial in community mental health. Partial hospitalization and emergency care represent highly desirable, indeed essential, extensions of the traditional clinical services and certainly move in the direction of greater flexibility and less disruption to normal patterns of living. Brief and partial hospitalization has proven to be cost effective (Endicott, Herz, and Gibbon 1978; Fink, Longabaugh, and Stout 1978). Yet the newer approach to community mental health through social systems such as family, school, neighborhood, and employment has further implications.

An important component of the community mental health center program and philosophy is that of prevention. The public health approach emphasizes prevention as a basic aspect of any health service program. To the public health practitioner, prevention is a tripartite matter: primary prevention involves attempts to reduce the incidence of new cases of illness; secondary prevention refers to efforts to reduce the prevalence of disease through such efforts as early case finding; and tertiary prevention means the reduction of long-term sequelae of disease through active rehabilitation programs. The CMHC very clearly shows, or should show, the public health orientation in its commitment to all three phases of preventive services.

There are various ways in which the CMHC can implement this orientation. For instance, the staff might conduct surveys and studies to locate the sources of mental stress; or it might conduct training programs for business managers, teachers, or clergymen to help them deal with the problems that they face on a day-to-day basis with employees, students, church members, and others. By providing mental health consultations to various client organizations—governing social agencies, health clinics, schools, courts, police departments, welfare agencies, churches, business, and industry—the staff of the CMHC can utilize its special knowledge to improve the quality of community and family life for all citizens. In effect, the staff increases the knowledge and skills of those community gatekeepers who have direct access to large segments of the population and to those people who may never seek out mental health treatment.

The CMHC can also provide consultation for the state mental hospital to which its community sends patients as a means of giving the hospital a constructive place within the context of the new CMHC approach to mental health. Ideally, these revitalized state hospitals will become integral parts of the comprehensive services offered to citizens of nearby communities. The CMHC–state hospital liaison has been demonstrated, in principle, to be viable (Boyd and Henderson 1978).

In accepting the important and difficult consultative role, mental health professionals of a CMHC must not presume to know how the institutions of a community should operate. Rather they should stress their contribution of a special perspective and special competencies that can aid the agencies and institutions to community life—in which people normally sustain and realize themselves. In this endeavor, the center staff needs to work in close cooperation with other key agencies and to share their concern for community betterment. The role of the CMHC is thus cooperative rather than superordinate. To promote coordination, representatives of various groups, such as local government facilities, social agencies, poverty programs, labor unions, and business organizations, should normally be included on the board responsible for center policies and practices.

**Other Service Providers**  Although the CMHC may be a primary caregiving agency in the field, it is by no means the only organization that provides mental health services. In every community there are family service agencies that are funded through the United Way and operated by members of the social work profession. Schools employ guidance counselors; colleges and universities have counseling psychologists on the faculty; and local and state governments finance numerous mental health programs, such as regional treatment centers (Ecklund 1978), satellite facilities (Hadley, Zuckerman, and Cymerman 1978), sheltered workshops, transitional living facilities (Holman and Shore 1978; Budson 1978), crisis intervention substance abuse programs, and specialized services. Voluntary groups such as religious organizations provide counseling services and education, and private practice groups and individuals serve significant segments of the population requiring mental health services. This includes the private psychiatric hospital and the psychiatric ward of a general hospital, the out-patient psychotherapist, and independent groups of private practitioners in the community.

The public mental health delivery system includes programs funded and operated by federal, state, and local governments as well as programs partially or fully funded by charitable organizations and foundations. Veterans Administration hospitals provide both in-patient and out-patient psychiatric services. Another service delivery system that has been operating informally with the public, voluntary, and private systems is the mutual-help service format. Membership in these groups is enormous, and the range of concerns is remarkably comprehensive.

The existing alternative human service technology developed primarily because of an unwillingness or inability on the part of professionals and their organizational structures to deal with particular problems of service delivery. One of the earliest of these systems developed because of the failure of traditional treatment techniques to reach the needs of individuals suffering from chronic psychotic disturbance and alcoholism. Drug or substance abuse programs developed somewhat later, with the rapid expansion of self-help groups, to meet this high-risk population. The intricate and crucial elements of mutual aid, including the unique benefits achieved through helping others and through participation in group process, are further described in chapter 8.

## IDEOLOGY OF SERVICE DELIVERY

Community mental health is one more recent in a long series of psychiatric ideologies or belief systems that affect the theoretical foundations and design of mental health caregiving networks (Baker and Schulberg 1967; Schulberg and Baker, 1969). Clearly validated etiological models of mental illness are as sparse today as they were a century ago. Consequently, practitioners are forced to function on the basis of psychiatric belief systems that are compatible with their own particular views of the relationship between man, pathological forces, and the illness process.

Three related yet significantly different frameworks have been prominent in the community mental health approach, as shown in table 1.4 (Sauber 1973).

The first of these, and the most commonly followed conceptual framework, defines pathology as primarily intrapsychic, that is, occurring within individual patients. This *clinical psychiatric approach* has much in common with the medical model of illness, in which the cause may be an environmental agent, such as a virus or an experience of deprivation, that is viewed as initiating processes within the individual that culminate in illness. Rather than attacking the offending agent before it can impair its victim, the treatment strategy of this medical-like model is usually to nullify or remove the pathogenic agent through the use of drugs or by intervention such as psychotherapy and rehabilitation programs that enable the patient's restorative forces to bring about recovery. The emphasis is upon intervening at the point where the individual's intrapsychic disturbance has reached a level that necessitates external assistance.

The services resulting from this intrapsychic conception of mental illness have generally been of high quality; however, they can reach only a small percentage of those requiring help. The general public has thus become increasingly dissatisfied with the relatively small contribution made by facilities using this approach toward reducing the community's overall burden. Consequently, there is a greater desire among mental health professionals to adopt the public mental health model as a guide to enlarging their scope of concern.

Under the *public health model,* the community mental health worker not only accepts responsibility for his individual patients but is also concerned with the needs of the total population. This approach assimilates the medical model of illness in that pathology is considered an internal phenomenon, but greater recognition is given to environmental factors. It also differs in that the public mental health practitioner uses case-finding techniques in addition to the diagnostic treatment functions of the clinical psychiatric practitioner as in the medical kind of model.

The third conceptional framework, the *human services model,* is markedly different from the individual-oriented frameworks as regards both structure and implication. Here illness is no longer perceived as an entirely intrapsychic process, but rather as a disequilibrium between certain individuals and their environment. This model focuses on problems-in-living in the social structure of a community and on the interlocking network of roles of its individual members, each of whom is expected to perform tasks and to receive privileges commensurate with his place in society. From this perspective, individual symptoms do not reflect internal pathology but rather signal an impairment in the individual's ability to assume an appropriate role and develop satisfactory relationships with others.

The implications of the socially oriented framework have radically changed the traditional boundaries of the mental health professionals' function. Because of the basic concern with the relationship of the environment and the welfare of total populations, it becomes especially necessary for the mental health professional to engage in activities of a preventive nature.

**Shortcomings of the Community Mental Health Center**   Despite its promise in preventive areas, the lack of impact of the CMHC in these areas has been a major shortcoming. There remain clinical, administrative, fiscal, and legal constraints on service (Elpers 1978). Other areas of difficulty that have impaired overall program effectiveness include planning, policy and priority setting, administration personnel and patterns, funding issues, and transition problems for state hospital personnel, patients, and alternative services.

Another shortcoming has been in effective evaluation of CMHCs and in use of evaluative results (Goldstein, Marcus, and Perkins 1978). During the first ten years of the area of the movement toward CMHCs, through the mid-1970s, a barrier to the evaluation of their success has been disagreement about the CMHC's definition of its major task and its respective priorities. Thus, due to the lack of clear-cut objectives, evaluative criteria have not been sufficiently formulated. Theoretically, the central tasks of the CMHC are the development of both a range of ''direct'' patient services and ''indirect'' mental health services such as program consultation and education.

There has always been some degree of controversy and confusion regarding the nature of indirect services, their development, and the values assigned to them. These are often referred to as an extension of the direct servicing system, since they provide consultation and training to community caregivers. The 1972–1973 annual NIMH inventory, however, indicates that less than 5 percent of staff time goes into direct preventive servicing in community mental health centers, despite the fact that the concept of prevention received special emphasis in President Kennedy's 1963 message on mental health. Using a broad definition of such activities, the 210 centers— out of a possible 295—that completed the NIMH-required inventory of activities for 1972 averaged only 10.3 percent of their staff hours in primary prevention. The categories included in compiling this figure are ''consultation,'' both program and case (4.4 percent), public ''information/education'' (1.5 percent), ''training'' other than in-service (2.3 percent), and ''community planning/developing'' (2.1 percent).

Because case consultation is frequently focused on secondary and tertiary prevention, primary preventive staff hours must obviously account for no more, and probably much less, than one-tenth of the total hours to which the nation's health centers commit paid staff.

Members of the President's Commission on Mental Health (1978) have argued that the absence of primary prevention programs should not be considered a failing in the CMHC movement because they were never really intended as a task priority of these centers. In fact, the researchers conclude, close inspection reveals that consultation and educational services have been overwhelmingly regarded as an extension of direct clinical services.

Of necessity, the development of indirect services implies a marked departure from the medical identity in terms of both organizational structure and ideology. Such services have required the development of programs in public health, consultation, and community intervention, which traditionally have been resisted by the clinical mental health profession. Primary interventions are aimed at the social and environmental factors that contribute to the incidence of disability of disease. With secondary preventive methods emphasizing early identification and intervention, the focus must shift from the individual patient to an entire population. From the experience of other countries, such as Canada, with CMHC-type operations, it has become clear that indirect services merit full funding, particularly if a national health insurance program is ever implemented (Tardiff 1978).

Despite growing awareness of the traditional doctor–patient model, of the manifest inadequacies of state hospital programs, and of the influence of social and environmental factors on psychological development, a clinical and individualistic ideology has continued to predominate. The result is that the CMHC has remained captive to the medical organization and the clinical professions. From the start, CMHC programs have had an overwhelming commitment to the clinical task; the indirect service component seems to have withered away, as if it had been an unsuccessful effort despite the fact it almost never received substantial support.

Other shortcomings have been attributed to the CMHC. For example, it has been alleged that some centers underserve psychotic patients. Data on three California CMHCs indicate that a substantial proportion of psychotic individuals in the community are served; that these patients had a significantly higher number of in-patient, day treatment, and out-patient admissions than did neurotic patients; and that they received more treatment in all major service modalities (Yarvis, Edwards, and Langsley 1978). Other problems concern the ways in which the CMHC is adopted to different types of communities—urban (Mesnikoff 1978) and rural (Jeffrey and Reeve 1978).

However, the rigid service and accountability requirements of P.L. 94-63 in 1975 produced "a dinosaur incapable of coping with environmental stress" (Sharfstein 1978).

**Problems of Administration**   At the time of CMHC development, few if any mental health professionals, and particularly psychiatrists, had been trained to administer complex organizations. Since the centers were thoroughly grounded in medical tradition, guidelines during the first decade of CMHC development required an M.D. as director, thus excluding professionals in other disciplines from the executive function. The naive argument that the knowledge of mental *illness* was essential to the leadership task and that psychiatrists should provide that function was generally accepted. On the other hand, when trained administrators have been employed, they too often have little knowledge of, or identification with, the field of mental health. In cases when both a mental health professional and a business manager work together, each an expert in his own area, the absence of a common frame of reference does not permit a unified approach.

To complicate matters even further, there is little useful literature on administration in mental health (Austin and Hershey 1982). The writing is so sparse that the designers of new training programs find little pertinent teaching material and are forced to rely on administrative data from outside the mental health field. Saul Feldman at the NIMH has made some attempt to respond to this need by starting a journal entitled *Administration in Mental Health* and editing a text on *The Administration of Mental Health Services* (1973).

Training programs still are not sufficiently tailored to delivery of mental health services. Generic administrative processes such as planning, budgeting, and decision making are always shaped by the environments in which they take place. While sharing a common base, administration in mental health is different from administration in other fields. Administrative technique is also determined by the needs and values of the various parties to the process as well as by the particular field in which it is applied. With very few training programs in mental health administration, the essential question—Training for what?—remains unanswered.

**Funding Issues and the State Hospital System**   The original mandate of community mental health centers to replace the public and state hospital requires further attention. Between the opening of the first federally funded centers, in 1962, and 1971, the number of state mental hospitals *increased* from 307 to 321. Total expenditures for the public hospital's in-patient services increased from $1.3 billion to more than $2 billion during the same period. One can contrast these figures to the $135 million appropriated by Congress for community mental health centers for fiscal 1972; the sum comprised about 25 percent of the total funds the centers could expect from all sources. In fact, in fiscal 1971 federal staffing grants accounted for only 27.4 percent of the reported CMHC total receipts from all sources (Kaplan and Borg 1976).

Today there are less than 800 CMHCs serving about half of the population; numerous funding and operational problems plague existing centers. It has become clear that the public mental hospital will probably survive.

Unfortunately, some attempts to "go community" have foundered. The causes of such failure include the fact that hospitals have at times been closed—and their patients precipitously discharged—with little regard for the sentiments of community groups or caregiving agencies. Planning for change has often occurred without sufficient appreciation of the participation demanded by communities. When hospital change has been introduced coercively, both patients and professionals, denied the opportunity to voice their opposition actively, have—in passive or indirect ways—sabotaged the efforts to change.

Schulberg and his colleagues (1976) advocated a five-year phase-down for the operations of public mental hospitals and the redeployment of funds to community services. Factors affecting the success of this program include a shift in the continuity of care for discharged patients, community acceptance of the mentally ill, and redeployment of personnel to community facilities.

Although the number of hospitals has increased, the number of patients in public mental hospitals has decreased in every year since 1955. To a great extent, this phenomenon can be explained by factors other than the development of the CMHC (Shun and Drotter 1974). Since the first centers did not begin operation until 1966, subsequent years of the decrease is de facto attributable to other factors: the most frequently mentioned is the growth of psychoactive drugging, a treatment that continues to the present.

A second element was the inception of the Medicare and Medicaid programs in 1965. The subsequent increase in the number of nursing homes has provided alternative care facilities, particularly for aged individuals who should never have been inside a psychiatric facility in the first place. For those "legitimately" diagnosed as mentally ill, Medicare and Medicaid policy toward the payment of benefits has contributed to the growth of a second alternative: psychiatric care in a general hospital. In a mental hospital, the government stipulates life-time maximum benefits with a specific number of covered days. In a general hospital, by contrast, mental illness is regarded in the same way as physical illness: that is, there is no lifetime maximum. Yet another factor has been the availability of Aid to the Totally Disabled as a major source of funding for the community care of former chronic mental patients (Kaplan and Bohr 1976).

Research by Baker, Issacs, and Shulberg (1972) indicates that there has been no significant increase in the involvement of state hospital services in the community-based caregiving network. Nor has there been a change in psychiatric hospital services, which in fact provide custodial care under the guise of "long-term" treatment. An interesting body of data supporting this contention shows that in 1970 more than 80 percent of the hospital personnel were in custodial, clerical, fiscal, or maintenance positions. Of this group, 46.3 percent of the total full-time personnel were aides or attendants, and 34.4 percent fell into the "all other" category, which was defined as including clerical, fiscal, and maintenance (Kanno 1971).

Impetus for change in the public sector is partly legal in origin. A number of recent court decisions have held public hospitals' administrative and professional staff responsible for their patients' inability to exercise their "right to treatment". In the private sector, health insurance companies, which have established a maximum number of days for reimbursible service, have provided impetus toward shorter periods of hospitalization and placed added responsibility for such patients on their community.

Several barriers to change have been noted. One is the existence of a power structure for whose membership the ideology is medical, the technology is clinical, and the expertise is psychiatric. Attempts to restructure mental health facilities from within have often been short-lived because, in order to implement the best of ideas, one must confront the day-to-day realities of the personnel who are being asked to operationalize the change. Another barrier to change has been the inability of relatively impoverished mental health facilities to underwrite the basic costs of anything new. They are generally financed and staffed at a level close to that needed merely to keep the organization functioning, so neither funds nor personnel can be spared. In this area, recent slashes in federal support for mental health services may serve as indicators of future trends.

The 1970 amendment calling for increased attention to the needs of poverty areas caused little change in the activities of those centers receiving the funds. The reasons cited in an NIMH-funded study of the amendment (Roy Littlejohn Associates 1973) are twofold. First, the inadequacy of government allocations has resulted from use of a formula in which actual allowable federal staffing percentages must be less than the legislated maximum for each consecutive year of operation except the first. Although the purpose of this fiscal arrangement is to encourage the community mental health center to seek alternative financing, the net result is frequently a shortage of funds as the center expands its area of activity. Second, many community mental health centers were in dire financial condition and needed preferential funds merely to retire their debts and survive at a maintenance level.

Kaplan and Bohr (1976) note that legislative changes will eventually have the greatest impact on mental health systems. They cite numerous examples with regard to the patient's "right to treatment" that will force authorities to provide minimum standards of treatment. Given the nearly impossible option of upgrading state hospitals sufficiently to allow them to treat the population traditionally housed within their walls, the pressure to seek alternative, community-based facilities for those labeled mentally ill is obvious.

**Specialization of Services and Providers**  The increased attention given to comprehensive mental health centers such as the community mental health center is due partially to a reaction against previous movements toward specialization. Mental health generalists are usually associated with comprehensive programs, and the term "specialist" is often referred to in terms of categorical services. This has resulted in the problem of relating the generalist to the specialist and relating general comprehensive services programs to specialized mental health services. Powerful lobby groups represent the various interests of the mentally ill, the retarded, the epileptic, the alcoholic, the narcotics addict, the paralytic, the unwed mother, the cancer patient, the heart diseased, and others. Such organizations want assurance that specialized services will be provided for their own constituencies and that the funds that they generate will be used entirely as they are intended. Nevertheless, in spite of the cogent arguments and strong social and political forces in support of a specialized service mental health system, the last few years have seen an increasing movement away from specialized services to general, comprehensive service programs.

One of the most basic and significant difficulties with the specialist mental health approach is its lack of continuity and the fragmentation of service delivery. The specialist generally does not consider it his responsibility to explore and examine problems other than those within his limited purview. He may inadvertently overlook factors that are, in fact, relevant to the patient. For example, the internist diagnoses a patient who has fallen off a ladder while painting his house. A fractured ligament is recorded in the hospital records rather than the fact that chronic alcoholism is the problem and the patient was intoxicated when the injury took place.

As another example, the child is participating in a behavior modification program at school while the welfare mother does not supervise or discipline her child at home. The siblings contribute to scapegoating this child by encouraging his troublemaking; consequently, the others remain identified as the "good children" and the mother continues to give them special privileges. Services in the school should not exclude the home influence; the child receiving specialized student treatment services without a general family approach is unlikely to make any significant advances. Personnel in education, welfare, and mental health systems need to coordinate their efforts concerning this child. The child must be understood within the context of his family and the social environment within which he resides, as opposed to as an individual in an empty sphere.

**Areas of Categorical Need**   Lieberman (1975) identified seven basic areas in which specified categorical needs exist. These require individualized services in order to complement the comprehensive approach to mental health services: children and youth services, the elderly and the aging, parenthood, mental retardation, risk taking and suicide, crime and delinquency in the correctional system, and substance abuse—alcohol, drugs, tobacco, and food.

For example, the last fifteen years have witnessed a growing concern with the number of mentally ill and emotionally disturbed children in the United States and an increasing dissatisfaction with the unavailability of mental health services. National recognition of this need and a mandate to establish the Joint Commission on Mental Health of Children was provided by the publication of the federal government entitled *Crisis in Child Mental Health* (1970). This document is more than a critique of clinical needs and problems related to mentally ill and emotionally disturbed children. It is also a protrayal of crises in our society that precipitate many kinds of intervention.

While the achievements of today's youth are indeed impressive, there are myriad indications of society's failure to provide the necessary supports. To the problems of the rising suicide rate, the high school dropout problem, and the large probation caseload may be added those of the unknown hundreds of runaway young people, the thousands of drug users, and the countless numbers who suffer from alienation. There appears to be no impending relief from societal problems of environmental pollution, over-crowding, weakening family structure, violence, delinquency, and rising youth unemployment. In spite of the obvious hazards facing youth, the overwhelming

**Figure 3.1**

THE CHINESE BOX SCHEMATIC REPRESENTATION OF SUBGROUP BREAKDOWN OF SCHOOL-
AGE POPULATION

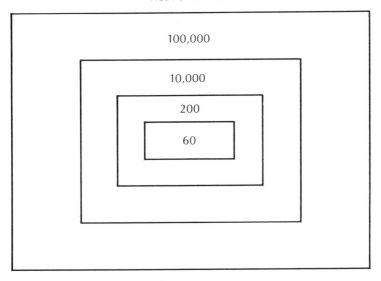

County School age Children ................... 100,000
Significantly disturbed ......................... 10,000
Mentally ill ...................................... 200
In residential treatment centers .................. 60

*Source:* Sauber 1975.

evidence of disturbance, and the knowledge that early intervention is essen-
tial-the mental health services available to children are grossly inadequate.
The time-honored American response to these problems has been the dispen-
sing of mental health, juvenile justice, child welfare, and education primarily as isolated care-giving systems.

Using the most conservative estimate from various school surveys, the
National Institute of Mental Health estimates that for an average community
of 100,000 age children, the statistics in figure 3.1 indicate reasonable expectations.

Estimates also suggest that mental health services are currently provided
to only a third of the children in serious need of attention. An additional 7
to 10 percent or more are estimated by school survey to need some help for
emotional problems. What happens to all the children who receive no help?
Here statistics become much less precise, since the vast majority of these
children are, literally, lost. They are bounced around from training schools

to reformatories to jails, and processed through all kinds of understaffed welfare agencies (Sauber 1975).

The Joint Commission (1969) has recommended the following priorities: comprehensive services that will ensure the maintenance of the mental health of children and youth; a broad range of remedial mental health services for the seriously disturbed, juvenile delinquents, mentally retarded, and otherwise handicapped children and their families; and the development of an advocacy system at every level of government, which will ensure the effective implementation of the desired goals for children's and adolescent's well-being. The recommended services would span the entire range of childhood, from systematic maternal and infant care to the transition stage from the adolescent and college age to effective young adulthood.

Another example receiving national attention is categorical services for the aging. In 1971 the U.S. Senate Special Committee on Aging published the document entitled *Mental Health Care and the Elderly: Short-comings and Public Policy.* The study cited widespread confusions and contradictions in public policy on mental health in the elderly causing heavy economic, social, and psychological cost among older Americans and their offspring. Psychopathology in general, and depression in particular, rises sharply with age. The suicide incidence reaches its zenith in elderly white males. The elderly need a social life, good health care, and special housing arrangements or assistance in maintaining themselves in their own homes—all elements of a total picture of which mental health is a part and to which it is linked. A primary problem is the scarcity of community resources, including mental health services, limiting the range of service choice. Should current trends of mental health service continue through the 1980s, it is projected that 80 percent of the elderly persons in need of mental health services will go without them.

Recent research suggests that functional (nonorganic) mental impairment in older persons is as responsive to treatment as in younger patients and that apathy, isolation, and regressed behavior can be reduced by adequate diagnosis and intervention (Butler and Lewis 1973). The date of that study indicates that negative attitudes presently permeate the area of geriatrics. It has been found that both administrative and treatment staff inappropriately fear that the elderly are unresponsive to treatment and rehabilitation attempts.

The elderly need a strong element of outreach, particularly since this group is reluctant to accept services in the first place (Moen 1978). Collaboration in the delivery of service is essential at the agency and consumer levels regardless of the separate purposes of the various agencies involved. Such goals are realistic: the Minneapolis Age and Opportunity Center, incorporated in 1969, provides an excellent illustration of the principles of comprehensive mental health practice applied at a community level and utilizing primary, secondary, and tertiary prevention strategies.

**State Planning**  The field of mental health has changed significantly in the past two decades, and it will undoubtedly continue to do so. Unfortunately, polemics, punctuated by the impassioned advocacy of various consumer interests, have sometimes obscured the reality that a quiet revolution has already taken place. There have, for instance, been changes in the "social" definition of mental illness, reflected in the widening of the boundaries of accepted behavior and in a more circumscribed "legal" definition of mental illness. In a dramatic redefinition of individual rights, the "right" to treatment has been asserted—now including the right to information, the exercise of informed consent, and the right to refuse treatment. The past few years have seen precedent-creating adjudication on behalf of patient plaintiffs in states as diverse as Alabama and Michigan. Further changes have been multiple and acting, involving such dimensions as the site of care, the content of care, the delivery, the caregivers and the models of professional practice, consumer interest, and the general public. Although resistance to state and local mental health planning still exists among those with strong ties to the status quo, the process is achieving general recognition as a legitimate function. Citizen and consumer groups, businessmen, legislators, and the press are among its strongest advocates. Even pressure groups that were originally most hostile to the concept have come to accept the idea that planning for mental health, previously left to the decisions of the market and the ingenuity of its participants, must now be subject to responsible private (voluntary) and public study.

Whatever the reasons have been for the lack of comprehensive mental health planning at the national, state, and local levels, there now seems to be an ever-increasing number of issues and problems that are becoming even more difficult to resolve. Some of the major problems are the definition of "optimum" mental health services and of goals and objectives, the composition of planning group governing boards, shortages of professionally trained planners and of community planning funds, the personnel shortage, inadequate distribution of resources, and state and federal legislation.

## THE ROLE OF THE STATES

Within the framework of comprehensive mental health planning and the larger spirit of creative federalism, the states have a major planning role. An attempt to assess and determine whether the state officials within departments of mental health were, in fact, inclined to follow in the reassertion of the responsibilities of state leadership that have been encouraged by current policies in intergovernmental affairs (Sauber 1976). The following states participated in this investigation: Arizona, California, Colorado, Illinois, Indiana, Maaryland, Massachusetts, Pennsylvania, and Rhode Island. Other states contributing data to the study on informal basis included Florida, Kentucky, New Hampshire, New York, and Virginia. Interviews were conducted with state officials from all of the above-mentioned states except New York and Florida. In these two states, interviews were held at the city and county level in the state of New York and at the State Training and Research Institute in Florida.

Among other things, the questions raised during these interviews asked for a description of the state's department of mental health; an assessment of the effects of national policies such as revenue sharing on the state planning for mental health services; a description of the situation in each state as regards the planning, organization, and delivery of mental health services; and a description of major issues and trends in the mental health system. A number of interesting findings emerged from the study and are summarized below.

**Ideologies**   Most fundamental to mental health policies were the ideologies held by commissioners and state officials—the commonly held systems of ideas or beliefs that serve to justify one's position and that acts as behavior rationales for mental health administrators, educators, and practitioners. As a result of the debatable nature of mental illness, the profound changes in the social environment, the American tradition of pluralism, competition, independence, and self-protection, and even changing fads, a succession of ideological movements has buffeted the mental health field during the nineteenth and twentieth centuries (Armor and Klerman 1968; Baker and Schulberg 1967; and Gilbert and Levinson 1957). Ideology has played an important role for some time in the development of psychiatric theory and practice. Consider, for example, the following ideologies: patient management in mental hospitals—custodialism and humanism; treatment orientations—psychotherapy, sociotherapy, somatotherapy; intervention strategies—clinical psychiatry and public health approaches; and service delivery systems—community mental health and human services.

In the study, most states classified their programs as falling somewhere between the clinical psychiatry and public mental health organizational models. Notable exceptions were the states of California, Colorado, Illinois, and Massachusetts. These states exhibited program variables lodged in the organization models of public mental health and human services. Only these states (to greater and lesser extents) offered evidence of comprehensive community mental health planning that incorporated all aspects of the program variables in each of the organization models, striving to achieve a human services delivery system (Sauber 1976).

**Organizational Structure**   With regard to organizational structure, there appeared to be a shifting in a focus from the level of a single organization, such as a state department of mental health, to that of a complex network of organizations and human services. There was also a tendency to speak of a state interorganizational system in which individual departments constitute components or subsystems. However, all organizational systems need not be assumed to be subsystems or components in some well-defined suprasystem. For example, two departments may be highly interdependent in terms of their exchange of information but may be mutually autonomous with regard to financial exchange (Baker and O'Brien 1971).

The changing balance between interagency "coordination" and comprehensiveness of services has resulted in the development of legislation that enables and encourages states and localities to unify and decentralize service components into areas of high need, to combine the resources of different programs, and to integrate services in proper sequence. This is a reaction against services that suffer from "duplication," "fragmentation," "specialization," "discrimination," "compartmentalization," "overlap," and "discontinuity of care."

Approximately twenty states have already combined several services, such as health and social problems, into a single department. Many other states are seriously considering similar reorganizations (O'Donnell 1969). In Massachusetts, for example, the new Executive Office of Human Services has combined the traditionally separate public health, mental health, and social welfare programs for the state under unified administrative control. Other interdepartmental reorganizations are exemplified in the states of Arizona and California, following the guidelines set forth by the National Institute of Mental Health; these states have created a division of mental health within the larger department of health. Maryland established a Department of Health and Mental Hygiene.

State inter- and intradepartmental trends toward mental health service reorganization in the 1970s favored a close association with the field of health, as opposed to its historical evolution from departments of public welfare in the early 1960s.

Intradepartmental changes include new organizational structures; developing new staff positions in the areas of planning, evaluation, prevention, and community services; resetting priorities (i.e., deinstitutionalization and the reallocation of existing state hospital funds for community-based program development); new plans for service delivery such as regional offices, county departments, and catchment area centers; and new staffing requirements and contract management. An example that highlights such changes is the creation of state offices of prevention and funded positions for mental health educators in the states of California, Florida, Kentucky, Massachusetts, New York, and Pennsylvania.

**Service Delivery Systems**   The boundaries between the fields of mental health and other human services, of course, have changed over a period of time, influenced by several interacting variables. Among them are historic events such as the War on Poverty and the community mental health revolution; the political climate, statutory developments, and the changing power of vested interests; the developing interrelationship among public agencies, the private sector, and voluntary service groups; interorganizational complexities of the caregiving system, such as fiscal and bureaucratic considerations; the prerogatives assumed in professionalism—for example, credentialism, confidentiality, and peer review; and the impact of new manpower patterns, training programs, models of practice, and methods of applied research.

The development of organizational models for community mental health and human services has required a redefinition of the boundaries and domain of both traditional organizations and professional disciplines. In general, there are five approaches to service delivery systems: federal, state, regional, county, and catchment area. The most influential role has traditionally been that of the federal level, and so on down the line. Today there is a trend toward community mental health program development and administration at the local catchment area level from block grants of the states.

An open-systems approach to organizational structure and dynamics may help one to view each state as a "bounded interacting set of components engaging in an input–output commerce with an external environment in the processing of material object, information, and people'' (Baker and O'Brien 1971). For example, Rhode Island is geographically small and has a population just short of one million; it operates exclusively at the state level, relying on the state hospital and private institutions that service the entire state.

Pennsylvania, by contrast, has many urban centers as well as large rural areas. Its staff at the State Department of Public Welfare, Office of Mental Health, consists of two mental health professionals and two business administrators. Therefore, the determination of services comes through the regional and catchment area administrators, who adopt a ''business management,'' as opposed to ''mental health,'' model of service delivery. The Massachusetts Department of Mental Health, with a 1980 budget of $366 million, employs 18,000 people in various areas, regions, hospitals, schools, community residences, and the central offices. There are seven regions, each with a director and several staff members; and there are thirty-nine catchment areas. The area director may direct a comprehensive community mental health center or coordinate a linking system of integrated services. In contrast to the Pennsylvania system, the state, regional, and area directors of Massachusetts are mental health professionals. This administrative and professional difference is clearly reflected in both therapy and practice, illustrating the extent to which the question of preference—the ''clinician executive'' versus the ''business manager''—is a major issue confronting state departments of mental health across the country.

The state of Illinois was a forerunner and leader in demonstrating the value of regionalism. In order to forge a partnership with the community, the Illinois Department of Mental Health has brought the resources of state institutions closer to the populations in need through a decentralized plan. For example, there are seven geographic regions (formerly called zones), each with state facilities, new mental health centers, and private grant-aided agencies. Region 2, the largest, encompasses the city of Chicago and nine counties with a population of more then 7 million. Region 2 services are divided into thirteen smaller geographic divisions, called subregions, which include fifty-three smaller divisions, called planning areas. The subregion staff coordinates public and state-aided mental health resources within each of its planning areas to meet the needs of each population.

A major shortcoming of regionalized systems of mental health services is that systems of welfare, corrections, rehabilitation, health, youth services, and education frequently have different regional boundaries. Inefficiency results because of program barriers and service gaps and makes planning, collaboration, and coordination extremely difficult. An exception to this problem is found in the legislature of Colorado, which has set common boundaries for all service providers. Despite the fact that the decision was based on geographic considerations rather than any conception of an integrated service delivery system, in each regional office coordinators from mental health, education, welfare, corrections, and so on are represented and plan in a collaborative manner. Systemic linkages will be developed whereby the elements of the systems come to be anticipated so that in some ways they function as a unitary system.

In the early 1970s, California dissolved its regionalized system in favor of centralized county programs, with liaison functions in the state headquarters. In a larger county such as Los Angeles, however, twelve mental health regions and twenty-five mental health districts were developed in order to further decentralize community mental health services. Table 3.1 illustrates the basic approach of this county.

**Future Planning Issues**   The attitude of most state mental health professionals in the mid-1970s was that there existed an unprecedented opportunity to develop mental health programs that are sound, effective, and realistic. To many, "community mental health" may have in fact been oversold; yet it still was seen as a "bold new step into the future." Local and state planners are now faced with the need to establish mental health services that reflect the best combined thinking and resources of all concerned. Although some localities and states are relatively better equipped than others to begin planning, they all face a series of confronting issues. These include:

1. conceptual problems in "mental illness-health and service delivery: philosophy and ideology;
2. increased politicization: politics inside and outside of the mental health profession;
3. accountability of service providers to clients;
4. indirect versus direct services: priority setting;
5. viable funding mechanisms; cost containment; management of cutbacks;
6. prevention of mental illness, versus promotion of mental health;
7. manpower development (professional, paraprofessional, and nonprofessional);
8. organizational structures: multiservice integration system versus linking-service network;

9. administrative practices: territorial (catchment areas) versus functional (high-risk groups);
10. leadership qualifications: medical versus nonmedial, and clinician executive versus business manager;
11. institutionalization versus deinstitutionalization;
12. citizen participation: community control versus professional control;
13. generic characteristics of helping activities (natural talent versus professional training; generalist versus specialist);
14. interdisciplinary versus multidisciplinary;
15. centralization, decentralization, and recentralization;
16. contractual management versus staffing;
17. approaches to service delivery: state-operated, regional control, or local ownership; and
18. human services versus mental health systems.

What is missing is a refined framework that provides conceptually and empirically based definition, description, and classification of these issues and system variables. State planning of mental health services is changing from a survey, forecast, and analysis system based on mental health methodology—which requires clinical training to understand and psychiatric knowledge to implement—to a more business-oriented approach. The latter view, a general theory of management evolving in recent years, focuses on basic administrative processes (planning, organizing, controlling, and communicating) necessary for the accomplishment of primary organizational goals and objectives. However, it is noteworthy that in the design, evaluation, and planning of human services organizations, as opposed to departments of mental health, systems concepts are gaining increasingly wide acceptance. Thus planning can be defined as the process by which resources of an organizational system are adapted to changing internal and environmental forces.

The caliber of statewide and areawide leadership provides the critical element that will determine the extent to which mental health planning will result in decisive, beneficial changes in the provision of comprehensive and coordinated community services. Both personal and environmental in scope, this goal endeavors to raise the mental health status and improve the social functioning of the population. A complete state plan must stimulate, support, and coordinate planning within its own regions and areas, as well as interpret national policy and coordinate with federal program administration and development. The leadership role of state mental health administrators

**TABLE 3.1**

**A PREFERENTIAL PLAN FOR MENTAL HEALTH SERVICES:**
**PLAN FOR LOS ANGELES COUNTY DEPARTMENT OF MENTAL HEALTH**

| Mental Health Dept. Activity | | Target Community Groups | | Individuals Affected | | Expected Outcome |
|---|---|---|---|---|---|---|
| **First Order Activities:** Community Analysis (analytic phase of community organization) Analyze and evaluate community phenomena productive of social and emotional handicap | → | Community at large | → | Mental Health Department staff | → | Knowledge of community's impact on citizen's lives |
| **Second Order Activities:** Community Action (community organization) Cooperate with and help constructive and remedial social forces within the community (includes planning). | → | Community at large Social action groups | → | All citizens Citizens at risk of alienation and dehumanization | → | Enrichment of community's support of healthy and productive living |
| **Third Order Activities:** Mental Health Education Educate groups and individuals to promote improvement of societal conditions and effective response to personal crises | → | Community at large Community caregivers | → | All citizens Persons at risk of becoming dependent on social service agencies Clients of caregivers | → | Optimum preservation and restoration of healthy social functioning without mental patient status |
| **Fourth Order Activities:** Mental Health Consultation Improve caregiver response by maintaining an active mental health consultation relationship to health, education, welfare, and other agencies supportive of healthy social functioning | → | Community caregivers | → | Clients of caregivers | → | Restoration to healthy social functioning Possible referral as mental patient |

I N D I R E C T

S E R V I C E S

Fifth Order Activities

Emergency and Crisis Treatment Services

Respond promptly and effectively with needed brief clinical services to individuals who, despite prior order activities, require the services of mental health professionals

D
I
R
E
C
T

Sixth Order Activities:

Out-patient, Brief Hospitalization and Partial Hospital Services

Provide high-quality definitive mental health professional care to those who are mentally and emotionally disordered avoiding development of chronicity

S
E
R
V
I
C
E
S

Seventh Order Activities:

Rehabilitative Services

Restore to optimum social functioning those who, despite prior order activities, require services to ameliorate chronic emotional handicap

→ (Preferably) clients of care-giver agencies referred when prior order services are not effective
Directly referred patients
Patients coming directly from the community

→ Patients within the mental health care system

→ Patients within the mental health care system

Restoration to healthy social functioning
→ Referral to nonmental health care-givers for further supportive services

Restoration to healthy social functioning
→ Where indicated, referral to care-giver support

Restoration to healthy social functioning
→ Where indicated, referral to care-giver support

*Note:* This diagram illustrates the basic approach of the Los Angeles County Department of Mental Mental Health to the delivery of community mental health services. Activities are specified in terms of their preferential order, such that higher order pursuits deal with those aspects of community mental health involving least direct intervention into the life-styles and personal behavior of individuals affected. This schema recognizes that the community is dynamic and changing, and that all seven types of activities must occur simultaneously if community mental health services are to be significant factors in achieving overall societal goals.

in the burgeoning fields of community mental health may largely be determined in the next few years by their own planning capabilities and by their ability to recruit, train, place, and retain experts in planning.

## CARTER'S WHITE HOUSE COMMISSION ON MENTAL HEALTH

Shortly after taking office, President Carter announced the creation of a new Commission on Mental Health, chaired by Mrs. Carter, a longtime member of the National Association for Mental Health. This commission was given a broad mandate with directions to prepare a comprehensive report for the President on a series of major issues—from the rights of the mentally ill to financing mechanisms for the delivery of mental health services. The commission has become the single most important national forum on the broad issue of mental health services.

Carter's executive orders specifically directed the commission to identify how the mentally ill, emotionally disturbed, and mentally retarded were being served, to what extent they were being underserved, and who was effected by such underservice. The report was to project needs for dealing with emotional stress during the succeeding twenty-five years, touching on the following areas:

> The ways in which the President, Congress, and the federal government can most efficiently support the treatment of the underserved mentally ill, emotionally disturbed, and mentally retarded.
> The various methods for coordinating unified approach to all mental health and people-helping services.
> The types of research that the federal government should support to further the prevention and treatment of mental illness and mental retardation.
> What the role of the various educational systems, volunteer agencies, and other people-helping institutions can perform to minimize emotional disturbance in the United States.
> As nearly as possible, what programs will cost, when the money should be spent, and how the financing should be divided among federal, state, and local governments and the private sector.

Although the president's order did not indicate it specifically, the commission's mandate also included drug abuse and alcoholism.

Presidential commissions derive their potential power in a number of ways. First, they bring together a network of influential people to consider the issues and to prepare a report that is widely disseminated. These opinion leaders in turn carry back the message to their agencies, constituencies, and the like. (In the case of the present report, not only were hundreds of mental health specialists involved in preparing it, but each of the commission's task forces had in turn a number of working groups whom they involved in the research.) Presidential commission reports also bring certain issues to the force then the President's stamp itself affects governmental agencies, particularly at the national level. Legislative and administrative action proposals also frequently emanate from such reports and, if implemented, provide another avenue of influence. Finally, and most importantly, various potential constituencies are activated and may even become better mobilized as an indirect effect of a report.

Production of the four-volume report involved the commission plus thirty-two task and subtask panels. Volume 1, the report itself, is only 40 pages long. According to Thomas E. Bryant, commission chairman, this length would ensure that the major findings would be read. Volume 2, 556 pages long, deals with a number of issues, including the nature and scope of the problem; community support systems; service delivery, with five subpanel reports on planning and review, organization and structure, community mental health centers assessment, access and barriers to care, and deinstitutionalization, rehabilitation, and long-term care; alternative services; personnel; and costs and financing.

Volume 3, covering 824 pages, addresses the mental health of American families, with subpanel reports on general issues and adult years, infants, children, and adolescents, and learning failure and unused learning potential; special populations, including subpanels on Asian/Pacific Americans, black Americans, Americans of European ethnic origin, Hispanic Americans, American Indians and Alaskan natives, the physically handicapped, and women and the elderly; rural mental health; migrant and seasonal farmworkers; and Vietnam-era veterans.

Finally, Volume 4, 792 pages, has reports on legal and ethical issues, research, prevention, public attitudes and use of media to promote mental health, arts in therapy and environment, and state mental health and liaison reports on mental retardation, alcoholism-related problems, and psychoactive drug use and misuse.

Many of the final report's 117 recommendations are aimed at three segments of the population: the underserved, notably minorities, children, adolescents, and the elderly; the unserved in rural areas, small towns, and inner cities; and the inappropriately served, most notably women, because mental health professionals are not prepared to deal with contemporary changes in women's roles. Recommendations were made in eight areas: community supports; responsiveness in the service system; insurance as provided by Medicare, Medicaid, and the private sector; better use of personnel; protecting the basic rights of patients; expanding the knowledge base through research; prevention strategies, especially with children; and improving public understanding of mental illness.

The major thrust of the report's recommendations was in three areas. First, a new federal grant program for community-based services was suggested. The program would eventually succeed the community mental health center program. This strategy would be more flexible than the present CMHC strategy because as few as one or two services might be required in a given community rather than the twelve now mandated. Second, efforts at preventing mental illness would be stressed, and programs for infants and children would be emphasized. The aim: to ensure that prevention would constitute 10 percent of NIMH's total budget within ten years. Third, much greater use would be made of "community support" systems. The commission recognized that people turn first to resources such as families, churches, schools, and clubs. There was noted a "need to develop linkages between these systems and the formal mental health services system" (*Mental Health Reports* 1978: 2). It was recommended that large state hospitals continue to be phased down and, where appropriate, closed.

The area that is likely to have the most impact relates to the significance of community support structures, particularly the self-help mutual aid systems and the natural neighborhood network. There are many reasons for this that are related to other forces in our society: the concern for decentralization and movement away from Washington; the alienation of large numbers of people who feel powerless in dealing with big government and the concomitant populist desire for smaller informal systems; the disillusionment with standard professional practice and its attendant paternalism, inflationary cost, and unresponsiveness to people and their problems; the consumer movement and the participatory ethos residual from the 1960s; the desire to strengthen the neighborhood and the community in light of the weakening of the family and religion; and finally, the recognition of the enormous need for human services, which most certainly cannot be met simply through paid work but requires a new kind of voluntary service (Riessman 1978).

The most controversial part of the report involved community-based services. Commission members conceded that this area was the most difficult in which to achieve consensus. While the accomplishments of CMHCs were noted, problems were also cited, leading to the conclusion that a more flexible approach is needed. Support of existing CMHCs would continue primarily as a stopgap effort. Ultimately, applicants for new grants would be either public or private nonprofit agencies. These would be funded initially for five years, with the federal government funding completely only where local matching funds were not available.

In general, reaction to the report was favorable. The few reservations that were expressed dealt with the recommended community-based services. The Mental Health Association endorsed a network of community-based services but noted that there were no concrete means of developing and maintaining such a system. The National Council of Community Mental Health Centers, on the other hand, indicated that the new grant program and the CMHCs could complement each other; there was disappointment that CMHCs were not emphasized more, however. There thus appears to be some ambiguity on the future of community mental health—not over whether it will continue to be stressed but over how services can best be delivered.

Before these recommendations could be implemented, the administration had to decide on how to implement them. Also, the public had to be convinced of the necessity of implementing them. In the 1980s it remained to be seen if any of the developments might come to constitute the nucleus of a fourth revolution in mental health.

## CONCLUSION

Proposed below is a conceptual framework for understanding the mental health system and the principal sources of variation within it. The framework for program analysis includes these components: (1) the organizational process, including decision-making system in process, responsibility interpretation and setting of goals, and resource acquisition and reduction of constraints; (2) the mental health transaction, including the helper, the nature of the service, and the direct recipient; and (3) the ecological placement, including the location of the transaction and the occasion or time of the service.

The process of resource allocation involves a series of choices about who will provide what service to whom, at what occasion or time, and in what location. The organizational process concerns resources, constraints, program responsibility, and goals. The establishment of a decision-making body, the acquisition and administration of resources, and the reduction of constraints would be part of the planning and politics of mental health. An operational framework would help guide one's assessment and formation of strategies in program development. Fiscal, administrative, and legal responsibilities must be incorporated into a working system, and the decision-making process must be codified or implicitly understood. At any given time, resources and constraints are relatively fixed quantities that determine the limits within which choices can be made at that time.

During most earlier periods of mental health ideology, goal setting was assumed to be the responsibility of the professional. Currently, the community members who are consumers of the services want to assume power, including the responsibility for goal setting and/or resource allocation. However, community members must be educated to assume this role properly (Silverman and Mossman 1978). The interpretation of program responsibility can lead to a variety of goals. Preventing new cases of personality disorder in children, making psychotherapy available to low-income groups, and reducing intrapsychic conflict are three examples of initial goal statements.

The mental health transaction involves three elements: the helper, the nature of the service, and the direct recipient. The specific caregiver is usually chosen because of certain personal characteristics, training, skills, and attributes. Examples of possible choices might include a clinical psychologist, clergyman, family care physician, guidance counselor, psychiatrist, and social worker. Further, services may be transmitted impersonally, such as through information provided in a pamphlet.

The nature of the service or the service of choice refers to the specific techniques, content, and process made available to the recipient. Examples include group psychotherapy, individual mental health consultation, rest and moral reeducation, psychoactive drug therapy, psychodiagnostic assessment, vocational counseling, family therapy, and even comic strips about the needs of infants.

The specific individuals who may be the direct recipients of such services constitute the next choice. They too may be identified as representatives of classes or special groups of individuals with whom they share certain characteristics. Examples include chronic schizophrenics, female college students, individuals thought to be possessed by demons, high school dropouts, industrial foremen, preadolescent boys who are thought by their teachers to be troubled, residents of a given area, and unwed mothers. It is sometimes useful to distinguish between the direct "recipient" and the "target group" and to recognize that a mental health transaction may have both a primary and secondary target. In some instances a sequence of transactions occurs, and the "direct recipient" in the first phase may become the "helper" in the second phase (e.g., consultation with teachers or clergymen).

The concept of ecological placement involves two important choices. Wide variations are possible both in the geographic and social setting where a mental health transaction may occur and in the temporal prerequisites for the timing of a service. The loci of transactions may include such diverse locations as a community general hospital, an elementary school, a private metropolitan office, a college dormitory, and a storefront near a bus stop. The occasion or time of the delivery and receipt of service provides another dimension of choice. On the transactional level, examples might include the following: after the birth of a premature infant; upon application to an elementary school; when self-referred; upon entering college; following the loss of a spouse; or when a particular symptom picture is recognized.

Since the early 1960s mental health workers in all fields have experimented with new community-oriented strategies and intervention and with the new organization of services in the community, such as the federal program of comprehensive community mental health centers. Subsequently, the need for new approaches to the problem of balancing patient care and the prevention of disorder has led many professionals to involvement in new roles. Care giving has progressed from the arena of the custodian to that of the therapist and now moves toward those of the mental health consultant, agencies, citizen groups, and human service workers.

The locus of influence has moved from the hospital asylum to the patient to the social forces that influence adaptation. Kelly, Snowden, and Munoz (1977) have applied concepts from biological ecology to understanding social systems and planning programs of intervention. His work illustrates a focus that is shifting from the intrapsychic and interpersonal to the broader social networks that are presumed to shape behavior.

Approaches to behavior classification have likewise shifted from the classification of internal psychodynamics to concern for adaptation by the individual within his social system. The importance of including social-psychological variables such as power, group status, and socioeconomic status has been recognized (Glidewell, 1971). The various attempts to define mental health and illness appear to have crystallized the idea of level of competence as a type of conceptual ''lowest common denominator.''

During the late 1960s the issues of responsibility, power, and control over all community institutions and services came into the foreground. These concerns are likely to continue as problems during the 1980s and into the 1990s. Dissatisfaction with the field of mental health at the community level has culminated in several related forms of innovation that can be loosely termed a community mental health approach. These included flexibility in the locations and occasions at which mental health services are made avail-

able and incorporated a number of treatment alternatives in helping strata-
gems based on varying the timing and location of interventions. The community approach also involved an increased variety of helpers trained to
provide useful services and numerous attempts to reach clinical groups that
had not previously been served. New services were also developed—notably
mental health consultation and education. Goals oriented toward disorder
prevention and optimization of effectiveness revealed the infusion of the
public health concept into the mental health field.

A social policy toward the mentally ill in the United States has developed
and is now based on a "right" and a "place." The "right" is the right to
treatment, and the "place" is the local community. Additionally, there is
increasing public expectation that treatment of mental illness, no less than
physical illness, be adequate for the needs of the individual patient. In requiring that treatment facilities be established within the local community,
the public is also beginning to realize that mental health services are provided as a responsibility of that community—to be financed through a variety of patterns, using public, private, and personal funds, as appropriate.

A first priority now is to expand the newly established social policy concerning the mentally ill into a social policy for the mentally healthy. This
approach has already begun to develop. Probably the most significant sign-
post of this development was the establishment, through provisions of the
community mental health centers, of consultation and educational services
as essentials in a program of community centers. Here, for the first time,
the provision of preventive services became mandatory in a publicly supported mental health program. The adoption of preventive services as a stated
public policy has not only added a new dimension to the mental health
program but has set a new direction for all health programs in the United
States.

Thousands of volunteers joined mental health professionals and members
of other professions in surveys of mental health resources and mental health
needs. The results of these planning efforts was the establishment of the
community mental health movement as a vehicle and a model which demonstrates that communities can expand and improve many kinds of services
using the techniques employed by the first citizen planners for mental health.

New ways are being found to involve community members in evaluation
and planning (Landsberg and Hammer 1978). Clinic mental health staffs, in
addition to treating the classic range of mental illness, are now beginning to
help clients with problems of housing, bill collection, reading, drug abuse,
alcoholism, and so forth that appear to be endemic in both the affluent and

deprived sectors of society. Psychologists, social workers, psychiatrists, psychiatric nurses, and a growing body of newly interested ancillary personnel are living and working together with people of all races in diverse communities. Even in their brief experience, these workers have learned that if the demands and expectations of the American people are to be met, effective mental health services must include a broad range of human services. Responsiveness of services may be a crucial predictor of utilization, for example, among minorities.

Establishing a comprehensive community mental health program with or without a CMCH involves the development of complex relationships with other community agencies and institutions. Besides creating the mechanisms required for efficient case finding and referral, prompt and appropriate treatment, and continuity of care, the mental health program must mobilize resources to meet the medical, financial, housing, and other needs of the person who is mentally ill or emotionally disturbed. One of the key problems in providing community health and welfare services has been the lack of effective coordination that would subordinate services to the needs of individual clients.

If the comprehensive community mental health program is to succeed, its planners, administrators, and clinicians must explore new ways to create interagency cooperation and to organize community facilities. These include improving the knowledge that organizations have of each other's functions and problems; recognizing and analyzing domain differences and trying to resolve them; educating community leaders about the interdependence of community mental health and other human services systems; educating referral sources about agency functions; informing the community in general about the resources of the agency; and other similar activities.

## REFERENCES

APA (American Psychological Association). 1972. Federal court upholds right to treatment. *APA Monitor,* 3(5):1.

Armor, D. and G. Klerman. 1968. Psychiatric treatment orientations professional ideology. *Journal of Health and Social Behavior.* 9:243–255.

Austin, M. J. and W. E. Hershe, eds. 1982. *Handbook on Mental Health Administration.* San Francisco: Jossey-Bass.

Baker, B. L., B. Seltzer, and M. M. Seltzer. 1977. *As Close as Possible: Community Residences for Retarded Adults.* Boston: Little, Brown.

Baker, F., C. D. Issacs, and H. C. Shulberg. 1976. The study of the relationship between community mental health centers and state hospitals. NIMH Contract No. HSM-42-70-107. Boston: Socio-Technical Systems Associates. August.

Baker, F. and G. O'Brien. 1971. Intersystems relations and coordination of human service organizations. *Journal of Public Health,* 61:130–137.

Baker, R. and H. C. Shulberg. 1967. The development of a community mental health ideology scale. *Community Mental Health Journal,* 3:216–225.

Baker, F. and H. Schulberg. 1969. Community mental health ideology: Dogmatism, political-economic conservatism. *Community Mental Health Journal,* 5:433–436.

Beers, C. W. 1937. *A Mind That Found Itself.* New York: Doubleday.

Bindman, A. J. Mental Health Conservation: Theory and Practice. *Journal of Consulting Psychology* (1959), 23:473–482.

Bindman, A. J. and A. D. Spiegel. 1969. *Perspectives in Community Mental Health:* Chicago: Aldine.

Bloom, B. 1972. *Community Mental Health: A Historical and Critical Analysis.* Morristown, N.J.: General Learning Press.

Boles, J. M. 1978. Midway Manor: A participant observation study of mentally ill residents of a community halfway house. Doctoral dissertation, Columbia University Teachers College. *Dissertation Abstracts International.* 38:6967A. University Microfilms No. 78-07, 045.

Boyd, C. and W. E. Henderson. 1978. Improving continuity of care through a state hospital, CMHC liaison program. *Hospital and Community Psychiatry,* 29(6):384–386.

Budson, R. D. 1978. *The Psychiatric Halfway House: A Handbook of Theory and Practice.* Pittsburgh: University of Pittsburgh Press.

Butler, R. N. and M. Lewis. 1973. *Aging and Mental Health-Positive Psychosocial Approaches.* St. Louis: Moseby.

Byers, E. S., S. Cohen, and D. D. Harshbarger. 1978. Impact of aftercare services on recidivism of mental hospital patients. *Community Mental Health Journal,* 14(1):26–34.

Caplan, G. and R. B. Caplan. 1966. Development of community psychiatry concepts in the United States. In A. M. Freedom and H. I. Caplan, eds., *Comprehensive Textbook of Psychiatry.* Baltimore: Williams and Wilkins.

Colvin, S. M. 1978. The cycle of hospitalization from the patient's viewpoint. *Hospital and Community Psychiatry,* 29(6):396–397.

Connery, R. H. 1968. *The Politics of Mental Health.* New York: Columbia University Press.

Cox, S. 1978. Fifteen years after *Asylums:* Description of a program for victims of the total institution. *Clinical Social Work Journal,* (6(1):44–52.

*Crises in Child Mental Health: Challenge for the 1970s.* 1970. Final report of the Joint Commission on Mental Health of Children, Inc., New York: Harper and Row.

Davis, J. E., T. W. Lorei, and E. M. Caffey. 1978. An evaluation of the Veterans Administration day-hospital program. *Hospital and Community Psychiatry.* 29(5):297–302.

Delaney, J. A., E. Seidman, and W. Grant. 1978. Crisis intervention and the prevention of institutionalization: An interrupted time series analysis. *American Journal of Community Psychology,* 6(1):33–45.

Demone, H. 1973. Human services at state and local levels and the integration of mental health. In G. Caplan, ed., *American Handbook of Psychiatry,* volume 4. Boston: Little, Brown.

Dunn, L. H. 1961. *High-Level Wellness: A Collection of Twenty-Nine Short Talks on Different Aspects of the Theme "High-Level Wellness" for Man in Society.* Arlington, Va.: R. W. Beatty.

Ecklund, L. A. 1978. The role of a regional treatment center in a model mental health delivery system. *Hospital and Community Psychiatry,* 29(6):279–283.

Elpers, J. R. 1978. Management and pragmatic constraints on community mental health services. *Hospital and Community Psychiatry.* 29(6):369–373.

Endicott, J., M. I. Herz, and M. Gibbon. 1978. Brief versus standard hospitalization: The differential costs. *American Journal of Psychiatry,* 135(6):707–712.

Favazza, A. R. 1975. Health and illness, physical and mental. In E. J. Lieberman, ed., *Mental Health: The Public Health Challenge.* Washington, D.C.: American Public Health Association.

Feldman, S. 1973. *The Administration of Mental Health Services.* Springfield, Ill.: Charles C. Thomas.

Fink, E. B., R. Longabaugh, and R. Stout. 1978. The paradoxical underutilization of partial hospitalization. *American Journal of Psychiatry.* 135(6):713–716.

Funding through the Operations of Community Mental Health Centers. *Executive Digest.* Volume 1. Washington, D.C.: Roy Little John Associates, 1973.

Gartner, A. 1971. *Paraprofessionals and Their Performance: A Survey of Education, Health, and Social Service Programs.* New York: Praeger.

Gilbert, D. and D. Levinson. 1957. "Custodialism" and "humanism" in staff ideology. In M. Greenblott, D. Levinson, and R. Williams, eds., *The Patient and the Mental Hospital.* Glencoe, Ill.: Free Press.

Ginsberg, E. 1948. Army hospitalization, retrospect, and prospect. *Bulletin of U.S. Army Medical Dept.* 8:38–47.

Glass, A. J. 1955. Combat psychiatry and the civilian medical practice. *Transactions of the College of Physicians.* 23:14–23.

Glidewell, J. 1976. Priorities for psychologists in community mental health. In G. Rosenblum, ed., *Issues in Community Psychology and Preventive Mental Health.* New York: Behavioral.

Goldstein, S., C. Marcus, and N. Perkins. 1978. The non-utilization of evaluation research. *Pacific Sociological Review.* 21(1):21–44.

Guerney, B. G. 1969. *Psychotherapeutic Agents: New Roles for Nonprofessionals, Parents and Teachers.* New York: Holt, Rinehart, and Winston.

Hadley, T. R., E. Zuckerman, and B. Cymerman. 1978. The impact of a satelite facility on the delivery of mental health services. *Hospital and Community Psychiatry.* 29(6):360–361.

Hobbs, N. 1964. Mental health's third revolution. *American Journal of Orthopsychiatry.* 34(5):822–833.

Hogan, W. 1978. Development of a rural psychiatric after-care group. *Psychosocial Rehabilitation Journal.* 2(1):9–15.

Hollingshead, A. and F. Redlich. 1958. *Social Class in Mental Illness.* New York: Wiley.

Holman, T. and M. F. Shore. 1978. Halfway and family involvement as related to community adjustment for ex-residents of a psychiatric halfway house. *Journal of Community Psychology*. 6(2):123–129.

Jeffrey, J. J. and R. F. Reeve. 1978. Community mental health services in rural areas: Some practical issues. *Community Mental Health Journal*. 14(1):54–62.

Joint Commission on Mental Health of Children. 1969. *Crisis in Child Mental Health*. New York: Harper and Row.

Joint Commission on Mental Illness and Health. 1961. *Action for Mental Health*. New York: Basic Books.

Jones, M. 1968. *Social Psychiatry in Practice: The Idea of a Therapeutic Community*. New York: Penguin.

Kanno, C. K. 1971. *Reviewing State and Local Mental Health Hospital Programs*. Washington, D.C.: Joint Information Service.

Kaplan, H. M. and H. R. Bohr. 1976. Change in the mental health field? *Community Mental Health Journal*. 12:244–251.

Kelly, J., L. Snowden, and R. Munoz. 1977. Social and community interventions. *Annual Review of Psychology*.

Kennedy, J. F. 1962. *Message from the President of the United States Relative to Mental Illness and Mental Retardation*. 88th Cong., 2d sess. February 5.

Kuhr, T. S. 1970. *Structure of the Scientific Revolution*. 2d. ed. Chicago: University of Chicago Press.

Landsberg, G. and R. Hammer. 1978. Involving community representatives in CMHC evaluation and research. *Hospital and Community Psychiatry*. 29(4):245–247.

Levenson, A. I. 1972. The community mental health centers program. In S. E. Goldan and C. Eisdorfe, eds., *Handbook of Community Mental Health*. New York: Appleton-Century-Crofts.

Lieberman, E. J., ed. 1975. *Mental Health: The Public Health Challenge*. Washington, D.C.: American Public Health Association.

Los Angeles County. 1972. Plan for mental health services of Los Angeles County: 1973, 1974; 1973, 1978.

*Mental Health Reports*. 1978. Vols. 1, 2, 3. Washington, D.C.: Government Printing Office.

Mesnikoff, A. M. 1978. Barriers to the delivery of mental health services: The New York City experience. *Hospital and Community Psychiatry*. 29(6):373–378.

Miller, S. M. and E. G. Mishler. 1959. Social Clan, Mental Illness, and American Psychiatry. *Millbank Memorial Fund Quarterly*.

Moen, E. 1978. The reluctance of the elderly to accept help. *Social Problems*. 25(3):293–303.

*National Action to Combat Mental Retardation: Report on the President's Panel on Mental Retardation*. 1962. Washington, D.C.

Neugebauer, R. 1978. Treatment of the mentally ill in medieval and early modern England: A reappraisal. *Journal of the History of the Behavioral Sciences*. 14(2):158–169.

NIMH. 1964. *Regulations: Community Mental Health Acts, 1963*. *Federal Register* Base. Washington, D.C.: National Institute of Mental Health.

O'Donnell, E. 1969. *Organization for State Administered Human Resources Program in Rhode Island: Report to the General Assembly by Special Legislative Commission to Study Social Services*.

Ohwaki, S. and S. E. Stayton. 1978. The relation of length of institutionalization to the intellectual functioning of the profoundly retarded. *Child Development.* 49(1):105–109.

Pepper, B. 1973. Working Paper. Baltimore: State Department of Health and Mental Hygiene, Mental Health Administration.

President's Commission on Mental Health, 1978. *Task Panel Reports,* vol. 3., appendix. Washington, D.C.: GPO.

President's Panel on Mental Retardation. National Action to combat mental retardation. Washington, D.C.: 1962.

Riessman, F. A. 1978. A new revolution in mental health? *New Human Services Review.*

Rockland State Hospital. 1971. *Multi-state Information System.* Orangeburg, N.Y.: Information Science Division.

Roy, Little John Associates. The Impact of Preferential Poverty: Funding through the operations of CMHC, *Executive Digest,* 1973, Vol. I. Washington, D.C.: Roy Little John Associates.

Sarason, I. G. 1966. *Personality: An Objective Approach.* New York: Wiley.

Sauber, S. R. 1973. *Preventive Educational Intervention for Mental Health.* Cambridge: Ballinger.

Sauber, S. R. 1975. Human services for children. Manuscript. Providence, R.I.: Brown University.

Sauber, S. R. 1976. State planning of mental health services. *American Journal of Community Psychology.* 4:35–46.

Schulberg, H. and F. Baker. 1969. Community mental health: The belief system of the 1960s. *Psychiatric Opinion.* 6:14–26.

Schulberg, H. C. and F. Baker. 1976. *The Mental Hospital and Human Services.* New York: Behavioral.

Schulberg, H., F. Baker, and S. Roen, eds., 1973. *Developments in Human Services.* Vol. 1. New York: Behavioral.

Schulberg, H. C. and M. L. Killilea, eds. 1982. *The Modern Practice of Community Mental Health.* San Francisco: Jossey-Bass.

Sells, S. B. 1969. Ecology and the science of psychology. In E. P. Williams and H. L. Raush. eds., *Naturalistic Viewpoints and Psychological Research.* New York: Holt, Rinehart, and Winston.

Sharfstein, S. 1978. Will community mental health survive in the 1980s? *American Journal of Psychiatry,* 135:1363–1365.

Shun, F. D. and S. Droher. 1974. The Madness Establishment: Ralph Nader's Study Group Report from the National Institute of Mental Health. New York: Grossman.

Siegel, B. and J. Lasker. 1978. Deinstitutionalizing elderly patients: A program of resocialization. *Gerontologist.* 18(3):293–300.

Silverman, W. H. and B. Mossman. 1978. Knowledge assessment of Mental Health advisory boards. *American Journal of Community Psychology.* 6(1):91–96.

Smith, D. E. 1978. "K is mentally ill": The anatomy of a factual account. *Sociology.* 12(1):25–53.

Snow, D. L. and D. M. Newton. 1976. Task, social structure, and social processes in the mental health center movement. *American Psychologist* 31:582–594.

Stockburger, D. W. and J. O. Davis. 1978. Selling the female image as mental patient. *Sex Roles.* 4(1):131–134.

Tardiff, K. 1978. Staff activities in a mental health service in Canada: Implications for funding services in the United States. *Hospital and Community Psychiatry.* 29(6):359–360.

Towery, O. B. and C. Windle. 1978. Quality assurance for community mental health centers: Impact of P.L. 94–63. *Hospital and Community Psychiatry.* 29(5):316–319.

Turner, R. J. and J. W. Gartrell. 1978. Social factors in psychiatric outcome: Toward the resolution of interpretive controversies. *American Sociological Review.* 43(3):368–382.

U. S. Congress. Senate. 1971. Special Committee on the Aging. *Mental Health Care of the Elderly: Shortcomings and Public Policy.* 92d Cong., 1st sess. Washington, D.C.

U. S. Congress. 1963. Mental Retardation Facilities and Community Mental Health Centers Construction Act. P.L. 88–164.

*Washington Report on Medicine and Health,* January 10, 1972.

*Washington Report on Medicine and Health,* October, 1972.

Weathers, O. D. and S. C. Bullock. 1978. Therapeutic group home care for adolescent girls: An interagency development. *Journal of the National Medical Association.* 70(5):331–334.

Weiss, C. H. 1978. The usefulness of social research for decision-making in mental health. Doctoral dissertation, Columbia University, 1977. Dissertation Abstracts International. 38(9):5730A. University Microfilms no. 78-02, 349.

Wheaton, B. 1978. The sociogenesis of psychological disorder: Re-examining the causal issues with longitudinal data. *American Sociological Review.* 43(3):383–403.

White, J. 1970. Administrative problems encountered in the operation of community mental health centers. Washington, D.C.: George Washington University School of Government and Business Administration, Dissertation Abstract.

Winston, A. and H. J. Lieberman. 1978. Family Life in a community residence. *Psychiatric Quarterly.* 50(1):50–54.

Yarvis, R. M., D. W. Edwards, and D. Langsley. 1978. Do community mental health centers underserve psychotic individuals? *Hospital and Community Psychiatry.* 29(6):387–388.

Zober, A. 1978. Measuring the impact of social and physical environmental characteristics within residential settings on selected adaptive and maladaptive behaviors of institutionalized retarded adults. Doctoral Dissertation, Brandeis University, Florence Heller Graduate School for Advanced Studies in Social Welfare. *Dissertation Abstracts International* 39(5):2484B–2485B. University Microfilms no. 78-21, 719.

# 4

# HUMAN SERVICES AND THE
# ADMINISTRATION OF CRIMINAL JUSTICE

## HAROLD J. VETTER

Public attitudes toward crime and criminals are deeply ambivalent. An understandable desire for vengeance and concern for preventing further crimes, particularly in the case of heinous offenses, conflicts with humanitarian impulses and liberal social philosophies. This ambivalence is equally apparent in public views of the criminal justice system. People want the criminal justice system to rehabilitate as well as punish; to reform as well as deter; to succor and nourish as well as to incapacitate the criminal offender. It is against the background of these conflicting, often wholly contradictory expectations that the human services performed by the criminal justice system must be reviewed and assessed.

To speak of human services in the context of criminal justice is to introduce a great many complex problems and issues. The traditional role of the criminal justice system—encompassing law enforcement, prosecution, the courts, and corrections—has been the apprehension, conviction, and punish-

Harold J. Vetter is Director of Graduate Studies and Professor of Criminal Justice, University of South Florida, Tampa.

ment of offenders. Despite many changes brought about by social progress in the past half-century, the underlying orientation of the criminal justice system is primarily punitive. If the reform or rehabilitation of criminal offenders has become a goal that is presently sought by the criminal justice system, it is one that remains subordinate to the major objective of social defense and the maintenance of public order.

## HISTORICAL DEVELOPMENT AND PHILOSOPHY

A crime is defined legally as the violation of one or more criminal statutes, the implication being that such behavior is harmful to the public and an offense against the community, state, or nation. But the legal conception of crime is unduly restrictive because it limits the area of concern to only those persons who have been officially adjudicated "criminal" or "delinquent." Thus, a great deal of nonofficially recognized antisocial behavior would remain unexamined. Criminologists and criminal justice professionals tend to consider criminal behavior as simply a part of the much more extensive spectrum of *deviant* behavior.

**The Deviance Perspective**  "Human behavior is deviant to the extent that it comes to be viewed as involving a personally discreditable departure from a group's normative expectations and elicits interpersonal or collective reactions that serve to isolate, treat, correct, or punish individuals engaged in such behavior" (Schur 1971: 24). This definition reflects the multifaceted nature of deviant behavior. First, it points to the fact that deviance encompasses quite diverse types of departures from normative expectations, ranging from law violations to minor departures from customary ways of behaving in informal situations. Thus, both the murderer and the individual failing to dress properly for a formal occasion may both be labeled deviant. In addition, it recognizes that deviance is a function of the extent to which behavior is condemned, punished, or ignored. For example, although individuals who use either marijuana or heroin are both viewed as deviant, those that use the latter substance are more likely to be condemned and punished.

The statement that "behavior is deviant to the extent that it is personally discreditable" emphasizes the point that violations do not equally reflect on the individual's identity. Hence, although occasional marijuana use is defined as deviant, this is not likely to affect an individual's self-concept or the way in which he is viewed by society because large sectors of our population do not see this as reprehensible behavior. On the other hand, the perpetration of a robbery, if discovered, is likely to have a material effect on an individual's identity because this behavior is viewed as an extremely serious breach of norms. In fact, an individual convicted of robbery is likely to be scarred for the rest of his life. Furthermore, this definition also specifies some of the possible reactions that are elicited from individuals or groups against those who engage in deviant behavior. The types of reactions elicited depend upon such factors as the degree to which the behavior threatens basic social values and is viewed as volitional and current beliefs regarding punishment versus rehabilitation. During the 1960s we began to see a move to decriminalize a variety of behaviors including homosexuality, alcoholism, and drug addiction because they came to be viewed as outside the control of individuals involved. In effect, this moved them from the criminal realm to the "sick" realm, which permitted the individuals involved to be treated rather than punished.

Finally, this definition alludes to the fact that deviance may vary with time and place. Over a period of time, acts may move along a continuum from criminality-sinfulness, to disapproval, to toleration without approval, to normal behavior. Examples of behavior that have moved along this continuum include homosexuality, participation in labor unions, divorce, and doing business on Sundays. In short, then, the deviance of an act or an individual is always relative, changeable, a matter of degree, and that degree depends mainly on the extent to which the behavior is viewed and responded to in certain ways.

The reaction of society to the deviant act and the possible labeling of the individuals involved is extremely important in understanding the nature of deviant behavior. All individuals engage in deviant behavior, some of which violates basic social values. However, there is ample evidence to indicate that many people are not officially labeled for their violative behavior. It is this act of censure by society that affixes the deviant label and results in changes in the way in which individuals are viewed by society and in their self-conception.

Lemert (1967) has used the term "primary deviance" to refer to deviant behavior that has not materially affected an individual's self-concept or social status. Included in this category are (1) those repeatedly arrested for drunkenness but who are still accepted by their families and employers; (2) drug users who are able to conceal their drug use from those who might take action against them; (3) juveniles who engage in delinquency but have not been arrested and/or adjudicated for their aberrant acts; (4) individuals who temporarily manifest some symptoms associated with mental illness;

and (5) adults who engage in occasional criminal acts such as shoplifting. The common thread that runs through all of these behaviors is that they are normalized and dealt with as functions of a socially acceptable role by an individual's associates or that the individual restricts his involvement to situations that will not result in the imposition of a deviant label.

Lemert used the term "secondary deviance" to refer to "the importance of societal reaction in the etiology of deviance, the forms it takes, and its stabilization in deviant social roles or behavior systems" (p. 40). First and foremost, this concept distinguishes between those who are viewed as deviant and those whose deviance does not affect their social identities. The decision on the part of the community to take action against those who are deviant is not a simple act of censure. It is, as Erikson (1964) suggests:

> a sharp rite of transition at once moving him out of his normal position in society and transferring him into a distinct deviant role. The ceremonies which accomplish this change of status ordinarily have three related phases. They provide a formal *confrontation* between the deviant suspect and representatives of his community (as in the criminal trial or psychiatric case conference). They announce some *judgment* about the nature of his deviancy (a verdict or diagnosis), and they perform an act of social *placement* assigning him to a special role (like that of prisoner or patient) which redefines his position in society. (p. 16)

Following these "status degradation ceremonies" there is a shift from viewing the individual's acts as deviant to viewing the individual as a deviant character. Labeling an individual rather than his specific acts as generally deviant may be a self-fulfilling prophecy. For example, once a youngster is labeled a delinquent, teachers, parents, and store owners tend to expect that the youngster will engage in further delinquency. Indeed, this youngster is generally the first to be accused when property is missing, damaged, or destroyed. Furthermore, other parents are likely to forbid their children to play with him for fear that he will influence them to engage in delinquency. Therefore, he is likely to be excluded from his peer group and also from adult-sponsored activities, such as church groups and Boy Scouts. Moreover, his ability to obtain after-school jobs is also likely to be restricted. Denied participation in conventional groups and activities, this youth is likely to graduate to delinquent groups and further delinquent activity. Movement into a juvenile gang can be viewed as the final step in the stabilization of the youngster's delinquency because it involves acceptance of a deviant identity. Gangs provide members with a system of rationalization that serves to neutralize and justify their deviant identities and delinquent behavior.

Erikson has suggested that part of the problem faced by deviants wishing to "shake off" their deviant identities results from the lack of any kind of terminal ceremony that marks the individual's relinquishment of his deviant status. "He is ushered into the deviant position by a decisive and dramatic ceremony, for example, a trial, yet, is returned from it with hardly a word of public notice. And as a result, the deviant often returns home with no proper license to resume a normal life in the community. Nothing has happened to cancel out the stigmas imposed upon him by earlier commitment ceremonies; from a formal point of view, the original verdict or diagnosis is still in effect" (1964:16–17). Deviance disavowal is also difficult because people believe that it is difficult, if not impossible, for an individual to change his character (for example, "once a con always a con").

**Theories of Crime Causation** Theories of criminality have a twofold purpose: they help to organize existing information about criminal behavior into a coherent, systematic framework; and they serve to point out directions for further research by indicating potentially fruitful leads to be explored. For example, a proponent of the theory that criminality is a biological phenomenon would attempt to integrate the available knowledge about crime and delinquency with the findings of biological research and would direct the continuing quest for explanations of criminality toward structures and processes within the human organism. Similarly, a proponent of the theory that criminality is a sociological phenomenon would attempt to interpret the available information on criminal and delinquent behavior to square with the results of sociological research and would orient the search for causes of criminality toward social organizations, groups, and institutions to which the individual belongs. In addition, theories of criminality may aim at establishing some rational basis for programs designed to control, reduce, eliminate, or prevent crime and delinquency.

The formulation of comprehensive theories of the origins and determinants is fraught with difficulties, not the least of which is the problem of accurately defining criminality. As Shore (1971) has observed:

> Antisocial behavior is not a diagnostic category or unitary phenomenon closely tied to cultural values and often dependent upon the interpretation given a behavior pattern by these agencies responsible for the regulation of social interaction. In certain communities, for example, the tolerance for deviance is lower

and certain behavior may be labeled antisocial which, in another context, would not be considered deviant at all. (p. 456)

Nevertheless, Shore points out, there are some people who engage in violent, aggressive behavior despite the advantage of the best social opportunities; others, on the other hand, who are subjected to extremely poor social conditions do not exhibit criminal or delinquent behavior. Thus, Shore concludes, "Aside from the need to understand and explain the social and cultural forces that foster criminal behavior, *there is need for a theory of individual behavior that can account for individual differences and the ways in which individuals interpret and respond to social forces"* (emphasis added) (p. 456).

Research on the cause of criminal behavior has, for the most part, focused on four broad areas of inquiry: biological factors and genetic predispositions; societal influences; individual differences in the organization and functioning of hypothesized *intrapsychic* structures such as "personality," "attitudes," and "motivation"; and behavior differences that reflect the learning experiences and reinforcement history of the individual. The biologist has sought explanations for criminality in the constitutional makeup of the individual; the sociologist has sought explanations for criminality in the processes that affect the behavior and experiences of people living in societal groups; the intrapsychically oriented psychiatrist and psychologist have sought explanations for criminality in the presumed personality configuration of the individual; and the behaviorally oriented investigator has sought explanations for criminality in the variables that affect the learning experiences of the individual.

A number of criminologists who are variously designated as "radical," "new," or "conflict theory" criminologists endorse a view of criminal behavior that is heavily influenced by Marxism, Leninism, and/or Maoism. These writers see criminality primarily as an expression of class conflict. According to their interpretation, behavior designated as criminal by the ruling classes is the inevitable product of a fundamentally corrupt and unjust society; law enforcement agencies are the domestic military apparatus used by the ruling classes to maintain themselves in power; the causes of crime lie within society and its legal system; and therefore crime will persist until or unless both are made to change.

At the present time, there is no "grand theory" of criminality that encompasses all approaches to crime and organizes the empirical findings of each discipline into some coherent, integrated schema. For the time being, at least, we must be content with either theories of the middle range, that is, those that account for only a limited number of facts about crime, or with microtheories, which are even further restricted in their range of content and generality than those of the middle range.

But criminological theories and theorists do not merely diverge along the clear lines drawn by professional specialization. In recent years deep-seated differences in value orientation and ideology among criminologists have created schismatic tendencies that cut into, as well across, disciplinary identifications. Moreover, these divergent ideological positions involve criminal justice practitioners—those who bear the burden of responsibility for providing the human services purveyed by the criminal justice system—in addition to academic criminologists. For this reason it is necessary to devote some discussion to ideological factors and their implications for criminal justice services.

## IDEOLOGIES AND SOCIAL VALUES

In 1973 the National Advisory Commission on Criminal Justice Standards and Goals published a series of task force reports covering the police, prosecution and the courts, and corrections and an overview of the criminal justice system and process. A later report (1974) was addressed to the issues involved in community crime prevention. A summary publication entitled *A National Strategy to Reduce Crime* (1973b) drew upon the recommendations that had been made in the other reports. This document is of considerable interest because it seeks to identify what the commission considered the leading contemporary issues confronting American society and the criminal justice system. Taken in their entirety, the volumes comprising the commission's deliberations and research constitute something approximating an "official" statement of significant contemporary issues.

High on the commission's list of priorities was a targeted reduction of from 25 to 50 percent in five categories of offense (homicide, rape, robbery, aggravated assault, and burglary) which had been identified as "high fear" crimes on the basis of public opinion sampling. In addition, the following were among the recommendations that received emphasis from the commission:

1. *Centralization.* Any police agency employing fewer than ten sworn officers should be combined with one or more other police agencies to improve efficiency.

2. *Diversion.* Police agencies should establish firm rules for diverting from the criminal justice system all individuals coming to their attention for whom other resources would be more appropriate.
3. *Crime Prevention.* Police agencies should establish crime prevention programs to encourage and assist the public in self-protection against crime.
4. *Education.* Recruitment for police agencies should concentrate on college-educated applicants and require for initial employment as patrolman at least one year of college-level education.
5. *Dissemination.* Uniform standards and procedures should be established to make full police file data available to other criminal justice agencies for official purposes.
6. *Plea Bargaining.* Bargaining between defendants and prosecutors concerning concessions to be made in return for guilty pleas should be abolished.
7. *Death Penalty.* The death penalty should be retained as an option.
8. *Recidivism.* The maximum sentence for most offenders should be five years, with no minimum sentence imposed by statute, except for "persistent, professional, or dangerous offenders," in which cases the maximum should range up to twenty-five years.
9. *Judiciary.* Judges should be nominated by a judicial commission appointed by the governor, and judges should stand for periodic uncontested election running against their records.
10. *Gun Control.* It should be made unlawful to possess, sell, or manufacture any handguns, their parts, or ammunition, except for official law enforcement or military purposes.

Walter B. Miller (1973) has pointed out that with regard to the criminal justice system, issues tend to be perceived and defined in accordance with a complex process that involves elements of ideology. His analysis helps to explain why certain issues in the above list are the focus of controversy and contention. In fact, on some issues (e.g., handgun control, the death penalty), among those who hold ideologically divergent positions, one group's solution is another group's problem.

What does "ideology" connote? Miller considers ideology to be the way a person believes that moral and political arrangements should be interpreted: "Ideological statements are unexamined presumptions taken loosely" (p. 142). Persons who hold these beliefs are strongly attached to them emotionally and are highly resistant to changes in those beliefs.

Gwynn Nettler maintains that "the theme common to ideological explanation is the *group-supported patterning of beliefs of inadequate empirical warrant, where such beliefs are energizing, in attack or defense of values, and comprehensive"* (1970:176–177). Thus, ideological orientations imply a dimension of dynamism or impetus toward action. Ideological positions, according to Miller, represent gradations. These positions are identified in terms of the general assumptions on which they are presumed to rest and the "crusading issues" that mobilize or "energize" beliefs in attack or defense of values.

Starting from a different set of premises, legal scholar Herbert Packer (1968) has arrived at conclusions that strongly support Miller's observations on ideology. In Packer's view, the source of many intramural conflicts in the criminal justice is two different conceptualizations of the criminal justice process. Packer has identified these conceptualizations as the crime control model and the due process model:

> The value system that underlies the Crime Control Model is based on the proposition that the repression of criminal conduct is by far the most important function to be performed by the criminal process. The failure of law enforcement to bring criminal conduct under tight control is viewed as leading to the breakdown of public order and thence to the disappearance of an important condition of human freedom. If the laws go unenforced—which is to say, if it is perceived that there is a high percentage of failure to apprehend and convict in the criminal process—a general disregard for legal controls tends to develop. The law-abiding citizen then becomes the victim of all sorts of unjustifiable invasions of his interests. His security of person and property is sharply diminished and, therefore, so is his liberty to function as a member of society. The claim ultimately is that the criminal process is a positive guarantor of social freedom. In order to achieve this high purpose, the Crime Control Model requires that primary attention be paid to the efficiency with which the criminal process operates to screen suspects, determine guilt, and secure appropriate dispositions of persons convicted of crime. (p. 158)

Implicit in the efficiency of operation of this approach is the assumption that the screening performed by police and prosecutors separates out a substantial majority of the innocent, leaving individuals who are probably guilty of criminal offenses. Thus it is the presumption of guilt that makes it possible for the system to process large numbers of people rapidly with more than 90 percent entering a plea of guilty. Stripped to its essentials, this model provides an administrative fact-finding process that results in either exoneration of the suspect or the entry of a guilty plea.

### SERVICE RECIPIENTS

A crime involves a perpetrator and a victim, either or both of whom may be an individual, a group, or a corporate entity. A forcible rapist may attack his victim(s) singly, with a partner, or as a member of a gang. Fraud may be perpetrated upon an individual, a group of individuals, or upon an industrial or business firm. Whom shall we regard as the client for human services—the victim who has suffered depredations of person or property at the hands of a criminal offender, or the criminal who may be himself a victim of long-standing and severe social inequities that are seen by many criminologists as causally linked to his criminal behavior? Or should *both* the victim and the criminal be considered as potential clients?

There is a further consideration. It is a well-embedded principle of Anglo-American criminal jurisprudence that a crime—*any* crime—is an offense against the state. Society itself is the plaintiff in all criminal actions. And it is the state that ultimately must bear the burden of providing protection for its citizens against domestic as well as foreign enemies. Shall we therefore consider the state as a client with respect to the delivery of human services by the criminal justice system?

The simplest and most obvious answer to the above questions is that the victim, the criminal, and society at large are *all* clients of the criminal justice system and the human services it provides. To state matters in this fashion, however, we must also recognize that there are competing, even contradictory, aspects to the services themselves and the means by which they are purveyed. Only in the writings of liberal social philosophers are individual and social welfare viewed as completely congruent. In the daily transactions of the criminal justice system the welfare of the individual client, criminal or victim, is frequently subordinated to the welfare of society, the exigencies of the criminal justice process, or any combination of a variety of special interests.

**Categories of Criminal Offense**   Crimes are typically classified as either felonies or misdemeanors. Felonies are the more serious crimes; they are punished by a year or more in a state prison. A misdemeanor, on the other hand, is generally accepted as an offense for which the sentence is confinement of less than one year, usually in a jail or workhouse. Misdemeanors can also be punished by the assessment of a fine. This broad definition varies from jurisdiction to jurisdiction, but the guideline of less than one year imprisonment is a fairly commonly accepted practice.

The legal definition of a misdemeanor is usually rooted in the statutes according to how severe the penalty is for the act, the level of government at which the offender is tried, or some specific list of offenses. In many cases the term is a catchall, with any crime that is not specifically listed as a felony automatically considered to be a misdemeanor. The gray area between a misdemeanor and a felony is even further confounded in some jurisdictions, which attempt to differentiate between "high" or "gross" misdemeanors and the regular garden variety. In general, however, the term "misdemeanor" applies to such minor offenses as drunkenness, vagrancy, disorderly conduct, breach of the peace, minor assaults, larcenies of small amounts, small-scale gambling and other forms of "vice," and shoplifting.

Felonies are a group of offenses that are considered serious enough to deserve strong punishment or even death in most societies. Although they vary somewhat in their wording and their specific names, the major felony crimes are remarkably similar no matter by which jurisdiction they are defined. In the United States, we have come to call many of the "common law" crimes felonies because of the inheritance of many of them from the English common law statutes. Under the common law there were three categories of crimes: treason, felony, and misdemeanor. Originally the distinction between the felonies and the misdemeanors was based on the fact that all felonies were capital offenses and also involved forfeiture of all lands and property of the perpetrator. It is fairly accurate to state that the early common law felonies were punishable by death, whereas the misdemeanors received lesser penalties. Although we adopted many of the aspects of the common law of England, in the United States the severity of felony punishment was modified to reflect the American way of life.

The most serious felonies are crimes against the person. They comprise four of eight major or "index" or part 1 offenses taillied in the Federal Bureau of Investigation's annual *Uniform Crime Reports.* They are defined by the FBI as follows:

1. Criminal homicide: (a) Murder and nonnegligent manslaughter: all willful felonious homicides as distinguished from deaths caused by negligence. Excludes attempts to kill, assaults to kill, suicides, accidental deaths, or justifiable homicides. Justifiable homicides. Justifiable homicides are limited to: (1) the killing of a person by a peace officer in line of duty; (2) the killing of a person in the act of committing a felony by a private citizen. (b) Manslaughter by negligence: any death which the police investigation establishes was primarily attributable to gross negligence of some individual other than the victim.

2. Forcible rape: Rape by force, assault to rape, and attempted rape. Excludes statutory offenses (no force used—victim under age of consent).

3. Robbery: Stealing or taking anything of value from the care, custody, or control of a person by force or violence or by putting in fear, such as strong-arm robbery, stickups, armed robbery, assaults to rob, and attempts to rob.

4. Aggravated assault: Assault with intent to kill or for the purpose of inflict-

ing severe bodily injury by shooting, cutting, stabbing, maiming, poisoning, scalding, or by the use of acids, explosives, or other means. Includes attempts. Excludes simple assault, assault and battery, fighting, etc. (p. 57)

These four crime categories—murder and nonnegligent manslaughter, aggravated assault, forcible rape, and robbery—are to the public the most emotion-laden of the felonies. These are the "headline crimes" that create fear and promote support for stronger law enforcement.

The remaining four part 1 offenses—motor vehicle theft, larceny-theft, burglary and arson—and most of the part 2 offenses are classified as crimes against property. They account for the majority of the more than 10 million criminal offenses reported each year in the *UCR*.

**Victims of Criminal Offenses**   Until rather recently, the victim of crime has received comparatively little interest or attention from criminologists and even less from the criminal justice system. The last several years have reversed this trend, and criminological interest in victimology, the specific study of criminal–victim relationships, has been paralleled by a steadily growing concern for the victim of crime within the criminal justice system and agencies of local, state, and federal government. While the criminologist has addressed the criminal–victim relationship as a factor in crime causation, concern for the victim within the criminal justice system and the government has concentrated upon the issue of compensation and restitution for the victims of criminal depredations. Efforts have been made to look closely at various groups within our society that are especially prone to victimization by criminal offenders (e.g., the elderly, children, the poor) and to develop models and programs for the delivery of services to victims who have suffered physical, psychological, or economic damage at the hands of criminal offenders. Some of these programs are examined later in this chapter.

## CURRENT DEVELOPMENTS IN BASIC AND ESSENTIAL SERVICES

The administration of justice in the United States, as in all modern nations, has become a task of epic proportions. As the roles and structures of government increase in response to the needs of a scientific and technological society, so also does the criminal justice system expand in size and scope. The image of a King Solomon meting out justice to his subjects with intuitive wisdom has been replaced by the reality of a huge bureaucratic structure of judicial administration reaching into many aspects of human life. The manner in which this system exercises its responsibilities influences considerably the functioning and direction of the society it serves.

The police officer is the most visible representative of this system. His visibility, however, is analogous to that of the iceberg tip; by far the larger portion of the criminal justice system, like the mass of the iceberg, is submerged and concealed from view. We are referring to the criminal and juvenile courts, judges, bailiffs, clerks, and other officials who handle the innumerable details of court administration; the prosecuting and defense attorneys; and those who are charged with the responsibilities of detention, corrections, probation, and parole. Taken in the aggregate, these individuals, the offices they hold, and the jobs they perform comprise the remainder of the criminal justice system.

The expression "criminal justice system," by the strictest rules of semantics, is a convenient fiction—an abstraction with no specific counterpart in reality. What we have referred to collectively as the criminal justice system is a system in the same sense that a government is considered a political system. Unfortunately, "criminal justice system" is a popular term; and although it is employed loosely, often by those who are unaware of the complexities or even contradictions concealed within its apparent simplicity, it nevertheless conveys a meaning that is difficult to capture with any other designation.

**The Police**   The police subsystem is the entry point of the criminal justice system for first offenders and the reentry point for the failures of the other subsystems. The police number more than 400,000 officers and civilians who serve approximately 40,000 separate local, state, and federal agencies with an annual budget in excess of $2.5 billion. Because they are the only component of the criminal justice system that is in daily interaction with both criminals and the public, the responsibilities of the police are more distinctive than those of other service agencies. Law enforcement policy is made by the policeman himself, a fact not generally recognized by the public. Kaplan (1973) observes: "A criminal code, in practice, is not a set of specific instructions to policemen but a more or less rough map of the territory in which policemen work. How an individual policeman moves around that territory depends largely on his personal discretion" (p. 74). The policeman's judgment is the principal determinant of whether or not the criminal process is invoked in each individual case.

Traditionally the two principal missions of the police have been maintenance of order and enforcement of the law. With the increasing complexity of society, numerous and varied demands have been put upon the police because of their unique authority. The National Advisory Commission on Criminal Justice Standards and Goals (1973b) recognized the following among the many functions that police agencies perform: prevention of criminal activity; detection of criminal activity; apprehension of criminal offenders; participation in court proceedings; assistance to those who cannot care for themselves or who are in danger of physical harm; control of traffic; resolution of day-to-day conflicts among family, friends, and neighbors; creation and maintenance of a feeling of security in the community; and promotion and preservation of civil order (pp. 104–105). These functions represent core elements in the contemporary police role. Among law enforcement personnel there is a great deal of controversy with regard to the emphasis that ought to be placed on each of these functions.

It has been estimated that only about 10 percent of the police officer's time and energy are taken up by law enforcement duties; the rest is occupied by what might be called "social welfare functions." One hears the complaint from police officers that there seems to be a contest among police departments to see who can undertake the largest number and most unusual kinds of non–law enforcement projects. One police administrator (Clark 1968) recommended that police departments move from delinquency prevention and family crisis intervention programs to various forms of offender *treatment* such as detoxification units, the responsibility of the correctional subsystem of the criminal justice program.

Much of the confusion about the role of the police officer, both from the viewpoint of the public and from the viewpoint of the officer himself, stems from confusion of the terms "law enforcement" and "crime prevention." Both are the designated duties of today's policeman, but they are not one and the same. The concept of the policeman evolved from the necessity for an agency of government to enforce the law. As a matter of administrative convenience, in this country he has also been charged with the prevention of crime. His existence, of course, serves as a deterrent to some crimes. What he does beyond that is left up to him.

**The Prosecutor**   The next component of the criminal justice system with which the individual charged with the commission of an offense has contact is the public prosecutor. This official possesses the broad discretionary power to dismiss the charges or reduce them to charges for which the defendant will plead guilty. Recent studies indicate that as many as 50 to 80 percent of the felony cases initiated by the police are dismissed by the prosecutor.

A high percentage of charges not dismissed are reduced through "plea bargaining" to a charge to which the defendant will plead guilty. While the Perry Mason type of trial gets much play in novels and the media, it is a fact that more than 90 percent of criminal cases are resolved by a plea of guilty. The usual explanation given for the prevalence of plea bargaining is that high caseloads and limited resources require the disposition of as many cases as possible in this fashion; otherwise the courts would be overwhelmed. Heavy caseloads may lead to this kind of situation, but they do not explain why some cases are prosecuted and others are dismissed. These decisions reflect the broad discretionary power given to prosecutors.

The effectiveness of a prosecutor is usually measured by the number of convictions he can obtain while he is in office. Since his political life depends in large part on success in securing convictions, it is not too surprising that he will dismiss or bargain away those cases that show little promise of conviction. He may even bargain for community supervision without prosecution ("deferred prosecution") in cases for which he sees no possibility of winning a conviction. The general public is seldom concerned about how their prosecutor secures his convictions, only that he gets them. As noted in Barnes and Teeters (1959):

> When a case finally reaches the trial court, the prosecutor earnestly prepares for a real battle, not for justice, but for a conviction. His professional reputation is at stake. He must resort to all the oratory and psychological trickery he can mobilize. He is ethically no better and no worse than the defense lawyer in this judicial bout. The average trial, unfortunately, becomes more a show or contest than a struggle for justice. The judge acts as referee—to see that there is something like fair play. The jury sits in amazement, at times flattered at the compliments paid them by the lawyers, and at times incensed at the threats and insults exchanged by the lawyers in reckless fashion. During the court recess the two lawyers may often be seen slapping each other on the back in perfect amity. Here is a basic American institution in action, with tragic implications that most Americans do not grasp. (p. 242)

The decision to charge an offender occurs after the police have made their arrest and present their information to the prosecuting attorney. Except in those few police departments that have legal advisors on call twenty-four hours a day, the prosecutor is the first legally trained individual to examine the facts. It is his job to decide whether to charge the suspect or to dismiss ("no paper") the case. (In a no paper action the prosecutor has decided there is insufficient probability of a conviction and, therefore, no reason to file an information.)

The legal decision to proceed depends on the presence of all of the "elements" of the crime alleged.[2] A good prosecutor can match up the intent and the unlawful acts more suitably, assuring a stronger case for conviction. If he thinks he can get the defendant to plead guilty to the lesser charge (and accept a lesser penalty), he may well bargain for it. If the defendant will not accept the lesser charge, the case is often dropped because of its low potential for conviction. In addition to wasting state money, it may also hurt a track record needed for reelection or advancement.

**The Courts**  The criminal court is at the core of the American criminal justice system. The courts are highly organized, deeply venerated, and rigidly circumscribed by law and tradition. As the deciders of the law, the rest of the system is dependent upon, and responsible to, the courts. The police and their procedures are guided and restricted by decisions of the courts; a prosecutor must weigh the legal and extralegal issues of cases before him in light of the court that will try them; and the correctional system is dependent upon the court for its workload. The formal processes that take place in the courtroom are not merely symbolic but often crucial for the protection of both the individual suspect and society.

Judges are either elected or appointed to office. In either case, they can be put into a position where they may have a political debt to their benefactors. Because of the corrupt practices of a very few judges, it is sometimes felt that they are responsive to pressure groups and will dismiss cases if told to do so by those in power. Actually, the judge in a criminal court is quite limited in his powers.

Dean Wigmore is credited by Roscoe Pound (1929) for the term "sporting theory" of justice as a description of a court trial. The trial is usually a legal "game" of sorts between two highly skilled lawyers with the judge playing the role of a referee. The adversary system of justice pits two lawyers against each other in an attempt to prove the *technical* guilt or innocence of the suspect, while providing him with all of his constitutional rights. The judge, who may sometimes be considerably less skilled at law than either the prosecutor or defense attorney, simply referees points of law. Many times his mistakes, when questioned on appeal,[3] result in the offender's going free. It is a basic concept of the American system of criminal justice that many guilty should go free because the system erred, rather than let one innocent person be convicted because of haste or in the name of efficiency.

Offenders may be freed and cases may be lost because the court finds there was a mistake in the charges or a misrepresentation of the facts and dismisses them at an early stage in the trial. The court itself may commit an error by allowing damaging or false evidence to be admitted, and then have the case reversed later by an appellate court. Also, the court may decide to divert the convicted person into treatment programs that it feels are more appropriate for a particular offender as alternatives to the state's correctional institutions.

Although the prosecuting attorney may have had good reason to believe an offense was committed by a certain suspect, charge him, and bring him to trial, he sometimes makes errors. These errors are usually brought to the attention of the court in the early stages of appearance before the judge. If the judge is convinced at this point that charges are in error, he can dismiss the case. He will usually accompany this dismissal with a few unkind words to the prosecutor for bringing such a poor case before him and wasting the court's time. It is this kind of problem that the ambitious prosecutor seeks to avoid at all costs.

In America's earlier days, a judge's choices were relatively simple. The suspect would be found guilty and sentenced to prison, or he would be found innocent and released. A few were found "not guilty by reason of insanity," but most of those convicted were sentenced to the fortress prisons of the nineteenth and early twentieth centuries in America. Today we have a broad range of alternative dispositional paths from which to choose following a finding of guilty. A few of these are mentioned in the following section on corrections.

**Corrections**   The corrections system is "that part of society's agencies of social control that attempts to rehabilitate or neutralize the deviant behavior of adult criminals and juvenile delinquents" (Fox 1972: 1). In theory, the correctional component of the criminal justice system begins to function with social and legal authority following the adjudication of guilt of an adult offender in the criminal courts, or when its services are invoked by the juvenile court authorities in the case of a minor charged with the commission of a delinquent act. In practice, however, the correctional function may be initiated informally prior to formal assumption of responsibility following court action. For instance, most police departments have juvenile officers on their staffs who specialize in work with juveniles and youthful offenders, and departments of social welfare provide protective services for children and adolescents with behavior problems. Such agencies may become involved with the youngster even before a referral is made to the juvenile court; indeed, they are often successful in keeping a juvenile out of court entirely.

The correctional process is a massive operation processing more than 2.5 million new offenders each year at a cost of more than $1 billion. Included in this process are jails and lockups, prisons, detention centers for juveniles, probation and parole programs, and community-based treatment centers of various kinds. The corrections system is plagued by an overlapping of jurisdictions, contradicting philosophies, and a hodgepodge of organizational structures. It has grown piecemeal, sometimes out of experience, sometimes out of sheer necessity, and sometimes out of folly.

Of all offenders under "correctional" care, only one-third are actually institutionalized. These security institutions, however, require more than 80 percent of the total correctional money and manpower available. Some form of supervision in the community oversees the remaining two-thirds of offenders but receives only 20 percent of the resources. Prison wardens estimate that perhaps 75 to 80 percent of their inmates could be released with little risk to the community, yet they claim that prisons are so overcrowded that control and security are their major problems. Rehabilitation programs, including vocational and educational training, suffer from acute budgetary shortages.

Surveys conducted by the Joint Commission on Correctional Manpower and Training in 1967 and 1968 revealed widespread personnel recruitment and retention problems created by low pay, heavy workloads, insufficient training, and lack of merit system employment in the correctional field. These problems have deprived the system of essential professional services and have resulted in programs that are often manned by personnel with little or no educational preparation or professional training for correctional work.

There is growing evidence that new programs making use of community approaches to corrections as alternatives to incarceration can be more successful and less costly to society. These programs are also a means of facilitating reintegration of the offender into the community following release from an institution. Community-based corrections recognizes the failure of massive, impersonal institutions far removed from population centers. It recognizes the importance of working with the offender in or near his home community, where his ties with family and friends can be used to advantage in his rehabilitation and reintegration into society.

There are many types of community and transitional release programs that have demonstrated value in rehabilitating the offender and reducing the social costs of recidivism. Among these are:

Probation

A court action that permits the convicted offender to retain his freedom in the community, subject to court control and the supervision and guidance of a probation officer. Probation sustains the offender's ability to continue working and to protect his family's welfare, while avoiding the stigma and possible damaging effects of imprisonment.

Parole

A procedure whereby prisoners are selected for release and a service whereby they are provided with the controls, assistance, and guidance they need as they serve the remainder of their sentences within the free community.

Halfway Houses

Small, homelike, residential facilities located in the community for offenders who need more control than probation or other types of community supervision can provide. Halfway houses are used also for gradual readjustment to community life for those who have come out of institutions. Halfway house programs usually offer supervised living and counseling services and draw upon the community for education, training, jobs, and recreation to aid in the rehabilitation process.

Work Release

Under this alternative, the offender is confined in an institution only at night or on weekends but is permitted to pursue his normal life the remainder of the time. Such a program makes possible a greater degree of community supervision but avoids total disruption of family life and employment.

Prerelease Centers

Supervised programs designed to ease the transition from total confinement to freedom by involving people from the community who come to the prison to provide information in areas of vital interest to the inmate who is about to be released. Subjects covered include such topics as employment, finances, family life, community services, and legal sources.

Goals for an expanded corrections program include the following: community-based programs, with emphasis on youthful offenders; improvement of probation and parole; marshalling of resources of the private sector; expanded use of halfway houses; replacement of outmoded jails with regional corrections facilities; new training centers for corrections personnel; and, finally, more effective research.

The shift to community-based corrections will eventually reduce the need for maximum security institutions. Experts agree that only 20 to 30 percent of inmates currently in prison represent a potential danger to society and must be kept under constant supervision in a security institution. If the remaining 70 to 80 percent can be rehabilitated in less restrictive local institutions, or under supervision in the community, only a few small security facilities will be needed for those considered dangerous and the least responsive to correctional treatment.

## INNOVATIVE STRATEGIES AND PROGRAMS

In response to the challenges posed by the failure of resources to keep pace with a rising crime rate, every sector of the criminal justice system has been taxed to develop innovative strategies and approaches to the accomplishment of its manifold tasks. The few examples that follow can scarcely hint at the diversity and originality exhibited by new programs in law enforcement, prosecution, the courts, and corrections.

**Law Enforcement** One of the most dangerous tasks a patrol officer is called upon to perform is dealing with family disturbances. In any given year, nearly 15 percent of all police officer killings and nearly 30 percent of assaults on policemen in the line of duty occur while they are answering disturbance complaints.

A pioneering study by Morton Bard (1970) demonstrated that training of police officers in the management of interpersonal conflict could improve their handling of domestic disturbances. In addition, research strongly suggested that the skillful performance of family crisis intervention was regarded by the community as a valuable service.

Bard (1973) notes that the special circumstances of police work place the police officer in a strategic position to intervene in crisis situations. Among the wide variety of crisis events that the policeman is likely to encounter, Bard lists the following:

1. *Crime victimization*. The victim of crimes, particularly those against the person, experience extraordinary stress reactions. A policeman trained in crisis intervention techniques can have the dual effect of helping the victim in stress while at the same time eliciting information necessary for the successful investigation of the crime.
2. *Natural disaster*. In this category are included such events as fire, flood, explosion, earthquake, and tornado. The suddenness and impact of the event leads to a "disaster syndrome." The dimensions of this syndrome and specific techniques for combatting it are essential knowledge for the police who must restore order after such an event.
3. *Notification*. A frequent police activity with little recognition by laymen, this involves informing the family or next of kin of the death or injury of a family member. In this circumstance, the police officer himself both causes the crisis reaction and can act as an agent in its resolution.
4. *Accident*. Ranging from vehicular homicides to falling objects, these events differ somewhat from the "disaster syndrome" in that the chaos is personal and exists in an otherwise ordered and intact environment.
5. *Psychotic reactions*. These reactions have profound effects upon others, particularly family members.
6. *Suicides and attempted suicides*. As with psychotic reactions, these occurrences profoundly affect others. Skillful intervention by police may offer significant preventive opportunities (p. 3).

Bard stresses the "unique potentials for crisis intervention in the police service delivery system." This is the positive dimension of what Bittner (1970), quoted earlier, refers to as the "distribution of situationally justifiable force." It is this outreach capacity of the law enforcement subsystem that permits the achievement of immediacy in time and place on the part of the policeman's efforts that is incapable of realization by other members of the "helping professions." Says Bard: "If there is a commitment to prevention in mental health, then there must be a challenge to develop means for utilizing the immediacy and authority of the police system" (p. 3).

**The Prosecutor**   The traditional discretionary authority of the public prosecutor to initiate or withhold criminal prosecution has been utilized by a growing number of prosecutors in programs aimed at pretrial diversion or intervention. The primary function of diversion is that of case screening, with the objective of removing from the sanction of the court defendants who do not need close control or supervision. The primary purpose of intervention, on the other hand, is rehabilitation of the offender. Intervention aims at identifying the defendant who needs treatment and arranging for the delivery of the appropriate services, with the expectation of providing a more effective alternative to criminal or juvenile justice system processing.

Diversion encompasses the removal of minimum-risk cases from overloaded court dockets; intervention implies the removal and treatment of defendants who require various services and presumably represent a greater level of risk to the community.

Closely allied to diversion are programs that provide facilities for *citizen dispute settlement*. Recognizing that, in many family and neighborhood disputes, the complainant is often the party who "wins the race to the police station," citizen dispute settlement programs are founded on the belief that the underlying causes of many squabbles can be resolved by bringing the disputants together and providing an opportunity for both confrontation and discussion. As the official report by the National Institute of Law Enforcement and Criminal Justice on a program in Columbus, Ohio (1974), has put it:

> In its simplest form, a Citizen Dispute Settlement Program offers an alternative "hearing process," outside of the normal court hearing procedures, for disputing parties to reconcile their differences with the aim of producing a lasting solution. The purpose of this informal hearing process is not to determine right or wrong and to impose sanctions of the law. Rather, the fundamental goal of a Citizen Dispute Settlement Program is to assist the complainant and the "defendant," or respondent, in reaching a mutually satisfactory settlement which can be implemented, whether that settlement is restitution or a promise to discontinue the problem behavior. (p. 1)

The "hearing officer" in the Columbus program is usually a law student, but he need not be a person with a legal background. The success of a citizen dispute settlement program is measured by the number of cases that can be resolved without resorting to formal criminal procedures. In the Columbus program, during its first ten months of operation, approximately one thousand hearings were held, and all but twenty disputes were settled without the necessity of invoking formal court processing. These disputes ran the gamut from malicious destruction of property and telephone harassment to landlord–tenant disputes and petty larceny.

**The Courts** Probation began with misdemeanants but subsequently underwent a transformation. Probation for misdemeanants was virtually abandoned and eventually was restricted to those who were convicted of felony offenses. Consequently, voluntarism in probation was replaced by the professional probation supervisor. It was not until 1960 that the idea of probation services supplied by volunteers received a substantial and renewed impetus.

Project Misdemeanant was founded by municipal court judge Keith Leenhouts in Royal Oak, Michigan. Beginning with eight concerned citizens, Judge Leenhouts developed the program Volunteers in Probation (VIP) into a nationwide organization affiliated with the National Council on Crime and Delinquency. The Royal Oak project demonstrated that "volunteers and professionals working together can provide intensive probation services that cannot be supplied in any other way" (NACCJS 6, 1974:9) and at a fraction of the cost of conventional probation services. In addition, the VIP program produced an impressive decrease in recidivism and a noticeable reduction in hostility among the probationers.

The success of the Royal Oak project led to immediate and widespread emulation. The Los Angeles County Probation Department developed a program called VISTO (Volunteers in Service to Offenders), which received federal fund support. In 1968, Florida became the first state to initiate a volunteer probation program on a statewide basis with felons, misdemeanants, and juveniles. At the present time, more than one thousand agencies in the criminal justice system have some provision for volunteer probation or parole services.

**Corrections**   It generally has been recognized that an offender who has served a long sentence in a total institution will suffer cultural shock when suddenly returned to the community from which he came. Just as astronauts must reenter the atmosphere in a series of shallow passes, so too the offender needs to reenter society in a gradual series of steps. This system, referred to as a *graduated release* program, is intended to ease the pressures of cultural shock experienced by institutionalized offenders. Some concepts designed to reduce the effect of reentry are presently being practiced; others must wait until there is a true correctional continuum in operation. Any preparation for release is better than none, but preparation that includes nonincarcerated periods is even more effective.

The periods immediately preceding and following the release of offenders are especially crucial to his adjustment to society. Fears and apprehension build as they approach release. Many inmates become "jack rabbits" shortly before they are freed, running away in fear of release. Others commit almost meaningless petty offenses within a short period after their release. These deliberate offenses allow them to return to total dependency afforded them in the institution. Recognition of this phenomenon has caused many thoughtful correctional administrators to establish prerelease and postrelease programs aimed at assisting the exoffender through this critical period. Topics covered in such programs include how to get a driver's license, how to spend money, how to find an apartment, family adjustment, sex, and credit buying.

The whole experience of incarceration is designed for the eventual release of the inmate. Unfortunately, the institutional environment has great difficulty in creating a copy of free life. The inmate is not allowed to earn a wage comparable to that of the private citizen, he is deprived of heterosexual relations, and he lives in an authoritarian world dominated by the needs of the institution. To expect an individual to switch readily from that situation to a free community is asking a great deal of even the strongest personality. Graduated release and prerelease programs are not either/or alternatives to incarceration, but they do recognize the destructive and dependency-producing effects of imprisonment.

A clear-cut effort toward an alternative to incarceration may be seen in the development of halfway houses. At the least, they afford the prison administrator a place where offenders who could benefit from work or education in the outside world, while residing in the community, may be sent.

Interest in the halfway house as an alternative to imprisonment has grown in recent years. Although the original concept of halfway houses was as a residence for homeless men released from prison, they have been used for a variety of purposes. Small residences that provide shelter have been managed by Prison Aid Societies for over a century. In recent years, more attention has been given to halfway houses as the possible nuclei for community-based networks of residential treatment centers. There is also a move toward using halfway houses as prerelease guidance centers.

In 1961 the Federal Bureau of Prisons established prerelease guidance centers in major metropolitan areas. The offender is sent to these centers from a correctional institution several months before he is eligible for parole. Staff personnel are selected on the basis of their treatment orientation and aptitude for counseling. The offender is allowed to work and attend school in the community without supervision and may participate in a number of programs in the halfway house itself. This approach has been copied by many states and appears to be a viable program when properly staffed and supervised. The prerelease guidance centers of the Federal Bureau of Prisons are probably the best known and most carefully researched of the halfway houses. As possible uses for the halfway house are explored and outcomes are verified, they will not only be places for short-term residency prior to placement on parole but will also serve as noninstitutional residence facilities for a number of different classes of offenders. When this occurs, genuine alternatives to institutional incarceration will be a reality.

## PREVENTION AND ALTERNATIVES TO DIRECT SERVICE

Crime control, the traditional task of the criminal justice system, and crime prevention, a current source of preoccupation among many criminal justice authorities and criminologists, are difficult to distinguish with any reliability or precision. If we build a residential or commercial structure that is impregnable to burglars, we are engaged in the prevention of the crime of burglary. If we arrest, convict, and imprison a burglar, we are preventing the crime of burglary—or at least those crimes that might have been perpetrated by that particular burglar. If we somehow manage, through psychotherapy, behavior modification, chemotherapy, psychosurgery, or moral suasion, to accomplish the rehabilitation of a burglar in or outside of prison, we are preventing further acts of burglary by the rehabilitated felon. If we create a society in which the causes of crime—whatever these are—have been abolished, then we are engaging in crime prevention.

All of these interpretations of crime prevention, together with several others, have been dealt with at varying length in the professional literature. Newman's (1971) work on "defensible space" and Jeffery's (1977) views on crime prevention through environmental design have directed emphasis toward those aspects of the physical environment that create vulnerability to criminal depredations. Proponents of mandatory flat-time sentencing, particularly of career criminals, conceptualize crime prevention largely in terms of incapacitation and deterrence. The rehabilitative ideal has been pursued by criminologists and correctional authorities who approach the problem from differing frames of reference and disciplines. With regard to the abolition of crime causation through social reorganization, the conflict theory criminologists, as pointed out earlier, have been most explicit in their advocacy of revolutionary aims through revolutionary means; but this type of solution, as Rhodes (1977) has pointed out, is implicit in nearly every contemporary theory of crime causation that assigns importance to socially inequitable arrangements as a primary determinant of criminality.

Although the preceding issues have received extensive coverage in the professional literature, perhaps the greatest amount of attention has been given to citizen and community involvement in crime prevention. Citizen action in crime prevention has a long history of sanction by Anglo-American tradition. The concept of mutual responsibility was the cornerstone of the early English peace-keeping system. A person was held accountable for the actions of his neighbors as well as his own; a citizen observing a crime was duty bound to raise the "hue and cry" and join in the pursuit of the wrong-doer. Just as the rise of specialization led to the replacement of concerned citizens by professionals in the area of social services, law enforcement evolved into its present form as citizens relinquished more and more of their responsibilities for crime prevention. We can now observe the beginnings of a reversal in this long evolutionary process. Volunteer programs and organizations are making an effort to promote increased citizen support for, and participation in, crime prevention activities.

Some communities have responded to the crime threat by seeking refuge behind deadbolts, German shepherds, electronic alarm systems, closed circuit TV cameras, and security guards. Other communities have taken a proactive approach toward self-protection. While recognizing the value and importance of security measures such as those mentioned above, their efforts have emphasized organized, collective community activities in support of conventional law enforcement agencies and operations.

**Crime Reporting**  It is assumed that the effectiveness of local law enforcement efforts can be increased to a significant degree by a citizenry alert to report crimes in the process of being committed, information that might help in the solution of crimes, and suspicious-looking persons and situations. This activity lends itself to both individual and collective effort. Under a variety of names such as Citizen Alert, Crime Alert, and Crime Stop, citizen organizations have conducted campaigns to enlist volunteers in crime reporting.

In Buffalo, New York, a program called Community Radio Watch (CRW) is supported by the efforts of 46 area firms employing over 2,500 drivers. These companies operate vehicles with two-way radios. Drivers are instructed to report any kind of emergency (fire, accident, crime) to their dispatchers, who transmit the messages to the appropriate authorities. CRW thus provides "a vast surveillance and communications network covering the entire county" (NACCJSG 1974:41).

In Battle Creek, Michigan, a citizen who reports a planned crime or witnesses a crime being committed may receive a cash award ranging from fifty to one thousand dollars. The Silent Observer Program, initiated in 1970 by the Battle Creek Area Chamber of Commerce, raises funds for the cash awards by the sale of posters that advertise the program and also from fam-

ilies of crime victims. In subsequent years, many civic-minded people re-
fused to accept any reward for the information they were able to supply to
the police.

**Property Identification**    In many parts of the country, law enforcement
agencies have developed programs to encourage citizens to register personal
property with the police. Local law enforcement agencies provide an etching
tool for community residents to use in marking their personal belongings
with their social security number or operator's license number. Each household is then supplied with a large display sticker, indicating that the residence is part of a theft-guard project, and a master list of identification
numbers is filed with the police department. One of the most successful
programs of this kind was carried out in Monterey Park, California. Property
registration produced a dramatic decrease in the burglaries that had plagued
area residents before the program was initiated.

**Neighborhood Security**    Volunteer safety patrols have been initiated by
residents of high-crime areas in a number of large cities. In New York, for
example, the city's Housing Authority Tenant Patrol program numbers more
than 11,000 members who provide security coverage for hundreds of buildings. Equipped with phones or walkie-talkies, local tenant patrols augment
the regular police surveillance of large housing projects. The Community
Vigilance Program of Philadelphia supplies volunteer wardens who patrol
designated areas in two-man teams. The wardens were recruited and trained
by the police department, and they contribute a minimum of three hours per
week. Although they are not permitted to make arrests, they patrol their
assigned areas in automobiles and report all violations to a base station,
which relays the reports to the police.

  Some idea of the range of surveillance provided by volunteer safety patrols is conveyed by the National Advisory Commission's (1974) description
of the activities of CHEC (Citizens Helping Eliminate Crime), a group organized by the Sertoma Club of Lima, Ohio, in cooperation with local law
enforcement authorities.

  Each participant is instructed to watch for a stranger entering a neighbor's house
  when it is unoccupied; a scream heard anywhere; strangers or strange cars in
  the neighborhood, school area, and parks; broken or open windows or doors;
  salesmen attempting to force entrance into a home; offers of merchandise at
  extremely low prices; anyone loitering in a parked car; persons leaving one car
  and driving off in another; anyone removing accessories, license plates, or gas-

oline from cars; anyone in a store concealing merchandise on their person; persons seen leaving or entering a business place after hours; the sound of breaking glass or other loud explosive noise; any vehicle parked with motor running; persons walking down the street peering into each parked car; persons involved in a fight; display of weapons, guns, and knives; strangers carrying appliances, household goods, luggage, or other bundles from a neighbor's home; persons loitering in secluded areas; and injured persons. (p. 41)

But security patrols do not confine their activities to observing illegal or suspicious behavior. They watch out for and report safety hazards, such as malfunctioning traffic signals and inadequate street lighting; they look in on community residents who are elderly or sick; and they even, on occasion, shovel snow from sidewalks.

The efforts of volunteers in neighborhood security patrols are augmented by the contributions of citizens who have joined auxiliary or police reserve units. In New York City, each precinct has an auxiliary police unit made up of volunteers who serve without compensation. Applicants are selected on the basis of requirements that are not appreciably different from those used in the selection of academy recruits, and they take an intensive ten-week training course. Auxiliary police members are supplied with uniforms and equipment but are usually not permitted to carry firearms. They have arrest powers and may use physical force when necessary. Members of the auxiliary units are on duty three nights per week and must average eight hours of duty per month.

## SPECIALIZED SERVICES AND HIGH-RISK POPULATIONS

**Victim Services**   In response to the growing public concern for the plight of victims of criminal offenses, a variety of programs have been developed within recent years to provide victim services. Such programs are addressed to both immediate and long-range goals, ranging from the use of crisis intervention techniques by police officers in the emergency treatment of victims of violent crime to the mobilization of community support for crime prevention activities. An extremely interesting proposal by Dussich (1973) is to provide a community with an ombudsman, who would assist victims of crime by intervening in the crisis and acting as a community facilitator for directing the victim to the community's resources. These programs and proposals might be construed as examples of the general tendency toward institutionalizing and formalizing the kind of community support and ameliorative actions that were supplied informally by neighborhood residents at an earlier period in our history.

Dussich (1975) has conducted a thorough analysis of victim service models and their efficacy, and the following discussion draws heavily on his account. In analyzing these programs, Dussich focuses upon the model or structure they employ and their various objectives or functions, which he categorizes as primary or secondary.

The primary function of most models is to deliver a broad range of services to crime victims on behalf of the respective agencies that operate as hosts for the programs. These services include

1. Assuming immediate responsibility for the victim at the crime scene.
2. Referring and/or transporting the victim to emergency medical or social service facilities.
3. Providing the victim with a companion during the period immediately following the crime.
4. Addressing the victim's family situation.
5. Protecting the victim from unnecessary exploitation by the media, police, or courts.
6. Conducting thorough followup procedures and assuring adequate delivery of public assistance services to victims.
7. Assisting victims with their responsibilities to the court as key witnesses.
8. Counseling the victims to prevent revictimization.
9. Utilizing contact information in community crime prevention planning.
10. Developing public awareness programs aimed at target hardening, i.e., making more specific and concrete the goals to be sought in victim-oriented services.
11. Coordinating victim volunteer programs to supplement existing manpower needs.
12. Assisting the families of victims with aftermath arrangements, e.g., insurance, funerals, compensations.
13. Conducting victimization surveys to help pinpoint high-victimization areas in need of attention.
14. Providing the victim with information about the progress of the case and his role and responsibilities in that process.
15. Institutionalizing community victim awareness.

Secondary functions include a variety of objectives or services that are unique to various models. These include such objectives as encouraging victims to report crimes to the police and gathering information from victims that would assist in police crime prevention efforts—functions specific to the police model—as well as notifying victims who are witnesses as to when they must appear in court and helping them to adjust their schedules to the court schedule, in the case of the district attorney model. There are some secondary functions appropriate to all models, such as maintaining a "hotline" for crime victims who are in need of immediate help or providing victims with a community services directory listing key resources that are available.

### High-Risk Populations: Psychotic, Retarded, and Psychopathic Offenders
Under our system of criminal jurisprudence, there are two methods by which an offender can be absolved of criminal responsibility for his actions: either by being found "not guilty by reason of insanity" or by being declared "incompetent to stand trial." In the first instance, the offender admits to having committed the act, but the defense claims that at the time of the act he did not have the capacity to understand the nature of the act or that it was wrong. The issue of competency to stand trial involves the common law criteria that a defendant must be able to understand the charges against him and to cooperate with his counsel in the preparation of his own defense. The procedures for determining competency vary considerably from jurisdiction to jurisdiction, but most require a court decision based on psychiatric testimony. In some states a jury may be impaneled if the defendant so requests, and in three states the court has the discretion to impanel a jury to determine competency (Brakel and Rock 1971). If a defendant is found to be incompetent to stand trial, he is usually committed to a mental institution until such time as he is certified to be competent by the medical or psychiatric authorities at the institution.

With the advent of legal insanity and incompetency as defenses against criminal conviction came the development of special asylums for the "criminally insane," which in most cases were just another form of prison, without due process protections. According to the National Institute of Mental Health (1972), these types of institutions are used for the following categories of persons:

1. persons adjudicated incompetent to enter a plea or stand trial;
2. defendants found not guilty by reason of insanity;
3. persons adjudicated under special statutes, e.g., "sexually dangerous persons," "defective delinquents," "sexual psychopaths";
4. convicted and sentenced offenders who have become mentally disturbed while serving a prison sentence and have been transferred to a mental health facility;

5. other potentially hazardous mentally ill persons requiring special security during the course of their evaluation and treatment.

There are presently seventy-three such institutions in the United States.

*The Mentally Retarded Offender.* Opinions concerning the possible relationships between mental retardation and criminality, according to Menolascino
(1975), have tended to converge upon the following "simplistic viewpoints":

1. The retarded are "born criminal"—i.e., congenital "moral idiots."
2. The retarded characteristically commit dangerous crimes because they lack
the capacity to grasp the social values of their culture—including its social and
legal definitions of "right" and "wrong."
3. The retarded cannot foresee the consequences of their actions and hence
cannot be effectively deterred by normal punishments.
4. The retarded are more highly vulnerable to suggestion and therefore respond indiscriminately to the criminal leadership of brighter persons.
5. Retarded individuals more frequently are reared in families and neighborhoods in which early and continuing identification with delinquent models is
common. (p. 57).

Interest in the mentally retarded offender, as Menolascino notes, had
"outstripped factual information." For example, the incidence of mental
retardation among incarcerated offenders is difficult to establish with any
reliability. The judgment that mental retardation is present requires psychometric evaluation, that is, an intelligence test, yet a survey by Brown
and Courtless (1971) of all correctional institutions in the United States
showed that, on the basis of 80 percent return of questionnaires, only about
half the inmates had been so tested. Approximately 9.5 percent of those who
had received psychometric evaluation had IQs below 70, and nearly 1,500
inmates had IQ scores below 55. Allen (1970), projecting the findings of
this survey on to the total prison population, stated: "There are in American
prisons today nearly 200,000 adult offenders (10 percent of the total prison
population) who are substantially impaired, some 3,300 of whom are clas-
sifiable as moderately to profoundly retarded" (p. 601). The nature of the
crimes committed by these offenders is not specified, but Allen indicated
that there is a higher incidence of crimes against the person among the retarded than among the nonretarded.

As Allen has pointed out, our society has pursued three different courses
with regard to mentally retarded offenders: "We have ignored their limita-

tions and special needs, or have sought to tailor traditional criminal law processes to fit them, or have grouped them with the mentally ill'' (p. 602). The lowered social-adaptative capabilities of the retardate that make him prone to commit illegal actions leave him particularly vulnerable in his constitutional rights, and he is not likely to comprehend the full import of the Miranda warnings when they are given to him by the arresting officer.

Contemporary services for the mentally retarded offender are perhaps the least of those provided for any category of offender. Conventional probation and parole procedures prove unsuccessful for the majority of retarded offenders, but neither the mental health nor the correctional authorities have been able to provide adequate institutional facilities for the care and management of such offenders.

Menolascino (1975) believes that the first obstacle to be overcome in improving programs for the mentally retarded offender is the problem of ''defining him by a common measure with stable dimensions.'' He suggests a classification that utilizes two age-specific categories, each subdivided into behavioral descriptions, as a basis for identifying the treatment needs of these individuals:

1. Mentally Retarded Adolescents and Young Adults

   (a) Behavioral problems: Teen-agers and young adults referred for the first time. Usually adolescents with IQs of 40 to 80 who are management problems, are sexually promiscuous, or lack salable or social skills required in our complex society.

   (b) Consistently antisocial, uncontrolled, or self-destructive behavior: Usually individuals who failed previously to respond to residential services or who have come directly from the community with a long history of social offenses.

2. Mentally Retarded Adults

   (a) Delinquent-criminal behavior with some community judgment of unsafe or unacceptable conduct: Individuals exhibiting a generally low level of successful socio-educational-vocational experiences before admission to an institution or a treatment setting; Actual or potential threat for physical assault toward others documented.

   (b) Severe retardation with a history of habitual unacceptable social behavior: Individuals admitted to an institution because their families or general society can no longer tolerate their low abilities and poor behavior. Typically, their problem behavior spills over beyond the power of the family, agencies, and community to control, modify, or contain them. (p. 63)

Allen (1970) has made a series of recommendations for improvement of the handling of mentally retarded offenders, beginning with the establishment of an ''exceptional offenders court'' to permit early identification of retardates who can be diverted from the criminal justice system. Emphasis is placed on the importance of special education and vocational training to help the retardate acquire skills needed to get along outside the institution, together with effective treatment of emotional problems and realistic prerelease planning. Reintegration into the community should be accomplished by the use of halfway houses and a parole system that uses officers specially trained in the management of mentally retarded offenders.

*The Antisocial (Psychopathic) Personality.* The nineteenth-century criminologist Cesare Lombroso endorsed the concept of the moral imbecile, noting that such individuals were guiltless, impulsive, highly aggressive, boastful, and particularly insensitive to both social criticism and physical pain. The term "psychopath" was used first by the ancient Greeks to indicate those behaviors not possible to identify through medicine. The etymological definition of the term "suffering mind" reveals the cautious approach of our ancestors toward this type of behavior, whose characteristics lacked sufficiently definable properties for medical classification.

While psychiatry continued to try to find a way to identify and treat this kind of condition, the law began to see special problems with this type of offender, one not troubled by various forms of delusions or other gross disturbances in affect or cognition. These offenders, when placed in a mental institution, were able to show rapid progress and were released, only to get into trouble again. The response to this perceived threat to society was the first of the psychopathy laws, passed by Massachusetts in 1911. Known as the Briggs Act, it created a distinct class of habitual criminal offenders, known as "defective delinquents" (Kittrie 1971).

## PROGRAM COSTS AND FUNDING MECHANISMS

Perhaps the most significant event in recent years for the criminal justice system in the United States was the passage by Congress in June of 1968 of the Omnibus Crime Control and Safe Streets Act. Although a modest law enforcement grant program had been in existence since 1965, the Crime Control and Safe Streets Act marked the first large-scale infusion of federal funds into the improvement of the criminal justice system. This landmark legislation resulted mainly from the work of the President's Crime Commission, which in its 1967 report, *The Challenge of Crime in a Free Society,* declared that financial resources at the local level were totally inadequate to deal with the necessity for innovation and change in approaches to crime. This legislation authorized the Department of Justice to create an administrative instrumentality, the Law Enforcement Assistance Administration, to provide criminal justice planning and program grants to state and local governments. It also authorized the establishment of the National Institute of Law Enforcement and Criminal Justice in order to stimulate, promote, and encourage basic research in the areas of crime, criminal behavior, and the criminal justice system.

The President's Commission supplied figures on public expenditures for law enforcement and the criminal justice system based on the situation as it existed in 1966. At that time, the estimated total cost of all operations was $4,212 million. The lion's share of this figure was the $2,792 million in expenditures for law enforcement made by the nearly 40,000 law enforcement agencies throughout the country. Salaries and wages accounted for approximately 85 to 90 percent of these costs. The second largest expense in the administration of criminal justice was for corrections, including parole, probation, and other rehabilitation programs, in addition to incarceration. Approximately 80 percent of all local and state expenditures in the correctional area were for institutional costs. The remaining expenses for prosecution, defense, and the courts totaled $386 million. It should be kept in mind that the majority of courts at all levels exercise both civil and criminal jurisdiction. Moreover, these estimates were made before the impact of court decisions on the right to counsel had begun to be felt throughout the criminal justice system.

Since 1969 there has been a steady and significant annual increase in overall criminal justice expenditure in the United States. A recent publication of the U.S. Department of Justice (1980) *Expenditure and Employment Data for the Criminal Justice System 1978* recorded an increase of 129.1 percent in criminal justice expenditure between 1971 and 1978. The federal government increased its expenditure by 154.3 percent during this period, state governments by 149.5 percent, and local governments by 116.3 percent. In absolute dollar figures, expenditures rose from approximately $10.5 billion in 1971 for the combined federal, state, and local criminal justice agencies to $24 billion in 1978.

The principal reason for the increases in expenditure noted above can be seen in the increase in the number of full-time employees in criminal justice services at all levels during the period from 1971 to 1978. The total number of full-time employees rose from 861,776 in 1971 to 1,157,335 in 1978, an increase of 34.3 percent. Although this cumulative increase was shared by all levels of government, state governments experienced the largest increase—50.9 percent—followed by the federal government with an increase of 33.8 percent, and local governments with an increase of 28.5 percent.

More than half of the $24 billion of the nation's total criminal justice expenditure went to pay for police protection; nearly one-quarter, $5.5 billion, was spent on corrections. Reflecting the fact that law enforcement is essentially a responsibility of local government, nearly two-thirds of their direct expenditure (64.7 percent or $9.3 billion) was for police protection activities. By contrast, state governments spent nearly half (47.5 percent) of their $6.7 billion on direct expenditures in the area of correctional services. These expenditure levels are undoubtedly going to continue to mirror cost increases as a function of inflation, but it seems improbable that employment figures will show much change in the immediate future. Despite increased needs for criminal justice services and personnel to provide them, many local governments have already experienced massive problems in meeting current criminal justice payrolls.

Legal Services Corporation is a private, nonprofit corporation established by an act of Congress in 1974 for the purpose of distributing federal funds to locally controlled, community-based programs that provide direct civil legal services to poor and disadvantaged persons. LSC lawyers advise and represent indigent clients in matters as diverse as family disputes, landlord harassment, consumer fraud, and claims for rightful entitlements such as Medicare, income maintenance, and food stamps. LSC, due for congressional reauthorization in 1980, is currently operating under a continuing resolution.

Proposed funding for LSC is as follows:

FY 1981   $321.3 million
FY 1982   FY 1982 funds for LSC contained in the third continuing resolution (H.J. Res. 370) are $241 million. This resolution, which expires on March 31, 1982, therefore, assures exactly half that amount, or $120.5 million. The administration proposes that any extension of the 1982 continuing resolution not include further funds for LSC.
FY 1983   The administration proposes that no further separate federal funding be provided LSC in 1983 or later years. In addition, the administration suggests that legal services activities can be provided at the various state's discretion through use of social and community services block grants with no concomitant infusion of federal funds to cover this additional task.

The continuing resolution includes a 1981 restriction that prevents LSC funds from being used in "promoting, defending, or protecting homosexuality." However, the reauthorization bill (H.R. 3480) and the appropriations bill (H.R. 4169) that have passed the House contain major restricting amendments, which include:

1. Restrictions on legislative advocacy,
2. a ban on class action lawsuits against local, state, or federal government agencies,
3. a prohibition against representing illegal aliens, and
4. a requirement that 60 percent of every local board of directors be attorneys appointed by the local bar association.

The administration proposes for 1983 that the LSC not be reauthorized and that funding already included in the continuing resolution be used for future needs relating to responsibilities for existing cases, separation costs of corporation and grantee staff, and related close-out functions.

## INTERSYSTEM AND INTERAGENCY COLLABORATION

**System and Process** To most people, "system" connotes merely an orderly arrangement of articulated parts according to some overall plan or design. The basic notion here is that relationships among elements or components in a system are deliberate rather than haphazard. Further, there is a strong implication that the arrangement exists to achieve some goal or purpose. A major characteristic of systems in their operating aspect is that anything that affects one part can potentially affect other parts as well as the system itself in its total functioning.

In recent years, a field called systems analysis has developed that makes use of sophisticated mathematical and statistical procedures in the study of organizational structures, operations, and problems. Systems analysis received contributions from a number of areas of inquiry: communications research, information theory, and cybernetics, to name but a few. Although the methods employed by systems analysts are rather complex and rigorous, some of their key concepts are readily understandable and widely applicable. One of these is the *linear process model,* a continuum—an orderly progression of events, from input to output. Hartinger (1974) has characterized the system: "The input is what the system deals with; the process is *how* the system deals with the input; and the output is the *results* of the process" (p. 9). In the criminal justice system language, "input" refers to selected law violations (i.e.; reported crimes), " process" refers to the activities of the police, courts, and corrections; and "output" includes the results (i.e., success or failure) obtained from the process.

This continuum can be seen more clearly in the diagram of the criminal justice system displayed in figure 4.1. This chart sets forth in a clear and simple form the structures involved in the process of criminal justice administration. The offender, if apprehended, will pass through most of the different parts of the criminal justice system on his way to prison. Many do not pass through every procedural step but fall out of the system at different points along the way. It should also be noted that felonies, misdemeanors, petty offenses, and juvenile cases receive different dispositions within the criminal justice system and thus follow separate paths in the process.

The criminal justice system is seen as a combination of four major subsystems—police, prosecution, courts, and corrections—each with its specific tasks. These subsystems are by no means mutually exclusive, however, and what is done in one has a direct effect upon another. Many subsystems of these four major components are required to interact at many different points in the criminal justice process. Courts receive their clientele from the police; the corrections sector receives its clients from the courts; and the cycle is often restarted when the released offenders commit another offense and are rearrested by the police. Increased efforts by the police produce an immediate impact on courts and corrections by overloading already heavy work schedules. Thus, if corrections is overburdened and cannot succeed in its rehabilitation efforts, the police become occupied with too many repeat offenders (recidivists). This circular process is the focal point for much controversy among the various components of the criminal justice system.

**Criminal Justice Systems 1 and 2**  The American criminal justice system is not a single system, but many separate systems and subsystems of institutions and procedures. In all of the thousands of towns, cities, counties, and states in the United States—and even in the federal government—there are criminal justice "systems" of sorts. Although they may appear similar in that they apprehend, prosecute, convict, and attempt to rehabilitate lawbreakers, no two are exactly alike, and few are linked together in any comprehensive manner.

But the situation is subject to even further complication. In another publication (1973a), the National Advisory Commission asserts the belief that "there are two criminal justice systems in the United States today, one of which is "visible and controversial," the other "submerged and usually ignored." The commission report identifies these as Criminal Justice Systems 1 and 2:

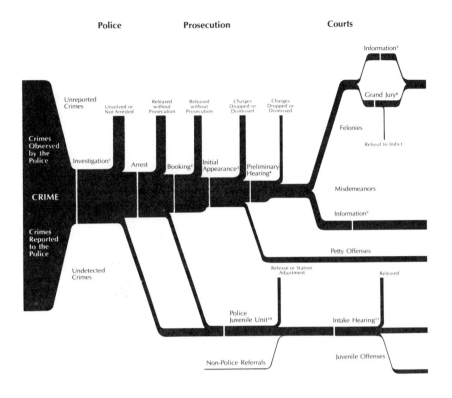

Police          Prosecution                    Courts

Information⁵

Grand Jury⁶

Unreported
Crimes        Unsolved or    Released      Released      Charges       Charges
              Not Arrested   without       without       Dropped or    Dropped or
                             Prosecution   Prosecution   Dismissed     Dismissed

Felonies

Refusal to Indict

Crimes
Observed
by the
Police      Investigation¹                                                      Preliminary
                          Arrest      Booking²   Initial          Hearing⁴
                                                 Appearance³

CRIME                                                                 Misdemeanors

                                                                      Information⁵

Crimes
Reported
to the
Police                                                                Petty Offenses

                                              Release or Station
Undetected                                    Adjustment                    Released
Crimes

                                     Police
                                     Juvenile Unit¹⁰          Intake Hearing¹¹

                    Non-Police Referrals                     Juvenile Offenses

'May continue until trial.                   'Before magistrate, commissioner, or       'Charge filed by prosecutor on basis of
'Administrative record of arrest. First step  justice of peace. Formal notice of          information submitted by police or
at which temporary release on bail may       charge, advice of rights. Bail set.         citizens. Alternative to grand jury
be available.                                Summary trials for petty offenses usually   indictment; often used in felonies,
                                             conducted here without further              almost always in misdemeanors.
                                             processing.                                 'Reviews whether Government evidence
                                             'Preliminary testing of evidence against    sufficient to justify trial. Some States
                                             defendant. Charge may be reduced. No        have no grand jury system; others
                                             separate preliminary hearing for            seldom use it.
                                             misdemeanors in some systems.

Criminal Justice System 1 is known well. It is the traditional series of agencies that have been given the formal responsibility to control crime: police and sheriffs' departments, judges, prosecutors and their staffs, defense offices, jails and prisons, and probation and parole agencies. Criminal Justice System 1 is an overt system, the one seen each day in operation, the one customarily understood and referred to in crime and delinquency literature. Even in this report, the phrase "criminal justice system" usually refers to Criminal Justice System 1.

But there are broader implications of the term. . . . Many public and private agencies and citizens outside of police, courts, and corrections are—or ought to be—involved in reducing and preventing crime, the primary goal of criminal justice. These agencies and persons, when dealing with issues related to crime

**Corrections**

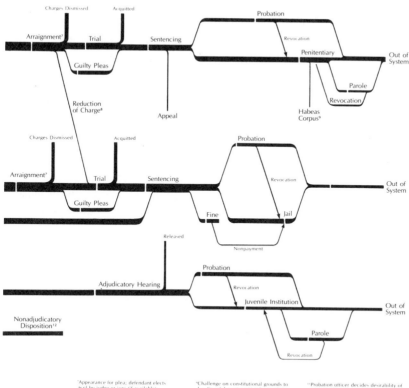

reduction and prevention, plus the traditional triad of police, courts, and corrections, make up a larger criminal justice system, a system which this commission
calls Criminal Justice System 2.

A state legislature, for example, becomes part of this larger criminal justice
system when it considers and debates any proposed law that might affect, even
remotely, any area of criminal justice activities. So also the executive agencies
of the state, educational administrative units, welfare departments, youth service
bureaus, recreation departments, and other public offices become a part of
Criminal Justice System 2 in many of their decisions and actions. Moving outside the state and local governments, community organizations, union offices,
neighborhood action groups, and employers may also be important functionaries
in the second system. (p. 1)

What the commission seems to be saying in the above passage has frequently been stated elsewhere in less formal terms: Coping with crime and its consequences is everyone's business in our contemporary American society. Unfortunately, as the commission notes, "Many public agencies and private citizens refuse even to acknowledge that they have a role in reducing crime" (p. 1). Moreover, the effectiveness of Criminal Justice System 1 is lessened by intramural conflicts among the police, courts, and correctional agencies.

If cooperation is poor among components of Criminal Justice System 1, it is markedly worse with respect to interactions involving Criminal Justice System 2. Many courts, law enforcement agencies, and correctional facilities have few or no working relationships with the various private and public organizations that might provide them valuable services for their clients. Worse, most have no clear policies for obtaining such assistance, even if there is awareness of its availability.

## ACCOUNTABILITY: EVALUATION AND PLANNING

The passage by Congress in 1968 of the Omnibus Crime Control and Safe Streets Act had two far-reaching implications for the criminal justice system. For one thing, it directed public attention to an institutional component of our society that had been almost totally neglected and ignored in spite of its crucial importance for the common welfare. Second, by creating an instrumentality called the Law Enforcement Assistance Administration—a title that, in retrospect, ought to have been the Criminal Justice Assistance Administration—at the federal level to supervise a massive transfusion of federal monies into the criminal justice system, it made many authorities suddenly aware of the fact that there was no apparatus, no administrative machinery, at the local and state levels to accomplish this transfer of funds in an orderly and meaningful way. As the National Advisory Commission on Criminal Justice Standards and Goals (1973b) pointed out:

> The actual funds received from the federal government under the Safe Streets Act may be less important in the long run than the stimulus the act provided to criminal justice planning. For the first time, state governments have a staff arm for closely examining criminal justice problems from a systemwide perspective. In a number of states, state planning agencies are becoming useful instruments for policy analysis and comprehensive reform. (p. 33)

The operative phrase in the above passage is "examining criminal justice problems from a systemwide perspective." The National Advisory Commission uses a homely but effective example to illustrate the kinds of difficulties posed for criminal justice planning when the needs of a whole system, rather than a single component or agency, are involved. The commission asks you to assume that you are taking part in a community decision where $250,000 in additional funds has been made available for law enforcement and crime prevention purposes. How should the money be spent? What will it buy? Says the commission:

> In an urban city, it will pay for 10 policemen for one year, including salaries, uniforms, training, equipment, overhead, and fringe benefits. The same money would pay for eight new prosecutors, together with their necessary support services. It might also pay for three months of special training in prerelease centers for each of 120 offenders or pay for an entire year of noninstitutional after care for 70 people in the system. The same money might greatly aid narcotics treatment centers, or maintain for one year two or three youth services bureaus that provide help for delinquent and troubled youth. (p. 44)

The decision-making process with respect to such highly diverse alternatives can be made more rational, the commission contends, by improved planning techniques. They recommend:

——Multiyear planning in each state, taking into account all federal, state, and local resources.
——Metropolitan area coordinating councils to plan across county and city boundaries.
——Expanded membership from non–criminal justice sources on criminal justice planning councils.
——Formalized exhanges of ideas and personnel between planning and operating agencies.

It has long been recognized in military circles that the key element in planning is the availability of up-to-date and detailed intelligence information. In criminal justice planning, the "intelligence" function is supplied by systematic program evaluation and evaluative research.

The importance of evaluation and systematic policy analysis, especially in the development of programs, cannot be overstressed. In addition to lack of information, some of the most conspicuous problems in the field of criminal justice can be attributed to unsystematic and often conflicting approaches in programming. Rational policy analysis and decision making should be implemented, and "accountability" should be the key word in the next few years of criminal justice planning. Rather than starting programs that are fashionable, criminal justice planners should evaluate new programs, recognize program failures, learn from their ineffectiveness, and develop rational alternatives.

With an emphasis on "experimental projects," criminal justice administrators should implement innovative programs, work to keep them operating efficiently, and then objectively and continuously evaluate them to determine whether continuance is merited. If such programs do not prove to be effective, they should be discontinued and other innovative programs tried.

A method of determining program effectiveness and development of new programs is "systematic experimentation." Rivlin (1971) suggests that through systematic experimentation of innovative programs, programs are initiated in several areas to establish the capability for determining the conditions under which they work best. Programs should be evaluated objectively, and the information about their effectiveness or noneffectiveness disseminated for use by other areas and jurisdictions.

Although determination of policy from program evaluation seems logical, criminal justice programs are often started and continued even when the program is not accomplishing its stated objectives. The above points suggest the definite need for more rational policy making and programming in criminal justice. Research and program evaluations should be conducted to determine the consequences of possible alternatives. Programs already implemented must be tested for accountability; if they are shown to be ineffective, serious consideration should be given to other alternative programs and their possible consequences.

Evaluative techniques that provide the analyst with information upon which to recommend policy are needed in the criminal justice field. Traditionally, program evaluation has not been extensively utilized in the policy-making process, due not only to the administrator's lack of interest in evaluation but also to the widespread utilization of inappropriate evaluative techniques by the evaluator.

Program evaluation should serve as a feedback process for future planning. For planning purposes, an evaluation must lend itself to providing data that are appropriate for planning needs, rather than to a simple formulation of statements regarding the effectiveness of an individual program. The role and responsibilities of the evaluator and researcher are bound to become more complex and important as their contributions to criminal justice planning are given increasing weight by criminal justice administrators at every level.

## UNIQUE CONTRIBUTION TO HUMAN SERVICES: TOWARD A SOCIAL JUSTICE MODEL

The clientele of the criminal justice system—and we must include in this designation the offender, the victim, and society at large—need services beyond those traditionally provided. Figure 4.2 illustrates the functions of a system that provides a maximum number of alternatives at each point in the process. The process begins when an offense is alleged to have been committed. In the present system, this leads to arrest and its collateral consequences. Under the social justice model, for minor offenses the offender would be issued a summons or a citation in lieu of an arrest. In the case of an arrest, maximum use would be made of bail, release on recognizance, or supervision. The social justice model also makes use of deferred prosecution and probation without supervision for those cases that the prosecutor feels should not be tried.

An individual may leave the system if he is determined to be unable to stand trial because of mental illness. Under the new model he would be sent to a probate court and then possibly committed to a state hospital for treatment. If, however, it is determined that mental health treatment in the community is a realistic alternative, the individual may be referred to out-patient care. Another key feature of a social justice model is the evaluation conducted after conviction. This evaluation is conducted by experts in several fields, not medical or psychiatric professionals alone; the panel would also include educators, social workers, vocational counselors, probation officers, and law enforcement personnel, who would examine the specific social and personal needs of the offender and determine the disposition that seems best suited to public safety and the individual's needs.

Disposition could range from economic sanctions, such as fines, to incarceration at the state prison. These sanctions could entail payment to the victim for losses or damage, or mandatory labor in some socially beneficial program. Offenders who present minimum risk could be placed on supervised probation and remain in the community, and their treatment plan reevaluated periodically. There could be several alternatives to incarceration for medium-risk offenders, depending on the availability of facilities and the evaluation of the individual offender. These offenders may be placed in halfway houses, probation hostels, or a community treatment facility. Other alternatives for this group may include weekend residence at a community treatment facility or mandatory attendance in group or individual treatment programs at a community correctional center.

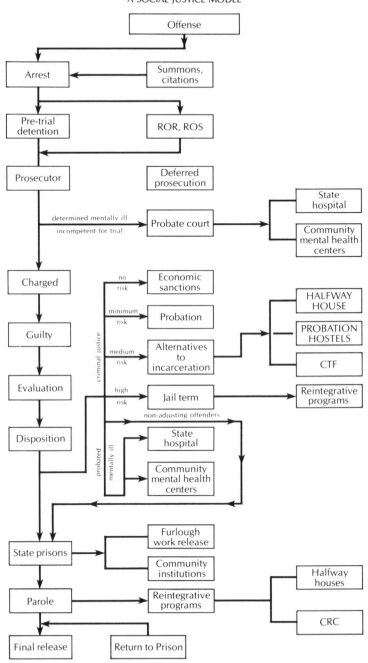

**Figure 4.2**
A SOCIAL JUSTICE MODEL

*Source:* Vetter and Simonsen 1976:336. Reprinted by permission.

High-risk offenders would first serve their sentences in the community correctional center. If the offender responds well to the center's programs, he may serve his entire sentence in the center and qualify for reintegration as soon as he is ready. If the offender is found to be so dangerous or maladjusted that he is a threat to himself and others, he will then be sent to a maximum security state prison. Upon qualifying for a trial work release program or return to a community correctional facility, the offender would be reintegrated into the community on a gradual basis. The reintegration process would take place in the same facilities used for other categories of offenders; both groups would participate together, regardless of offense or sentence.

This system is still perhaps more of a dream than a reality. Yet the elements for this type of system are available in most jurisdictions today. The major difference between the social justice model and the standard criminal justice model is the establishment of graduated and integrated levels of correctional treatment, without regard to the offense, that treat the offender as an individual with a unique set of problems and needs. Most social agencies are doing these things on a piecemeal basis now, but the added element of coordination and control would assure that all programs made the fullest contribution toward solving the offender's basic problems. The social justice model seems to be the most logical evolution from the present system of corrections.

## NOTES

1. "Plea bargaining" refers to the practice of prosecutors in dealing with the defendant in order to find out about other crimes, secure information on other offenders, or in the situation where the case is weak, to accept a plea of guilty to a lesser charge. To achieve the granting of a plea of guilty to a lesser charge, the defendant agrees to "bargain" away the more serious offense.

2. "Elements of a crime" refers to specific and precise statutory conditions of fact that *must* exist in order for that crime to have taken place (e.g., it must be *dark* for "burglary in the night season" to have taken place).

3. "Appeal" refers to the "removal of a case from a court of inferior to one of superior jurisdiction for the purpose of obtaining a review and retrial" (Kerper 1972:506).

## REFERENCES

Allen, R. C. 1970. The law and the mentally retarded. In F. J. Menolascino, ed., *Psychiatric Approaches to Mental Retardation.* New York: Basic Books.

Baker, N. 1933. The prosecutor: Initiation of prosecution. *Journal of Criminal Law, Criminology, and Police Science* 23:771.

Bard, M. Alternatives to traditional law enforcement. In E. F. Korten et al., eds. 1970. *Psychology and the Problems of Society.* Washington, D.C.: American Psychological Association.

Bard, M. 1973. *Family Crisis Intervention: From Concept to Implementation.* Washington, D.C.: U.S. Department of Justice.

Barnes, H. E. and N. K. Teeters. 1959. *New Horizons in Criminology.* Englewood Cliffs, N.J.: Prentice-Hall.

Bittner, E. 1970. *The Function of the Police in a Modern Society.* Chevy Chase, Md.: National Institute of Mental Health.

Brakel, S. and R. Rock. 1971. *The Mentally Disabled and the Law.* Chicago: University of Chicago Press.

Brown, B. S. and T. F. Courtless. 1971. *The Mentally Retarded Offender.* Rockville, Md.: National Institute of Mental Health.

Clark, B. 1968. Is law enforcement headed in the right direction? *Police* 12:31–34.

Cleckley, H. 1970. *The Mask of Sanity.* St. Louis: Mosby.

Coffey, A., E. Eldefonso, and W. Hartinger. 1974. *An Introduction to the Criminal Justice System and Process.* Englewood Cliffs, N.J.: Prentice-Hall.

Dussich, J.P.J. 1973. The victim ombudsman: A proposal. manuscript. Tallahassee, Fl.: Florida State University.

Dussich, J.P.J. 1975. Victim-service models and their efficacy. Paper presented to the International Advanced Study Institute on Victimology and the Needs of Contemporary Society, Bellagio, Italy.

Erickson, K. T. 1964. Notes on the sociology of deviance. In H. S. Becker, ed., *The Other Side: Perspectives on Deviance.* New York: Free Press.

FBI. 1977. *Uniform Crime Reports: 1976.* Washington, D.C.: Federal Bureau of Investigation.

FBI. 1979. *Uniform Crime Reports: 1978.* Washington, D.C.: Federal Bureau of Investigation.

Fox, V. B. 1964. Dilemmas in law enforcement. *Police* 9:28–31.

Fox, V. B. 1972. *Introduction to Corrections.* Englewood Cliffs, N.J.: Prentice-Hall.

Glueck, S. 1962. *Mental Disorder and the Criminal Law.* Boston: Little, Brown.

Jeffery, C. R. 1977. *Crime Prevention Through Environmental Design.* Beverly Hills: Sage.

Kaplan, J. 1973. *Criminal Justice: Introductory Cases and Materials.* Mineola, N.Y.: Foundation Press.

Kerper, Hazel B. 1972. *Introduction to the Criminal Justice System.* St. Paul, Minn.: West.

Kittrie, N. 1971. *The Right to Be Different.* Baltimore: Johns Hopkins University Press.

Lemert, E. M. 1967. *Human Deviance, Social Problems and Social Control.* Englewood Cliffs, N.J.: Prentice-Hall.

Lewis, J. H. 1972. *Evaluation of Experiments in Policing: How Do You Begin?* Washington, D.C.: Police Foundation.

McCartt, J. M. and J. Mangogna. 1973. *Guidelines and Standards for Halfway Houses and Community Treatment.* Washington, D.C.: Government Printing Office.

Menolascino, F. J. 1975. A system of services for the mentally retarded offender. *Crime and Delinquency* 21:57–64.

Miller, W. B. 1973. Ideology and criminal justice policy: Some current issues. *Journal of Criminal Law and Criminology* 64:141–162.

NACCJSG. 1973a. *The Criminal Justice System.* Washington, D.C.: National Advisory Commission on Criminal Justice Standards and Goals.

NACCJSG. 1973b. *A National Strategy to Reduce Crime.* Washington, D.C.: National Advisory Commission on Criminal Justice Standards and Goals.

NACCJSG. 1974. *Community Crime Prevention.* Washington, D.C.: National Advisory Commission on Criminal Justice Standards and Goals.

NIMH. 1972. *Directory of Institutions for Mentally Disordered Offenders.* Washington, D.C.: National Institute of Mental Health.

Nettler, Gwynn. 1970. *Explanations.* New York: McGraw-Hill.

Newman, O. 1971. *Architectural Design for Crime Prevention.* Washington, D.C.: Government Printing Office.

Packer, H. 1968. *The Limits of the Criminal Sanction.* Palo Alto, Calif.: Stanford University Press.

Pound, R. 1929. *Criminal Justice in America.* New York: Holt.

PCLEAJ. 1967a. *The Challenge of Crime in a Free Society.* Washington, D.C.: President's Commission on Law Enforcement and Administration of Justice.

PCLEAJ. 1967b. *Task Force Report: Crime and Its Impact—An Assessment.* Washington, D.C.: President's Commission on Law Enforcement and Administration of Justice.

PCLEAJ. 1967c. *Task Force Report: The Police.* Washington, D.C.: President's Commission on Law Enforcement and Administration of Justice.

Rhodes, R. P. 1977. *The Insoluble Problems of Crime.* New York: Wiley.

Rivlin, A. M. 1971. *Systematic Thinking for Social Action.* Washington, D.C.: Brookings Institute.

Schur, E. M. 1971. *Labeling Deviant Behavior: Its Sociological Implications.* New York: Harper & Row.

Shore, M. F. 1971. Psychological theories of the causes of antisocial behavior. *Crime and Delinquency* 17:456–468.

Silberman, L. 1974. Keynote address to the annual meeting of the National Conference of State Criminal Justice Planning Administrators. *LEAA Newsletter* 4:6–8.

Stone, A. 1975. *Mental Health and the Law.* Washington, D.C.: Government Printing Office.

Ulberg, C. 1973. *A Report of the Background and History of the Washington Criminal Justice Education and Training Center.* Seattle: Battelle Human Affairs Research Center.

U.S. Department of Justice. 1980. *Expenditure and Employment Data for the Criminal Justice System 1978.* Washington, D.C.: Government Printing Office.

# 5

# THE SOCIAL
# WELFARE SYSTEM

## HAROLD H. WEISSMAN

What is social welfare? To the average person it is something in the form of money or food or clothing that is given to people who cannot take care of themselves, either through misfortune or through lack of will. Although this definition in no way mirrors reality, it does illustrate a basic problem in the field. There is no one precise agreed-upon definition of social welfare; there are several.

In the Preamble to the Constitution, we, the people, specifically note our intention to promote the general welfare. Did the framers have in mind the general welfare of the country or the general welfare of citizens? Are they the same? What actually would government do to promote the general welfare? Presumably the answers were to be spelled out in later times and generations, in a continually evolving process.

Harold H. Weissman is Director of the Center for Study of Social Administration and Professor of Social Work, Hunter College of the City University of New York.

We might not have had a constitution ratified, had specific answers been attempted in 1789. The problem then, and the problem now, is the same. There are great philosophical and practical disagreements over what should be done for and what constitutes the general welfare.

At the present time these same disagreements hold true for social welfare. The main points of disagreement have been characterized as the residual and institutional views of welfare. The former holds that the general welfare is promoted by family and religious, political, and economic institutions. Only when these institutions break down is there a necessity for social welfare— activities and services that are given to individuals who either through their personal failings or the failings of society are unable to take care of themselves.

This residual view of welfare has been espoused by the Reagan administration. The institutional view of social welfare assumes that in an increasingly complex society, religious, economic, political, and familial structures cannot deal adequately with the problems of individuals. Social welfare services are needed as part and parcel of the fabric of society. They are not safety nets, or safety valves; they are first-line structures (Wilensky and Lebeaux 1965:139).

Both views of welfare rest on certain value premises. They represent different views of society. In both conceptions, the major social structures are viewed as ineffective to some degree in meeting people's needs. The key issues are, "To what extent is this an anomoly reflecting mainly the deficiencies of some individuals and the small margin of institutional malfunctioning? To what extent is it a regularly anticipated consequence reflecting the inherent limitations of both institutional adaptations to change and individual efforts to deal with the exigencies of life in modern industrial society?" (Gilbert and Specht 1974:7).

Basically one answers these questions in terms of the meaning and degree of importance given to such values as personal freedom, security, equality, justice, and humanitarianism. These values affect society's approach to welfare issues: Shall financial assistance to those in need be organized through voluntary and religious organizations, or shall it be a responsibility of government? Shall services be offered to certain categories of people, such as veterans or the aged, or shall they be offered to every citizen? Are services to be given on the basis of need, or are they to be given as a right?

Whichever view one takes, social welfare generally "denotes the full range of organized activities of voluntary and governmental agencies which seek to prevent, alleviate, or contribute to the solution of recognized social problems, or to improve the well-being of individuals, groups, or communities" (Pumphrey 1971:1446). Given this definition, it is difficult to put parameters on the field.

Social welfare is not concerned with the kinds of help that family, friends, and kinship groups give on an informal, individual basis. Social welfare activities are first, formally organized under social auspices, in that society sanctions the purposes and methods of social welfare organizations, and insists that these organizations be held accountable for their actions.

Services organized on a commercial, profit-making basis, e.g., recreational programs, private insurance schemes, are not generally considered to be part of social welfare, although their availability and effectiveness influence the provision of welfare services. (Wilensky and Lebeaux 1965:141–142) Wilensky and Lebeaux make one basic distinction—social welfare organizations take a comprehensive view of human needs and personalities. They are concerned with seeing the totality of a person or individual's life (1965:145).

There seems to be no clear conceptual reason why in the public mind, and in actuality, certain organizations and fields are not considered to be specifically social welfare. In England, for example, public education is considered to be one of the social services. Here in the United States, education is a separate category, as is health. The reasons appear to be pragmatic. "No matter how identified with welfare a field may have been in origin, once it becomes highly developed, widespread in its incidence among the population, and professionally staffed by persons other than social workers, such organizations tend to be excluded from the social welfare category" (Kahn 1973:23–26).

Social welfare as an institution is much older than the profession of social work. Gilbert and Specht (1976) make the point that, among professional groups, social work is the one most strongly identified with the institution of social welfare because it provides the greatest amount of manpower for the varied areas of social welfare. A public health officer and a teacher are generally trained to work in a rather limited number of programmatic arrangements, in contrast to the social worker. This breadth of training is to a considerable extent related not only to the variety of programs where social workers play a part but also to the twin mission of social work as a profession.

Social workers have generally considered themselves to be concerned both with the rehabilitation of individuals who have problems and with the reform of those structures of society that affect individual and social life. Social workers are therefore engaged in both reform and rehabilitation.

Rehabilitation activities include education, advocacy, information giving, referral, and counseling. These activities are the major subject matter of social casework, social group work, and those aspects of community organization in which direct services are provided to community groups. Reform activities are concerned with bringing about a better adjustment between human needs and social resources by creating organizational arrangements through which society can deal with recognized social problems. These activities are the major subject matter of the indirect services—community organization, planning, administration, and evaluation—for which the social welfare specialist is trained.

The dual focus on social services and social reform has created considerable internal tension for social workers as well as tension in their relationships with other fields of practice. At times social workers have been caught in the dilemma of criticizing the services which employ them. At other times they have been faced with the issue of working in or administering a service they felt was inadequate. At other times they have questioned the value of providing services that may be temporarily ameliorative but do nothing about solving the longer-run problems such as unemployment or poverty without whose solution individual problems will continually recur.

## HISTORY

A dual purpose was evidenced early in the history of organized social welfare in our country. Two types of social agencies dominated the early history of the field. Charity organization societies, (COS), which sprang up in the 1880s and spread through every large and mid-sized city in the country, were organized to provide administrative efficiency in response to the seemingly inefficient hundreds of small voluntary and church-related charities that existed at the time. The COSs attempted to register all those seeking help and to divide each city into districts where friendly visitors would visit the poor and "uplift" them, always ensuring that what alms were dispensed were in fact needed (Axinn and Levine 1975).

The settlement house movement, which began roughly in the same period, sprang from a different impetus. The workers in these agencies actually lived in the neighborhoods. They were concerned not so much with simply helping individuals as they were with the social conditions that affected individuals' lives. From these settlements sprang child welfare legislation, housing regulations, minimum wage concerns, laws against sweatshops, sanitation regulations, public health campaigns, and the like.

Out of the settlement house movement with its concern for social reform came leaders such as Jane Addams and Lillian Wald. Their philosophical orientation was toward a multicausal view of social problems. The idea that poverty was really a personal problem or a personal defect was clearly rejected.

Ultimately this multicausal view affected social workers working in the COSs, who increasingly over the years identified themselves as members of the social work profession. Originally charity workers were volunteers, but gradually, as economic depressions recurred and deepened and caseloads increased, there arose a necessity for people who would be available on a regular five-day-a-week basis.

Thus, starting in 1898 with a summer school at the New York Charity Organization Society, courses of study were developed. Gradually the idea emerged that the social worker's skill lies in gathering facts in family situations—the social facts, the personal facts, and the environmental facts— and then making a diagnosis of what a family would require for stability. Expertise was substituted for the moral supremacy that the original charity organization workers felt (Chambers 1967:87–106).

The increasing professionalization of the field was evident not only with the development of schools of social work but also in the increasing functional specialization that occurred. For example, in 1905 the first medical social workers were hired at Massachusetts General Hospital. Their early concerns were related to the relationship of family and environment to the treatment of tuberculosis. In 1906 Greenwich House in New York City hired the first visiting teachers, as the early school social workers were called. In 1907, also at Massachusetts General, the first psychiatric social workers were hired to concern themselves with the environment and its effect on mental patients. Even earlier, in 1879, the National Conference of Charities and Corrections was established, with a strong emphasis and concern with the rehabilitation of criminals.

By the end of World War I and certainly during the 1920s, social work took on much of its present structure. A separation occurred between public and private social welfare programs. The emphasis in private welfare shifted temporarily from reform to rehabilitation, and in rehabilitation a movement occurred away from concern with the social to concern for the psyche.

Social work's long and sometimes ambivalent relationship with psycho-analysis began in 1921 with the Commonwealth Fund experiments. These experiments, organized in New York City, attmepted to utilize psychoana-lytic knowledge and insights in helping students to overcome learning and emotional disabilities that limited their normal school functioning.

Social workers and social agencies participated in the experiments. Psy-choanalytic ideas had a profound impact. There is no sharp line between the normal and the abnormal, behavior is neither good nor bad, but functional or dysfunctional. Social workers began to reconceptualize their work in these terms. Could the money-granting function of welfare be handled differently? Yes, the key issue for people on welfare is the meaning that money holds for them. What is its relationship to emotional dependency?

By 1930 Virginia Robinson, in *A Changing Psychology in Social Case-work* (1930), was claiming that all social casework is psychotherapy. Yet changes in social welfare are generally related to changes in the social and political structure of our society. No matter if in the 1930s social workers were enthralled by ideas of dynamic psychiatry, the country was in the midst of a great economic depression. Fifteen million people were unemployed and three-fourths of these were in great personal and economic distress. President Hoover believed in individual state and local responsibility as well as voluntary organizations and community service to deal with the economic problems of individuals.

The New Deal under Roosevelt took a different view: It is the responsi-bility of government to revive the economy and provide relief to the unem-ployed. Harry Hopkins, a social worker and a former director of New York's Charity Organization Society, became a key aide to Roosevelt. He and other social workers helped to write the Social Security Act of 1935 as well as to promote the development of a variety of governmental agencies that have become legends, the WPA, FERA, CCC, PWA. The Social Security Act, besides providing for old age and survivors' disability insurance, also pro-vided matching grants to states for old age assistance, aid to the blind, aid to the disabled, and aid to dependent children. The Social Security Act, through the dedication of federal power for individual welfare, inaugurated a new phase in the history of our country.

In the aftermath of World War II, as society moved back to normalcy, social work shifted its emphasis once again from reform. In such periods, invariably, there is an identity crisis. In the early 1950s the question that came forth strongly was, What is the knowledge base of social work? What qualifies us as a profession? The answer at that point seemed to lie with social science. The impressive development of ideas and concepts about socialization, reference groups, role networks, therapeutic milieus, communication systems, and the like were waiting for adaptation and implementation.

The methods of group work and community organization that developed in the 1920s and 1930s in the settlement houses and local community centers were ripe for social science ideas and techniques. The profession itself was seeking to improve its standing and expertise.

In 1956 this quest for professionalism, status, and expertise culminated in the formation of the National Association of Social Workers out of seven different existing professional associations of social workers. Many doctoral programs were started in schools of social work during this same period. Specializations were created—alcoholism, gerontology, work with street gangs—which addressed the idea that the totality of the individual's life space must be understood before treatment can be given. Group workers debated the difference between group work and group therapy, community organizers talked about change agents, targets, and systems. Caseworkers concerned themselves with crisis intervention and raised questions about the aptness and applicability of traditional casework models for the hard-to-reach and sometimes openly apathetic and resistant clients.

As the 1960s began there was concern in the field about the adoption of social science ideas. Questions were raised as to whether the understanding of a problem from different theoretical perspectives really adds much to what to do and how to solve that particular problem. In other words, does all this new knowledge really contribute to the development of helping skills?

Gradually an answer emerged. Social workers would have to pick and choose among social science ideas, and the profession may very well have to develop a cadre of social workers familiar and capable enough to utilize and adapt those ideas of social science that are theoretical but not operational. It is up to social workers to make the ideas workable to help individuals, groups, and communities.

While social workers in the 1950s had talked about the hard-to-reach client, in the 1960s they were talking about the hard-to-reach agency and social work's disengagement from the poor (Epstein and Cloward 1967). If the poor were "culturally deprived" and different from others in their value system and perspective on life, their sexual behavior and child-rearing patterns, the emphasis must be on restructuring our educational, health, and criminal justice system to make them accessible and fair. As one observer noted at the time: "Pupils don't fail, schools do."

Lloyd Ohlin and Richard Cloward in response to such concerns developed opportunity theory. "The lack of congruence between the aspirations of youth and the opportunities open to them lead to delinquency" (Cloward and Ohlin 1961). Neighborhoods are to be saturated with opportunities for job training, education, health, case services, recreation, housing, and legal assistance.

Another issue of the 1960s raised by the proverty program was the importance of power. Nothing can be changed without requisite political power was the rallying cry of the period. Community action agencies, created to help poor residents of ghetto areas to have some voice on issues that affected their lives, were its embodiment. These agencies were in line with a basic social work value or belief system. Citizen participation is important, both as a democratic right, and as a necessity if change is to occur, as well as a means of combatting alienation and helplessness in people (Weissman 1969a).

As part of the same concern over power and powerlessness in the 1960s, social work agencies moved quickly to hire paraprofessionals, which meant basically black, Puerto Rican, and other minorities, who suffered from some of the same problems as clients. Pressure was applied as well as self-imposed by agencies to ensure that professional staff were representative of various ethnic groups. Issues were raised as to the relative importance of having more skilled service or ensuring that staff had an appropriate racial mix. As the 1970s dawned, these issues were not resolved.

The poverty program did not eradicate poverty (Weissman 1969a). Programs such as the Job Corps, VISTA, Head Start, New Careers, Neighborhood Youth Corps, and Legal Services for the Poor were aimed at training and educating people. The poverty program did not include a job creation program; thus one could be trained and still not get a job. It was insufficiently funded and ultimately lost political support because it promised what it could not deliver.

Nevertheless the program had profound effects on the field of social work. It introduced new categories of staff, indigenous workers and case aides, as well as a variety of new service technologies. Case advocacy was restored to an appropriate place among social work techniques; neighborhood service centers were created where advice and referrals could be given; and legal services for the poor were developed and a host of self-help organizations created (Kahn 1976:33).

The period also clarified one issue that increasingly has come to the fore in the 1970s. Social workers deal with clients through organizations. Social workers therefore must come to grips with knowing and understanding how organizations operate and how they can be made more effective in achieving their social ends.

Thus, with the 1970s, as government's interest in funding large-scale service programs waned, questions about social organizations, schools, hospitals, welfare departments, and mental hospitals changed. No longer were demands for new programs and organizational reform heard; rather questions were put as to their effectiveness and efficiency. How accountable were these organizations for the dollars given to them? Schools of social work respond by creating sequences or concentrations in administration. Public welfare departments begin to look to schools of business to staff their higher administrative levels. In some public agencies the MBA became more valuable than the MSW for advancement. The value of social services was actually in question.

As welfare costs skyrocketed during the inflationary 1970s, the question of cost constantly impinged itself on the decade's if not the century's debate as to who should be the beneficiary of services. Should only special categories, such as the worthy, or the lame, or the blind receive services? Or should services be available on a universal basis, to all in society as a matter of right, similar to public education?

The larger overriding issue similarly raised and debated during the 1960s was not resolved in the 1970s. Can social problems be eradicated in a free and capitalist society, or must the solutions of these problems wait until a more socialist economic system is instituted? Are we concerned about equality in an absolute sense, or are we concerned merely about equality of opportunity? Those who need services the most tend to utilize them the least. The poor have more trouble gaining access and manipulating service programs for their ends than does the middle class.

As a byproduct of the concern with the shrinkage of funds and resources in the 1970s, the relationship of social workers to other human service professionals has become an important issue. At times questions have been posed in a positive manner related to how various professionals can cooperate, how different types of organizations such as schools, courts, and social service agencies can integrate their services. At other times the questions have been negative: Whose turf or prerogative is it to man certain agencies or certain programs? Whose skill is greater?

Battles have been and are currently being fought over licensing issues in state legislatures as to who may be permitted to do what. They have tremendous economic ramifications in terms of reimbursements for services from private and public insurance funds and as such presage the dilemmas in the human service professions.

## FIELDS OF PRACTICE

To understand these dilemmas from a social work point of view, a brief review of what social workers actually do is required. One way of dividing social work fields of practice are those that are manned primarily by social workers and those in which social work services are adjunctive and complementary to the services of other professionals. The former are agencies related to child welfare, for example, foster care agencies, child-caring institutions, and adoption agencies; family service, where counseling and therapy are given to individuals and families in stress; community centers and settlement houses, where recreation, informal education, and group programs provide a variety of services; and welfare departments, where money and service are both dispensed. In some of these settings, such as family service agencies and the child-caring institutions, social workers predominantly are professionally trained and possess a master's degree. In the centers and welfare departments, professionalization is not as strong, if training is taken to be the major criterion (Kahn 1973:29–33).

There are a host of other fields in which social workers provide services in conjunction with other professionals. Social workers, for example, are increasingly involved in unions, providing personal services to union members, from counseling and retirement planning to information and referral for a variety of legal and personal difficulties. Social workers operate in housing, often planning for social services in new housing developments as well as offering direct services to individuals, and forming organizations of tenants. Legal services for the poor often employ social workers to provide information and referral and do background studies for lawyers in relation to pertinent aspects of clients' cases.

Social workers provide a variety of services for the retarded; they work in alcoholism, drug addiction, nursing homes, and innumerable types of services for the aged. While it is beyond the scope of this chapter to discuss in detail the development and issues in each of these fields, the four that are dealt with in other articles in this book present issues and concerns that are systemic to the field of social welfare.

## SYSTEM INPUTS

From a systems point of view social welfare can be conceptualized as a system that transforms a set of inputs into a series of outputs. Problems at any one point in this system will have ramifications throughout the total system.

The four basic inputs the social welfare system needs are money, staff, legitimacy, and clients. Scarcity or even an overabundance of these resources is best viewed not simply as a problem to be eradicated like a disease but more as an enduring concern that must be managed and adjusted to as conditions change.

**Funding**  The first national organization of social welfare in the late nineteenth century was called the National Conference of Charities and Corrections. The word "charity" in the title conveyed the private nature of the funding of the charities.

In the one hundred years since the founding of this organization there has been a radical change in the funding apparatus of social welfare. In the nineteenth century private funds accounted for the vast majority of funds, whereas public monies accounted for only a miniscule amount.

The shift to public funding has not been accompanied by the demise of private agencies. What has occurred is that a larger and larger share of the budgets of these agencies derives from public funds through fee-for-service contracts on a percapita basis for services such as adoption and meals-on-wheels or outright grants to provide services such as day care and information and referral.

When an agency receives 80 to 85 percent of its budget from public services, is that agency still private? Should its board still have the right to set policy as to who should be served, what services should be given, at what cost, and so on?

The answer to such questions lies in the importance one imparts to private agencies. Traditionally these agencies were thought to have more flexibility to develop innovative programs and to be able to serve specific types of clients who might need services that the public services either did not have available or were not authorized to give. Traditionally, sectarian private agencies served this latter need.

There are those who argue that public services can be innovative and that the fee-for-service arrangements maintain large private agencies and retard the development of public services. They contend that private agencies are too selective in offering services; thus segments of the population remain unserved or underserved because of the lack of public services that would be open to everyone. Proponents of this point of view contend that a municipality that relies on purchased service without a public capacity to provide that service—a public presence capable of defining needs and assuming accountability—inevitably becomes a hostage of the providers, and there is then little or no effort to change or improve the quality of purchased services (Kahn 1973:101–106).

Another major problem with the current pattern of funding in social welfare is related to the overlapping boundaries and multijurisdictional nature of the funding bodies. Myriad rules and regulations plus such factors as constituencies, patterns of exchange and trade-off, administrative conditions, desire for visibility on national and local fronts, and differing values, philosophies, aims, and techniques form some of the baggage that each agency and its personnel bring. Attempts to coordinate and fill in gaps in service ultimately must deal first with the problems presented by multiple and uncoordinated funded streams, which tend to overwhelm efforts of coordination and rationalization of services (Kahn 1976:23–56).

For example, the federal government has increasingly supplied the largest portion of funds for mental health services. In the 1970s, when federal policy began to shift toward revenue-sharing approaches, competition was intensified between mental health and other human services for federal, state, and local support. Inevitably funding arrangements that create a necessity for organizations, professions, and services to compete also make less likely the possibility of effective integration and coordination of services.

**Legitimacy**   Who gives agencies the right to offer services? This sanction is a precious commodity, for without it agencies might lose their funding, source of clients, or legal entitlement to carry out their functions. In private agencies, the boards of directors, once empowered by the state to set up a nonprofit organization, provide the sanction from the community. In public agencies, sanction comes directly from laws passed by legislatures, councils, and Congress.

Legitimacy in social agencies is never total. Many programs that agencies offer or would like to offer are not sanctioned by large segments of the population at particular times. In past decades family planning agencies were often denied access to United Funds or Community Chests because of the controversial nature of their program. Work release programs for prisoners are often roundly condemned. Anger at public welfare programs is a regular feature of political campaigns.

Such disputes are related to the earlier-mentioned value conflicts that exist in society—self-reliance versus cooperation, freedom versus security.

Ultimately value conflicts find expression in the political arena. Thus social welfare issues inevitably are political issues, as it is through politics that the legitimacy of programs is renewed, changed, or withdrawn. Because of this, social welfare can never be adequately considered solely from a professional, technical, or methodological point of view.

**Clients**   The arguments over who should be the beneficiaries of social welfare go back hundreds of years to the English Poor Laws, which distinguished between the worthy (sick, aged) and the unworthy (able-bodied) poor. The history of the field could be written from the point of view of the constand expansion of the range of beneficiaries of social services.

The welfare state defines all citizens as potential beneficiaries. Much of the current debate in social welfare in America revolves around this issue and the issue of just what is meant by the concept of meeting needs.

Does social welfare only meet the needs of selective groups, that is, aged, veterans, orphans, or does social welfare meet universal needs, that is, medical care, housing, food? Some say these latter services, if offered, are best viewed as public utilities—as needed as gas, electricity, or water. Such disagreements over needs and services are at the heart of the dispute mentioned earlier between the residual and the institutional nature of social welfare.

Currently most social welfare programs are organized on a selective basis: aid to the blind, veterans' benefits, senior centers, and the like. This selectivity results in wide gaps in services, overlap, and lack of access for certain groups. It also results in groups with broad and more powerful constituencies getting more adequate services than those less organized—say, the aged as opposed to the delinquent. It also results in a certain amount of "hucksterism" when each year brings a new group suddenly selected out for experimental and demonstration programs—runaways, battered women—because of its political appeal or notoriety.

Such a system might not be too dysfunctional if newly "selected out" groups could be tied into existing service systems. This seldom happens. The result usually is another fragmented, inaccessible, inadequate, and inefficient service system (Kahn 1973:78–84).

Another systems issue in social welfare focuses on whether a service-oriented strategy is really helpful to clients when these services too often only ameliorate problems and do not prevent them. Social services that aim to change people's behavior, attitudes, or values are not substitutes for social or economic reform, nor are they cures for social problems. Only employment or income transfer of some sort will affect poverty. Yet some social services are necessary both for a humane society and for individuals who need immediate assistance and cannot afford to wait for social reforms.

In addition, social programs that combine provisions and services have an important part to play in the resolution of social problems. They can help to clarify the nature of such problems, which are seldom really solved, but are redefined and moved toward resolution as the limitations and potential of problems, conceptions, and programs are understood (Bernard 1975).

**Manpower** Currently social welfare offers employment for millions of people, depending on the paramenters one sets, and is a field of practice for a host of professions. There are a variety of issues related to the recruitment, selection, and training of staff.

At the present time, three trends seem to portend considerable conflict in the field. One is increasing professionalism and specialization. Each of the helping professions—social workers, doctors, nurses, psychologists, rehab counselors—tends to define more and more specialization with increasing educational requisites. Similarly, licensing requirements are imposed. Entrance to the profession is tightly controlled through a system of graduate schools and professional licensing boards.

Current debate centers around the virtues of professionalism. Do professional associations and professionals act in the best interests of clients, or are they merely self-serving guilds? Do they block the development of new and innovative approaches? Do they inflate salaries and lower productivity? Can we actually produce sufficient numbers of highly trained professionals to man all of the needed services (Gross 1978)?

During the 1960s, with the exponential increase in social services, the answer to the last question was negative. New careers were developed. So-called paraprofessionals, often recruited from the ranks of clients and would-be clients, were hired as case aides, counselors, case managers, and the like. These paraprofessionals often lived in the neighborhoods where agencies were situated. They were accessible after office hours and could serve to explain agency programs to the community and to explain clients' attitudes and values to middle-class professionals. The results of this manpower trend, known as new careers, have been mixed.

Clearly a great deal that is done to serve clients does not require graduate education. Yet training is important. Paraprofessionals could be trained on the job, but such training is expensive if it is to be comprehensive. Additionally some paraprofessionals quickly lost their sense of community with clients and were no more accessible than the most encrusted bureaucrat (Grosser 1967).

The new careers movement has argued that most paraprofessionals were hired for dead-end jobs; therefore motivation for continued growth was lacking. The dilemma has revolved around maintaining service while providing time off from work to attend classes often located at universities a great distance from agency sites. How to provide training for those who wish to enlarge their scope of responsibility and supervision for those who do not conceptualize their job as a career is as yet an unresolved issue. The danger is that paraprofessionals will be hired because they are cheaper, kept poorly trained, and then blamed for not producing results.

A third important manpower trend relates to the use of volunteers. Traditionally volunteers were recruited and then assigned to particular agency tasks under the supervision of a paid staff member. During the 1960s and 1970s a different pattern developed. Increasingly, more and more self-help groups were formed following the model of Alcoholics Anonymous—Schizophrenics Anonymous, Parents Anonymous, Fortune Society, and a host of therapeutic drug treatments.

A final input issue deserves mention. For many years social workers tended to resist unionism, seeing it as antithetical to professionalism. Increasingly under the pressure of large-scale organizations, when decisions are made far from the local base, along with pressures of inflation, social welfare staffs are turning increasingly to unionization. To date unions have won increased salary, job security, and fringe benefits for their members. They tend to be dominated by such bread and butter issues. On the programmatic side, this domination has made it more difficult for agencies to fire incompetent workers. Although the plusses and minuses have yet to be totaled, unionism is here to stay in social welfare, although at this point the majority of private social agencies are not unionized (Cole 1977:1559–1663).

## SYSTEM THROUGHPUTS

As changes in sanction, funding, and types of clients served have occurred, there have been commensurate pressures to change the conversion or throughput system in social welfare. These later changes include the structure through which services are delivered, treatment modalities and the technology of providing service, interprofessional relationships, and perspectives about the integration of services.

**Treatment Modalities**  Schools, mental health agencies, criminal justice institutions, and health organizations have undergone a number of similar changes. There has been increasing use of behavioral techniques in such settings. Similarly, crisis intervention, which involves observations of the normal coping processes of the ego, focuses on the here-and-now stress factors of the person in a situation, and aims for limited goals, is increasingly utilized in a variety of settings.

In the health-related fields of social welfare for example in recent years, along with new treatment modalities, strong critiques have been directed at the medical model. In this model, the worker searches out the relevant data, decides what is wrong, labels it, and then prescribes procedures he deems necessary to set it right. Alternate approaches are more interactional, in which the worker and client share various responsibilities as they continually redefine their purpose in working together. Change and help occur through an interactional process.

Although human service workers work with many different types of clients, organizations, and problems, have a variety of skills, and often disagree as to their relative importance, they have a great deal in common. What they share is best termed "process" or practice, a systematic series of actions directed toward some purpose (Pincus and Minahan 1973:98). For example:

a worker in a community mental health clinic who has been asked for help by a mother of a teenage boy experimenting with drugs who has been in trouble with the police, courts, and the school must decide if he should (1) try to involve the whole family in an action system, (2) work alone in the action system with the boy, (3) place the boy in an action system with other teenagers, (4) work individually with school personnel, police, and court workers, or (5) ask the boy and/or his family to accompany him to meetings with school and court personnel. The worker may decide to form several action systems to accomplish these goals.

Further, the worker may realize that the private troubles of this one family in its interactions with one another and with community institutions are similar to many other problems he and other workers in the clinic have encountered. Therefore he could conclude that the clinic should work on the public issue of the social problems of drug use and abuse, and the worker and his agency could establish the goals of (1) coordinating existing community services for drug abuse, (2) changing police practices, (3) creating new services, (4) changing existing drug laws, or (5) establishing a drug education program for teenagers, parents, and staff from community institutions. To achieve these goals the agency could form one-to-one action systems to influence a chief of police, a school superintendent, or a prominent legislator, or it could form group action systems composed of people able to influence the targets of change.

The worker's decision on the most effective and efficient size action system to use is influenced by two major factors: the purpose he hopes to achieve, and the characteristics of the target, although in practice these two factors are related. (Pincus and Minahan 1973:195)

In some settings the therapeutic orientation shifted focus from the dynamics of "individual case" to the social roots of mental illness. Social workers became more involved in the control, organization, and programming of social systems. The psychiatric social worker moved toward an indirect service model in which the emphasis was in the use of consultative, supervisory, community organization, and educational techniques. (Nacman 1977:902).

Although this pattern is certainly not currently predominant, it does illustrate how shifts in one part of the service system affect other parts. For example, the deemphasis on hospitalization of the mentally ill has resulted in a large out-patient population, which requires a variety of specialized services such as day or night hospitals, halfway houses, quarter-day houses, workshops, socialization, vocational training, job placement, and out-patient chemotherapy and psychotherapy programs. Some new programs have been created, but there have been tremendous gaps in services in the community and a need for coordination of services. Inevitably, when coordination becomes an issue, the skills of workers trained in coordinative techniques will be in demand.

Likewise, in recent years there has been an increasing trend to place upon the school responsibility for racial conflicts among students and to pay more attention to pupil's rights in relationship to matters of discipline, suspensions, curricular tracking, placement, and special education as well as concern about access to pupils' school records (Costin 1977:1241). Inevitably such issues, especially racial ones, move schools to enlist the aid of the skills of workers trained in community organization and group work. In addition, increasing attention to the need for compensatory education systems for students who are not making effective use of their learning opportunities creates situations where social agencies are more involved with the educational process.

**Conflict and Integration**  New roles and role repertories have resulted in considerable interprofessional and organizational conflict. For example, the health advocate or ombudsman is a role that insures that clients receive effective services. Advocating for clients often brings social workers into conflict with other professionals in health settings.

The traditional areas of conflict between social workers and physicians are over who shall make referrals for social services and who shall define the nature of social work service. In prior years social workers received their clients on referrals from doctors—the traditional red slip on which "social work" was checked among boxes for "X ray," "hematology," and so forth. Social workers have traditionally resisted this role and are increasingly successful in gaining authority in hospitals to do their own case-finding for those who may need their services.

Another area of conflict lies in discharge planning for patients. Often hospital administrators wish to discharge patients because the economics of chronic illness make it necessary to have an effective turnover of patients, when monies cannot be recouped from chroniclly ill patients. Thus social workers have felt that their services are often used to discharge rather than to plan effectively with the family or community for the patient's return. The emphasis on the optimal utilization of hospital beds puts an additional burden on medical social work consultants to document the lack of resources and gaps in programs that prevent maximum health care benefits. Thus medical social services are moving into the planning and organization spheres of medical and health care.

Two recent trends, the articulation of patients' rights and the ethical issues related to transplants and the like, in addition to pressure from consumers to be involved in the planning of health services, have increased the range and scope of social welfare personnel as well as the potential for increased interprofessional conflict. Growing concern about disease of the aged, concern with issues of death and dying, has cast social workers in a variety of different settings and roles, such as the training of medical personnel in geriatric care. The whole relationship of social work to health services is completely tied up with definitions of health, illness, treatment, and goals, about which there is considerable dispute in and among the human service professions (Phillips 1971:623–625).

As the 1980s begin, the same flux and necessity for role redefinition and reintegration are apparent. For example, from a variety of quarters there have been pressures to change many aspects of the present criminal justice system. These changes include deinstitutionalization; decriminalization and diversion; reducing time spent in institutions; alternatives to institutionalization; making the period of institutionalization productive; and restoring civil and personal rights. In some ways each of these new trends is concerned with relating the institutional experience as closely as possible to the community to which the offender must return and on maintaining him as an active participant in his normal role relationships (Studt 1977).

The same role flux can be seen in the educational system. Social workers in schools originally were concerned with children who did not come to school. The first school social workers in many ways began as part of the criminal justice system, although they were hired by schools.

Costin (1977) makes the point that, in the face of a wide diversity of conceptions of school social work practice, job titles, sizes, resources, and other characteristics of public schools, it is difficult to define what school social workers really do, since they do so many things in different places. The school social worker deals with individual pupils, offering case services as well as group work. They may offer pupils factual information, advice, suggestions, or direction (related to their peers, teachers, learning problems). They may help them develop personal goals and values to understand their abilities and interests (p. 1241).

They often offer knowledge about neighborhood or relevant information about a child's home situation; they may consult with teachers about relationships in the classroom among various groups, assist teachers in diagnosing the cause of a pupil's problems, and advise administrators in developing a working relationship with community agencies as well as how to deal with the general school atmosphere (p. 1242). Many social workers, although aware of the individual factors in students' personal and cultural background and of how these factors affect their ability to learn, are also aware that the school itself as an institution has an effect on students' learning.

Similarly, social workers in mental health settings in the 1970s and 80's have broadened their concerns, as have other professionals, under the press of demands for quality assurance and the rights of patients. Both of these current concerns have effected system changes. The 1972 Amendments to the Social Security Act (P.L. 92-603) mandated the establishment of professional standards review organizations (PSROs) for care given under the auspices of Medicare, Medicaid, and child health services. An inevitable result of PSROs will be a focus on how various professionals work together.

Initially PSROs have focused on particular services, with social workers developing their own standards and procedures. Ultimately this must lead to greater interprofessional concerns, because clearly no one professional group can be effective in mental health settings without cooperating with others.

These interprofessional relationships will have to deal with questions of status and power.

A variety of mechanisms and techniques have already been developed, but they nevertheless need refinement. The "team approach," for example, had as its intent avoiding departmental rivalries and interprofessional conflicts. The essence of the team, whether in a mental hospital, prison, or residential treatment center, is that it contains each of the roles and disciplines needed to provide service to a client. Rather than moving a client from one department to another, the team is available to serve the client.

The team's virtue lies in its smallness, which makes it more likely that each member of the team will be concerned with the results achieved with clients rather than with his or her own particular skill or process. Small size makes it less likely that what is actually happening to a client can be avoided, that professional ideologies will hold sway in the face of repeated failures, that clients will be anonymous, and that they will be seen as parts rather than as wholes. Smallness also makes it possible for various professionals to get to know each other on a daily basis, to develop informal arrangements, and to lessen the distance that often exists among them.

Ideally team members are selected on the basis of their ability to contribute to objectives. There is to be sharing of responsibility as well as authority, flexibility in roles, open communication, sharing of suggestions and ideas, full staff participation in planning, and a problem-centered, client-centered, rather than discipline-centered, approach.

There are, however, a variety of problems that have been noted in the team approach (Wertz 1966:43–49). These problems illustrate the dilemmas surrounding interprofessional cooperation. First, when teams are found in institutions, such as mental hospitals or prisons, what is often neglected in planning for the team is consideration of the patient or client. Often in total institutions the clients have their own developed system of coping with the institution. Creating a team ostensibly to improve service to the client is not always viewed that way by the client. Very often the client is most concerned about the low-status member of the team—guard, attendant, cottage parent.

These low-status members usually control what the client most wants: weekend passes and small dispensations such as movies, trips to towns, easy jobs, and the like. Clients who have developed an accommodation to these staff often feel threatened by a change in the team structure. They will play one staff or one group off another: guards versus social workers, attendants versus nurses. The clients can thus confound interprofessional cooperation.

Another difficulty with the team approach is the lack of congruence at times between the person who is the team leader and the skill required to lead the team. Physicians, for example, or psychiatrists are often made team leaders by virtue of their status and their ultimate legal responsibility for clients. Yet they usually have very little training in leading a group of workers. They are not trained to know how to elicit cooperation, to insure that there is follow-through on decisions or to deal with the variety of work-related conflicts.

A related problem is the issue of salaries. It is easy to talk teamwork and cooperation but they are difficult to achieve. When a suggestion is made that everyone is a ''therapist''—the attendant and the psychiatrist—and if they are, in fact, both acting therapeutically and sharing responsibility, then how can one make $12,000 and the other $45,000? Disparity in salaries militate against cooperation in the long run.

Another systemic problem related to the team approach is that there is a tendency to lapse back into old perspectives, especially when a crisis occurs, such as an escape from prison, a suicide in a mental hospital and the like. Who gets blamed for these crises? If the guards and attendants get the blame, they will soon get the message that they really aren't therapists, that there really isn't any shared responsibility. It is in fact just talk. There must be some institutionalized way of setting priorities in dealing with inevitable conflicts.

A final concern about the team approach is symptomatic of concerns about all types of systems changes. For example, when shifts are made to the team approach, there must be standards of success, ways of determining whether this technique in fact leads to better service for clients. Because it makes the staff happier, and raises the status of some and lessens the distance between others does not necessarily mean that clients are going to get better service. Some way of determining this has to be set up. Otherwise, the team approach merely becomes a new structure that is dysfunctional. Accountability, as will be noted in the concluding section, is crucial.

Sebring (1977) suggests that there are a number of sources of interorganizational and interpersonal conflict: past unsuccessful encounters among personnel; misunderstanding about each other's environmental pressures and constraints; differing organizational goal orientations, reward structures, time orientations, and formality of structure; as well as failure to formalize and standardize interorganizational relationships and a general reluctance of groups to develop reciprocal and open relationships. Other conflict factors include managerial style; constraints of operating procedures of the groups; separation among the cooperating groups; gripes about professionals and organizations; and formalized rules, control procedures, and formal reporting relationships.

Unless each human service profession can understand the reality of the other, there is little basis for hope that there will be real cooperation. Often conflicts are muted and people informally agree to cooperate while formally there is a good deal of conflict. Since not all professionals are able or adept at making informal relationships, the working situation is actually one of conflict.

**Delivery System**   Human services generally include health, corrections, education, mental health, income transfer, housing, employment, and a variety of social services, termed personal social services. Kahn and Kamerman (1977:4) include among these child welfare, including adoption, foster home care, children's institutions for the dependent and neglected, and protective programs for children; family service and counseling; community services for the aged; protective services for the aged; homemakers and home helpers; community centers; day care; vacation camps for children, the handicapped, the elderly, and average families; information referral programs; congregate meals and meals-on-wheels; self-help and mutual aid activities among the handicapped and disadvantaged groups; counseling programs for adolescents; protective residential arrangements for youths; and specialized institutions for several categories of children and adults.

As noted earlier, these programs may be organized in particular communities, counties, or states in a variety of different forms. In some cities, for example, a private family service agency will offer family counseling, operate a residential home for foster children, as well as provide adoption services. It may also operate a day care center, a counseling program for adolescents, and a meals-on-wheels program.

In another city, the same services may be available only at the public department of social services. In a third, social services may be offered through a county department of social services and in that same city private agencies may offer services similar to those offered in the public agencies, although not necessarily completely similar.

The confusing part of the picture is that in the first city, where the family service agency provides an array of services, it actually may be offering these services on a per capita or contract basis, with the department of social services paying for the services. The picture is further complicated by the fact that, as of the mid-70s, the federal government provided roughly 50 to 75 percent of the cost of some of these programs and the total cost of others.

Perhaps the simplest way of looking at the delivery system of services is to distinguish between public assistance, which includes all those cash transfer governmental programs that aid and assist needy individuals, and other programs that are part of the broad public welfare system—Medicare, Medicaid, child welfare, mental helath and mental retardation programs, and programs for the aged, as well as a variety of other social services such as homemaker, housing, and legal aid.

Cash transfer programs are always governmental programs administered either by a city or county governmental department of social services or human resources administration that is directly accountable to the state's department of social services, which in turn is accountable to HEW for federal funds.

The current system of public assistance money payments began in the 1930s, when the Depression produced great numbers of unemployed. The Social Security Act provided for grants to states for the care of the aged, the blind, and families with dependent children, now called AFDC—that is, to those persons generally outside the labor market. Aid to the disabled is also now included.

The most significant changes in the Social Security Act since 1935 are

1. The provision for aid to the aged, the blind, and the disabled are now covered by the Supplemental Security Income program (SSI), administered and financed by the federal government with optional state supplementation.
2. Medical payments are now provided for those over sixty-five years of age and those covered by SSI's Medicare program.
3. Medical assistance for the poor has been instituted under the Medicaid program; eligibility is determined by the states.
4. A broad social services program has been established, with a $2.5 billion federal expenditure ceiling (Title XX).
5. The Work Incentive program (WIN) has been strengthened including provision for penalties for the refusal of training or work. This has been administered nationally by the U.S. Department of Labor through state and county offices (Berman and Lourie 1977:340).

The general principles of the public assistance program are:

1. Aid should be in the form of money payments, rather than "in kind." (Food stamps are an exception.)
2. There should be objective criteria for eligibility determination.
3. The cost should be shared among the federal and other levels of government.
4. The basic decisions on eligibility and payment levels should be made by the states within broad limits set by federal law. (Thus, the considerable variation among states.)
5. As a component of state responsibility, the state must prepare a plan indicating commitments and the level of care to be provided.
6. In order to protect the individual against capricious acts, states must provide a fair hearing in all cases, and recipients' records must be kept confidential.
7. A merit system should cover employees administering the program (Berman and Lourie 1977:341).

Excluding Medicare and Medicaid, the largest and most controversial deviation from the money payment principle is the food stamp program. In the early 1980s, it has been estimated, 9 percent of the population, approximately 18.8 million people, are receiving food stamps. Basically this program allows those below a minimum income level to purchase stamps at a reduced rate, and these can be cashed in at local food stores.

In addition to direct cash payment programs, the federal government provides a variety of other programs that offer services rather than cash. These include Title IVB of the Social Security Act, which authorizes states to establish services for all needy children in each political subdivision. This program is not a cash assistance program. It assists states in providing services that can include adoption, foster care, and including institutional care, programs for unmarried mothers, child protection, child care, and delinquency prevention.

Similarly, Title XX of the Social Security Amendments of 1974 directed HEW to pay to each state according to a formula based on population, a sum not to exceed $2.5 billion for the nation to provide for a variety of services including those directed toward family planning, self-support, achieving and maintaining self-sufficiency to prevent, reduce, and eliminate dependency, preventing and remedying neglect and abuse, preventing and reducing inappropriate institutional care, and providing for community-based, home-based, and other forms of care among many others. In providing such services, a state through its designated agency may itself provide or enter into contract with local community agencies for the actual delivery of these services. Thus a private agency can receive a contract for the provision of services.

In similar fashion, the Older Americans Act, first enacted in 1965, provides for a wide array of services, which can include hot meal programs, some part-time employment opportunities, a number of social services and recreational programs, homemaker services, counseling services, residential, repair, and transportation. This act includes similar federal, state, and local relationships with the possibility of contracting for services.

Nevertheless, the Reagan administration, through the Omnibus Budget Reconciliation Act of 1981, greatly increased the powers and scope of state responsibility. It consolidated a very large number of programs and grants under the aegis of the Health and Human Services Department into seven block grants. These grants will be funded by the federal government but administered by the states. They include:

——Social Services: consolidating former Title XX programs in social services, day care, and local staff training.

——Maternal and Child Health: consolidating programs in maternal and child research, services and training; crippled children services; childhood lead-based paint poisoning prevention; sudden infant death syndrome information and counseling; hemophilia diagnostic and treatment centers; genetic disease testing and counseling services; adolescent pregnancy prevention services; and disabled children programs.

——Alcohol, Drug Abuse, and Mental Health: consolidating alcoholism state formula grants; alcohol abuse and alcoholism project contracts and grants; special alcoholism project grants; drug abuse state formula grants and contracts; drug abuse community service projects; mental helath centers and services.

——Preventive Health and Health Services: consolidating health incentive grants; rodent control; emergency medical services; hypertension (high blood pressure); home health services and training; fluoridation grants; health education and risk reduction grants; and rape crisis projects.

——Primary Care: consisting of programs covering community health centers, hospital affiliated care centers and primary care research and demonstration grants.

——Community Services: consisting of former Community Services Administration programs in community action; community food

**TABLE 5.1.**
PROJECTED OLDER AMERICANS ACT AND RELATED LOSSES DURING THE REAGAN ADMINISTRATION

| | 1981 Appropriations | | | 1982 Appropriations [a] | | | 1983 Proposals | | | N.Y. City Reductions, 1981–1983 | | Reductions Adjusted for Inflation |
|---|---|---|---|---|---|---|---|---|---|---|---|---|
| | U.S. | N.Y.S. | N.Y.C. | U.S. | N.Y.S. | N.Y.C. | U.S. | N.Y.S. | N.Y.C. | $ | % | |
| Older Americans Act Title IIIB (social services) | $252 | $20.5 | $ 8.9 | $241 | $19.1 | $ 8.3 | $216 | $ 16 | $7.0 | $1.9 | 21.2% | 35.6% |
| Title IIIC-1 (congregate meals) | 300 | 23.9 | 11.1 | 287 | 22.7 | 10.4 | 258 | 18.6 | 8.5 | 2.6 | 22.9% | 37.3% |
| Title IIIC-2 (home-delivered meals) | 50 | 4.5 | 2 | 57 | 4.6 | 2.1 | 48 | 3.3 | 1.5 | .5 | 25.5% | 39.9% |
| Title V (older workers employment) | 277 | 20.5 | 3.2 | 266 | 19.8 | 3 | 0[b] | 0 | 0 | 3.2 | 100% | 100% |
| Dept. of Agriculture Community Foods | 85 | 8.3 | 5.3 | 95 | 9 | 5.8 | 84 | 8 | 5.1 | .2 | 4% | 18.4% |

*Source:* CSS 1982.

Note: All figures are rounded and compare New York City with New York State and the nation. Inflation adjustment is based on the Congressional Budget Office rate of 14.4 percent.

[a] Based on annualization of the current continuing resolution level, which expires March 31, 1982.

[b] No appropriation is requested for Title V for FY1983. The administration request includes $200 million for a new block grant under the Department of Labor to reach special target groups, including older workers. Funds may become available through this grant to maintain some elements of the current Title V program. No further information is available at this time.

and nutrition; older persons community action; older persons' opportunities and services; community economic development (local initiative); state economic opportunity offices support; and various other training, technical assistance and public information projects.

——Low-Income Energy Assistance: converting the existing assistance program into a block, at reduced funding.

The major critique of the block grant system is first its adequacy. Much less money was voted for the seven block grants than for the prior grants. There is considerable danger that service programs and systems will engage in intense competition at the state level, further disintegrating what was never a very adequate or coordinated system.

Second, by placing responsibility at the state level for making additions in funding for programs should more adequate services be desired, there is a danger in times of economic recession of burdening those states which are most hard hit and which will need services the most, with a responsibility that they cannot fulfill during hard times.

Third, the array of programs and services presents a variety of problems. Perhaps the most basic problem from a recipient or client point of view is that some of these services are mandated and others are not. Thus in any one area there may be certain services, and in another area twenty-five miles away these services may not be available. Although in every county in America there is an absolute mandate for a department of social services that will offer some form of cash assistance, there is no such mandate, for example, that all services available under Title XX will be available. Each state is entitled to develop a service plan, and, once accepted by HEW, then that plan is in effect in that state.

The assumption is that each state should have the flexibility to develop a service package that meets the needs of most of its citizens. Ideally this would be acceptable if in fact it worked according to planning for need. It is often largely a pass-through device and funding mechanism by which to deliver categorical services to the clients of specialized agencies or existing agencies. If there isn't sufficient money available, then states tend to support the established services in their area and not to add new services.

A dilemma, especially for needy clients, is the adequacy of cash payments. Although food stamps help, they do not close the gap between accelerating food costs and available money for food for these public assistance families. Inflation has affected public assistance families in every area of life's necessities: gas and electricity, food costs, clothing costs. Every group has felt the impact of inflation, but public assistance families' budgets have been hit the hardest, with less purchasing power as compared with SSI beneficiaries (couples) and gains by factory workers.

Besides the question of level of government, types of services available, and adequacy of cash payments, there is an over-riding issue over process or, in colloquial terms, what is help? Is the key ingredient of help forming a trusting relationship with clients to help them to overcome fears and resistances to utilizing services and to help them to change attitudes and values that have caused them personal and social problems? Or is help more the simple provision of adequate services, ensuring that these services are easily accessible to clients, that they are delivered in a manner appropriate to the client's background and personal aspirations, that they are not stigmatized, and that there is an accountable work force that delivers these services in an efficient and humane way?

These disagreements plus others related to professional rivalries, jurisdictional battles among agencies with competing services, and general public disappointment with the lack of effectiveness and efficiency of social agencies led to an interest in services integration in the 1970s. This interest spawned a number of developments.

One development was to create a category of human service worker called the case manager. The responsibility of this worker was to see that immediate and long-term assistance is given to clients. The case manager would have the same relationship with families and clients as did and does the traditional medical general practitioner, giving general assistance and counseling.

The case manager also would be able to make referrals to a variety of services, such as homemaker, day care, medical care, registration for job training, and help with problems of eligibility for financial aid. In addition to helping the client get these services, the case manager would be accountable. He would have the responsibility of finding out if the services were delivered, and, if not, ensuring that they are.

The following example is from an agency organized on the case manager style (Weissman 1978; 62–64).

The client is a Vietnam refugee with four children aged six to fourteen years. She lost her husband and her youngest son in Vietnam. She has no relatives or friends in this country and does not speak English. (The case manager communicates with her in Cantonese.) Her small apartment was completely bare except for two beds. The small allotment received from public assistance was not sufficient to buy furniture or clothing, and no special allowance had been provided for these purposes. The situation was potentially serious—all the family possessed was warm weather clothing, and winter was approaching. The children, because of their home situation and inability to communicate, had problems in school. The fact that the family had been affluent in Vietnam compounded their difficulties, and the mother felt that she might be on the verge of a breakdown.

The case manager worked with the client to determine the family's service needs. They identified five major areas including: (1) financial—more money required for family's basic needs; (2) socialization—human contact needed particularly by mother; (3) language—need by all family members to learn English; (4) health—children's teeth particularly in need of work; (5) housing—need for larger apartment.

A meeting was scheduled with potential service providers and a service plan was formulated. The case manager monitored the provision of services and the participation of the client. The following services have been provided to the family:

1. After considerable negotiation, the International Rescue Committee supplied $600 for furniture, $275 for winter clothing, and $80 for a sewing machine.
2. A neighbor agreed to help the mother shop and along with the family union worker (who initially visited the woman four times a week), provided some of the human contact that was needed.
3. The mother and children were enrolled in special English classes provided by the Board of Education and Immigration Social Services. The immigration service, which ordinarily charges a fee, agreed to waive it.
4. Gouverneur Hospital gave all members of the family physical checkups and provided the dental work required by the children (root canal work and teeth extraction).
5. A local agency, It's Time, contracted to work with the family in finding more appropriate housing.

Since the mother still had considerable time on her hands, especially when the children were in school, and since she was still hard pressed to make ends meet, she agreed to seek employment. The mother knew of an opening for an assistant clerk at the grocery store where she bought her food each day but had been afraid to ask for the job since she had never worked in Vietnam. The case manager helped her to ask for the job and spoke to the store owner about the family's situation. The store owner hired the client. The mother is pleased with the job. Besides providing additional revenue, she has been able to meet a number of new people through her work. The family is now able to cope better with their situation. The case manager currently meets with the family once a week to check on how things are progressing, to assess any new developments, and to help the family begin to do some longer-range planning. As an additional precaution, since a new crisis could erupt at any time for the family, the case manager has arranged to make emergency help available to this woman and her family twenty-four hours a day.

Without assistance, it is conceivable that within a short time the four children would have wound up in foster care. Communication was a major ingredient in developing a successful working relationship with the client. In providing services to the family, the case manager was able to coordinate: (1) public agency services (Board of Education, Immigration), (2) voluntary agency service (It's Time); (3) charitable organization (International Rescue); (4) neighborhood supports (neighbor assists with shopping); (5) overall management supports (LESFU).

Through the case managers efforts, the family was kept intact and has now been informed that the husband and son who had been assumed dead in Vietnam have been located and will be joining the family in New York.

Kamerman and Kahn have expanded the above case manager approach into what they call a personal service system, which would include geographic assignments of responsibility with front-line generalist social workers carrying out case integration as well as basic counseling and service brokerage functions. Kahn and Kammerman take the basic point of view that there must be experimentation among the personal social services as to which auspice they should be under, what the administrative structure should be, what programs should be included, what the relationship to other systems should be, who should provide the services, and so forth.

Thus they feel that the personal social services should be integrated among themselves so that the following tasks can be carried out, more effectively:

(a) contributing to socialization and development by offering daily living and growth supports for ordinary, average people (not just problem groups), a role shared with other nonmarket services, but involving unique programs; (b) disseminating information about and facilitating access to the services and entitlements in all six social service areas; (c) assuring for the aged, handicapped, retarded, and incapacitated a basic level of social care and aid necessary for them to function in the community or in substitute living arrangements; (d) arranging substitute institutional or residential care or creating new permanent family relationships for children whose parents are not able to fulfill their role; (e) providing help, counseling, and guidance to assist individuals and families facing problems, crises, or pathology to reestablish functional capacity and overcome their difficulties; (f) supporting mutual aid, self-help, and activities aimed at overcoming problems of community living; (g) integrating the variety of programs and services in response to consumer needs to assure maximum benefit; (h) controlling or supervising deviant persons who may harm themselves or others, offering care assistance, guidance, growth, and change. (Kahn and Kamerman 1978: 99)

They are opposed to overall human service integration of health, education, income transfer programs, housing, employment, and the personal social services. They make this assessment of the literature on human services integration:

While professional rhetoric stimulates unanimity on the issue of multiservice delivery outlets and integration of all human services as a goal, multiservice delivery where successful means two or three subsystems integrated on a well-focused task where roles can be clearly defined (child abuse, community services for specific groups of the handicapped, or employment program). Nor is this development surprising, given the differences among the several systems (health, education, housing, income transfer, employment) with regard to mission, special equipment, location, intervention orientations, the relationships with clients, sanction, and mandate (Kahn and Kamerman 1978: 96).

It is just as reasonable to draw the conclusion that

a multi-provider, pluralist system with many relatively small units may meet the innumerable needs and wants of a large and diverse population much more satisfactorily than a large hegemony of integrated or tightly controlled and coordinated subunits. Good data is simply lacking to decide what small units may be more flexible, effective, and responsive and for what conditions of distress, and when large units can overcome the cumbersomeness of size through mobilization of resources. (Morris and Lescohier 1977: 11–12)

The debate over the proper type of service integration will continue in the 1980s. The Reagan administration block grants could provide the impetus for experimentation at the state level. The 60s and 70s provide a rich experience to draw upon. This experience includes multiservice centers where one facility houses a variety of services; super agencies such as human resources administrations in cities and counties that assume overall planning and accountability functions; generalist workers akin to the family physician role who serve as case managers; citizens advice bureaus that serve as information and referral centers; and public–private ventures where one group provides the service and the other assures accountability (Agranoff 1977: 527–552).

## SYSTEM OUTPUTS

In the 1950s and 1960s the question was asked, Why is there not more program evaluation in social agencies? In the 1970s the similar question was asked, Why is there not better management in social agencies? These are not unrelated questions. One of the requisites of better management is a workable system of program evaluation that can provide ongoing guidance to program managers. The key to improving the impact of the outputs of social welfare in the 1980s lies in improving the related systems of planning and accountability.

**Planning**    In the 1960s the Johnson administration, with the active cooperation of Congress, initiated a host of programs designated to eliminate poverty, create employment, improve medical care and education, and revitalize cities and rural areas.

> Traditional patterns of dispensing federal funds were often abandoned, resulting in the direct allocation of sizable sums to local communities where they were spent by a diverse group of public and private agencies, many of which were created especially to administer them. States were often bypassed or given only enough money to permit limited monitoring and technical assistance. (Hansen 1977: 1445).

The 1960s were a period of great optimism about the possibilities of planning human services. New structures and mechanisms were developed. Funding levels were high. Professionals from a variety of fields were involved.

> In a brief period, however, program deficiencies, escalating costs, and the political realities of using public funds combined to blunt the enthusiasm of both legislators and reformers. Local decision making gave way to congressional mandate, community control was returned to elected officials, funding limits were established, and the brakes were applied to new initiatives. The type of national planning and programming that made possible Head Start, Vista, Job Corps, Legal Services, and Foster Grandparents was effectively curtailed. (p. 1445)

The real incentive for increased planning comes from federal and state legislation along with funds earmarked for such purposes. For example, planning funds have been included in the Older Americans Act, Comprehensive Employment and Training Act, and Comprehensive Medical Facilities Planning. Similarly, in January 1975, President Ford signed the National Health Planning and Resources Development Act of 1974 (P.L. 93-641) authorizing a billion-dollar three-year program of health planning.

Perhaps the most significant bill for planning in the human services field is the Allied Services Act proposed by HEW in the late 70's. Although not yet enacted, it would authorize monies to states and through them to local governments for the development of "allied services plans," which are intended to promote the coordination of services. States would be permitted to transfer funds from one HEW program to another. Administrative and technical barriers could be waived if they impeded coordination. The political debate over this bill will continue in the 1980s.

> Even though the bill was not passed the fact that local public officials are close to citizens, are in the public view, and are usually expected to do something (even if the problems are not of those officials' making) argues for the conclusion that the responsibilities of local government vis-à-vis the human services will probably grow in the future rather than decline and they will have to engage in more rather than less planning. (Morris 1977: 11)

**Accountability**   Perhaps the key to discovering the most effective and efficient way for improving the impact of human services in the decades to come lies in increasing their accountability so that the effects of various staff combinations and delivery systems can be evaluated. Problems seemingly solved often revert to their prior state because the conditions that nurtured the problem in the first place were not adequately monitored (Weissman 1973: 132–137). Thus accountability involves structuring roles within and without an organization (Who is accountable to whom for the quantity, quality, and cost of service?); the method or procedures by which this accountability is determined; and the reallocation of rewards and costs that buttress the accountability and ensure that progress will be maintained.

The structure of an accountability system is related to who shall be accountable to whom, both inside and outside the organization, for the quantity, quality, and cost of services. Fiscal accountability and accountability for efficiency and effectiveness of an agency has traditionally been left to its board of directors. The history of such welfare boards has not been sanguine in terms of holding agencies accountable. Yet their capacity to carry out this function can be strengthened. There is, in fact, little recourse, as it is highly unlikely that social work or any other profession can adequately police itself. Conflicting pressures and interests are too great.

A major problem with welfare boards of directors is that in most cases they are almost completely dependent on the administration of an agency for information about the agency. It is highly unlikely that most executives will provide information that calls their own competence into question. Welfare boards must have a means of independently assessing the work of an organization, rather than depending on the staff and the administration to provide it for them. This in no way precludes staff from doing their own evaluation but merely serves as a basis for comparison and discussion.

Some have argued that, even if all of the above procedures, as well as others, were included, boards would inevitably get bogged down in policy disputes: quotas of staff based on ethnicity, internal politicking based on status drives, animosity to certain staff members, factionalism. More access to information would merely create more disputes.

During the 1960s for example, experimental community school boards were set up in many areas without guidelines for judging effectiveness of the schools. Without objectives, the interplay of representation from various groups—parents, community, researchers, and students—was dissipated in vague dialogues on racism and educational ideology. The only answer is that a limit can be put on such disputes if there is a focus on measuring the results an organization achieves.

Brown (1975) makes the point that none of the accountability systems or techniques works very well. Each has strains and certain inherent dilemmas. Yet he concludes that "the operationally important form of accountability is the mixture of formal devices and conventions, rooted in our political culture, for publicizing the workings of a system, so that those who are interested can spot errors and imbalances" (p. 278). For him the touchstone is neither formal accountability nor citizen participation, but openness.

The error of the 1960s was to assume that the appointment of clients to boards could automatically assure such a challenge without any ongoing systematic feedback of information about agency methods or results. The key issue is what an organization does with the information that is available to it through its accountability structure and technology.

The 1970s have been called the age of accountability in social welfare, but little has been accomplished. Hindsight makes the reasons for this limited progress clear. The spate of new technologies such as PSROs, program budgeting, zero-based budgeting, and management by objectives have too often not been related to the dynamics of organizational life.

Social institutions cannot be improved by simply hiring better trained and qualified technicians. These institutions are not baseball or football teams, where better players usually make a better team. Schools, welfare departments, and hospitals are complex structures. When they try to cure, teach, prevent, research, and rehabilitate at the same time, disagreements over priorities, desires for status, and control inevitably lead to waste and working at cross-purposes. There are often several competing and even antagonistic teams in one institution. Because of this, many felt during the 1970s that what is needed are top-flight managers, people who understand the meaning of the "bottom line." Yet when Ford produces an Edsel, an alarm goes off in the organization. Something or someone must be changed. If not, Ford may go out of business. But when social Edsels are produced, training programs that fail to train and therapy programs that fail to rehabilitate, no such alarm goes off because the survival of schools and hospitals is not directly related to profits.

Ford can get rid of the Edsel, but New York City can't rid itself of an ineffective prison system. Social programs can never be judged solely on fiscal considerations. The businessman-manager used to having profits as a guide is often lost without them.

While not as precise as profits, goals need not be as vague as "doing good." Scientific management, with its array of techniques, PERT, zero-based budgeting, management information systems, operations research, and MBO—each surrounded by an army of consultants—was available in the 1970s.

Yet these techniques are limited. An efficiency expert might suggest refusing service to those who are at high risk, yet a rehabilitation agency is not a credit department. Is drug addiction a disease or a crime? Does welfare cause dependency, or is it a symptom of a sick economic system? No answer is provided, nor does management technology relate to how to cure an addict, reduce dependency, or teach.

Yet the concepts and language of accountability have become clearer over the last decade. For example, the crucial and perhaps central concept of "system," can now be seen both in its potential for improving service delivery as well as in its potential for snaring this delivery.

Previously, the positive aspects of a system approach have been stressed: it has the advantage of mapping out a rational conception of a service delivery design;

it stimulates service programs to become more precise about their accomplishments; it provides a method of gathering data to be fed back for decision making and organizational changes. Though these advantages are so readily apparent, it is necessary to caution that the systems framework contain within it some special limitations and problems; a few caveats are therefore in order. One caution is that while the systems model is at once value free, it operates within the value context. The establishing of goals is inherent in a systems approach, but the determination of these goals often emerges from the arena of conflicting interest groups and political decision makers. In reality decisions about priorities are ultimately based upon values; therefore, serivice staff must be aware that they are influenced by these and may in turn be able to influence choices. They can choose as technicians to mechanistically carry out the mandates from state and federal officials, who in turn are highly sensitive to political pressures, or they can prefer to use their growing technical expertise to influence political value judgments.

Similarly the systems model provides concepts in the language that may permit staff to disengage from those they are to serve. The systems parlance permits designating unserved clients as ''wastes''; it allows that ''client input overload'' will result in shutting off the intake valve; it fosters the gathering of data to give the illusion that accomplishments are occurring when in fact they may not be; it can tolerate the establishing of objectives that may be achievable, though not necessarily challenging. In short, systems concepts can create ''gamesmanship'' situations in which staff too readily accept reality and use systems concepts to enhance their own survival rather than to stretch their effort to reach beyond present performance. A third danger inherent in the systems model is the emphasis given to those activities that lend themselves to measurement, i.e., to repetitive events, simple goals, and well-defined products. This may be one reason why individual and family counseling services are being deemphasized. Such activity is difficult to quantify. Though it is important to identify service accomplishments, in their quest to do so, staff of social service programs may choose to improve their own self-maintenance by concentrating on services where success can be demonstrated while abandoning the more difficult and more challenging objectives. (Rosenberg and Brody 1974: 68–69)

## CONCLUSION

As the social welfare system enters the 1980s it is stronger because as a field it has remained true to its basic functions of reform and service. The desire to serve more effectively fuels the analytical drive that creates such critiques and caveats about systems approaches as noted in this chapter.

The impulse to reform can be expected in the 1980s to focus on local delivery systems as social welfare responds to such pressures as result from the changing structure of governmental funding, the quest for equality, technological change, urban decay, and demographic shifts.

It may be that it is these latter shifts toward an increasingly aged population and increasingly aged cities with their attendant desire and need for services that will determine the ultimate fate of social welfare, whether it remains as a residual function in society or whether it is accepted as an integral institution. Should the latter be the case, the face of society at the conclusion of the decade will have many different contours.

# REFERENCES

Agranoff, R. 1977. Services integration in W. Anderson, B. Frieden, and M. Murphy, eds., *Managing Human Services*. Washington, D.C. International City Management Association.

Axinn, J. and H. Levine. 1975. *Social Welfare: A History of American Response to Need*. New York: Dodd, Mead.

Berman, C. S. and N. Lourie. 1977. Public Welfare. In W. Anderson, B. Frieden, and M. Murphy, eds., *Managing Human Services*. Washington, D.C.: International City Management Association.

Bernard, S. 1975. Why service delivery programs fail. *Social Work* 20: 206–210.

Brown, R. G. S. 1975. *The Management of Welfare*. London: Martin Robertson.

Chambers, C. 1967. *Seedtime of Reform*. Ann Arbor. University of Michigan Press.

Cloward, R. and L. Ohlin. 1961. *Delinquency and Opportunity*. Glencoe, Ill.: Free Press.

Community Council of Greater New York. Research Note no. 37. November 1979.

Cole, E. 1977. Unions in social work. *Encyclopedia of Social Work*. Washington, D.C.: National Association of Social Workers.

css. 1982. Briefing on 1983 Reagan admnistration budget proposals, March. New York: Community Service Society.

Costin, L. 1977. School social work. *Encyclopedia of Social Work*. Washington, D.C.: National Association of Social Workers.

Epstein, I. and R. Cloward. 1967. Private social welfare's disengagement from the poor: The case of family adjustment agencies. In G. Brager and P. Purcell, eds., *Community Action Against Poverty*. New Haven: Yale University Press.

Gilbert, N. and H. Specht. *The Emergence of Social Welfare and Social Work*. Itasca, Ill.: Peacock. 1976.

Gilbert, N. and H. Specht. 1974. *Dimensions of Social Welfare Policy*. Englewood Cliffs, N.J.: Prentice-Hall.

Goldberg, S. P. 1971. Accounting in social welfare. *Encyclopedia of Social Work*. New York: National Association of Social Workers.

Gross, S. J. 1978. The myth of professional licensing. *American Psychologist* 33: 1016–1019.

Grosser, C. 1967. Class orientation of the indigenous staff. In G. Bragor and P. Purcell eds., *Community Action Against Poverty*. New Haven: Yale University Press.

Hansen, J. 1977. Social planning, governmental: Federal and state. *Encyclopedia of Social Work*. Washington, D.C.: National Association of Social Workers.

Kahn, A. J. 1973. *Social Policy and Social Services*. New York: Random House.

Kahn, A. J. 1976. Service delivery at the neighborhood level: Experience, theory, and fads. *Social Service Review* 50: 23–56.

Kahn, A. J. and Kamerman, S. B. 1977. *Social Services in International Perspective*. Washington, D.C.: Department of Health, Education, and Welfare.

Kahn, A.J. and S. Kamerman. 1978. Delivery system options for the personal social services. In J. Vigilante and D. Thursz, eds., *Social Service Delivery Systems*. Vol. 3. Beverly Hills: Sage.

Knee, R. and W. Lamson. 1977. Mental health services. *Encyclopedia of Social Work*. Washington, D.C.: National Association of Social Workers.

Miller, S. J. 1977. Human service professions. *Encyclopedia of Social Work*. Washington, D.C.: National Association of Social Workers.

Moroney, R. 1977. Social planning: Tools for planning. *Encyclopedia of Social Work*. Washington, D.C.: National Association of Social Workers.

Morris, R. 1977. The Human services function and local government. In W. Anderson, B. Frieden, M. Murphy, eds., *Managing Human Services*. Washington, D.C.: International City Management Association.

Morris, R. and I. H. Lescohier. 1977. Service integration: Real vs. illusory solutions to welfare dilemmas. Paper presented at the Conference on Issues in Service Delivery in Human Service Organizations, Racine, Wisc.

Nacman, M. 1977. Mental health services: Social workers in. *Encyclopedia of Social Work*. Washington, D.C.: National Association of Social Workers.

New York State Department of Social Services. 1977. Comprehensive annual social services program plan for New York State, October 1, 1977–September 30, 1978. Title XX, Federal Social Security Act.

Phillips, B. 1977. Health services: social workers. In *Encyclopedia of Social Work*. Washington, D.C.: National Association of Social Workers.

Pincus, A. and A. Minahan. 1973. *Social Work Practice: Model and Method*. Itasca, Ill.: Peacock.

Pumphrey, R. 1971. Social welfare: History. *Encyclopedia of Social Work*. New York: National Association of Social Workers.

Robinson, V. 1930. *A Changing Psychology in Social Casework*. Chapel Hill: University of North Carolina Press.

Rosenberg, M. and R. Brody. 1977. *Systems Serving People*. Cleveland: Case Western Reserve, School of Applied Social Sciences.

Sebring, R. 1977. An organizational environment perspective on state government–university interorganizational conflicts: The case of the five million dollar misunderstanding. Paper delivered at twenty-fourth Annual Meeting of the Council on Social Work Education, Phoenix.

Studt, E. 1977. Crime and delinquency: Institutions. *Encyclopedia of Social Work*. Washington, D.C.: National Association of Social Workers.

Walker, R. 1972. The ninth panacea: Program evaluation. *Evaluation* 1: 50–53.

Weissman, H. H. 1969. Epilogue. In H. Weissman, ed., *Justice and the Law in the Mobilization for Youth Experience*. New York: Association Press.

Weissman, H. H. 1969. Social Action in a social work context. In H. Weissman, ed., *Community Development in the Mobilization for Youth Experience*. New York: Association Press.

Weissman, H. H. 1973. *Overcoming Mismanagement in the Human Service Professions*. San Francisco: Jossey-Bass.

Weissman, H. H. 1978. *Integrating Services for Troubled Families*. San Francisco: Jossey-Bass.

Wertz, O. 1966. Social workers and the therapeutic community. *Social Work* 11: 43–49.

Wilensky, H. and C. N. Lebeaux. 1965. *Industrial Society and Social Welfare*. New York: Free Press.

# EDUCATION AS
# A HUMAN SERVICE

## MARIO D. FANTINI

"System," as it applies to education (indeed, as it applies to most social institutions), refers to a network attempting to deliver specific services through an organized and coordinated process. The more complex and sophisticated the society, the more complex and sophisticated the system(s), and therefore the more extensive the services to be provided. Similarly, the simpler the society, the simpler the system(s) and the more circumscribed the services. Before looking at how our present educational system incorporates as well as complements the human services, it might be appropriate to see how our educational system has evolved from the earliest years of our history, how it is currently organized and governed, and what are some of its goals and ongoing issues.

Until the nineteenth century, schooling was, by modern standards, a very unfettered and unencumbered process. There were no school boards, com-

Mario D. Fantini is Professor and Dean of the School of Education, University of Massachusetts, Amherst.

missioners, or superintendents of education; there were no compulsory education laws, standardized tests, and the like. Major decisions about education—whether schooling was to be provided at all, whether poor children were to be included, what, exactly, schooling should consist of, how the school, a teacher's salary, books, etc, were to funded—were basically arbitrary and were left to a limited number of people. It was not until the early nineteenth century that state school laws were widely enacted, thus marking the beginning of the public school system as we know it today: a highly complex and stratified comprehensive network, staffed by scores of specially trained personnel, supported by the levying of state and local taxes, broken down into specially chartered school districts governed by school boards and/or committees, accountable to a host of elected and/or appointed officials, characterized by a graded elementary and secondary lavel, separated from the church, and so forth. (The tremendous increase, incidentally, in the number of religious and private schools during the nineteenth century was a direct result of our Constitution, which mandated the separation of church and state.) By 1900, a complete American school system was established (Cordasco 1967:136), and by 1918 compulsory education laws were operating in all of the states, insuring, at least theoretically, educational opportunity for all. (In 1880 the number of students enrolled in elementary and secondary schools totalled 9,868,000; in 1930, there were 28,239,000 students enrolled in the public schools; and by 1970 there were 51,319,000) (Bureau of the Census 1980:135, 369).

## THE GOVERNANCE AND MANAGEMENT OF OUR PRESENT-DAY SCHOOL SYSTEM

An educational system that is responsible for servicing over 50 million individuals will, understandably, be a complex system, consisting of various components and administered by numerous people. As it is presently constituted, our educational system may be represented by the model in figure 6.1.

While there might be slight variations in this model depending upon the particular state and size of a given community—many rural communities, for example, by virtue of their small size, do not have enough school-age children to be included in a district, and therefore a local school committee takes the place of a district board of education—diagram 6.1 is a fair representation of how, and by whom, our educational system is governed and managed. According to this model, each state is responsible for enacting

**Figure 6.1**

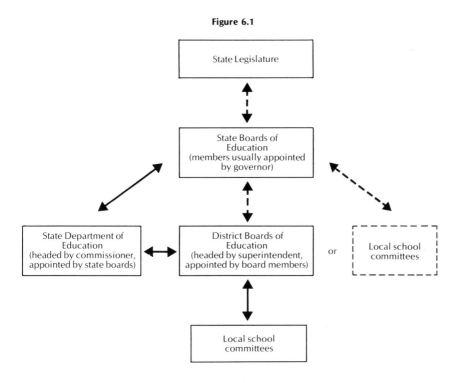

statutes and laws concerning the education of its citizens and for the management of public education. The individual states, therefore, and not the federal government, are vested with all the power and authority with respect to educational matters. There is no mention whatsoever in our federal Constitution about education, and powers not specifically delegated to the federal government have consequently been delegated to the states by the Tenth Amendment (Grieder and Romine 1855). Only if the educational practices within a state conflict with a constitutional right—as, for example, some states' practices in the 1950s conflicted with the constitutional guarantee of equality for all people—can the federal government intercede. The federal government can also provide grants and financial assistance to the individual states with respect to educational programs and services, as it did with the National Defense Act of 1958 and the Elementary and Secondary Act of 1965. But even here the states have the power to accept or reject proffered federal assistance. The states, therefore, individually enact educational policies and manage their schools as they each deem proper and suitable. And all other bodies—the state boards of education, the state department of education, the district boards of education, and/or the local school committees—are charged, in large measure, with adherence to the implementation of those state policies.

## EDUCATIONAL GOALS AND RESPONSIBILITIES

Naturally, every educational system attempts to respond to the needs of its particular constituency as well as to the needs of the larger society. Traditionally, one of the fundamental objectives of education has been to teach youngsters "the basics"—reading, writing and arithmetic. These basics, however, were for many years, particularly during the Colonial Period of our history, subordinated to still another "basic," namely, to providing religious instruction to children, whether it was instruction in the Puritan, Lutheran, Quaker, Presbyterian, or other faith (Cordasco:110). Basic literacy was seen as a vehicle for instilling religious beliefs and moral values. With the constitutional separation of church and state, however, that originally dominant motive for teaching the 3 R's was altered, although the teaching and learning of the 3 R's themselves have always remained one of the fundamental aims of education. No doubt the 3 R's will continue to remain basic in education (witness the current "Back-to Basics" movement throughout the country) as will other fundamental aims, such as creating healthy citizens, of good moral character, who are civically and socially responsible, etc. Economic, political, and social factors will, however, impinge upon such broad aims or make one aim, at any given time, take precedence over another. During the first half of this century, for example, when so many immigrants were arriving in the United States with diverse languages and customs, one of the dominant concerns of the schools was providing these immigrants with language skills that would ultimately allow them to be assimilated into the mainstream society. Because this assimilation was an overriding political and social priority, learning English was therefore one of the primary goals of education. (Helping immigrants to assimilate our language and culture has always been a national priority and therefore has always been reflected in our educational institutions. However, when there was a tremendous influx of immigrants, as there was in the 1830s and 1840s, there was a correspondingly greater concern to give people the language skills to adapt easily and quickly.)

With the advent of minority rights groups in the 1960s and 1970s, a different philosophy and priority introduced itself. The philosophy of revising one's native heritage came into currency, and different cultural groups strove to not "sacrifice" that linguistic and cultural heritage to the needs or dictates of the state ("state" defined, in this instance, by national as well as territorial boundaries). Hence, we saw the inception of bilingual and multicultural education. Similarly, when the cold war and the arms race with Russia began after World War II (and especially after Russia successfully launched Sputnik), a furor arose concerning the Soviet Union's emphasis in school curricula, the sciences, and the fear that our schools were not emphasizing the sciences as much and would therefore "lose ground" to the Soviet Union. The National Defense Education Act of 1958, which provided the states with federal funds designed to strengthen programs in science, math, and foreign languages, was a direct outcome of this furor. Thus the curricula in the schools were affected by the politics of the day.

To get an even more dramatic example of how such political considerations affect education, one need only recall the 1960s. Those were the years during which many people were particularly vociferous about their discontents and dissatisfactions with American public education. Parents were especially unhappy with the schools and with what they perceived as the "failures" of the schools—in particular, their inability to encompass and serve the divergent needs and demands of people, especially minority people. Furthermore, parents demanded, and got, more community participation and community control in the schools—in particular, more parental input into decision-making policies which directly affected their children, more public "accountability" from professionals involved in education.

The 1960s were also years in which the federal government gave a great deal of financial assistance and support to state and local school districts as well as to institutions of higher learning. The Elementary and Secondary Act of 1965, mentioned earlier, was designed specifically to assist economically disadvantaged students and to deal with such problems as school segregation and racism. The federal financial support amounted to a 7 percent share in the costs of financing public education, quite a generous amount of money when one multiplies that percentage by the large number of educational institutions throughout the country that were the recipients of such assistance. Within another ten years, however, the economic situation changed so that federal and state funds for educational programs were cut and financial aid to the public schools was further undermined by a growing loss of public confidence in the schools.

The point to be understood here is that "the aims of education are constantly being refashioned" (Brubacher 1962: 119) by the political, social, and/or economic considerations and needs of the time. Such considerations and needs notwithstanding, the *ultimate* aim and responsibility of education—at least in terms of the educational theories to which most public institutions and educators subscribe—is to assist every individual in the perfecting of all his/her powers (p. 114), and to foster and encourage human growth. Thus, the ultimate aim of education is *the actualization and realization of every human being's potential*. From this philosophical perspective, the concept of education as a human service becomes far more intelligible since, as we shall see in the next section, this fostering and encouraging of human growth and the development of one's potential ties all of the human services and education together.

## EDUCATION AND THE HUMAN SERVICES

As has already been pointed out, the process of public accountability that began in the late 1950s and continued into the 1960s and 1970s, resulted in accelerated activity from legislative and judicial quarters. The Supreme Court decision, *Brown v. the Board of Education,* in 1954 ushered in efforts to achieve school desegregation, which continue to the present. The Russian launching of Sputnik triggered extensive debate over the possible shortcomings of our schools in the areas of science, mathematics, and technology. This resulted in the National Defense Education Act of 1958, which recognized education as a part of America's national defense system. Because people expressed so many dissatisfactions with public education and raised so many questions about equal as well as quality education, there was a concerted effort on the part of government to respond to criticism and thus bring about educational reform. In the process, however, two things happened. First, the schools were delegated more and more additional responsibilities, which, predictably, made it all the more difficult for them to deliver the myriad services they were already charged with delivering. Second, many of these "add-on" services which were delegated to the schools (e.g., programs designed especially for the handicapped, for vocational education, special education, adult education, remedial education, etc.) became extremely costly as well as duplicative. By the early 1970s, it was clear that the schools could no longer bear the heavy load that had been layered upon them, and that they simply could not attempt to do *everything*. In fact, it appeared that our educational system was becoming dysfunctional and that a different method of delivering educative services to people had to be devised. By the middle of the 1970s, therefore, there was a call for an educational system that would reverse the trend to *de*centralization in the 1960s.

A more *centralized* system was envisioned so that (1) educational services would not be as costly; (2) there would be less duplication of services; and (3) most important, the system of education would be characterized by collaboration, rather than separation, between various educative and rehabilitative agencies.

In 1978, the U.S. Congress established a policy destined to make schools an integral part of the local human service delivery system. In doing so, Congress was attempting to deal with economic concerns as well as to promote the kind of collaboration and interlinking between heretofore separate educative and rehabilitative systems. Congressional amendments to Title VIII of the Elementary and Secondary Education Act of 1965 established the Community Schools and Comprehensive Community Education Act of 1978. In its findings and policy statement (Section 802), Congress found that:

(1) the school is an integral part of the local human service delivery system;
(2) the school is a primary institution for the delivery of services and may be the best instrument for the coordination of frequently fragmented services including benefits obtained by energy savings and parental involvement in the delivery of such services;
(3) community schools provide a great potential for the use of needs assessment as a basis for human resources policies.

The purpose of this title is "to provide in collaboration with other public and non-profit agencies educational, recreational, cultural and other related community and human services, in accordance with the needs, interests and concerns of the community through the expansion of community education programs." This act would also "serve to coordinate the delivery of social services to meet the needs and preferences of the residents of the community served by the schools."

With the establishment of such a policy, Congress was merely catching up with the realization that schools have been performing as human service centers for decades. For many people, however, conceptualizing the school as an integral part of the human service delivery system may need further clarification. Certainly the inclusion, until recently, of "education" within the framework of Health, Education, and Welfare helps in associating education with the more established human services. Most people know and understand that educational institutions have nurses and doctors on their staffs, that general health issues were considered in school organization and curricula, and that the schools have always been involved with youth problems that concerned the courts, juvenile justice, counseling, and the like. Moreover, many citizens also realize that other "hidden" services of a more menial nature are also performed by the schools, and that schools perform "custodial" as well as educational functions.

The schools do much more, however, with respect to the human services. At the most basic level, they are concerned with *human growth and development*—of each learner with identifying and facilitating the conditions that foster such growth and development and with identifying and minimizing the conditions that thwart such growth and development. The schools have always dealt with such human development, particularly by concentrating on the intellectual aspects of learning. The well-known 3 R's that are so much a part of our folklore and culture can be viewed as a human service in that they are predicated upon the commitment to enhance the development of people and to increase their chances for success in the larger society. Persons who have not mastered the basics of reading, writing, and arithmetic may be "handicapped" developmentally and limited in their future opportunities. In the same way, vocational and avocational services provided by the schools are also aimed at increasing opportunities for individuals to grow and to prosper through cooperative life careers. Because the schools deal with a myriad of learning outcomes and because motivation, behavior, and learning are the principal activities of the schools, the schools have become increasingly concerned with the psychosocial dimensions of growth. Teachers engage in diagnostic and prescriptive teaching, have concern for positive mental health, relate the effects of nutrition to motivation and learning, and have close contact with parents and community agencies such as the courts, the judicial system, halfway houses, and the like. Therefore, it is not at all surprising that Congress has viewed the school as an integral part of the community human services network.

Other community-based social agencies, such as rehabilitation programs, recreation departments, and scores of other agencies that are prominently associated with human services, are *also* concerned with human growth and development. *Human growth and development is, in fact, the unifying concept that ties all of the human services agencies and education together.* It is the common denominator of both the human services agencies and education, with the ultimate goal of both being to assist each human being in realizing his or her full potential. Nevertheless, for a variety of historical reasons, the schools have become isolated from the other social agencies. It is only in recnt times that the full impact of larger societal forces upon education has been realized. Industrialization, the dramatic changes in the marketplace, democratization trends, communications, and the like have transformed the needs and desires of society and its citizens. The schools have discovered that they do not have the capacity to deal with all of the responsibilities delegated to them over the decades.

In attempting to respond to these responsibilities, schools often duplicated services being provided by other community agencies, pushing themselves into a more self-contained operation. As a matter of fact, the inability of the schools to deal independently with many of these services has, in many ways, accelerated the need for better human services—especially for the school-age population. The increase in remedial and rehabilitative services is, in part, designed to offset some of the factors identified by the community that appear to impede human development. In addition, the isolation of the schools from their natural allies in fostering human development has led to a mode in which the primary thrust in compensatory—rehabilitative or curative—rather than preventive. That is to say, when the family or the school was unable to provide an environment that fostered positive human development, a secondary system of counseling and compensatory services took over with the task, once again, of trying to rehabilitate the person to fit into "normal" institutional patterns.

The dramatic increase in compensatory and rehabilitative services, both within the school system and the community, is vivid testimony to the failure of an uncoordinated network of human services related institutions. To many observers, this *fragmentation* in the delivery of human services is, in part, responsible for this failure; to others this duplication is also viewed as costly, in a fiscal sense; and to still others the total approach is seen as unsuccessful because it is now basically oriented towards cure rather than towards prevention. The need, therefore, is to foster a collaborative model of services promoting positive human growth and development in the community.

Ironically, the realitites of the energy crisis and the increased economic constraints have assisted in facilitating more coordination of the human services agencies, with the schools being a key member of this association. The evolution of a community human service system which includes the schools and promotes human development in a collaborative way needs to move toward a *preventive* rather than a *curative* mode. To be sure, there will be a period of transition from what is primarily a compensatory structure to one geared toward prevention; but such a collaboration can begin to emphasize the tailoring of programs that fit individuals rather than the other way around, as is still often the case today. The more, in fact, that the human services groups collaborate, the more likely they will match services to the developmental style of the person, and the more they may be able to draw from the total resources of the community. Furthermore, the more collaborative the model, the more far-reaching the enterprise and the more likely it is that the full impact of accumulative wisdom and know-how of the participating agencies and institutions can be brought to bear on the primary mission of designing environments that enable the person to develop, as fully as possible, as a unique being.

Our expanding knowledge base is guiding us increasingly toward individualized procedures. Since human variability is a fact and no two persons are alike, then the need to tailor programs to fit individuals takes precedent over masses of people adjusting to standardized procedure.

Further, since evidence points in the direction of all people having the capacity to learn *under the right conditions,* the concept of matching learner to appropriate learning environments becomes basic. This leads not only to the recognition and acceptance of diversity but the need for more *options and choices.*

The emerging model of human services which includes the schools and is tied to human life span development is really a simple one. There are several advantages to such a model. To begin with, the base of human and material resources available would not only be enlarged but would be fully known to all participants. Furthermore, the orchestration efforts of this expanded base of resources can lead to more tailored approaches to human development.

A more coordinated human services delivery system is already taking various forms. One popular form pioneered and supported by the Mott Foundation is the school as the community *center* of human services. Since the schools deal with each succeeding generation of young people, they become the focal point for contact with those young people. The earlier and more coordinated the service is, the more useful and appropriate, as well as preventative, are the consequences. This has the additional advantage of avoiding duplication, including energy services (referred to in community studies and in the Community Schools and Comprehensive Community Education Act in 1978). Under this model, state unemployment offices assign special rehabilitative counselors to the school; recreational departments offer programs after school and in the evenings; mental health agencies provide staff to the school, either during the day or evening; and the school is opened weekends and becomes a center for community service to assist not only the school-age population but adults as well. In certain places this model has the additional advantage of creating an ''intergenerational'' context in which adults, including the elderly and the retired, serve as role models and as teaching aides for the young, and vice versa.

The direct connecting of schools to the other human services in the community is probably best facilitated by the counseling and psychology groups that are already in existence. Many schools already have social workers, psychiatric personnel, special education therapists, and similar professionals who are able to lead in this direction. More important, the leadership—whether it is among the school boards, educational administrators, or leaders of the social service agencies, religious, civic and political leaders—need to be convinced that this is also the direction that can maximize the effectiveness of *all* the human services. The realization that there is so much duplication and that a rehabilitative model is costly without yielding the expected impact may result in an alternative model of collaboration and cooperation for a more viable human service network.

There is yet another reason for a more coordinated human service delivery system. The advent of public alternative schools has resulted in a growing realization that the schools per se are not the only places where learning can and, indeed, does take place, nor are those who "teach" limited to people within the walls of a school. We have known for some time now that education extends beyond the four walls of the schools and that for human development to be maximized, all of the "educators" of the young have to be mobilized in a more integrated fashion. This means that parents, peer groups, media, community—all the so-called "socializers"—need to become part of a team that cooperates in creating conditions that foster the maximum development of each and every person under its influence. As we move into the 1980s and beyond, there are increased calls for options and choices, for cooperation and collaboration between parents, teachers, business and industry, as well as between the host of social agencies that are in the business of socializing the young. The contemporary move to deinstitutionalize and to seek alternative forms of delivering human services is, in part, a recognition that many of the institutional formats have not been as responsive to the wide range of individual differences as they need to be. This has had a predictable effect on parents and others who are now seeking greater control over their own lives and over the development of their children. It appears that the schools are caught up in the same social force that have occasioned the trend toward deinstitutionalization of the human services. The public school system is increasingly unable to deliver services as it has in the past.

There is, therefore, a type of deinstitutionalization now going on in the schools which takes the form of options and choices, with a whole gamut of alternative schools, including more community-based mini-schools which encourage and enable parents and other agents in the community to play a greater role in educating people. Through this process, the discovery of the community as a basic setting for education has been advanced. In the future we will be talking not so much about a *school system* as about an *educational system,* in which all the resources of the community will be delineated and orchestrated to fit the learner. The conversion of a school system into an educational system tied to the resources of the total community and structured around the coordination of the human services can be depicted in figure 6.2. This move towards making the schools an integral part of the human services delivery system represents a recognition that the school is essential in tying together the human service agencies in a more coordinated framework.

Human development—that is to say, maximizing the growth in each and every person as a distinct human being, fostering those conditions that promote that distinctiveness, having each person assume a greater sense of control over his/her own destiny, and creating a structure in which each individual can tap all of the resources available in a community—is the very business of education, and as such, inherently involves all the human services as participants. Accomplishing this goal of human development, however, is not an easy task. There is a host of issues, some of them deeply conflicting, which can potentially thwart the full realization of this goal and even undermine the progress we have made thus far. It may be useful, therefore, to examine and come to grips with some of these problematic issues and potential impediments.

The problems of the public schools are very much on the public's mind, with aspects of these problems presented almost daily through reports in newspapers, magazines, television, and radio. A great deal of concern and attention has been focused on the vandalism in the public schools, and on the violence of students toward teachers, or toward each other. There is also concern over the number of teenage pregnancies and the high incidence of venereal disease among teenagers, raising questions of the school's proper role and responsibility in providing or perhaps in orchestrating an adequate sex education program. Teachers' morale is low, with fear of lay-offs and increasing evidence of the phenomenon of "teacher burnout." There is also an increasing politicalization and polarization within the schools, with teachers aligned against administrators, and the rapid turnover of educational administrators compounding the problems. According to the Gallup Poll (1982: 38), the general public perceives the lack of discipline as the major problem confronting the public schools, closely followed by the lack of proper finan-

**Figure 6.2**

SCHOOL STRUCTURE

EDUCATIONAL SYSTEM

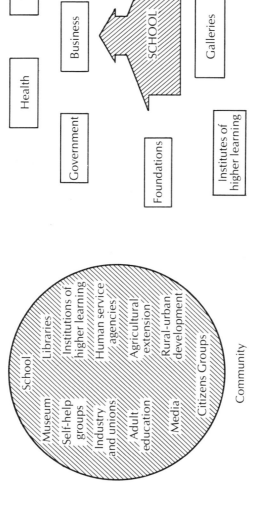

*Source:* Fantini, Reed, and Loughran 1979:13–14.

cial support and the use of drugs. Poor curriculum and/or low academic standards and difficulty getting good teachers were also high on the list. Integration and busing (combined as one item in the poll) and the lack of interest on the part of teachers, parents and students were also significant causes for concern.

These issues, among others, undermine the ongoing struggle by professional educators to achieve the goals of equality, quality, and efficiency in the delivery of school services. Efforts to offer true equality of educational opportunity have operated in a number of arenas, including attempts to eliminate racial discrimination, a concern for bilingual and multicultural education, and attention to the rights of special needs students.

Despite the fact that the Supreme Court's historic decision occurred twenty-five years ago and despite the fact that the desegregation of schools has been legally implemented in all parts of the country, many of our public schools remain segregated, or have "resegregated" over the years, and the issue of "equality" continues. In an article entitled "Desegregation: The Unfinished Agenda," authors Green et al. point out: "Even in districts where school enrollments have been adjusted to eliminate the most obvious evidence of the separation of the races, subtle forms of continuing segregation have been used to maintain a dual system of education, resulting in two standards of outcomes: one for majority students and one for minorities," (1981: 282).

Among these "subtle forms of continuing segregation" is the tracking of minority students in desegregated schools into special education programs, remedial, and vocational courses. The result is that minority students are underrepresented in college preparatory classes and overrepresented in noncollege bound classes. Another form of segregation which occurs in otherwise desegregated school systems involves discriminatory disciplinarian practices. "While minority students comprise approximately 25 percent of the nation's school population," the co-authors of this article note, "they make up 40 percent of all suspended and expelled students." Furthermore, the authors state: "Black students are not only suspended more frequently, their suspensions are also for longer periods of time. Thus, these students lose time in schools, drop out of school, or fail to meet graduation requirements; they enter the job market with few work skills, destined to join the overflowing ranks of the unemployed" (Green et al. 1981: 282).

The institutionalized practice of classifying students also contributes to subtle discrimination. Standardized tests, for example, can be used to identify "able" from "less able" students. Such learner classification systems provide labels such as "bright" or "dull," which in turn leads to self-fulfilling prophecy (Rosenthal 1968). Teacher attitudes reinforce the expectations signaled by the classification. The child labeled "slow" is treated as a slow learner, is defined as a "slow" learner, and eventually *becomes* a "slow" learner.

Another national issue concerns bilingual and multicultural education. Bilingual programs have been supported by federal funding through Title VII of the 1965 Elementary and Secondary Education Act, passed in 1968. Since that time, many states, Florida and California among them, have voluntarily enacted into law their own bilingual education acts. In 1974, however, the Supreme Court, through what is commonly referred to as the Lau decision, mandated local school districts to provide limited-English-speaking students with access to appropriate and understandable education. Because Hispanics are the nation's largest group of non-English-speaking minorities, they have naturally been more directly affected by the Lau decision than has any other ethnic group. However, this decision applies to *all* non-English-speaking people—Vietnamese, Chinese, Haitians, Italians, etc. School districts all over the country have implemented bilingual programs as well as English as a second language (ESL) programs to provide such youngsters with an equitable education and to help them achieve competency in English language skills. During the late 1970s and early 1980s, bilingual policies began to undergo review at national, state, and local levels.

Education for special-needs students has also proved to be a controversial issue. PL 94–142, the so-called "Bill of Rights for the Handicapped," mandates the need to design "least restrictive environments" for the education of students with special needs. Many earlier compensatory programs attempted to rehabilitate the learner to fit the school. A more recent trend reverses this process, with responsibility falling on the schools to develop individual education programs, custom-tailored to the needs of each student. While initially conceived for special needs students, the idea of individualized programs could apply beneficially to all learners. The need to fit students' learning styles with teaching styles has also become increasingly recognized (Fantini 1973, 1976) with the development of increasingly refined techniques to determine learning styles (Dunn and Dunn 1978). Furthermore, such an approach encourages parent participation in designing the child's program and depends on the expertise of human services professionals both within the school system and outside the schools in the community.

With this expansion in the concept and scope of educational services, the demands placed on teachers have also changed. In response, professional educators mobilized to demand recognition along the same lines as members of other professions, such as medicine or law. Professionalization brought increased authority and control for teachers and administrators. At the same time, this increase in professional authority meant a decrease in community control and parental input. The schools became isolated in the community, just at the time they needed to become more fully integrated into community networks. Public accountability also emerged, in which responsibility for students' achievement and competency went hand-in-hand with increased authority.

In the area of concern for *quality* in education, the whole definition of "quality education" has become under fire. The question is two-fold: how appropriate is current curriculum to contemporary needs, and how effective are the schools and the process of schooling? Doubts and debate over the excellence, or even the adequacy, of public education continue to this day, intensified by the changing demands of new technology. From the business sector came serious doubts that public school graduates are equipped to meet contemporary manpower needs. In response to these doubts, many businesses and industries are beginning to develop their own educational programs. A host of new literacies have arisen—including computer literacy—to join the traditional "3 R's." This, in turn, has occasioned serious concern over redefining the components of quality education. Once the components of quality education are redefined, however, there is also the issue of how to best deliver educational services. A number of studies are beginning to surface, examining the exact nature and factors of school effectiveness (Averch et al. 1974; Comer 1980; Goodlad 1979; Rutter et al. 1979; Weber 1979). In addition, a focus on the problems of secondary level public education has led to a series of major reform projects, each attempting to reform the structure and/or curriculum of the high school (Gray 1982: 564–568).

One of the most pressing issues facing education today concerns the diminishing financial support from federal, state, and local sources. The economic realities of the late 1970s and the 1980s have significantly altered the funding patterns and possibilities for public education. There is a marked decrease in large-scale federally funded programs that characterized educational reform efforts in the 1960s, and a similar marked decrease in school funding on the local level. The so-called "citizen tax revolt" also affected fiscal pollcies, including a reduction of support to public schools. Both Proposition 13 (in California) and Proposition 2½ (in Massachusetts) were designed to put a ceiling on property taxes. (From such property taxes, of course, come the revenue for schools as well as for public services, including police and fire protection, public transportation, disability benefits and the like.) While the exact nature and extent of the ramifications from such tax ceilings remain unclear, some predictions are possible. With reduced financial resources available to the schools, direct educational services are limited, staffs are reduced, and certain programs—often in art, music, physical education, or other areas not perceived as "basic"—are cut. As these attractive "extracurricular" activities are eliminated, more and more middle-class parents are turning to the private sector for education. Increased interest in a variety of tuition tax credit plans and voucher proposals, which would grant parents rebates for the expenses of private school education, are indicators of this shift. While this opens up increased avenues of choices for families, it also further erodes the financial base of support for public education. However, this need not necessarily mean *overall* educational services will be curtailed, especially if education is viewed as part of the human services system rather than as an isolated institution, apart from other community agencies. There is an increased emphasis on "doing more with less" in education, as in many other community agencies. Many communities across the country are exploring the possibility of utilizing community resources, facilities, and expertise for educational efforts. This expands educational efforts and involves the school more closely with its surrounding community. In addition, such exploratory developments avoid costly duplication of efforts, in which the schools struggle to reproduce services or facilities better offered elsewhere, and help keep the costs of public education closer to the price the public is willing to pay. Along with quality education and equal access to education, efficiency is emerging as a goal and expectation.

In recent years, we have seen a number of major changes in politics, economics, and educational theory, all of which have had an impact in changing the role and responsibility of the school. Many of these changes are still in motion, and the ultimate outcomes remains unclear. It is important to remember that the problems in the schools, and in the overall delivery of educational services, are merely reflections of problems in the larger society. The various confluent trends in the schools and in society can serve as guidelines toward establishing new policies and integrating education into the human services system. It is equally important to realize that, rather than merely reflecting the problems of a transitional state of affairs, these problems offer an opportunity for evaluation and improvement.

# REFERENCES

Averch, Harvey A. et al. 1974. *How Effective Is Schooling?* Englewood Cliffs, N.J.: Educational Technology Publications.

Brubacher, John S. 1962. *Modern Philosophies of Education.* 3d ed. New York: McGraw-Hill.

Bureau of the Census. 1980. *Statistical Abstract of the United States.*

Comer, James P. 1980. *School Power.* New York: Free Press.

Cordasco, Francesco. 1967. *A Brief History of Education.* Totowa, N.J.: Littlefield, Adams.

Dunn, Rita and Kenneth Dunn. 1978. *Teaching Students Through Their Individual Learning Styles: A Practical Approach.* Reston, Va.: Reston.

Fantini, Mario D. 1973. *Public Schools of Choice.* New York: Simon & Schuster.

Fantini, Mario D., ed. 1976. *Alternative Education: A Source Book for Parents, Teachers, Students, and Administrators.* Garden City, N.Y.: Doubleday/Anchor Books.

Fantini, Mario D., Horace Reed, and Elizabeth Loughran. 1979. Community Education: Toward a Definition. Manuscript.

Gallup, George H. 1982. The 14th Annual Gallup Poll of the Public's Attitudes Toward the Public Schools. *Phi Delta Kappan* (September).

Goodlad, John I. 1979. *What Schools Are For* (Phi Delta Kappa Educational Foundation).

Gray, Dennis. 1982. The 1980s: Season for High-School Reform. *Educational Leadership* (May).

Green, Robert L., Margaret A. Parsons, and Frances S. Thomas. 1981. Desegregation: The unfinished agenda. *Educational Leadership* (January).

Grieder, Calvin and Stephen Romine. 1955. *American Public Education.* 2d ed. New York: Ronald Press.

Rosenthal, Robert. 1968. *Pygmalion in the Classroom.* New York: Holt, Rinehart and Winston.

Rutter, Michael et al. 1979. *Fifteen Thousand Hours.* Cambridge, Mass.: Harvard University Press.

Weber, George. 1979. *Inner City Children Can Be Taught to Read.* Washington, D.C.: Council for Basic Education.

# 7

# HEALTH SERVICES

## F. DOUGLAS SCUTCHFIELD

The World Health Organization has defined health as "a state of complete physical, mental, and social well-being and not merely absence of disease and infirmity (1960: 1). This definition, cited in the WHO constitution, has a number of implications for the human services system. First, it includes mental and social well-being along with more traditional definitions relating to physical wellness. It indicates that the health care system shares with other systems of human services a concern for these two important elements of the individual's total health. In addition, it states a very positive definition of health, that is, that health does not exist merely in the absence of disease and infirmity. This provides the health care system with a charge to care for asymptomatic patients and to maintain the health of the individual and society. These two components of the definition of health broaden significantly the consideration of what issues the health system should address.

Further examination of this definition leads us to some additional considerations. Current research indicates that life events can have an impact on

F. Douglas Scutchfield is Professor of Medicine and Director of the Graduate School of Public Health, San Diego State University, California.

physical health. It has been demonstrated that when a large number of social events occur in an individual's life there is an increased possibility of illness—illness for which the medical care system is contacted (Holmes and Ray 1967). Thus, it is necessary that those responsible for the health care system recognize social contributions to the physical health of the patient. Further, there is increasing recognition that social problems, in and of themselves, significantly affect health over and above their contribution to the subsequent development of physical disease. Therefore, what have traditionally been regarded as social problems are of concern to the health care system. Awareness of these social contributions to health and a broader definition of health have been responsible for the increasing incorporation of social services into the practice of medicine and the growing concern among physicians for social problems.

There have been significant historical trends in the development of a definition of health. In many situations conditions that are now considered diseases were once considered normal. For example, during the 1930s and 1940s intestinal parsitosis was so common in the South that it was almost considered normal. Similarly, there have been historical trends in mechanisms for dealing with the problems of illness and disease. DuBose, in his classic book *Mirage of Health* (1959) has traced some of these. He reflects that in the "olden days," as defined by both Indian and eighteenth-century European cultures, individuals in the "natural" state had good health with no disease. He points out that this feeling for a "return to nature" was responsible for many of the sanitary reforms of that period, which, in turn, caused significant declines in morbidity and mortality. In the late 1800s yet another revolution was experienced—the development of increasingly technological approaches to illness and disease. The germ theory of disease and the advent of Pasteur, Koch, and Lister gave rise to the philosophy that more technology would contribute significantly to the control of disease.

These changing attitudes mirrored a changing disease incidence. The etiology of the most common causes of mortality in the early 1900s was acute infectious disease. These diseases declined with improvements in sanitation, general socioeconomic status, diet, and immunizations. When these declined, there was a concomitant increase in the chronic disease mortality. Many of these chronic diseases are attributable, in part, to contemporary life-styles. Thus, although we have learned more about the nature of disease, the nature of society and the personality of people underlie much of the changing incidence and nature of illness.

## MEASUREMENT OF HEALTH AND DISEASE

Specifically, how does one go about the process of measuring health and illness? Over the years attempts have been made to develop indices of health. The initial effort to quantify illness probably dates back to the 1800s and the development of the death registry by Southwick. This registry was the forerunner of our current vital statistics. The following formulas illustrate some of the types of statistics obtained and the most common rates for these particular vital events.

$$\text{Crude birth rate} = \frac{\text{Number of live births during the year} \times 1000}{\text{Mid-year population}}$$

$$\text{Fertility rate} = \frac{\text{Number of live births during the year} \times 1000}{\text{Mid-year population of women 15–46 years old}}$$

$$\text{Crude death rate} = \frac{\text{Number of deaths during the year} \times 1000}{\text{Mid-year population}}$$

$$\text{Maternal mortality rate} = \frac{\text{Deaths during the year due to puerperal causes} \times 10,000}{\text{Number of live births}}$$

$$\text{Infant mortality rate} = \frac{\text{Number of deaths of children less than 1 year old} \times 1000}{\text{Number of live births}}$$

Vital statistics, while important, can and often do give false or misleading impressions of the health or illness of a community, either through inadequate or inappropriate reporting, vagueness and differences in definition of the various conditions with which one is dealing, or statistical problems such as small variations in the rate.

The most commonly used statistical mechanism for comparison of health is the infant mortality rate. It has become an international, national, and interstate vehicle for comparison of the health of groups of individuals. For example, infant mortality rates among the various nations of the Western industrial world are frequently cited to illustrate that the United States remains far behind other countries in provision of health care. Reporting problems and definition differences, as mentioned above, give rise to concern about the accuracy of citing this statistic as proof that one system of medical care is better or worse than another.

The majority of these vital statistics deal with mortality, with little consideration given to morbidity or disability, two major contributions to the quality of life. Several attempts have been made to examine morbidity and disability as a mechanism for measuring health. These have resulted in large numbers of derived indices of health. The most accepted measurement of morbidity is lost-work days and bed-disability days. This measure has been used extensively by the National Center for Health Statistics (Bureau of Vital Statistics 1975). Terris (1975) has pointed out that a good way to dichotomize and thereby measure health is to look at health and illness as a continuum, with function being the yardstick for measurement. He defines function as performance and looks at studies of capability of performance and of performance itself as it relates to the extent to which an individual is "ill" or "healthy." Obviously, none of these definitions, indices, or other machinations has reached universal acceptance. This definitional problem is important, for the medical care system probably has little effect on mortality but does have a significant impact on the quality of life.

## MEDICINE AND HEALTH

As a rule, when individuals examine the health care system they are looking at the medical care system. Health, as we have indicated earlier, is comprised of physical, social, and mental well-being. Generally the medical care system, as opposed to a health care system, does not deal with social ills and/or the impact of social systems on the physical health of individuals. The only contribution from the medical care system to mental health is psychiatry. Clearly many factors other than psychiatry are involved in the development of an effective mental *health* system.

The remainder of this chapter will focus primarily on the medical care system; however, it is important to remember that environment, life-style, and social institutions also influence health.

In order to discuss medical care, a framework must be developed. While the medical care system has been charged with being a "nonsystem," this is not the case. It is a ritualized and very organized system with interrelationships and interdependency of the various components of the system. The model that I will use to discuss the medical care system is drawn from Kissick (1971) and is illustrated in figure 7.1. Kissick has divided the medical care system into three major components: resources; organization and finance; and services to consumers. Under resources he has included manpower, facilities, and technology. Rather than deal specifically with the ser-

**Figure 7.1**

MODEL OF THE HEALTH CARE ENTERPRISE

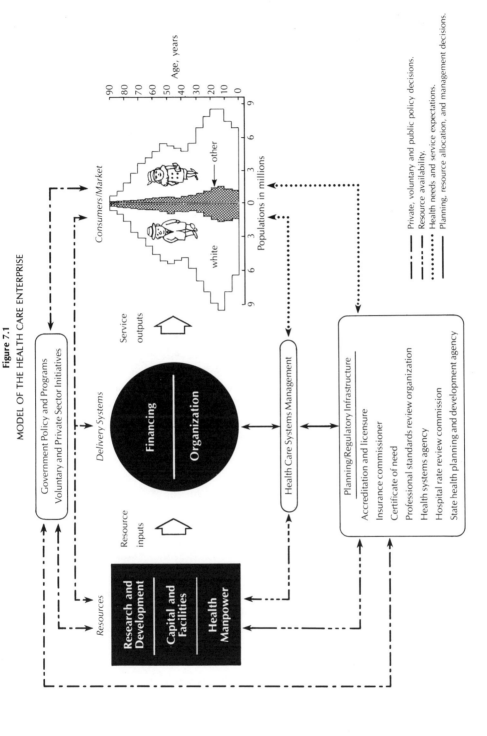

vice component as the output of that model, I will deal with the issues of consumers and consumerism in medical care as a reflection of the services received by the population. The parts of the system are interdependent, and alteration of one unit of the system will change the character of the other units. To recognize the character of this interdependence, one need only examine the effects of legislation in specific areas of this system on other parts of the system.

For example, one of the initial efforts to improve medical care services during the 1940s was the development of the Hill–Burton program. This program provided funds for the construction of hospitals. The result was the building of a large number of hospital beds, many in remote and isolated areas of rural America. Because of this thrust, there is the contention that the United States is "overbedded" and that the pressure to maintain a high occupancy rate in those beds has resulted in an escalation in the cost of hospital care. This, in turn, has increased costs to consumers and made a significant alteration in our financing system for medical care.

The mid-1960s saw the first attempt by the federal government to fund services directly for a limited segment of the population, that is, Medicare and Medicaid. This was done entirely through a financing mechanism, with no thought given to reorganization of the system. Rather the existing system received a massive infusion of resources. This lack of organization resulted in escalation of medical care costs. Thus, the consideration of one component of the medical care system without regard for the others is inappropriate and can result in disastrous consequences. This instance also serves to illustrate that the medical care system is just that, a system, and that there is a significant interdependence of each part in this system.

It would be capricious to leave these initial discussions of this model without pointing out another problem of the medical care system: confusion of inputs and outputs. The average American consumer, and to a certain extent provider, tends to confuse the resources needed for the provision of services with the services themselves. The resulting cries are "Give us a hospital," or "Give us more doctors," with the automatic assumption that there will be an increase in services. This is an invalid assumption because it does not consider organization and finance mechanisms. It is important to interpret this plea for additional resources as actually reflecting a concern for availability of services.

Any attempt to deal with the medical care system requires the perspective of a number of disciplines and their consideration of the problems and potentials. To consider problems of financing and organization without including economists and administrators does not utilize the expertise that is available. Similarly, if we are to concern ourselves with services and consumers, it is appropriate to recognize the significant contributions in our understanding of the issues that can be made by the social sciences. Our concern for the system must reflect the fact that interdisciplinary approaches involving a number of expertises will assure the best possible input in decisions concerning the system.

## MANPOWER

In 1973 an estimated 4.4 million people were employed in health fields and related occupations. Of these, only some 345,000 were physicians and osteopaths actively involved in the practice of medicine. Therefore, when we discuss health manpower we must consider not only physicians, dentists, and nurses but also allied health personnel. The ratio of allied health personnel to physicians has increased from approximately two-to-one in the early 1900s to fifteen-to-one in the 1970s. This change reflects our increasing technology and the need for technicians and specialists to operate and maintain the machinery and activities inherent in that technology. This change also reflects an increased recognition of the importance of social and environmental influences on the health of the patient. This recognition has resulted in a rapid increase in the number of such activities as social service departments and nutritionists and dietitians available to care for the patient, both in the hospital and in ambulatory care settings. The importance of these individuals working together as a team to deal with the total patient is self-evident. However, while much lip service is given to training the health care team, very little actual training as a team occurs. Since patients come with not one isolated problem but with a constellation of them, resources from any of the individuals engaged in health occupations should be available to that patient.

**Physicians**  Physician manpower, of course, is a major concern in any discussion of health manpower. Traditionally the physician has been responsible for the direction of patient care, and only under his orders are health resources mobilized for the patient. The physician has enjoyed much respect, dating from the time of the Hippocratean physician-priests. Despite some decline in physician prestige from around 1400 until the early 1700s, the physician has reassumed the role of an influential and powerful individual in the community.

The past decade has seen rapid increase in the number of physicians educated within the United States. Since 1950 there has been a 74 percent increase in the total number of physicians, reducing the ratio of persons per physician from 672:1 in 1950 to 562:1 in 1973 (HEW 1971). This growth is largely the result of increased federal funding for health manpower education, particularly physicians. There has been an increase in enrollment in medical schools, an increase in the number of medical schools, and, in some areas, a shortening of the medical school curriculum from four to three years.

Recently we have seen a shift in federal policy on physician manpower. There is now a concern that there are too many physicians being trained and that by the end of the twentieth century we will have a physician glut. In addition to the increases in enrollment and the formation of additional medical schools, substantial increases have occurred in the number of foreign-trained physicians practicing in the United States. For example, in 1963, 11.2 percent of the country's physicians were foreign-trained. By 1973 the percentage had increased to 19.5 percent.

There are three levels of complexity of medical care: primary, secondary, and tertiary. Primary care is provided by the health professional of first contact. This person assumes responsibility for continuity of care, coordination of all sources of health care, and assurance of the comprehensiveness of that care. Primary care is generally ambulatory in nature and is usually provided by the physician in his office. Secondary care occurs in the community hospital. Such care usually has an intermittent level of technological orientation. The tertiary, or the most complex level of care, is very sophisticated and occurs in the university medical center. It represents a subspecialist-level service with high use of complex technology, equipment, and staff.

Physician specialties that are usually considered as primary care providers include family medicine, internal medicine, and pediatrics. Though debate has raged about whether or not obstetrics and gynecology is a primary care specialty, it is not included in the primary care specialty training programs funded by national legislation.

The proportion of physicians engaged in family or general practice has declined from approximately 80 percent of all physicians during the 1920s to some 20 percent currently. This decline might be offset by the increased numbers of physicians specializing in internal medicine and pediatrics. However, in 1973 only 15 percent of practicing physicians were in internal medicine, and only 6.5 percent in pediatrics. Thus, less than 50 percent of physicians are currently practicing primary care.

Kerr White (1973) has developed a paradigm that reflects the problems of primary care. During a one-year period, in a population of 1,000 individuals approximately 720 will visit a physician's office, 100 will be hospitalized in an acute general hospital, and 10 will be admitted to a tertiary care center. Therefore, fewer than 50 percent of the physicians will provide the care for the 720 physician office visits, whereas over 50 percent of the physicians will be responsible for the 100 hospital admissions. This is the problem of specialty maldistribution. What has prompted this lack of commitment by physicians to primary care specialties? While there are a number of factors, one of the most serious contributors to specialty maldistribution has been the growth of technology. The National Institutes of Health have supplied large amounts of money to subspecialty teaching and research activities in major medical centers. As a result of these allocations, the role models of general and family practice have been lost in medical education environments. In addition, physicians in training have become dependent upon the specialized resources that accumulate in tertiary medical care settings. Medical students and resident physicians alike have had very little exposure to primary and ambulatory care.

There are also financial incentives that mitigate against primary care. Most health insurance policies provide coverage for hospital-based physician services, as opposed to out-patient care, particularly out-patient care of a preventive nature. In addition, surgical and medical subspecialists have a higher level of income because of the more expensive technological procedures and activities they perform, so there are financial differentials between primary care physicians and subspecialists.

A correlary to the specialty maldistribution is the geographic maldistribution of physicians. In general, the distribution of physicians weighs very heavily toward major metropolitan areas, where the physician-to-patient ratio may average 500:1. The comparable ratio for rural communities is 2,000:1. The reasons for geographic maldistribution are very similar to those for specialty maldistribution. Specifically, there is frequently a higher fee paid for a procedure performed in a metropolitan area than that paid for the same procedure performed in a small rural community. In part this is the result of health insurance reimbursement formulas. Further, a physician must practice in a metropolitan area close to a large hospital in order to have access to the highly technical equipment and personnel necessary to practice a subspecialty. Previous research has also demonstrated that concerns about education, cultural, and social opportunities in rural areas mitigate against increasing numbers of physicians locating in these underserved areas

(Scutchfield 1976). It is also very difficult to form a group practice in a rural area, due to the fact that there are inadequate numbers of patients to support such a group. Problems of geographic isolation also exist in inner-city environments.

**Dentists**   In 1973 there were 100,780 active civilian dentists for a ratio of 1 dentist per 2,088 persons. This contrasts to a dentist-to-patient ratio of 2,100:1 in 1960. This improved ratio is the result of federal funding for dental schools, which resulted in an increase in enrollment, the construction of new dental schools, and a shortened dental school curriculum. The enrollment in dental schools has increased dramatically, almost 50 percent, since 1960. Dentistry has not had the technological revolution that medicine has experienced, so the ratio of allied health personnel to dentists is approximately 2:1. In fact, the majority of allied health personnel currently involved in dentistry are dental assistants rather than hygienists or expanded-duty auxiliaries.

**Nurses**   Nursing constitutes one of the largest health professions. In 1973 there were approximately 815,000 registered nurses, 460,000 practical nurses, and 1 million nursing aides, orderlies, and attendants. Nurses comprise the largest single group of health professionals, although 30 percent of registered nurses were not employed in 1972. While the majority of those under twenty-five years of age were employed, the percent employed falls off rapidly thereafter.

The largest single employer of nursing personnel are hospitals, with 65 percent of nurses employed by these institutions. Only 6.8 percent of nurses are employed in physician's offices.

Nursing education is at a crossroad. Prior to the 1950s, the majority of nursing education occurred in hospitals. Nurses were trained for three years, awarded a diploma, and then expected to pass a nursing registry examination. However, in the 1950s came the advent of the baccalaureate degree in nursing, with many nurses opting for a four-year curriculum leading to the bachelor's degree. These nurses are also required to sit for the registry examination.

A further development in nursing education is the associate degree program, a two-year curriculum that qualifies a student to sit for nursing boards and thereby become a registered nurse. Nursing educators have envisioned the development of two classes of nurses, the professional nurse with a baccalaureate degree and the technical nurse with an associate degree.

As with physicians and dentists, there is a geographic maldistribution of nurses. In the south-central states there is 1 nurse to every 400–500 persons, while in the New England states there is 1 nurse to every 150–210 persons.

Nursing is attempting to adopt a more professional role than that of "handmaiden of the physician." In addition, a growing number of nurses are completing postbaccalaureate training, such as certified nurse midwifery and family nurse practitioner programs. The majority of these programs have a one-year postbaccalaureate curriculum and can lead to either a master's degree or certification. There is also a trend toward the utilization of the family nurse practitioner in freestanding primary care programs. There are those who feel that the family nurse practitioner will replace the old-style general physician and provide primary care in underserved areas. Programs in states such as North Carolina and Colorado have demonstrated that not only is the nurse practitioner an acceptable alternative to the physician, but the quality of care is just as good for those conditions with which the family nurse practitioner is equipped to deal (Levine et al. 1976). Attempts are currently underway to allow Medicare to provide for reimbursement to family nurse practitioners, and in some states Medicaid will pay for an office visit to a family nurse practitioner.

**Allied Health Manpower** As I pointed out in the beginning section of this chapter, in the early nineteenth century there were two allied health workers, including nurses, for every physician. However, there are now large numbers who assume responsibility for various aspects of health care. In fact, the Bureau of the Census lists over two hundred health-related occupations. There has been a rapid proliferation of new job titles in the health professions, largely as the result of an increased technology and the development of additional therapeutic and diagnostic equipment. This new technology requires specific skills, thereby increasing the employment opportunities available in the allied health professions. One of the problems with the technological innovations has been that they are not labor saving but rather labor intensive and require additional personnel. This increases the total employment in the health professions without saving existing manpower.

It is impossible in so brief a chapter to describe all of the various types and characters of allied health manpower, but it would be well to point out some problems with these new occupations. The first problem is one of licensure and credentialing. The purpose of licensure is to assure the public that practitioners of a profession possess adequate knowledge and skill to practice their profession. Licensure is a two-edged sword and can also be used to restrict the number of practitioners of a particular health profession. This restriction can result in a decreasing supply of those professionals and, in the face of steady demand, increase wages and prices.

The second problem of licensure is the question of who is to license the allied health professional. Presently, most of the licensing boards are comprised of members of the profession being licensed. However, in some circumstances, another professional group is responsible.

The third problem has to do with struggles over who will be allowed to do what. For example, physical therapists might restrict through law what the physician's office nurse might do with a diathermy machine, thus increasing the demand for physical therapy services and, concomitant the cost of services.

In spite of these problems, with new technology there is little question that the numbers and types of allied health manpower will continue to grow. In addition, we might expect more delegation of responsibility for certain components of existing health professional activities to members of these new allied health professions. It is important to recognize, however, that problems do exist and that cooperative and collaborative efforts among all of the health professions are necessary to assure satisfactory working relationships for the benefit of the patient.

**Mid-Level Health Manpower**   The terms ''midlevel health worker'' and ''physician extender'' are generic. The types of personnel who inhabit these categories are basically of three groups. The first is the nurse practitioner, discussed in the section on nursing. The second is the physician's assistant, who has two to four years of specialized medical training. The third is the Medex, a one-year training experience for individuals who have had previous health-related jobs, such as Armed Forces corpsmen. There has been a rapid growth in all three of these programs, and it appears unlikely that there will be anything less than a continuing increase in the numbers of these individuals.

The midlevel health manpower category was originally viewed as a mechanism to improve access to health care in underserved areas and to increase the efficiency of the physician in the provision of care. Generally, these workers are expected to handle preliminary data gathering, such as the history and physical examination; to perform some laboratory procedures; to make some initial judgments concerning the health or illness of the patient; and to take appropriate action, in conjunction with the physician. In addition, it is expected that these midlevel health workers, operating under a protocol or a series of standing orders from the physician, will be able to diagnose and treat a number of common, acute illnesses. These midlevel practitioners will assure that the patient understands and is capable of dealing with the problems of his own disease. Studies have demonstrated that a majority of conditions can be cared for by these individuals and that only some 15–25 percent of patients require referral to a physician for a more thorough evaluation and/or management (Demens, Lawrence, and Collen 1976). In addition, the quality of care of those conditions for which protocols have been prepared seems to be at least on a par with that provided by physicians. Although data seem to indicate an increased productivity in practices using physician extenders, issues and concerns about cost-effectiveness have yet to be answered (Levine et al. 1976).

## FACILITIES

There are two major types of facilities with which I will deal: the acute general hospital, and the long-term care facility or nursing home.

**Hospitals**   Hospitals have their origins in antiquity. They were originally called hospices. Uusally only the poor used these hospices, and then only to die. Later hospitals became the sites of care of acute illness, where it was anticipated that progress could be made in the condition of the patient.

The three major categories of hospitals are governmental, proprietary, and nonprofit. There are two kinds of government hospitals, federal and those funded by state and local governments. Government hospitals were originally formed for the benefit of the public rather than the individual. The first public hospitals were for tuberculosis and mental illness, problems that were seen as having a significant impact on society and that necessitated patient isolation for society's benefit. Following that movement, city governments constructed acute general hospitals to serve the indigent population of their communities. In the early 1900s, small hospitals were owned by a physician, or a small group of physicians, for the purpose of hospitalizing their patients. With more involvement of the nonprofit sector as a result of Hill–Burton legislation, there was a decline in the numbers of these kinds of facilities in the first half of the twentieth century. Since the advent of Medicare and Medicaid, there has been a growing number of beds operated by the proprietary, investor-owned segment of the economy.

The acute, general, nonprofit hospital has an even longer history, as most of the hospices mentioned above were founded by religious orders to care for the poor and the transient. The nonprofit, short-term hospital received major impetus in the mid-1940s with the passage of the Hill–Burton legislation. This legislation provided funds to nonprofit corporations or state and local governments to construct hospitals and other health facilities. Since its passage, $12 billion have been spent on hospital construction, approximately thirty percent of it provided through Hill–Burton funding. To a large extent these hospitals were located in rural areas, in an attempt to redress significant differences between the numbers of hospital beds in urban and rural areas. In fact, this is the only indicator of health resource allocation in which the Southern and Midwestern states have fared as well as New England and the West Coast. Largely as a result of this legislation, the number of hospital beds rose from 3.4 per thousand in 1948 to the current 4.3 per thousand. Some argue that as a result of Hill–Burton programs we have too many beds and point to the Western European countries, where the number of beds is much lower, running 2.5—3.5 per thousand population. They also point to the fact that health maintenance organizations, which have an economic incentive not to hospitalize, have a bed-to-person ratio of approximately 2.2 per thousand. The proposition that the United States is overbedded is further bolstered by the fact that the national occupancy rate is approximately 75 percent.

To assure that hospitals were constructed where there was a demonstrated need, and to try to avoid overbedding, the Hill–Burton advisory councils were formed. These councils were to assist state governments in making decisions about funds for hospital construction. Such councils were the forerunners of the comprehensive health planning councils and subsequently the health systems agencies.

With the rapid growth in the number of acute short-term general hospitals, there has been a concomitant decline in the number of governmental hospitals from approximately 1.7 beds per thousand in 1946 to 0.7 per thousand in 1973. Similarly, the nonfederal psychiatric and tuberculosis hospitals have decreased significantly both in total beds and beds per population as new methods of treatment for these problems have become available. This has resulted in a reduction in these facilities from 10.3 beds per thousand in 1946 to 7.3 beds per thousand in 1973.

Hospitals are unquestionably one of the most expensive resources within the health care system. The current estimated cost of constructing a hospital bed is $60,000. While this is an impressive figure in and of itself, it must be added that the operation cost for that bed is approximately $40,000 per year. Moreover, the fixed cost of that bed comprises three-quarters of the total cost of maintenance. Therefore, even if the bed is empty, an average of $30,000 annually is required to maintain that empty bed.

The hospital has also become the center of our advanced medical technology. As I pointed out in my discussions on allied health manpower, increasing technological innovations have resulted in the expansion of services traditionally provided by hospitals. These are such innovations as computerized axial tomography, coronary care units, open heart surgery, and other very expensive technologies. Major concerns in this technology have centered around two issues. First, as we have pointed out, it is very labor intensive and, rather than saving other resources, is an additive cost. Further, such technologies are felt to add prestige to a hospital, forcing unnecessary duplication of these units in facilities. As a good example of this, Washington, D.C., currently has more computerized axial tomography machines—at a cost of approximately $700,000 each—than the entire British Isles. High-technology services have a low utilization rate when they are duplicated in many facilities, but because the fixed cost of running such units remains essentially the same, the cost per unit of service must increase in order to cover the total cost of providing that service. This increases the cost of hospital care.

The hospital is rapidly becoming a center for health care. Increasingly, hospitals assume responsibility for ambulatory patient care through their outpatient clinics and in many of their emergency rooms. Many hospitals sponsor such nonbed-related services as home health and provide out-patient services for physical therapy, respiratory therapy, and the like. In addition, there are increasing indications that medical group practices can and will associate with hospitals, either administratively or geographically.

**Nursing Homes** With the decline in birth rate and some slight increase in longevity in the United States, there is a growing geriatric population. In 1970 approximately 11.5 percent of our population was over sixty-five. If the current trend continues, it is likely that within a few decades we will see 15–20 percent of our total population in the over-sixty-five age group. This increase in the number of elderly people, combined with the growing loss of the extended family structure, has created a demand for nursing and personal care homes to assume responsibility for our geriatric population. In response to this demand, as well as to availability of funding through Medicare and Medicaid, there has been a tremendous increase in the numbers of nursing and personal care homes in the United States.

The three major types of long-term chronic disease care facilities are the skilled nursing facility; the intermediate care facility; and the personal care home. Care in a skilled nursing facility can be paid for by Medicare, and as a result there has been tremendous impetus for this type of nursing home care. Patients confined to this type of facility must require skilled nursing care in order to justify payment from Medicare. These facilities were seen as a mechanism to decrease the pressure for acute general hospital beds by providing a level of care somewhat lower than that in hospitals at a proportionately lower cost. Such facilities usually have nursing care available around the clock.

The personal care home is intended to assist the patient who has no need for skilled nursing care but must be assisted with the activities of daily living. The intermediate care facilities fall somewhere between these two and usually have nursing care available on a one-shift-per-day basis. Medicare and Medicaid do not pay for personal care. Medicaid will, in some states, pay for intermediate care, again providing impetus for construction and development of these facilities. A number of these units are proprietary in nature, and the majority are freestanding, that is, not associated with an acute general hospital.

## TECHNOLOGY

The beginning of the technological thrust in American medicine occurred around 1910, largely as a result of the Flexner Report. Unitl 1910, most medical schools in this country were proprietary in nature and operated on an apprenticeship system. Flexner, a nonphysician educator, was commissioned by the Carnegie Foundation to examine medical education in the United States. In his investigations he found that the majority of these schools to be inadequate and suggested that they be closed. He felt that it was necessary to have a research base for medical education so that the model of the inquisitive mind could be encouraged. This, in large measure, was the result of his visits to European medical schools, where there were outstanding models of medical research in the late 1800s. His recommendations caused research to become an increasingly important component of medical education. In our technologically oriented society it is felt that technology will provide answers to problems of morbidity and mortality in the United States. We have seen the giant strides that were made with the introduction of antibiotics and the development of innovative surgical techniques. Research received renewed emphasis in the late 1930s and early 1940s with provision of research grant support through the National Institutes of Health. The next twenty years were the halcyon days of medical research. Large research establishments in medical schools were developed, and significant advances occurred in the understanding of basic physiologic and biologic mechanisms that relate to health and disease. In large measure as a result of that funding, an explosion of medical technology has occurred. More technology requires more manpower, and much of this technology is not labor saving, but rather adds to the cost of care. The computerized axial tomography is an illustration. While unquestionably a technological marvel, with its capability of visualizing internal organs, there are those who ask whether it actually improves mortality and morbidity and, if it does, what is the marginal cost of this additional information. Similarly, while we have developed heart transplants, the issue of the extent to which this technical procedure can and will influence morbidity and mortality from heart disease still exists.

In addition to these questions, the issue of targeted versus untargeted research has become a major concern. In the past, the National Institutes of Health spent major amounts of their resources on investigator-proposed research. It was thought that, through the development of information in basic biologic disciplines, the necessary information to cure disease and disability would develop. However, this approach has come under increasing criticism, and with the decline in funds available for research more funds have been spent on contract research with specific research objectives, and less on untargeted investigator-proposed research. This has prompted criticism from the biomedical research community, which feels very strongly that research in basic disciplines is necessary to understanding etiology, pathophysiology, diagnosis, and treatment of those chronic diseases that currently plague us.

This national debate will certainly continue on the extent to which research should be funded over service or educational activities and the extent to which research should be targeted as opposed to untargeted. While these debates go on, it remains true that ours is a technologically oriented society and that research about disease processes will continue.

## FINANCING

I will discuss two components of financing of medical care. The first component concerns the cost of medical care itself, the trends in those costs, and some interpretation of the reasons for the changes in cost. The second component is payment for medical services.

**Costs of Medical Care**   Health care has become a major business. In 1973, 7.7 percent of the gross national product, $99 billion, was expended for medical care by the public and private sectors. There has been an increase in both percent of gross national product expended and the total expenditure for health care. In 1929, only 3.5 percent of the GNP was expended on health care, with an average per capita expenditure of $29.49, as opposed to $463.00 per person in 1973. These are only the direct costs and do not include indirect costs inherent in illness, such as lost wages and transportation costs to and from health care facilities.

A major cause for the escalation in health care costs has been the funding of Medicare and Medicaid. As a result of these two programs, the rate of growth for health expenditures exceeded 12.5 percent in the latter part of the 1960s, but has slowed somewhat to about 10.4 percent since 1971.

Public sources of funds are responsible for an increasing proportion of funding for personal health services. In 1929, public expenditures paid for 8.9 percent of the personal health care costs in the United States, as opposed to 37.6 percent in 1974. There has been a steady but progressive rise in expenditures by the public sector, primarily through payments from Medicare and Medicaid.

According to the U.S. government's budget for FY 1981, expenditures for Medicare have increased from $32 billion in 1979 to about $45 billion in 1981, or an increase of over 40 percent in two years. Medicaid spending during the same period is expected to grow from $13 billion to $16 billion. In contrast, health services supported by the U.S. Public Health Service, such as those provided in community health centers and maternal and child health programs, are shown in the FY 1981 budget as growing from $1.7 billion in 1979 to $2.1 billion in 1981, or a growth rate of about half that of Medicare. But where the pinch will really come is in grants to states for social and child welfare services, which are budgeted to decline from $3 billion in 1979 to $2.7 billion in 1981. Thus, the combined growth in Medicare and Medicaid from 1979 to 1981 is about 36 percent; for other health services 24 percent; and social services will actually drop 10 percent. National health insurance is no longer considered inevitable; indeed it may not even be desirable in the absence of a workable method of controlling health care costs.

Medicaid funding funding for the year 1982 is estimated to be $17.89 billion for federal vendor payments (program costs) to states and the federal share of state and local administrative costs.

Reduction of federal payments to states by 3 percent (and by 4 percent in

1983 and 4.55 percent in 1984) is expected. States can offset these reductions by 1 percent each by operating a qualified hospital cost review system, recovering amounts from fraud and abuse equal to or exceeding 1 percent of the national average. States can also qualify for a dollar-for-dollar offset of their reduction if they limit increases in FY 1982 to less than 9 percent of their FY 1981 expenditures (and for FY 1983 and 1984 if the increase is less than the medical care expenditure component of the consumer price index for these years).

Proposed by Reagan for FY 1983 is $17,006,000 for federal vendor payments to states and $810,000,000 for state and local administrative costs. Costs incurred in administering Medicaid, food stamps, and Aid to Families with Dependent Children are to be combined in a block grant.

Program changes for 1982 allow states greater flexibility to cope with the reductions. Among other things, states may now (1) if they cover the medically needy, cover some medically needy and not others; (2) eliminate many services for the medically needy because requirements governing the service package for this group have been eliminated; and (3) limit recipients' freedom of choice of health providers.

States are allowed to obtain waivers from the secretary of the Department of Health and Human Services to provide coverage for a range of noninstitutional services (case management, homemaker/home health aide and personal care services, adult day care, habilitation services and respite care; room and board is not included) to persons who are likely to need care in a skilled nursing or intermediate care facility but who choose home care. The cost of home care cannot exceed the average cost of nursing home care.

Proposed by Reagan for FY 1983 include the following:

1. Reduce the federal match for optional services for the categorically needy and all services for other beneficiaries by 3 percent.
2. Establish copayments of $1 per out-patient visit for all Medicaid beneficiaries and $1 and $2 per in-patient day for the categorically needy and other beneficiaries, respectively.
3. Allow states greater flexibility to recover long-term care costs from beneficiary estates and relatives.
4. Combine federal support for administrative costs in a single fixed payment to states for the administration of Medicaid, food stamps, and Aid to Families with Dependent Children.
5. Eliminate the federal match for state Medicaid payments to enroll eligible Medicaid beneficiaries in Medicare Part B.
6. Eliminate the special higher matching rates for family planning (now

90 percent) and state certification activities (now 75 percent).

7. Phase in full state responsibility for erroneous payments through reducing the acceptable error level by one percentage point per year.
8. Shorten the automatic extension of Medicaid eligibility for individuals who lose their eligibility for AFDC as the result of increased earnings from four months to one month.
9. Eliminate people from Medicaid through eliminating more people from AFDC and SSL.
10. Reduce Medicaid costs through program changes in Medicare that impact on Medicaid.

Given the fact of rising expenditures for health care, both in terms of absolute dollars and as a percentage of the GNP, it is necessary to examine factors that have been important in these increases. There are three major components of the cost increase. The first is the expanded cost of a unit of service, the price component. Price increases account for about half of the escalation in expenditures for theperiod 1965–1975. These declined somewhat between 1971 and 1974, largely as a result of the wage–price stabilization program, which placed an artificial ceiling on increases in wages and prices of goods and services. Economists argue that the increasing price of medical care is not merely paying more for the same service, but that the character of the service itself has changed; that, with the development of technology and the increase in manpower available to provide care, the quality of care has increased and the consumer is buying a better product than he did previously.

The second component in increased costs is the increased use of medical services. This use has risen with an increased awareness of health services and with an older population with more chronic disease. Removal of some of the financial barriers to health care has also increased the demand for health services. The medical care system does not follow a "market philosophy" of increased price causing a decreasing demand. For example, in 1900 there were 2.5 doctor's office visits per patient per year, and 750 hospital days per 1,000 people per year. In 1973, there were 4.7 doctor's office visits and 1,200 hospital days per 1,000 people. This increased utilization took place in the face of a rising price, which theoretically should have decreased demand.

Inflation is the third component of cost increases in the medical sector. While inflation has increased the cost per unit of service, it has been more striking in the medical care sector than it has in other areas of the economy.

For example, the cost of all goods and services increased 61 percent from 1950 to 1970, while medical care had an inflation factor of 125 percent.

It seems appropriate in the course of this discussion to look at the components of health care cost and ascertain exactly which sector is responsible for the majority of this price increase. Figure 7.2 illustrates that the major

**Figure 6.2**
GROWTH IN MEDICAL PRICES 1960–1970

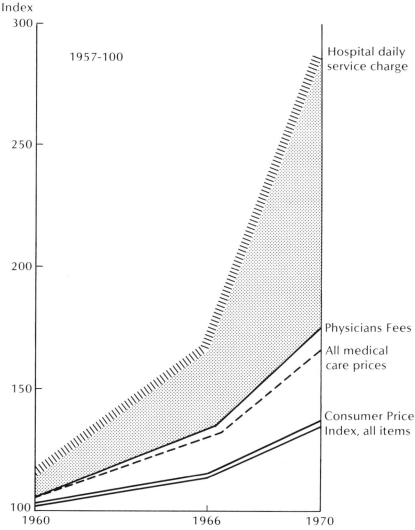

1957-100

Hospital daily service charge

Physicians Fees

All medical care prices

Consumer Price Index, all items

*Source:* USDC 1972.

cost increase is in hospital care. The average cost per in-patient day for community hospitals has risen from $62.82 in 1969 to $107.30 in 1973. Much of this increase occurred around 1966, when Medicare and Medicaid, Title XVII and Title XIX of the Social Security Act, were passed.

It is clear that the cost-reimbursement formula currently used by Medicare and Medicaid fueled an increase in medical care costs. Under the cost-reimbursement formula, there is no incentive for economy in hospital spending, since the reasonable cost of a hospital stay is reimbursed, regardless of what is calculated in the cost.

The major influences on the increase in hospital costs are: wage increases, new technology, and the increase and change in the mix of the hospital work force. New, expensive technology has been developed that improves services, such as coronary care units. However, equipment developed with this new technology does not increase productivity, as in other industries, but rather requires additional, specially trained manpower. Therefore, technological innovation does not decrease the labor force but, in fact, increases it. Again, coronary care units are a good illustration of a very labor-intensive, highly developed technological innovation.

Hospitals are a labor-intensive industry. Currently, the average hospital has three employees per hospital bed, and recent technological changes have resulted in an alteration of the mix of workers so that they are now more highly skilled and more highly paid.

**Medical Insurance**   Through the preceding section I have traced the development of rising costs of medical care and examined the development of these costs and some of their antecedents. The usual mechanism for dealing with the costs of medical care is health insurance.

It is useful to define the "insurance model" and examine this definition briefly. If 1,000 people had 100 admissions to a hospital during a year and averaged a stay of 8 days, this group would have an "experience" of 800 hospital days. This experience, multiplied by $100 per day bed costs, would make the hospital expense for this group $80,000. Each member of this group would then be asked to pay a "premium" of $80 per person per year to cover the cost of hospitalization. This "premium" is "pure premium" because it does not include administrative costs, or "costs of insuring." Obviously, in our insurance model, we would want people with "average" attributes. If we insured only old people, poor people, or people with previous existing disease, they would use more hospital days and could bankrupt the insurance company. If that happens, there is an "adverse selection of risk.'' The differential attraction that medical insurance has for old people or people with preexisting disease usually introduces adverse selection of risk.

Private medical insurance comes under three broad areas of organizational sponsorship: (1) the private insurance industry, such as Metropolitan and Aetna, (2) provider-sponsored, such as Blue Cross, State Hospital Association; Blue Shield, State Medical Association; Delta-Dental, State Dental Association; and (3) independent, such as union-sponsored or consumer co-ops. The fastest growing and largest insurer is the private insurance industry. There are almost half again as many private health insurance policies in force as there are Blue Cross/Blue Shield policies. The continued growth in health insurance has resulted in third-party payments now covering two-thirds of personal health expenses, as opposed to approximately 30 percent in 1950. Stated another way, while health insurance has grown rapidly, 35 percent of the cost of medical care must still come directly from the consumer, as out-of-pocket cost.

There are two major management mechanisms involved in the disbursement of funds under health insurance plans: cash-indemnity plans, and service plans. The first diagram below indicates disbursement under the indemnity plan. In this mechanism, an individual visits the provider and then receives a certain amount of cash from the plan, which he pays to the provider for services rendered. Frequently, the provider will ask the subscriber to assign the payment to him, so that the provider collects directly from the plan. This formula is most commonly seen in the private insurance sector.

The service plan is illustrated in the following diagram. The subscriber pays the premium to the plan, and the provider then bills the plan.

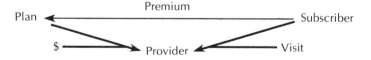

This type of plan is more common in the Blue Cross/Blue Shield plans and many of the independents, such as the union-sponsored plans. Both of these mechanisms have advantages and disadvantages.

Why are private insurance policies growing so rapidly and maintaining a lead over the Blues and the independent plans? There are four major reasons: more aggressive sales of policies; more flexibility in the plans; encouragement of individual enrollment; and their function as a "loss-leader," so that the company loses money on its health insurance to obtain life insurance on the same person.

The pressures of the private health insurance are toward the "classic insurance" model, as in life or auto insurance. The characteristics of this insurance model are that the risk is precisely defined, there is a significant magnitude of loss, the risk occurs infrequently, the occurrence is unwanted, the occurrence is beyond control of the insured, and existence of insurance does not increase utilization. Medical insurance obviously does not fit this model because it is sometimes difficult to define the risk; there are small, repeated losses rather than one major loss; medical care is a wanted service; the insured person controls the amount of medical care he receives; and people with medical insurance use the system more than those without it. This latter point is called the "moral hazard" of health insurance.

The pressure then is for commercial insurance to make medical care insurance better fit the classical model. This is done through a number of means, such as limited enrollment periods, physical exams prior to issuing the policy, cost-sharing arrangements, and insuring hospital care rather than out-patient physician care. In spite of the growth that has been projected in the amount of private and public health insurance, the type of benefits provided remains uneven. Figure 7.3 lists the types of benefits and the percent of the population covered by these various benefits. The figures in all categories have increased somewhat since 1970, when this figure was current. For example, in 1973 nearly 90 percent of hospital expenses were covered by third party payors, but only 61 percent of physician services and 14 percent of dental services were covered.

It is also important to point out that insurance coverage varies by several demographic characteristics. Such variations are responsible for influencing the proportion of family income spent on health care. For example, in families with an income under $2,000, 12.6 percent of that income was consumed by medical care in 1970, as opposed to only 3.5 percent for families with an income of $7,500 and over.

Public insurance for medical care costs is based on Medicare and Medicaid. The development of Medicare and Medicaid was a slow evolutionary process and represented a great many compromises along the way. Medicare is comprised of two parts: Part A, Hospital and Basic Coverage; and Part

**Figure 7.3**
HEALTH INSURANCE BENEFITS

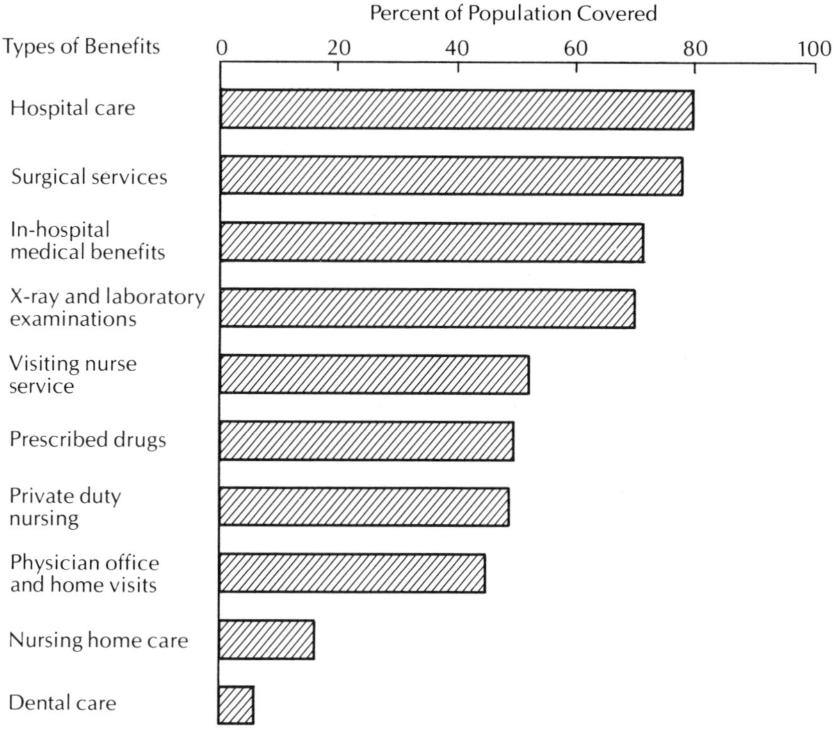

Percent of Population Covered

Source: Kolodrudetz 1972.

B, Supplemental Medical Insurance. Medicare is financed by deduction through Social Security taxes. These deductions are placed in a trust fund against which disbursements are made. In order to examine Parts A and B, it is important to look at them on the basis of coverage, premium, major type, and benefits.

Part A is universally available for everyone over sixty-five years of age and those individuals under sixty-five who are disabled or have end-stage renal disease. The total insurance premium is paid up at the time the individual reaches sixty-five years of age or is declared disabled. It is not necessary to pay any additional premiums. Part A of Medicare is a service policy and is usually administered through an "intermediary," such as an insurance company. The intermediary is responsible for receiving bills and disbursing funds. The basic benefit structure under Part A of Medicare includes hospitalization, post-hospital home health service, and the use of skilled nursing facilities. Part A of Medicare does not include co-insurance, payment of a fixed percentage of the total bill by the patient. However, it does include deductibles, the amount of money that must be paid prior to the insurance scheme beginning to pay for care. Medicare also limits the number of days that may be spent in a hospital or a skilled nursing facility or the number of visits by a home health service. Under Part A of Medicare, the patient must stay in an acute hospital prior to being admitted to a skilled nursing facility or a home health service.

In Part B of Medicare the coverage is voluntary, and a monthly premium must be paid by the subscriber. Part B is a cash-indemnity plan in which the basic benefits include physician and other professional out-patient services and home health services without the patient's having had prior hospitalization. Part B includes not only a deductible, but also a co-insurance. These deductibles and co-insurance must be independently collected by the provider. Because of the deductibles, co-insurance, and uninsured benefits, as an aggregate, Medicare covers only about fifty percent of the total costs of medical care for individuals over sixty-five years of age.

The Medicaid program, unlike Medicare, is a joint federal–state program in which the state determines eligibility and benefits and serves as administrator of the program. The federal government contributes a share of the total cost of the Medicaid program, based on a formula reflecting the state's poverty level.

The recipients of Medicaid benefits fall into two broad groups: categorically needy, and medically needy. All states participating in Medicaid are required to assume responsibility for the categorically needy. These include individuals who receive cash payments for their subsistence, such as old age assistance, aid to needy blind and permanently and totally disabled, and aid to families with dependent children. The medically needy are those individuals who are eligible under one of the four public assistance categories outlined above, whose income is adequate to provide food, clothing, and shelter but inadequate to cover the cost of medical care. The income requirement varies from state to state and from year to year.

To receive federal funds for Medicaid, all programs must include certain benefits: (1) in-patient hospital care; (2) out-patient hospital services; (3) laboratory and X-ray services; (4) extended care facilities; (5) early and periodic screening, diagnosis, and treatment of defects in eligible children; (6) family planning services; and (7) physician services. Additional services may be provided at the discretion of the state, such as care by podiatrists and chiropractors, home health services, private duty nursing, dental services, physical therapy services, drugs, dentures, or eyeglasses, tuberculosis or mental hospital care, transporation, whole blood, Christian Science sanitoria, emergency hospital services, and intermediate care facility services. In addition to those services provided for by Medicare and Medicaid, Medicaid will pay the Medicare deductible, co-insurance, and premiums for persons receiving old age assistance benefits.

**Health Maintenance Organization**   One additional financing mechanism is the health maintenance organization (HMO). The HMO operates somewhat like the insurance company but is usually a management system involving physicians, hospitals, and allied health personnel. In the HMO a prospective payment is made to the organization to cover the total cost of medical care. If the amount paid by the individual or family is more than the cost incurred for care, the profits received as a result of this are usually divided among the providers of care. Proponents of this system point out that it creates a situation in which benefits can accrue to the providers as a result of economies in their care of the patient.

The principal economy that has been realized is a decrease in the number of patient-days of hospitalization. The Kaiser-Permanente Plan, one of the largest health maintenance organizations, has demonstrated that they can substantially decrease the number of hospital days, and they point out that their patient-to-bed ratio of 2.2:1,000 is half the national average (Warsinger et al. 1976). There has been a rapid growth in the HMO movement. This has been the result of increased federal funding for development as well as the requirement that firms with over twenty-five employees offer a health maintenace organization as an alternate to more traditional private insurance, if an approved plan is available within the community.

## ORGANIZATION

Paul Elwood (1972) contrasted three models of organization of the health care system: the central planning model, the health maintenance organization model, and the professional model. Because health maintenance organizations were briefly considered under financing mechanisms and there are many who feel that HMO is more a financing system than an organizational system, it will not be discussed in this section.

Elwood defines the professional model as the existing health care system, with physician domination being its most important characteristic. The patient chooses the physician, and the physician arranges for and handles the remainder of activities in the care of that patient. The industry revolves around a series of small independent firms with little or no vertical integration of services. The economic characteristics of the professional model are such that a series of separate financial transactions occur following each contact of the consumer with the health care system. Prices are determined by the providers, either in terms of usual, customary, and reasonable fees or on a cost-plus basis, in the case of hospitals.

The central planning model, in contrast, is based on the idea that there should be political control over resource allocation and planning, rather than the market system allocating resources as it does in the professional system. This model attempts to develop a reasonable vertical integration of all the components of the health care system, including physicians, hospitals, nursing homes, and the like. It revolves around progressively complex levels of care, including regional medical centers, district hospitals, and primary or ambulatory care units based on geographic area, population, and estimated need for services in each of these areas. The economic characteristics of this system focus around resource allocations from some regional or national group. This model advocates a centralized method of paying for medical care, such as a national health insurance.

Basic assumptions underlying these two models should be examined briefly. The professional model assumes that physicians have a high body of technical knowledge and that they are the only ones who can organize and govern the health services system; that the consumer knows when he needs medical care and is free to select the physician of his choice; that the demand for medical care is directly related to fees for rendering medical services, which are, in turn, directly related to needs; and that the distribution, both geographic and specialty of health services, would correct itself if there were an increase in the supply of physicians.

The central planning model reflects some other assumptions: that physicians will not locate, either geographically or by specialty, in the most appropriate way for consumers; that reliance on the traditional price system of resource allocation has resulted not in a decrease of cost but rather in unnecessary duplication of services with a concomitant increase in cost; that Western European health systems have been very effective in controlling infant mortality and other indicators of health status and that we would do well to emulate them; and that public planning bodies can and will design a much more efficient and effective system. Elwood points out that the question of control is a very sticky one. There are some who believe that consumer control is possible and even important, whereas others believe that planning and allocation are very technical activities and require professional planners. These are clearly two competing models of the health care system, and each of them has significant subsets.

One of the major subsets of the professional model is group practice. The United States has seen progressive increases in group practice. In 1960 only 5 percent of physicians were involved in group practice, as opposed to almost 20 percent in the mid-1970s. Physicians are increasingly attracted to group practice because it offers more free time, greater professional contact and consultation, a lower initial outlay of money to buy and equip a building, and financial support until the practice develops.

The recent passage of Public Law 94–641 empowers the development of health systems agencies. These agencies have their roots in the comprehensive health planning councils, which were themselves the offshoot of the Hill–Burton advisory committees.

The intent of the comprehensive health planning councils and subsequently the health systems agencies is to involve consumers in decisions about resource allocations. Although the health systems agencies are required to have a decision-making board with more than 50 percent consumers, the low level of technical knowledge usually possessed by consumers and the fact that they have less interest in the issues than have the providers frequently resulted in provider domination of these boards. In addition, the old comprehensive health planning councils had very little authority in most states. The health systems agencies legislation, however has changed a number of those features.

These regional bodies will have the responsibility for approving any and all capital construction requests in excess of $100,000, and the issuance of certificates of need for new facilities within the region. The control that can be imposed for the construction of nonconforming beds is that Medicare and Medicaid will not pay for patients occupying these nonconforming beds. Similarly, the health systems agencies will now have the authority to approve or disapprove any and all federal grant funds expended within a region for health care. In addition, resources are to be allocated to the health systems agencies that they, in turn, can allocate to various activities and programs, according to a previously established set of priorities. Certainly the health systems agencies legislation is a major step toward implementation of the central planning model developed in the preceding section. At one time it was even suggested that these regional bodies be responsible for setting the reimbursement rates in the various components of the health care system, particularly hospitals. In the future, it is likely that more responsibility will be given to the health systems agencies for decisions about resource allocation.

## CONSUMERS

For many years, hospital boards have served as one method for assuring community input into professional decisions concerning medical care institutions. This role was institutionalized even further with the implementation of the Hill–Burton legislation, which required consumer participation. Similarly, involving consumers in medical care decisions had further impetus with the development of the OEO-funded neighborhood health centers. This legislation called for maximum feasible participation in the administration of the centers by its patients. The most recent step in the consumer movement is the requirement that the majority of health planning council boards, and their descendant, the health system agency boards, will be comprised of consumers. Thus, we have seen the institutionalization and legitimizing of consumer involvement in various levels of decision making about medical services. While much controversy exists about the extent to which consumers can effectively involve themselves in health planning and decision making, evidence has demonstrated that consumers, even in rural isolated areas, are sophisticated enough to recognize, as readily as providers, the major health issues which confront them.

Kane and Kane (1974) have defined the five steps in the development of programs to assure improved health services. These are identification of community health problems; development of alternates; choice of a solution; implementation; and evaluation. It is clear that the consumer and the provider will share in each of these steps to different degrees. The consumer can and should have a major voice in identifying a community's health problems. They, after all, are the recipients of the services and understand the various medical care problems which confront them. As much as possible, information should be generated from objective data as well as from the community to assure that the problems selected by a group are, in fact, representative of the basic problem. The development of alternates, including cost-benefit analyses and advantages and disadvantages of alternates are related to technical input and should be provided by outside consultants. The choice of a solution should be a shared responsibility between consumers and the providers who must implement it. Just as there is a planning and control cycle in the business community, so should there be one in the health community. The model we have described will assure consumer involvement in the total health care system. Through this method we will more likely achieve a more responsive system and one that more appropriately meets the needs of the community.

## SUMMARY

Within this chapter we have attempted to define and understand health in its broader context. To repeat: health, as defined by the World Health Organization, is a complete state of mental, physical, and social well-being, and not merely the absence of disease. Thus health interrelates with other systems of human services. This chapter has attempted to delineate the difficulties with this definition of health, particularly as it relates to our current system of care. There is more to health than just the medical care system. However, major energies, expenditures, time, and effort currently are focused on the very narrow therapeutic and curative aspect of health care. Very little attention is focused, by our current medical care system, on outside forces which can and will make a significant impact on the total health of the individual and the community. Recognizing these difficulties, I have attempted, using a system structure suggested by Kissick, to develop a broader understanding of the medical care system by looking at the various components of manpower, facilities, technology, organization, financing, and consumers in medicine.

Perhaps through a broader understanding of the total system, its interrelationships and workings, there can be a striving for a more thorough integration of other components of human services in the health care system. Perhaps we can assure that those individuals responsible for services other than medical care can most appropriately draw on the medical care resources to deal with the physical concerns of their clients. In addition, perhaps this understanding of the broader context of health will enable providers and potential providers of health services to cultivate a broader understanding of the social and mental components of the health care system and their importance to the total health of the people they serve.

## REFERENCES

Bureau of the Census. 1972. *Statistical Abstracts of the United States, 1971* 83:62.
Bureau of Vital Statistics. 1975. *Prevalence of Selected Impairments, United States, 1971.* Series 10–99, Rockville, Md.: Department of Health, Education, and Welfare.

Demens, J. L., D. Lawrence and W. B. Collen, 1976. *Educating New Practitioners; The Medex Northwest Approach.* Seattle: Medex Northwest.

DuBose, R. 1959. *Mirage of Health.* Garden City, N. J.: Doubleday Anchor Books.

Elwood, P. M. 1972. Models for organizing health services and implications of legislative proposals. *Milbank Memorial Fund Quarterly* 50:67–95.

Holmes, T. G. and R. H. Ray. 1967. Social readjustment rating scale. *Journal of Psychosomatic Research* 11: 213–218.

Kane, R. A. and R. L. Kane. 1974. Galloping consumption: Consumer participation in health programs. In Robert L. Kane, ed., *Challenges of Community Medicine.* New York: Springer.

Kissick, W. L. 1971 Health policy directions for the 70's. *New England Journal of Medicne* 282: 1343–1354.

Kolodrudetz, W. W. 1972. *Social Security Bulletin* 35:1.

Levine, D. M. et al. 1976. The role of new health practices in a prepaid group practice. *Medical Care* 326–347.

Scutchfield, F. D. 1976. Physician recruitment: A proposal for the community and the health science center. *Medical Digest* 22: 11–18.

Terris, M. 1975. Approaches to an epidemiology of health. *American Journal of Public Health* 65: 1037–1045.

Warsinger, R. et al. 1976. Inpatient hospital utilization in three prepaid comprehensive health plans compared with a regular Blue Cross plan. *Medical Care* 14: 721–731.

White, K. 1973. *Life, Death and Medicine: Scientific American.* San Francisco: W. H. Freeman.

WHO. 1960. Constitution. Geneva: World Health Organization.

HEW. 1972. *Health United States 1971.* Publication no. (ARA) 76–1232. Rockville, Md.: Department of Health, Education, and Welfare.

# 8

# THE MUTUAL-HELP
# MOVEMENT

Connections between members of various groups within a society have long been recognized and referred to by a variety of terms. Not uncommon have been such words as networks, primary and secondary groups, cliques, social systems, action sets, and social fabrics. But the conceptualization and study of such interconnections as a system of service delivery are more recent developments. The concept is now attracting increasing and widespread attention.

## HELPING NETWORKS: GENERAL CONSIDERATIONS

The development of network analysis can be traced from the exploratory work of three English anthropologists, J. A. Barnes, Elizabeth Bott, and J. Clyde Mitchell in the early 1950s. A definition of a network evolved from these efforts: "a specific set of linkages among a defined set of persons, with the . . . property that the characteristics of these linkages as a whole may be used to interpret the social behavior of the persons involved" (Mitchell 1969). A more recent text on natural helping networks has been written by Collins and Pancoast (1976). It describes the network as either a personal type—which refers to the individual member—or as a general type—which describes the perspective of an outside observer.

Craven and Wellmen (1973) have described three aspects of networks that are theoretically useful: density, range, and pathways. If all the relationships in a network are known, its density can be expressed as the ratio of actual to potential links in a network. "Range" refers to the number of individuals involved in a network. Range and density can vary independently.

A path that consists of an indirect link between one individual and another through at least one intermediary can be an important access to resources outside the individual's immediate circle of contacts; this serves to extend the range of a network. Relatively dense networks are generally small, and the linkages among the members quite strong. Loosely knit networks tend to be large, and their members less deeply involved with one another. In general, large loosely knit networks appear to expedite access to tangible resources, while dense networks with strong ties expedite access to intangible, emotional resources. However, loosely knit networks sometimes supply more tangible resources in an emergency or crisis situation. Craven and Wellmen find these variables particularly useful as generalizations about the variables relevant to network analysis. The research on natural support systems has concentrated on such global characteristics as the concept of social support and its relationship to mental health.

In the sociological and anthropological literature, density has been identified as the most important structural feature of social networks (see Whitten and Wolfe 1973). Mitchell (1969) defined density as the total number of relationships within an individual's social network as a proportion of the total possible number of such relationships. Thus, if all the members of a person's social network are also friends with each other, density = 1; if none is friendly to another, density = 0.

Hirsch (1977) empirically examined the utility of this concept. The purpose of his research was to assess the effect of density on the quality of emotional support, using students' final examinations as an environmentally imposed stress factor. His measurements consisted of a social network questionnaire and a daily interaction rating form. In the questionnaire his subjects listed, in matrix form, up to fifteen significant others with whom they were likely to interact at least twice daily during any two- or three-week period. They also indicated, with an "x" whether these people were themselves friends with each other, using the same criteria employed in the initial list. Density was calculated by the formula, "Let $x$ = the number of $x$'s on the matrix, and let N = the number of people listed in the social network (SN). Then density = $x$ (N-1)/2N.

On the interaction rating form, the students were asked to record daily the quantity and quality of the social and emotional support they received. Emotional support was operationalized as interactions that involved sharing feelings or personal concerns.

The study showed that the level of stress significantly affected three variables: (1) the total amount of social support received, as measured by the total time spent with others; (2) the number of people from whom emotional support was received and the time spent with them, as measured by the lengths and frequencies of interactions that involved the sharing of feelings or personal concerns; and (3) satisfaction with the emotional support received, as measured by satisfaction expressed with that aspect of their interactions that involved the disclosure of feelings or personal concerns. Density had a wide ranging effect on the variables: students in high-density social networks received significantly more social and emotional support than did students in low-density social networks. Moreover, higher levels of density decreased the probability of communicating empathically, resulting in decreased satisfaction. This kind of study suggests that natural social networks provide considerable social and emotional support for individuals under stress. Future research should use these variables in assessing a greater variety of populations.

Individuals usually belong simultaneously to a number of networks. These can be based on kinship, friendship, employment, recreation, education, politics, ethnicity, religion, or whatever other interests or elements people have in common. Within the area of helping networks, these groups can take on positive and negative balances. For example, a negative network might consist of juveniles committed to a juvenile detention center, or of preadolescent boys living in a high-risk crime housing project or attending a junior high school in a low-income area where the norm is truancy and disruptive behavior in the classroom. The association of any individual with this network is likely to result in his taking negative qualities of the particular group; the entire network will have an adverse effect on individuals within it.

Positive helping networks may be thought of as the opposite of juvenile gangs. Examples of such groups include those involved in a Big Brothers program; Alateen, a mutual-help group for adolescent alcohol abusers or children of alcoholics; and La Leche League, a group of mothers reaching out to new mothers interested in learning about specific methods of newborn care.

"Networks" refer to the various individuals each of us turns to for coping with daily and more serious problems of living. They are not groups. They often do not know each other. They are a combination of people we look to in helping to solve a problem: a spouse, a neighbor, friends, relatives and co-workers. Together they form the "natural helping networks" of an individual. Research shows that these social bonds provide 80 percent of problem coping for the average person. This compares with only 20 percent for doctors, clergy, teachers, police, social workers, and mental health professionals.

Life stresses, crises, and transitions may challenge some individuals but overwhelm others. Recent evidence shows that those who have social supports are protected in crisis from a wide variety of pathological states, both mental and physical. It is thought that these supports buffer the individual from the potentially negative effects of undergoing crises and changes and can facilitate coping and adaptation. It may be possible to provide additional social supports to those lacking them and thereby mitigate some of the potentially negative outcomes of life stress (President's Task Panel on Community Support Systems 1978).

Dumont (1967) has described an unrecognized mutual help network among a tavern population, which is as foreign to most human service workers as are peoples in remote places studied by anthropologists. The tavern was described by Dumont as offering homeless men the "only home" they had, a place affording a sense of belonging and physical comfort that their lives would otherwise lack. Since they had long been alienated from their families and had little or no identity as part of a labor force, these men had only each other as a reference group. The bartender was also the proprietor of the boarding house for single men and had a central position in the network. Men frequented the bar only when he was there and asked him to handle their welfare checks. They borrowed money from him when they were destitute and accepted his regulation of their drinking and "pesty" manners. The bartender had to differentiate between his roles as friend and landlord and at the same time remain sensitive to the emotional and physical needs of the men and demonstrate a willingness to invest effort in trying to solve their problems.

Shapiro (1969) described buildings offering single-rooms occupancy. Here the neighborhood was organized around tenants in a building. Small groups served familylike functions. Each of these groups had its own leaders, in spite of the severe physical and emotional problems among them. Shapiro found expressive and forceful personalities and a wide range of emotions displayed toward members of their "families" and toward those outsiders with whom they had built close relationships. The leaders had established rapport with outside sources of power whenever possible. They made contact with local policemen, welfare investigators, managers, and other service people on whom the tenants depended. Sometimes a mutual bargaining process developed between the leader and the service people, and a byproduct was better service to the tenants.

## SUPPORT SYSTEMS

The nature of helping networks as social support systems is really not a new phenomenon. On the contrary, the support system has operated for centuries. However, it has not been used consistently by human service workers as a viable strategy and approach to reaching individuals and groups of people in need. Professor Gerald Caplan (1974) of Harvard University was one of the first to rediscover its value and bring it to the attention of human service professionals. Support systems essentially offer an alternative and possibly complementary service delivery system to that of the institutionalized, bureaucratized system.

The term "support system" denotes an enduring pattern of continuous or intermittent relationships, connections, or networks that play a significant part in maintaining the psychological and physical integrity of the individual over time. The various elements of the support system may be spontaneous; that is, it need not be organized in a planned way by someone who is interested in promoting the health of the individual or the population. It emerges, rather, from the needs of the individual and the natural biosocial responses of the people in his community or from the values and traditions of his culture in society.

Natural support systems have been regarded as the reason for much "spontaneous remission" of psychological systems (Bergin 1971;), as well as an important contribution to the rehabilitation of the exhospital patient (Fairweather et al. 1969). More recently, the possible role of natural support systems in the prevention of mental disorder has received increased attention (Kelly et al. 1977). It is hypothesized that individuals with strong natural support systems are less likely to develop psychological and physiological symptoms under stress than are individuals with weak or nearly nonexistent support systems (Cassel 1975; Kaplan, Cassel, and Gore 1973; Schulberg and Killilea 1982).

**Functions**  Several studies have attempted to investigate more directly the relationship between social support and mental health. Maddison found that measures of social support were able to differentiate healthy from nonfunctional outcomes in widows (Maddison and Walker 1967), while Tolsdorf (1976) found that hospitalized schizophrenics had fewer supportive relationships and valued supports less than did nonpsychiatric hospital patients.

In an unorganized or disorganized society, such spontaneous support systems may be inadequate, especially for marginal people. And it is particularly in such situations and for such people that community-based feedback is likely to be insufficient—and the need for individually oriented support systems greatest. In these cases, the risk of illness will be the highest unless someone takes special steps to organize a planned support system to fill the gap.

Caplan (1974) has emphasized the importance of considering the health-promoting functions of such social units and has suggested the use of the term "support system" to refer to such spontaneous and organized social arrangements that aid individuals in coping with a wide variety of crises, life transitions, and other problems-in-living. Natural support systems include family and friendship groups, local informal caregivers, voluntary service groups not directed by caregiving professionals, and mutual-help groups.

He described support systems as groups of social aggregates that provide individuals with opportunities for feedback about themselves and for validations of their expectations about others. Support systems may thus offset deficiencies in these communications within the larger community context. People have a variety of specific needs that demand satisfaction through enduring interpersonal relationships—needs for love and attention, for intimacy that provides the freedom to express feelings easily and unself-consciously, for validation of personal identity and worth, for satisfaction of nurturance and dependency, for help with tasks, and for support in handling emotions and controlling impulses.

Most people develop and maintain a sense of well-being by involving themselves in a range of relationships that together satisfy these specific needs. Such relationships are diverse and include marriage, parenthood, other forms of loving and intimate ties, friendships, and membership in religious congregations and social, cultural, political, and recreational associations. Other relationships include those with colleagues and workers; acquaintanceship with neighbors, shopkeepers, and providers of services; intermittent relationships of a health-seeking nature from professional caregivers such as doctors, nurses, lawyers, and social workers; and continuing dependence for education and guidance on teachers, clergymen, intellectuals, and community leaders and men and women of authority and influence.

A special attribute of these buffering relationships is that the person is dealt with as a unique individual. Other people are interested in him in a personal way. They speak his language. They tell him what is expected of him and guide him in what to do. From this point of view, feedback is provided in two ways: first, individuals may collect and store information about cues in the outside world and offer guidance and direction to the individual so that he can find safe paths to travel and interpret in a balanced, reality-based way, feedback cues that would otherwise be incomprehensible to him. Second, such relationships may act as a refuge or sanctuary to which the individual may return for rest and recuperation between his sorties into the stressful environment—a kind of island of stability and comfort in the turbulent sea of daily life.

An individual who is fortunate enough to have several supportive and social ties strategically situated in the community, at home and at work, in church, and in a series of recreational sites may move from one to the other throughout the day and be almost entirely buffered against the stressful world.

Unfortunately, the term "support" often has negative connotations, associated with weakness. The concept that should be advocated is not one of pampering or offering refuge to an individual in danger, but rather one of augmenting a person's strength so as to facilitate his mastery of his environment.

The term "system" expresses more than an occasional or fortuitous relationship or aspect of a social association. Toffler wrote in *Future Shock* (1970), about the rapidity of changing relationships, environments, demands for goods and materials, and mobility in a technological society. Understandably, a need exists for a continuity of social aggregates to provide members of a community with opportunities for feedback about themselves to validate about their expectations about others. These functions may offset deficiencies in communications within the larger environmental and institutional context.

The purpose of feedback within the framework of support systems is to provide consistent, rather than confusing, communication on expectations, assistance, evaluation of performance, and reinforcements. The dimensions for understanding support systems include (1) time, a more or less enduring set of relationships (support in critical problems-of-living or short-term supporters); (2) elements for supporters (help to mobilize resources or assistance in tasks, to provide extra supplies such as money, materials, and food), (3) direction (support in seeking out or taking refuge or resting); and (4) frequency (continuous or intermittent support leading to steady-state maintenance).

**Classification**   In order to understand better the complexity and dimensions of support systems, three broad classifications are proposed: (1) natural and spontaneous support systems; (2) organized support systems not directed by professionals; and (3) organized support systems influenced by professionals in human service organizations. The natural and spontaneous support system is comprised of informal caregivers who may be either generalists or specialists. The generalist is recognized in the neighborhood as being knowledgeable about people and community services. This person may be a pharmacist in a drugstore, a manager of a grocery storey, a beautician or hairdresser, a bartender in a tavern, or a policeman in the neighborhood. Often these generalists have emotional problems of their own, but they are nonetheless sought out by others in the community as offering supportive assistance.

Specialists in the natural and spontaneous support system are those individuals known to be "in the same boat"; they have their own personal experiences with the problems of the person needing help. Such people are often known as specialized local informal helpers. For example, in the adjustment of parents who have given birth to a premature or retarded baby, other parents who have themselves gone through a similar experience may make themselves available for assistance. Offering help to others going through a similar experience is a highly adaptive way of coping and crisis resolution for the helper. As another example, widows are often more helpful to the bereaved family than are friends and physicians who urge the widowed person to "keep a stiff upper lip." By contrast, those who have lost spouses are likely to encourage others in the same situation to go through the grieving and mourning processes because they have "been there" themselves.

The characteristics of natural and spontaneous support systems are as follows: (1) direct person-to-person influence; (2) authenticity and spontaneity, rather than scientific knowledge; (3) coordinated, rather than hierarchal or super-subordinate, relationships, with no "put downs"; (4) a mutual and reciprocal quality in the interactions in which there is a giver and receiver, both of whom benefit from the contact; (5) a voluntary arrangement between the helper and helped and the absence of any kind of financial payment; and (6) intimacy, in which sincerity and personalized attention with loving kindness are offered, with the relationship of interpersonal boundaries being more intimate than they would be in the office of a professional. In the latter situation, one can observe an egalitarian atmosphere that is nonjudgmental in its sharing of the problems of daily living.

The second type of support system organizes support groups that are not directed by professionals and includes the subcategories of voluntary service groups, mutual-help associations, and religious denominations. Examples of voluntary service groups include the American Association of Retired Persons, which has initiated innovative service projects in which volunteers give service to specific groups in trouble. There are also many voluntary service groups in which organized student volunteers work in mental hospitals, nursing homes, and underprivileged neighborhoods.

Mutual-help associations include such groups as Alcoholics Anonymous, Parents Without Partners, widows' associations, Disabled War Veterans, mastectomy and ileostomy associations, Parents of Retarded Children, and various counterculture groups that form as a result of the perceived ineffectiveness of professional caregivers. A mutual-help group may be defined as a group or organization in which membership is limited to people with a common problem. The members use their common experience to find solutions to their problems or to learn from each other ways of dealing with it. To qualify as a helper in such a program, one has to have coped successfully with the same problems and to be willing to use the experience to help others. The programs are run by members, for members (Silverman 1972). "Old-timers" help the newcomers to master crises and provide social contacts and activities that serve as psychosocial replacements and attachments. No longer are these individuals with problems perceived by others as "deviant," and social isolation and depression may thus be avoided.

Religious denominations comprise the third category of mutual-help groups. Such congregations are located in every neighborhood; regular meetings and broad ranges of activities are offered. Theology, values, traditions, common identity, and cohesion provide service programs to reach people in times of crises.

Human services organizations can also play a significant role in developing helping networks. Professional caregivers may organize or initiate new support systems by working within or outside of a particular identified group of individuals; or they may consult with an already existing, already organized social support system.

The organization of a new support system may take place within a community institution such as the Helping the Helpers to Help Program in the Episcopal church, described by Caplan (1972), or within a school system such as the training of junior high students as peer counselors which has been used to help sixth graders in making the transition from elementary to junior high school.

The qualifications of a successful human service consultant include his knowledge and skills in crisis intervention; expertise in guidance; ability to organize peer groups in which individuals "in the same boat" can be brought together for mutual problem solving; emotional support through shared successes and failures; the ability to moderate discussions with outside leaders of higher status; and the ability to provide a reference point or group supports in terms of ideology and problem solving for normative behavior.

Human service professionals may provide program development skills within or outside any institution. An example of the latter is the widely recognized project of Phyllis Silverman known as the Widow-to-Widow Program (1972). Consultation may also be provided to existing groups, as in the support system for alienated and runaway youths in Chicago called Looking Glass. Here, a staff of young people has benefited from mental health consultation at the case and administrative levels. This is an example of an organized group that needs and accepts assistance. In contrast, there are unorganized existing groups that reject professional input and influence.

A number of studies describe the social support system. These studies document the existence of an informal support system for the elderly. While the scope of these studies varies, there are important commonalities that are helpful for practitioners and policy makers concerned with relating to informal support systems in an effort to provide more effective services to the elderly population at high risk.

## SELF-HELP GROUPS

The development and rapid proliferation of self-help groups may be seen as a natural evolution—meeting specialized needs of our modern society, given the decline of traditional integrating and bonding structures such as the family, the church, the neighborhood, and the formal caregiving institutions. Sidel and Sidel (1976) offer the following perspective:

> The self-help and mutual aid movement is a response to a number of different factors in our society which make human services unavailable or unresponsive to those who need them: the pervasiveness of technology and its rate of development, the complexity and size of institution and communities, with their ac-

companying depersonalization and dehumanization; the alienation of people from one another, from their communities and institutions, and even from themselves; and the professionalization of much which in the past was done by individuals for themselves or for one another. (p. 67)

Some basic characteristics of groups may be identified within the mutual-help and support system network (Killilea 1976): common experiences of members; mutual help and support; the helper principle; differential association; collective willpower and belief; the importance of information; and constructive action toward shared goals.

The characteristic of *common experience of members* consists of the sharing of personal problems—defining membership status in the self-help groups despite many individual differences. A peer and self-help group thus has a commonality or mutuality of concerns with others (Katz 1970). Silverman (1970) believes that the primary characteristics of mutual-help associations are "that a recipient of service can change roles to become a caregiver; and all policy and program is decided by a membership whose chief qualification is that they at one time qualified and were recipients of the services of the organization (p. 547).

The second element is that of *mututal help and support,* as exemplified in Recovery, Inc. Lenneberg and Rowbotham (1970) note that the successful expatient can demonstrate a good outcome for the patient currently suffering from a hazardous or stigmatized condition. Mutual exchange is a central process in each of the following stages:

Stage 1. Contact between individuals with a common problem: identification.

Stage 2. Expansion of the identification with another individual into identification with a group: passive acceptance of the program.

Stage 3. Expansion of group identification into identification with its program: active participation.

Reassurance and goals for both the patients and the caretakers are established when the expatient appears in person; his degree of success becomes temporarily the model. Access to such a model promotes the visualization of the self with the condition, and when the model has been successful, positive identification can take place in the patient. This mechanism of the psyche, which happens in all human situations, is the root of mutual aid between troubled and previously troubled people.

The third characteristic, that of the *helper principle,* has been described by Riessman (1965), to find ways to transform recipients of help into dispensers of help, thus reversing their roles, and to structure the situation so that recipients of help will be placed in roles requiring the giving of assistance (p. 28). Skovholt (1974) summarized the benefits received from helping others into four factors that make the helper-therapy principle potent:

1. The effective helper often feels an increased level of interpersonal competence as a result of making an impact on another's life.
2. The effective helper often feels a sense of equality in giving and taking between himself or herself and others.
3. The effective helper is often the recipient of valuable personalized learning acquired while working with a helpee.
4. The effective helper often receives social approval from the people he or she helps. (p. 62).

The fourth element, that of *differential association,* is based on Sutherland's (1974) theory and a general symbolic interactionist theory (Cressey 1955: 118–119). These theories are formally summarized in Cressey's principles dealing with the use of anticriminal groups as a medium of change. For example,

> If criminals are to be changed, they must be assimilated into groups which emphasize values conducive to law-abiding behavior and concurrently alienated from groups emphasizing values conducive to criminality. Since our experience has been that the majority of criminals experience great difficulty in securing intimate contacts in ordinary groups, special groups whose major common goal is that of reformation of criminals must be created.

The fifth element in group change, *collective willpower and belief,* is based upon the notion of persuasive power, in which each person looks to others for validation of his attitudes and feelings. Hansell (1972) discovered in his research of TOPS that part of its group philosophy is that "everyone can lose weight." With the decision, willpower, stick-to-itiveness, concentration of energies on it, and the help of friends and TOPS members, one can achieve and maintain a target weight—they constantly correct each other, looking for "hocus-pocus methods" or "blue-sky schemes." They establish reducing pals to assist each other. In specific rituals, the members stand in a circle and covenant each other to assist in their purposes. They watch over any person who makes headway and then stops for any reason. They assist each other when an individual waivers in resolve, challenging him to recommit himself to a decision of extraordinary importance. They give each other what they term willpower booster shots.

The sixth characteristic refers to the *importance of information.* Education is the process of promoting greater understanding, addressing the facts on the problem, associated conditions, and solution of the problem. The information is technical and serves as an agent for anticipatory guidance on the expectable problems and phases that one goes through in relating to the problem.

Ladas (1971) hypothesized that women, with support and information of the type given by La Leche, would have a better outcome in regard to breast-feeding than most women without them. She found that her hypotheses were confirmed: information relates to outcome of breast-feeding. Support related to outcome. Any combination of information and support relates more highly to outcome than either alone. Some support, even with opposition, was as effective as much support.

Ablon (1974) studied Al-Anon groups, finding that the transmission of information in its own specialized form is the most prominent process element in the Al-Anon experience. The sharing and exchange of strategies for, and reaction to, common problems provides alternatives for the new member to consider, to choose for use if she wishes, or to reject. The very act of consideration of these as presented by others provides a basis for graphic comparison with our own typical modes of operation, and the stimulation for the process of self-examination leading to new insights.

The seventh element identified by Killilea is that of *constructive action toward shared goals*. Activities help to overcome a greater sense of personal responsibility. The emphasis is upon doing rather than on intellectual pursuits or emotional cathartic release (Barish 1971). Toch (1965) states,

> One service every self-change movement seems to provide is to build a fire under its members by stressing the intolerability of their fate. By spelling out the undesirable consequences of the member's condition, the movement defines his problem. The result is to reinforce the member's conviction that he must take action. The next step is to demonstrate that action is feasible, and that the goal is attainable. Self-help as a group process is a social movement to collectively promote individual change. (pp. 83–84)

**Professionalism**   Gartner and Riessman's more recent book, *Self-Help in the Human Services* (1977) uses the terms "self-help groups," "mutual-aid groups," and "mutual-support groups" synonymously. They characterize this approach as an "important advance in human service technology," a new form of service that is productive, nonbureaucratic, and aprofessional. The term "aprofessional" is used to refer to interventions that are generally based on experience, intuition, and common sense rather than on systematic knowledge. The emphasis of Gartner and Riessman is upon the relationship of the aprofessional to the professional. They pay particular attention to how the two can work or may work together as a dialectic unity, each having its strengths and weaknesses. They stress consumer intensivity, that is, the role the consumer plays as a producer of services and how the consumer increases the effectiveness and the quality of the services, and the "helper therapy principle," which asserts, in essence, that those who help are helped the most—or help giving is help getting.

In essence, the self-help approach reflects a series of dimensions that might be termed aprofessional. The following list, taken from Gartner and Riessman (1977), presents a schematic, ideal-type contrast between the professional and aprofessional modes of human service.

| Professional | Aprofessional |
|---|---|
| 1. Emphasis on knowledge and insight, underlying principles, theory, and structure. | 1. Emphasis on feeling and affect (concrete, practical). |
| 2. Systematic. | 2. Experience, common-sense intuition, and folk knowledge are central. |
| 3. "Objective"—use of distance and perspective, self-awareness; control of "transference." | 3. "Subjective"—closeness and self-involvement. |
| 4. Empathy; controlled warmth. | 4. Identification. |
| 5. Standardized performance. | 5. Extemporaneous, spontaneous (expressions of own personality). |
| 6. "Outsider orientation." | 6. "Insider" orientation; indigenous. |
| 7. Praxis. | 7. Practice. |
| 8. Careful, limited use of time; systematic evaluation; curing. | 8. Slow; time no issue; informal, direct accountability; caring. |

The self-help group may further be seen as representing a new dynamism in the practice of human services, a momentum that is likely to lead to new forms of service delivery. It is a system built on competency or what a person can actually do, a system of greater spontaneity and flexibility. With less bureaucracy and adherence to traditional, outmoded approaches, it utilizes more innovative, people-serving, and consumer-based methods. This movement for change is having an impact and is playing a role similar to that of the paraprofessional force of the 1960s. The basic thrust of the self-help approach is deeply antibureaucratic and antihierarchical: self-help rests on the assumption that the efficiency of the system comes at the point of relationship between the consumer and the server, not within the service system itself—unless the changes in the latter are fundamentally related to the consumer. With the rising interest in the self-help group and the widely recognized need for the expansion of resources, professionals have developed new interest in relating to self-help organizations and, in many cases, in starting or crystallizing them themselves.

**Classifications of Approaches and the Nature of Help Giving**  A variety of models for the professional relate to the self-help activity. Gartner and Riessman (1977) demonstrate the first of these in the assertiveness training model, in which a professional psychologist typically trains a group of lay people in becoming assertive and then may train them to become trainers of others. Lay trainers may return from time to time to the professionally led groups for added skill training. The multiplier effect of this model is obvious: a small number of professionals have an effect that radiates out to many groups. A second model is found in the peer-group "rap session," in which a professional trains the large number of youths in mutual or reciprocal counseling (often called cocounseling); the expert assumes a consultant role in the rap-group meetings as well as in other community and school settings.

A third model consists of technology programs in colleges at the A.A. or B.A. levels. Here, professionals train paraprofessionals to set up various types of mutual-aid groups in the community and other caregiving institutions.

A fourth model is exemplified by various health groups that have been established by the American Cancer Society and other professional agencies. In these instances, professionals not only initiate the mutual-help approach but also maintain close supervision and consultation, as in Laryngectomy, Inc., Reach to Recovery, and the Stroke Club. Some disease-specific groups depend on medical technology, as in hemophelia; other groups, such as those concerned with cystic fibrosis, rely on a combination of medicine and secondary support services.

Fifth, there is a youth-tutoring-youth and children-teaching-children model in education. The professional educator assumes an important function in setting up the program, training the participants, and serving as an ongoing consultant. The young tutors or teachers have the freedom to develop their own ways and means of tutoring and teaching others in need.

The sixth model familiar to professionals in the mental health field is Recovery, Inc. (Low 1950). This organization stipulates that professionals may not hold office or become leaders of that organization, although they may and sometimes do become members. The history of this group shows a shift from professional dependency to lay peer-group independency. By contrast, in Parents Anonymous a professional is typically involved in a supportive or consultative role, and a professional was influential as well in the establishment of the method. Daytop Lodge was also sponsored and developed by professionals, utilizing the basic self-help approach modeled after Synanon. Finally, many parents' groups, such as Parents of Retarded Children, have close working relationships with professionals.

A seventh model is found in social action groups, as exemplified by tenants welfare rights groups. Professional organizers have frequently played a major role in forming such groups, catalyzing them and assisting them in various ways, including advice, organizational training, and skill development. In the eighth model, professionals have assisted in the development of groups for hypertensive and diabetic patients.

The ninth model is exemplified various mutual-aid groups for the aged, such as Foster Grandparents, Resources to Serve in Volunteer Programs (RSVP), and Senior Companions. These have been organized by professional agencies with professional assistance. These groups, while having an attachment or connection to the backup human service agency, are essentially autonomous units.

Particularly in the health care field, sequential relationships between professional and self-help groups have developed. The doctor provides the acute intervention, surgery, for example, while the self-help groups takes primary responsibility for the development of adaptive behaviors.

Finally, a tenth model is found in groups formed on the basis of self-help literature or coping books such as *Transcendental Meditation, Guide to Successful Marriage, Becoming Orgasmic: A Sexual Growth Program for Women, Systematic Training for Effective Parenting, A Guide to Rational Living,* and *Psycho-Cybernetics.*

**Interface**  In systems language, a useful concept for understanding boundary relationships is the concept of interface, which may be defined as the area of contact between one system and another (Baker 1977). Available information indicates that a community's natural support system exists as a necessarily separate set of individuals and groups from the community's professional caregiving system. Separate systems may engage in numerous types of transactional processes at the interface across the boundaries of these systems. A number of types of transactional interdependencies can be identified. In one type of relationship, the two systems may actively engage in competition for clients, members, or converts. The professional caregiving system may feel that natural support systems offer poor alternative services for the same individuals whom the professional caregiving system seeks to treat. In such a competitive situation there may be bad feelings between the two systems, and considerable political jockeying may occur.

In another "pure" type of relationship, the two systems may engage in an active exchange of resources, including information, people, and material and financial resources. In such a collaborative arrangment, under optimal circumstances, the two systems will complement each other.

A third pattern that may be found in some communities is one in which the two systems engage in very little direct interaction but influence one another through the effects they have upon individuals in the community who need care and support.

Theoretically, we would suggest that support systems and professional support systems exist in a certain balance with regard to one another. Natural support systems come into existence or disappear in a cyclical sequence in counterpoint to developments in the professional caregiving network of a particular community. When a problem becomes acute among a significant element of a population without being given adequate attention and recognition by formal caregiving systems, natural support systems arise to meet the need. As these natural support systems spontaneously evolve, they tend to move toward a formal structure, and the leaders of the movement become increasingly professionalized. Examination of the natural histories of support systems in a community should be undertaken in order to test this hypothesized sequence of interdependent development of natural and professional helping systems (Baker 1977).

**Current Status** Clearly, professionals and paraprofessionals can play numerous roles in relation to self-help activity. They can initiate such a group; they can refer persons to such a group; they can develop a group; they can consult with a group; they can staff a group; and, finally, they can help the group become independent of the agency and the professional worker. The basic issue, of course, is whether the self-help approach will be compromised through partnership with the professional sector. The mutual-help approach often serves as a challenge to the professional or as a supplemental service. At other times it offers an alternative, a way of expanding and enriching professional practice and total human service delivery. Rarely does it displace the professional when the professional's expertise is appropriate.

To a great extent, self-help groups have developed because of the unwillingness and inability of professional organizations to deal with the kinds of problems that self-help groups tackle. In addition, many professionals have exhibited an overintellectualized distancing orientation, excessive credentialism, and limited reach with regard to various populations.

There are, however, critics of the movement. Ralph Nader and his supporters are cautious about self-help approaches that detract from the need for system responsibility. They believe that these groups may encourage demands to "clean your own streets rather than demand better service from the sanitation department"; or "get rid of crime in your neighborhoods by organizing your own block patrols rather than obtain improved police protection."

Professionals also raise legitimate concerns about the self-help approach. Among self-helpers are large numbers of those who may be labeled "professionalized clients." Rather than offering a substantially different alternative to professional services. These people seek "service" themselves. Rather than change the content of the help, they merely alter the agency that does it. The danger of "professionalized clients" is that they are more concerned with how they feel, or with who is helping, than with what works.

Among other criticisms that have been directed at the self-help group is that it fosters dependence, sometimes life-long, on the part of the participants. Some groups are seen as authoritarian and as imposing a new orthodoxy, frequently a very simplistic one. Further, there is a lack of record keeping, and the overall nonsystematic approach leads to great difficulties in determining accountability and effectiveness. Many groups have a strong antiprofessional bias that prevents a useful integration of the professional and his professional approaches. Such groups run the risk of blaming and stigmatizing the victim if the service fails in any way because of their emphasis on an individual responsibility and their neglect of the social causation of problems. Finally, they have a tendency to fragment social change, as each group "does its own thing."

Gartner and Riessman (1977) have summarized possible dangers to both the professional caregiving system and the consumer. To the professional caregiving system:

1. The self-help approach may be used as an argument for the further curtailment of the services.

2. It may be used to reduce professional and system responsibility.

3. The recent concern for accountability and evaluation may be reduced to mean no more than customer satisfaction, and the goal of finding and developing objective indices of service performance may be sacrificed.

4. The self-help approach may be thoroughly coopted by the professional establishment, which could then use the form of self-help groups as appendages of traditional agencies.

To the consumer:

1. When self-help is emphasized, a particularly pernicious form of victim blaming is possible.

2. Persons engaged in mutual-aid activities may get participation but not help.

3. Where cures are available and where professional expertise appropriate, involvement with self-help may divert attention from such resources.

4. Dependence may be encouraged—the self-help participant may come to believe that only by remaining in the group can he or she stay healthy.

As the role of the consumer expands, both in self-help activities and in other human services activities, the extent of these dangers is likely to be mitigated. However, the struggles with these dangers are ongoing.

Frank Riessman, codirector of the National Self-Help Clearing House and member of the Task Panel on Community Support Systems of the President's Commission on Mental Health, has emphasized that a major purpose of his organization was to show professionals the various models of relating to the self-help movement; he made the point that self-help and professionalism do not have to be competitive. Dr. Matt Dumont of the Laboratory of Community Psychiatry at Harvard Medical School has referred to self-help as "a way of doing business that is more cooperative, less competitive, more reciprocal and supportive." Since more than a half-million groups function currently, the trend does suggest that the movement has revolutionary potential. There are self-help groups for check bouncers, convicts, crooks, divorcees, suicides, debtors, the unemployed, mistresses, former mental patients, and every disease listed by the World Health Organization—for example, Cancer Anonymous, Checks Anonymous, Convicts Anonymous, and other "Anonymous" groups with the following surnames: crooks, delinquents, disturbed children, divorcees, dropouts, fatties, gamblers, stutterers, sexual child abusers, rich kids, migraines, narcotics, neurotics, overeaters, parents of youth in trouble, psychotics, recidivists, relatives, retirees, schizophrenics, smokers, youth, parents, mothers, and suicides.

What seems to be a common denominator of most groups as Reissman (1977) observed, is "dedication and deep commitment, particularly to the service ethic that has been watered down in professional settings." He has argued that human service professionals who spurn self-help activities are, in effect, "cutting off their noses to spite their faces," first because fiscal cutbacks in manpower shortages—what he called "the service crisis to society today"—have created an environment in which the rise of self-help is especially propitious. Moreover, Reissman, has pointed out that many of today's mental health problems relate to one or another form of addiction, an area that is ripe for self-help groups because professionals often cannot and usually do not like to deal with it. Among other reasons described why professionals ought to welcome a mutual-aid boom are the decline of the family, the school, the church, and other traditional institutions, the failure of the criminal justice system, and a new awareness of the special problems of dying and bereavement.

Riessman (1977) issued a call for research on a movement that clearly has come a long way since Alcoholics Anonymous was founded in 1935. AA alone now has 27,000 chapters, with more than 500,000 members. Potential researchers should ask, How do self-help groups work? How effective are they, and for whom? Will they work for all socioeconomic groups, not just the middle class? Reissman offered a warning to self-helpers that cooperation with professionals could possibly lead to cooptation:

> One of the major dangers that the self-help movement will face in the coming decade is that it may well be more closely allied with the professional institutional structures. In many cases, professionals will attempt to dominate and socialize self-help groups to existing professional norms. The self-help approach may then become an appendage of the professional structure.

Surely the most exhaustive analysis of the literature of self-help has been done by Killilea (1976), who has catalogued what she describes as the "categories of interpretation" (p. 39). The following uses Killilea's categories (pp. 40–66), while the examples are hers and those of others.

1. *Social assistance,* a factor in evolution. This is the interpretation of Peter Kropotkin who, as we have noted, emphasized mutual aid as a form of group life that was, and is, critical for human survival.

2. *Support systems.* This is the formulation of Caplan (1974), who defines support systems as "an enduring pattern of continuous or intermittent ties that play a significant part in maintaining the psy-

chological and physical integrity of the individual over time'' (Killilea 1976:7).

3. *A social movement.* Various interpreters of self-help have described it as a social movement, some emphasizing the focus on changing the group's members (Toch 1965), others focusing on societal effect (Gussow and Tracy 1973; Vattano 1972).

4. *A spiritual movement and a secular religion.* Mowrer (Mowrer and Vattano 1976) views his integrity groups as filling some of the roles that religious groups did in an earlier period, while Synanon now styles itself as a secular religion (Newmark and Newmark 1976). Of course, there is a spiritual dimension in AA (Hurvitz 1974; Blumberg 1977), as well as in such offshoots as GA, Gamblers Anonymous (Scodel 1964). Groups such as Recovery (Wechsler 1960) and even the dieting groups (Allon 1973) also have a religious quality.

5. *A product of social and political forces* that shape the helping services. Several authors (Glaser 1971; Levine and Levine 1970; Lewis and Lewis 1976) have seen self-help as a development in the human services.

6. *A phenomenon of the service society.* Gartner and Riessman (1974) note the development of consumer-intensive services as a central feature of the service society, self-help being a prime example.

7. *An expression of the democratic ideal,* consumer participation. This formulation is strongest in Vattano (1972), although Katz (1972) questions whether the ''power to the people'' rubric that Vattano uses fits all self-help groups. Dumont (1974) and Sidel and Sidel (1976) offer a more restrained version of this characterization.

8. *Alternative caregiving systems.* For groups and problems that the traditional caregiving system disdains or serves poorly, the self-help groups provide an alternative. This may well be one of the most central characteristics of self-help groups.

9. *An adjunct to the professions,* a solution to the manpower problem. In many ways, those groups concerned with ''after-care'' fit this category. These include Recovery, the -ostomy groups, Reach to Recovery, the laryngectomy groups, and the stroke clubs.

10. *An element in a planned care system.* To some extent, mental health programs are now including activities modeled on AA as part of their caregiving system. And at Queens College, City University of New York, workers in mental health agencies are being trained to become organizers and ''sponsors'' of self-help groups. In the health field, the ''activated patient'' activities (Schnert 1975) and

other aspects of "self-care" (Levin, Katz, and Holst 1976) fit this category.

11. *An intentional community.* Such various drug treatment programs as Synanon (Yablonsky 1965), Gaudenzia, Inc. (Glaser 1971), and Delancey Street (Hampden-Turner 1976; Sales 1976) are examples of intentional communities.

12. *A subculture,* or way of life. To some extent, each of the self-help groups is a subculture, particularly those that provide a new community for their members (for example, Parents Without Partners and the widow groups), as well as the behavior change groups.

13. *A supplementary community.* Weinberg (1968) describes Little People of America as a supplementary community, as does Weiss (1973) in discussing Parents Without Partners.

14. *A temporary/transitional community.* The various ex-patient groups in the mental health field play the role of temporary and transitional communities.

15. *Agencies of social control and resocialization.* To some extent, many of the self-help groups act as agencies of social control and resocialization, including all of those concerned with behavior change (AA, GA, the drug groups, and the weight reduction groups), as well as those more formally a part of the criminal justice system (Volkman and Cressey 1963).

16. *Expressive/social influence groups.* Self-help groups serve both to meet the self-interest of their members ("expressive") and to influence the larger society ("instrumental").

17. *Organizations of the deviant and stigmatized.* To some extent, the tendency to destigmatize is a characteristic of all of the self-help groups, although, of course, the extent of the stigma varies. Sagarin (1969) has identified this as the central characteristic of the groups, and Steinman and Traunstein (1976:356) note that a majority of the members of the self-help groups they studied stated that their most important objective was to change the public's definition of their condition from "deviant" to "different."

18. *A vehicle to aid coping with long-term deficits and deprivations.* The various health groups concerned with ostomates, laryngectomees, and mastectomees fit this categorization, as does the Center for Independent Living (Kirshbaum, Harveston, and Katz 1976).

19. *A vehicle to aid in coping with life-cycle transitions.* La Leche League, Parents Without Partners, and the various widow groups all serve this function. It is interesting to note that these groups are almost exclusively female.

20. *A therapeutic method.* Each of the various groups has its "way,"

ranging from AA's "Twelve Steps" to the Integrity Groups' "Ten Commitments." Antze (1976) describes this way as the unique "ideology" of the groups, while Hurvitz (1974) has conceptualized an entire alternative therapeutic modality that he says characterizes peer self-help psychotherapy groups.

**Self-Help Processes**  Professional attempts to study self-help groups have included the structural classifications, they have also examined the nature of the help giving. The basic elements include face-to-face interactions; the origin of the group is usually spontaneous; and personal participation is an extremely important ingredient. Bureaucratization is perceived as the enemy of the self-help organization. The members usually agree on and engage in certain actions, and the group develops from a condition of powerlessness. Then the group fills the needs by providing a reference group, a point of connection and identification with others, a basis for activity, and a source of ego reinforcement. Levy and others (1977) have also described patterns of help giving in self-help groups.

Table 8.1 illustrates the activity and its definition; table 8.2 shows the correlations between mean ratings and frequency of occurrence of twenty-eight help-giving activities by members of seven self-help groups; and table 8.3 indicates the factor structure of help-giving activities and means of ratings for the frequency of occurrence in all groups.

**Examples**  Each of the different service systems, whether mental health, health, education, criminal justice, or social welfare, has a mutual-help network associated with its particular service system. The type of self-help groups may not be easily classified or exemplified within a particular system, however, but are more likely to overlap. Kaplan (1974) has distinguished between those self-help groups designed to help members break a harmful habit (such as alcoholism, drug abuse, smoking, or overeating) and others that emphasize the formation of a new community in which members undergoing role transitions can immerse themselves.

The second category includes parent groups such as those for people alone, widows' associations, adolescent and older persons' groups, Parents Without Partners (PWP), and women in the process of becoming mothers. "The association with others in the same situation combats the social isolation that would otherwise be the lot of those who feel themselves, and are perceived by others, to be deviant in an ordinary society" (Caplan 1974:21–22). Both the parent and the "people alone" groups not only provide emotional and

**TABLE 8.1.**
DEFINITIONS PROVIDED BY SELF-HELP GROUP MEMBERS OF HELP-GIVING ACTIVITIES

| Activity | Definition |
| --- | --- |
| 1. Behavioral prescription | When a personal problem is brought up by a group member, other group members suggest things the person might do to overcome his or her difficulty. The group sometimes even makes very direct suggestions, such as *"Do this* and see what happens." |
| 2. Behavioral proscription | When a personal problem is brought up by a group member, other group members often identify actions that they believe are things he or she shouldn't do. The group even makes the direct suggestion, *"Don't do this."* |
| 3. Behavioral rehearsal | When a personal problem is brought up by a member, other group members often suggest how the person might act to handle the problem and then ask the person to *practice these behaviors in the presence of the group.* |
| 4. Positive reinforcement | When a member does something that the group approves, the group often *applauds* this behavior, or in some way *rewards* the member for acting in this way. |
| 5. Punishment | When a member does something that the group disapproves, the group often *criticizes* this behavior, or in some way *punishes* the person for acting in this way. |
| 6. Extinction | When a member says or does something that the group disapproves, the group members often *ignore* the person's behavior. |
| 7. Modeling | Group members often explain how they would go about handling a problem brought up by another member. In order to give this member a clear idea of what they have in mind, members often *demonstrate* just how they would react if they were faced with this person's problems. |
| 8. Self-disclosure | Group members often disclose to other members experiences, fantasies, thoughts, or emotions that are very personal and that they *normally wouldn't tell other people.* |
| 9. Sharing | Group members often share past and present experiences, thoughts, or feelings with other members. These things are not as private as those in #8 above, but serve to let other members know *what's going on* in each others' lives with respect to a whole range of areas, for example, coping with a problem, family life, financial matters, past events of interest. |

| Activity | Definition |
|---|---|
| 10. Confrontation | Group members often *challenge* one another, sometimes in a *demanding* or *threatening* way, to explain themselves or account for their behavior. |
| 11. Encouragement of sharing | When a group member brings up a personal problem, other members often *ask the person for additional information* or explanation about this problem, but do so in a way that is *not challenging.* |
| 12. Reflection and paraphrase | In order to clarify how a member thinks or feels about something, other members often put in other words what they believe the person has said; they may also make some statements to him concerning how they believe he is feeling emotionally. |
| 13. Requesting feedback | A group member often asks other group members how he impresses them, and how they feel about him. |
| 14. Offering feedback | Group members often disclose their feelings toward and impressions of another group member, and do so face to face. |
| 15. Reassurance of competence | Members often assure one another that they are *capable* of handling their problems. |
| 16. Justification | Members often let other members know that they were justified in feeling or acting as they did in response to some situation. |
| 17. Mutual affirmation | Members often assure one another that they are *worthwhile, valuable* people. |
| 18. Empathy | When a person expresses his emotions in the group, other group members let that person know that they *understand and share his feelings.* |
| 19. Normalization | When a person describes his actions or emotions as somehow strange or abnormal, other group members often *assure him that his behavior is normal.* |
| 20. Reassurance | Group members often reassure other members that their problems will eventually be worked out positively. |
| 21. Personal goal setting | A group member often sets his own goals and checks the progress he has made toward these goals. |
| 22. Establishing group's goals | Group members often *discuss goals* that they believe the group should adopt. |
| 23. Reference to group's norms | The group seems to have rules concerning how members should feel and think and act. Group members often refer to these rules in one way or another during group meetings. |

**TABLE 8.1.** (continued)

DEFINITIONS PROVIDED BY SELF-HELP GROUP MEMBERS OF HELP-GIVING ACTIVITIES

| Activity | Definition |
|---|---|
| 24. Consensual validation | Members often use the group as a way of determining whether their personal view of the world is the "best" or "most accurate" way of looking at the world. This process generally involves three steps: (1) a group member tells other members how he feels about certain issues, situations, or other people; then, (2) this group member learns from other group members how they feel about the things he has mentioned; and (3) the member evaluates his view. If other group members disagree with this person's view, he tends to feel that his opinions are right. If other group members disagree with this person's view, he tends to feel that his views need to be corrected. In short, *the group helps the member determine whether his or her own point of view or way of seeing things is accurate or not.* |
| 25. Functional analysis | Group members often try to understand a problem by *breaking it down* and determining such things as what went on before the problem situation arose, how the person reacted, and what happened after the difficulty arose. |
| 26. Discrimination training | When a group member describes a situation happening at the present time as similar to situations that happened in the past, other group members often point out in what ways these situations or emotional reactions are different. |
| 27. Explanation | Members provide explanations that help other group members *to better understand* themselves or their reaction to a situation. |
| 28. Catharsis | The group often emphasizes and encourages the *release of emotions.* |

*Source:* Levy et al. 1977.

*Note:* Group members were not given names of activities in their questionnaires.

social support "but they usually provide detailed information and specific guidance in increasing their members' understanding of the issue involved in their predicament and in practical ways of dealing with the expectable day-to-day and long-term problems" (p. 23).

**TABLE 8.2.**

CORRELATIONS BETWEEN MEAN RATINGS OF FREQUENCY OF OCCURRENCE OF TWENTY-
EIGHT HELP-GIVING ACTIVITIES BY MEMBERS OF SEVEN SELF-HELP GROUPS

| Groups | AA | TOPS | PA | OA | PWP | EA |
|--------|-----|------|-----|-----|-----|-----|
| TOPS | .76 | | | | | |
| PA | .64 | .51 | | | | |
| OA | .80 | .73 | .78 | | | |
| PWP | .77 | .67 | .72 | .67 | | |
| EA | .79 | .63 | .60 | .72 | .88 | |
| MTC | .67 | .56 | .78 | .81 | .64 | .70 |

*Source:* Levy et al. 1977.

*Note:* AA = Alcoholics Anonymous; TOPS = Take Off Pounds Sensibly; PA = Parents Anonymous;
OA = Overeaters Anonymous; PWP = Parents Without Partners; EA = Emotions Anonymous; MTC =
Make Today Count. All correlations are significant beyond the .01 level.

Parents Without Partners was started in 1957 and is the largest group of single parents, with more than 250 chapters and some 250,000 members, about three-quarters of whom are women (Gerwik 1981). Unlike in the "anonymous" and expatient groups, membership in PWP is subject to considerable turnover; during its first ten years, over 100,000 persons were members at one time or another (Gould 1968). Weiss (1973) pointed out that the organization is responsive to the marital loss itself, as well as to the defects of the life of a single parent.

Members are more likely to be divorced or separated than widowed, and the organization meets the needs of these individuals to be able to talk to understanding and sympathetic listeners about their feelings, their concerns, and their plans. For others who have already made the transition from marriage to life on their own, PWP meets their needs for relationships and provides a sustaining community, an opportunity to meet and see friends, and the presence of a supportive group. It thus functions to provide members with the sense of worth and encouragement to go on and, to some extent, with a replacement for the absent emotional attachments. The leaders of PWP deemphasize the charge that their organization is simply a dating service, both because they wish to avoid the pejorative implications of that accusation and its attendant loss of attraction of "nice people" and because they see their work as having broader scope (as indeed it does). Support systems have also developed within the criminal justice field. Prison Families Anonymous, Inc., an excellent example, was formed in 1974.

**TABLE 8.3.**

FACTOR STRUCTURE OF HELP-GIVING ACTIVITIES AND MEAN OF RATING OF THEIR
FREQUENCY OF OCCURRENCE IN ALL GROUPS

|  | Mean |
|---|---|
| Factor 1. Cognitive-Emotional Interventions (49.5% of variance) | |
| reflection and paraphrase* | 3.17 |
| empathy* | 4.20 |
| consensual validation* | 2.92 |
| functional analysis* | 3.30 |
| discrimination training* | 3.30 |
| explanation* | 3.89 |
| catharsis* | 3.59 |
| self-disclosure | 3.67 |
| reassurance of competence | 3.41 |
| support for feelings and actions | 3.35 |
| justification | 3.61 |
| Factor 2. Support and Relationship Building (15.4% of variance) | |
| reassurance* | 3.82 |
| sharing | 3.83 |
| encouragement of sharing | 3.57 |
| mutual affirmation | 3.94 |
| Factor 3. Group Sanctioning of Behaviors (12.5% of variance) | |
| positive reinforcement* | 3.66 |
| punishment | 1.65 |
| confrontation | 1.65 |
| establishing group's goals | 2.78 |
| reference to group's goals | 2.39 |
| Factor 4. Normative Advice (10.4% of variance) | |
| behavioral proscription* | 2.62 |
| behavioral prescription | 3.40 |
| normalization of experience and behavior | 3.39 |
| Not loaded on any factor | |
| modeling | 2.25 |
| behavioral rehearsal | 1.79 |
| requesting feedback | 1.76 |
| offering feedback | 2.01 |
| extinction | 2.17 |

Source: Levy et al. 1977.

Note: The four factors together account for 87.8 percent of variance. Factor loadings are all greater than .42. Mean frequency ratings are the means of the group means. Higher ratings indicate greater frequency of occurrence.

*Factor loading greater than .60.

Self-help groups are most common and best known to those in the mental health field. AA, Alcoholics Anonymous, is the largest, and need not be described here; another, Recovery, Inc., offers an interesting example of a unique kind of mutual-aid group. Recovery, Inc., provides a systematic method of providing self-help, an after-care approach to prevent relapses in former mental patients and chronicity in nervous patients. Developed by the late Abraham A. Low, M.D., the self-help organization is operated, managed, supported, and controlled by patients and former patients trained in the Recovery method. The Recovery approach consists of studying Dr. Low's book, *Mental Health Through Will Training,* (1950) and other literature, plus records and tapes recorded by Dr. Low (plus regular attendance at Recovery meetings and the practice of Recovery principles in one's daily life).

People live longer today. They are thus subject to a broad range of chronic disorders such as diabetes, mental illness, cancer, heart disorder, hypertension, arthritis, and emphysema. Additionally, there are behavior-related disorders that stem from speedy driving and from smoking, drinking, and taking drugs. The major health problems of our times are the result of overeating, oversmoking, overdrinking, overdriving, oversitting, overworking, overheating, and underexercising. Self-help groups have also emerged as a major remedy for these problems.

Strauss (1973) has described three steps that help sufferers of chronic illness to cope with their medical problems. The first is the ability to read signs that portend a crisis, for example, a diabetic's ability to recognize the signs of oncoming sugar shortage or insulin shock or an epileptic's ability to recognize an oncoming convulsion. In a sense, this ability is a form of self-diagnosis. The second is the ability to respond to the crisis of the moment, for example, diabetics carrying sugar or candy or insulin and epileptics stuffing handkerchiefs between their teeth just before convulsions. These are, in a sense, forms of self-treatment. Finally one can note the ability to establish and maintain a regimen. The extent to which a person is able to do this depends on his or her belief in the efficacy of the regimen. All three of these abilities are central characteristics of a consumer-centered model of health care.

In the past three decades, patients have added a new dimension to medicine and rehabilitation based on mutuality between persons with a difficulty in common. Many organizations of people with health problems exist. Alcoholics Anonymous was the first, followed by Narcotics Anonymous, Cured Cancer Clubs, Laryngectonees, Inc., Diabetes Groups, and Organizations of Parents with Retarded Children, Deaf Children, Emotionally Disturbed Children, and so on. This list of groups is large and grows continuously; its range can be seen in the following list of self-help groups in health care, classified according to the World Health Organization disease categories (from Gussow and Tracy 1973).

Addiction
    Addicts Anonymous
    Al-Anon
    Alateen
    Calix Society
    Gram-Anon
    Gamblers Anonymous
    Synanon Foundation
Blood Conditions
    Candlelighters (cancer)
    Cooley's Anemia Blood and Research Foundation for Children
    National Rare Blood Club
Bronchopulmonary Conditions
    Black Lung Association
    Emphysema Anonymous
Endocrine Conditions
    Human Growth, Inc.
Health Maintenance Groups
    Anti-Coronary Club
    Medic-Alert Foundation International
    Saved by the Belt Club
Intelligence
    Association for Advancement of Blind Children
    Association for Children with Learning Disabilities
    Association for Children with Retarded Mental Development
    Association for the Help of Retarded Children
    Mongoloid Development Council
    Mothers of Young Mongoloids
    National Association for Gifted Children
    National Association for Retarded Children
    New York Association for Brain-Injured Children
    Orton Society
    Retarded Infants Services
Infant Mortality
    National Foundation for Sudden Infant Death Syndrome
Mental Illness
    American Schizophrenia Association
    Mental Patient Liberation Project
    Mental Patients Political Action Committee
    Mental Patients Resistance
    Mothers Anonymous (Parents Anonymous)
    National Society for Autistic Children

Neurotics Anonymous International Liaison
Radical Therapists
Recovery, Inc.
Schizophrenic Anonymous International
The Bridge, Inc.
Neuromuscular Disorders
California Association for Neurologically Handicapped Children
Committee to Combat Huntington's Disease
Syautonomia Association
Louisiana Epilepsy Association
Myasthenia Gravis Foundation
National Tay-Sachs and Allied Disease Association
Stroke Club
Obesity
Buxom Belle, International
Fatties Anonymous
TOPS (Take Off Pounds Sensibly)
Overeaters Anonymous
Weight Watchers, International, Inc.
Physical Disabilities
American Wheelchair Bowling Association
Disabled Officers Association
National Amputation Foundation
National Association of the Physically Handicapped
National Wheelchair Athletic Association
Paralyzed Veterans of America
Sensory Disorders
American Federation of Catholic Workers for the Blind
Association for Education of the Visually Handicapped
Athletics for the Blind
Blinded Veterans Association
Choose, Inc.
International Parents Organization
Myopia International Research Foundation
National Association of the Deaf
National Federation of the Blind
National Fraternal Society
National Industries for the Blind
Retinitis Pigmentosa Foundation
Skin Disorders
Leanon Chapter
Psoriasis Research Foundation

Surgeries
>    International Association of Laryngectomees
>    Mended Hearts
>    Reach to Recovery
>    Society for the Rehabilitation of the Facially Disfigured
>    United Ostomy Association

At first glance this list might suggest a typical outgrowth of an organization-happy American society, where almost any common interest is seized upon to justify a club, an organization with officers, or a corporation through which interest becomes, first of all, approved. Belonging is, in and of itself, a positive value in our society. But why do patients choose to belong to patient groups rather than—or in addition to—parent–teacher associations and church groups? Groupings of people occur where previously there had been a gap between felt needs and their fulfillment by the given people in the existing environment, in this case the medical professions.

Advances in medical care and in understanding of psychological forces have raised the hopes of people beyond anything dreamed of even thirty years ago. Yet such rapid advances cannot be uniform on professional fronts; nor is the supply of personnel adequate for the demand of care. With the voluntary help agency movement firmly established in America as a means for the public to participate in relieving human suffering, the stage for mutual-aid, or self-help, groups, has been set. Thus, the development of mutual-aid groups of patients or parents of child patients should be viewed (1) clinically, as a healthy effort at self-help toward an ultimate goal of rehabilitation-independence; (2) sociologically, as an outgrowth of the increasing participation of the American public in matters of physical and emotional well-being; and (3) as fulfilling a need in a unique way—through mutuality, limited to people with common problems who may learn from each other, where coping with problems and the willingness to help others having the same problems is the basis for membership. One of the first of these groups was the Ileostomy Group Movement, which began about 1950. Today there are hundreds of ileostomy and colostomy patient groups in the United States and Canada. Most are affiliated through a federation, the United Ostomy Association, with headquarters in Los Angeles. Great Britain and Ireland have ileostomy associations consisting of over fifty branches with a total membership of over 5,000. The work of the groups is accomplished through meetings, visits to new patients and candidates for surgery, correspondence, preparation of literature, lectures to professional groups, and prosthetic equipment testing. For the ileostomy patient, rehabilitation had been lagging because hospital personnel were obviously unable to solve the patient's practical problems. When they returned home with many unanswered questions and often unmanageable problems of daily existence, patients found the need to consult each other for advice on the basics of keeping oneself clean and functioning in everyday pursuits. Thus began the self-help group.

Today, visits by the new ostomy patient to the hospital have become a standard routine, and followup programs are recommended by the medical and allied staff. Literature, such as the manual for the ileostomy patients, is used as a standard reference for both lay and professional people, as is the periodical, *Ileostomy Quarterly,* which began publication in 1956 and is now published by the United Ostomy Association as *Ostomy Quarterly.*

The ileostomy group serves as an excellent model of the kind of reciprocal relationships needed along the mutual-help group and professionals and service organizations. With such cooperation, the exchange of information and knowledge leads to referrals and assists collaborative and coordinated efforts. The success and effectiveness of mutual help for ileostomy patients points the way toward equally beneficial results for members of other self-help groups.

Recognition is also growing that natural support systems have unique qualities and that many individuals in modern society need the kind of support and feedback that are provided by self-help groups. This explains systems of support that are artificial in terms of organizational network but that take on the functions of a natural support system. Artificial networks tend to be more feasible when they replace those operated under professional auspices, when natural support systems already exist—even though they function minimally, and when the natural network is readily accessible to the potential clients. The impetus for developing artificial networks has come from the theory of crisis prevention, which holds that the outcome of a crisis in the individual's life depends largely on the help immediately available when the crisis occurs.

For example, an impressive project was implemented by Hamburg and Vorenhorst (1972) who organized an artificial network to meet the needs of students within a school system. The rationale for the project was described as follows:

> The modern American nuclear family with its smallness, mobility and relative isolation from other kinship ties has need of a network of non-familial supports. The schools have become the social institution which would appear to have the necessary ingredients for playing a major role in meeting these needs. The role of teachers and counselors as parent surrogates can be clearly seen. The role of

students as surrogates, models, bridging persons and sources of useful information for each other has been somewhat overlooked.

## CONCLUSION

The significance of helping networks and support systems can be viewed from at least two perspectives: first, in the ways in which the mutual-help approach relates to the character and quality of human services delivery; and, second, in the relevance of the mutual-help worldview to social and political change. The first view is associated with consumer involvement; this affects not only the quantity but also has an important fundamental effect on the quality of all human services, whether in education, mental health, social welfare, criminal justice, or health care.

Much of the effectiveness of human services depends on the involvement and motivation of the consumer. Furthermore, every person who needs help should also have the opportunity to play the role of helper, whether that person is a child underachieving in school, an alcoholic, or a drug addict. Human service strategy should be directed at devising ways of creating more helpers. To be more exact, the strategy should find ways of transforming the recipients of help into new dispensers of help—that is, reversing their roles—and of structuring the situation so that the recipients of help will be placed in roles requiring the giving of assistance. This helper-therapy principle operates universally. The form that this search for help takes may consist not only of face-to-face encounters but also of letters (Caplan 1982), hotlines (McGee 1974), radio talk shows, and the print media, including newspaper reader exchange pages such as the "Confidential Chat" of the *Boston Globe* and advice columns (Dibner 1974).

In connection with the second view, that of worldview, the self-help approach seems particularly responsive to new problems that demand our attention, such as the character problems associated with drug addiction and alcoholism, the highly resistant help-related behaviors, such as smoking and overeating, and the chronic health problems associated with an aging population. Pearlman (1976:19) sums up the issue with regard to grass-roots self-help groups:

Both the pitfalls and the potentials are great. The key questions are: (1) whether these groups will be able to sustain the motivation and mobilization of their membership; (2) whether they will be able to overcome the limits of their localism and take on larger-scale issues and struggles; (3) whether they will survive the inevitable attempts at cooptation and/or repression once they begin to pose more of a threat to established interests; (4) whether they can unite to forge a national federation of grass-roots groups; (5) whether they will begin to develop political consciousness and ideological clarity; (6) whether they will be able to build alliances with labor; and finally (7) whether they contain the seeds of a new radical party or a movement to transform the Democratic Party. Whatever the future may hold, people are coming to understand the issues and identify the enemy, are learning to fight strategically on their own behalf and are gaining confidence in their collective abilities.

The ethos of the self-help movement is critical of traditional institutions, professional behavior, and human services delivery practices. As a basic characteristic the trend toward self-help is locally directed and focused on specific problematic areas. Unfortunately, as with professionals and caregiving agencies, little liking and coordination characterizes the essentially fragmented system of mutual-help networks.

At present, too, the political and social influences of self-help are marginal compared with the organized professional delivery system. Such impact remains peripheral, since the self-help purpose is largely to function so as to help its own members survive in a negative environment.

To some extent, the women's movement is an exception, but recent data indicate that the consciousness-raising unit is increasingly moving away from a political perspective and more toward an interpersonal one (Lieberman and Bond 1976). To what degree the women's consciousness-raising groups mesh with a larger national feminist movement at this time is unclear and uncertain. Unless the priorities of mutual-help associations are focused on such fundamental problems as the distribution of resources, inflation, employment, and social and economic planning, the resolution of social symptoms will be found in self-help groups that reach out on a fragmentary, single-issue basis rather than deal with the global issues of the larger system that produces these large-scale difficulties. This is not to say that mutual-health movements should redirect their focus to national issues, but that they should have a greater awareness and attitude toward accomplishing this mission as a consequence of a broadly defined mandate at the local level. Gartner and Riessman (1977) express their hypothesis: The self-help approach can contribute significantly to social change by reducing the alienation and increasing empowerment.

More information is needed about the way in which mutual-help approaches work, with what populations, and for how long. Politicians need to study the principles and methods that are employed in the various natural networks; social scientists and professional evaluators should examine the networks' effectiveness.

# REFERENCES

Ablon, J. 1974. Al-Anon family groups. *American Journal of Psychotherapy* 28(1):30–45.

Allon, N. 1973. Group dieting ritual. *Society* 10:36–42.

Antze, P. 1976. The role of ideologies in peer psychotherapy organizations. Some theoretical considerations in three case studies. *Journal of Applied Behavioral Science* 12:323–346.

Baker, F. 1977. The interface between professional and natural support systems. *Clinical Social Work Journal* 5(2):139–148.

Barish, H. 1971. Self-help groups. In *Encyclopedia of Social Work.* Vol. 2, no. 16. New York: National Association of Social Workers.

Barnes, J. A. 1954. Class and committees in a Norwegian island parish. *Human Relations* 7:43.

Bergin, A. J. 1971. The Evaluation of therapeutic outcomes. In A. E. Bergin and S. L. Garfield, eds., *Handbook of Psychotherapy and Behavior Change: An Empirical Analysis.* New York: Wiley.

Bild, Bernice R. and Robert J. Havighurst. 1976. Senior citizens in great cities: The case of Chicago. *Gerontologist* 16(1).

Blumberg, L. 1977. The ideology of a therapeutic social movement: Alcoholics Anonymous. *Journal of Studies on Alcohol* 38(11):2122–2143.

Bott, E. 1971. *Family and Social Network.* London: Tavistock.

Cantor, Marjorie H. 1973. *The Elderly in the Inner City.* New York: Office for the Aging.

Caplan, G. 1974. *Support Systems and Community Mental Health: Lectures on Concept Development.* New York: Behavioral.

Caplan, G. 1982. Epilogue: Personal reflections. In H. C. Schulberg and M. Killilea, eds., *The Modern Practice of Community Mental Health.* San Francisco: Jossey-Bass.

Cassel, J. 1975. Social science in epidemiology: Psychosocial processes in theoretical formulation. In E. Struening and M. Guttentag, eds., *Handbook of Evaluation Research.* Vol. 2. Beverly Hills: Sage.

Collins, Alice H. 1973. Natural delivery systems: Accessible sources of power for mental health. *American Journal of Orthopsychiatry* 43(1).

Collins, Alice H. and Diane L. Pancoast. 1976. *Natural Helping Networks: A Strategy for Prevention.* Washington, D.C.: National Association of Social Workers.

Craven, P. and B. Wellmen. 1973. The networks city. *Sociological Inquiry* 43(3–4):57–88.

Cressey, D. 1955. Changing criminals: The application of the theory of differential association. *American Journal of Sociology.* 61(1):116–120.

Cressey, D. R. 1965. Social-psychological foundations for using criminals in the rehabilitation of criminals. *Journal of Research in Crime Delinquency* 2(2):49–59.

Dibner, S. S. 1974. Newspaper advice columns as a mental health resource. *Community Mental Health Journal* 10(2):147–155.

Dumont, M. 1967. Tavern culture: The sustenance of homeless men. *American Journal of Orthopsychiatry* 37:938–945.

Dumont, M. P. 1974. Self-help treatment programs. *American Journal of Psychiatry* 131(6):631–635.

Fairweather, G. W. et al. 1969. Community Life for the Mentally Ill: An Alternative to Institutional Care. Chicago: Aldine Press.

Gartner, A. and F. Riessman. 1974. *The Service Society and the Consumer Vanguard*. New York, Harper & Row.

Gartner A. and F. Riessman. 1977. *Self-Help in the Human Services*. San Francisco: Jossey Bass.

Gerwin, K. 1981. Parents Without Partners. *The Single Parent*.

Gould, E. P. 1968. Special report: The single parent family benefits in Parents Without Partners, Inc. *Journal of Marriage and the Family* 30:666–671.

Gussow, Z. and G. S. Tracy. 1973. Voluntary self-help health organizations: A study in human support systems. Mimeo. Progress Report, January–May.

Hamburg, B. and B. B. Varenhorst. 1972. Peer counseling in the secondary schools: A community mental health project for youth. *American Journal of Orthopsychiatry* 42(4):566–581.

Hampden-Turner, C. 1976. *Sane Asylum*. San Francisco: San Francisco Book.

Hansell, N. 1974. Study of activities of self-help groups: Take Off Pounds Safely. Mimeo. Department of Psychiatry, Northwestern University School of Medicine.

Heisel, Marsel A. 1973. Social interaction and isolation among a group of elderly blacks. Paper presented at 26th annual meeting of Gerontological Society, Miami Beach, Florida.

Hirsch, B. J. 1977. The social network as a natural support system. Paper presented to the American Psychological Association, San Francisco.

Hurvitz, N. 1974. Peer self-help psychotherapy groups: Psychotherapy without psychotherapists. In P. M. Roman and H. M. Trice, eds., *The Sociology of Psychotherapy*. New York: Jason Aronson.

Kaplan, B. H., J. C. Cassel and S. Gore. 1973. Social support and health. Paper presented at the meeting of the American Public Health Association, San Francisco.

Katz, A. H. 1970. Self-help organizations and volunteer participation in social welfare. *Social Work* 15(1):51–60.

Katz, A. H. 1972. Self-help groups. *Social Work* 17(6):120–121.

Kelly, J. G., L. R. Snowden, and R. F. Munoz. Social and Community Interventions. *Annual Review of Psychology* (1977), 28:323–361.

Killilea, M. 1976. Mutual-help organizations: Interpretations in the literature. In G. Caplan and M. Killilea, eds., *Support Systems and Mutual Help: Multidisciplinary Explorations*. New York: Grune and Stratton.

Kirschbaum, H. R., D. S. Harveston, and A. H. Katz. 1976. Independent living for the disabled. *Social Policy* 7:59–62.

Kropotkin, P. *Mutual Aid*. Boston: Extending Horizons Books, 1914.

Lennenberg, E. and J. C. Rowbotham. The Iliostomy Patient. Springfield, Illinois: Thomas, 1970.

Levin, L., A. H. Katz and E. Holst. 1976. *Self-care: Lay initiatives in health*. New York: Prodist.

Levine, M. and A. Levine. 1970. *A Social History of the Helping Services: Clinic, Court, School and Community*. New York: Appleton-Century-Crofts.

Levy, L. H. 1977. Patterns of help-giving in self-help groups. Paper presented at the American Psychological Association convention in San Francisco.

Lewis, J. A. and M. A. Lewis. 1976. *Community Counseling: A Human Services Approach*. New York: Wiley.

Lieberman, M. A. and G. G. Bard. Problem of being a woman: Survey of women in consciousness-raising groups. *Journal of Applied Behavior*, (1976), 13(3):363–379.

Low, A. A. 1950. *Mental Health Through Will Training: A System of Self-Help in Psychotherapy as Practiced by Recovery, Inc.* Boston: Christopher.

Maddison, D. and W. Walker. 1967. Factors affecting the outcome of conjugal bereavement. *British Journal of Psychiatry* 113:1057–1067.

Mitchell, J. C. 1969. The concept and use of social networks. In J. C. Mitchell, ed., *Social Networks in Urban Situations*. Manchester: University of Manchester Press.

Mowrer, O. H. and A. J. Vattano. 1976. Integrity groups: A context for growth in honesty, responsibility, and involvement. *Journal of Applied Behavioral Science* 12:419–431.

Newmark, J. and S. Newmark. 1976. Older persons in a plain community: Synanon. *Social Policy* 7:93–99.

Pearlman, M. 1976. If you need a shoulder, I have two. Manuscript. New York: National Commission on Resources for Youth.

Perleiser, B. 1977. *Research Utilization Briefs* 1(5):2–10.

Riessman, F. 1965. The "helper" therapy principle. *Social Work* 10:27–32.

Sagarin, E. 1969. *Odd Man In*. Chicago: Quadrangle Books.

Sales, G. 1976. *John Maher of New York*. New York: Norton.

Schulberg, H. C. and M. Killilea, eds. 1982. *The Modern Practice of Community Mental Health*. San Francisco: Jossey-Bass.

Scodel, A. 1964. Inspirational group therapy: A study of Gamblers Anonymous. *American Journal of Psychotherapy* 18:115–125.

Sehnert, K. 1975. *How to Be Your Own Doctor (Sometimes)*. New York: Grossett and Dunlop.

Shapiro, J. Dominant leaders among slum hotel residents. *American Journal of Orthopsychiatry*, 39(4):644–650.

Sidel, V. W. and R. Sidel. 1976. Beyond coping. *Social Policy* 7:67–69.

Silverman, P. R. 1972. Widowhood and preventive intervention. *Family Coordinator* (January):95–102.

Skovholt, T. M. 1974. The client as helper: A means to promote psychological growth. *Counseling Psychologist* 4(3):58–64.

Smith, Sarah Alexander. 1975. *Natural Systems and the Elderly: An Unrecognized Resource*. Portland, Ore.: Graduate School of Social Work, Portland State University.

Steinman, R. and D. M. Traunstein. 1976. Redefining deviants: The self-help challenge to the human services. *Journal of Applied Behavioral Science* 12:347–362.

Strauss, A. 1973. Chronic illness. *Society* 10:26–36.

Toch, H. 1965. *The Social Psychology of Social Movements*. New York: Bobbs-Merrill.

Toffler, A. 1970. *Future Shock*. New York: Bantam Books.

Tolsdorf, C. 1976. Social networks, support, and coping: An exploratory study. *Family Process* 15(4):407–417.

Vattano, A. J. 1972. Power to the people: Self-help groups. *Social Work* 17(4):7–15.

Volkman, R. and D. Cressey. 1963. Differential association and the rehabilitation of drug addicts. *Americn Journal Sociology* 69(2):129–142.

Wechsler, H. The self-help organization in the mental health field: Recovery, Inc. *Journal of Nervous and Mental Disorders* (1963), 130:297–314.

Weinberg, M. S. 1968. The problems of midgets and dwarfs and organizational remedies: A study of the Little People of America. *Journal of Health Social Behavior* 9(1):65–72.

Weiss, R. S. 1973. The contribution of an organization of single parents to the well-being of its members. *Family Coordinator* 22(3):321–326.

Whitten, N. E., Jr., and A. W. Wolfe. 1973. Network analysis. In J. J. Honnignann, ed., *Handbook of Social and Cultural Anthropology*. Chicago: Rand McNally.

Yablonsky, L. *Synanon: The Tunnel Back*. New York: MacMillan, 1965.

Zablocki, B. D. 1967. Christians because it works: A study of Bruderhof communitaranism. Doctoral dissertation, Johns Hopkins University.

# INTEGRATING AND COORDINATING
# HUMAN SERVICES

The concept of integration as an ideal in human services has existed for a number of decades. In an age less specialized, that ideal was probably closer to reality than it has been in recent years (McKenzie 1978). This disparity, as well as the rising costs of providing services, has given impetus to movements toward integration. These efforts have also been launched as extensions of the community mental health belief in continuity of care (Baker and Northman 1978).

The concept of integration has proven to be complex and elusive, as is discussed in the first part of this chapter. The remainder of the chapter discusses concepts and problems involved in coordinating efforts at integration and in the area of community organization, where integration has historically been most in evidence.

## INTEGRATION

The necessity of integrating the delivery of human service programs is typically illustrated by the needs of a hypothetical family living in dilapidated housing. The mother is in poor health and functionally illiterate; the father has a prison record, so jobs are difficult to obtain and hold. One son has been sentenced for theft and is thought to be on drugs, another appears to be retarded, and a daughter is pregnant.

**Rationale**   The needs of such a family can only be met through a variety of services: financial assistance, counseling on various problems, health diagnosis and care, education and training, and correctional programs. These services are rendered by a number of government agencies, each with its own system of entry, diagnosis, referral, treatment, reporting, and followup. Similar services may be offered by separated agencies; other services may not be available in the locality. The problem in general is that services have been delivered in a fragmented and confusing manner, with different and often conflicting goals and objectives. Moreover, the programs lack accountability and become self-perpetuating with the result that they do not provide attention to prolonged needs.

The concept of human service integration is addressed to overcoming these problems and to meeting the needs of people. Services integration is difficult to define. Sometimes the integration effort is described as the creation of a new flexibility in accountable systems of delivery in response to locally determined priorities. Flexibility makes possible new combinations of services across agency and program lines. The goal: to respond to an individual's or a family unit's total problems rather than to take a piecemeal approach. Gans and Horton (1975) offered the definition: "The linking together by various means of the services or two or more service providers to allow treatment of an individual's or family's needs in a more coordinated and comprehensive manner" (p. 32).

The definitions of services integration have also included the following: "A service delivery system which can provide all those services needed by a given client or community—constrained only by the state of the art and the availability of resources" (Gardner, et al. 1971).

According to a memorandum from the past DHEW Secretary Elliot Richardson (1971) services integration is aimed

> . . . at developing an integrated framework within which ongoing programs can be rationalized and enriched to do a better job of making services available within the existing commitments and resources. Its objectives must include such things as: (a) the coordinated delivery of services for the greatest benefit to people; (b) a holistic approach to the individual and the family unit; (c) the provision of a comprehensive range of services locally; and (d) the rational allocation of resources at the local level so as to be responsive to local needs. (p. 1)

As a process or activity, services integration may be defined by the ways in which particular services are combined or related across agency and program lines. These are basically what have been identified as "integrative linkages" in this text.

The various definitions, as well as the Gardner report (1971) indicate that services integration must involve significant redirection of ongoing programs and resources—even to the point of institutional change—rather than the overlay of new service activities on a fragmented base of continuing operations. Moreover, although services integration has attempted to overcome fragmentation at the delivery level, at the state level, and at the federal level, Secretary Richardson recognized that the "primary focus" is "the integration of services at the local level for the purpose of maximizing their actual benefits to people" (p. 1).

The concept of services integration has developed in response to a fragmented pattern of service delivery in which separate programs, each individually developed over the years, meet separately defined needs. That categorical approach treats "the individual not as a whole being, but as a person with separate and separable problems which can be treated in isolation from one another" (Gardner 1971:24). The limitations of such an approach clearly demand some revision: "Since needs are related, the consumer who has (several problems) must deal with a system which seems totally irrational. Rationalization of the service delivery system must occur from the bottom up" (Richardson 1971:1).

The President's Commission on Mental Health pointed out that the interface between mental health and physical health has all but been ignored (Long 1979:46).

Three types of problems are involved in the organization and distribution of social services: the dispersal of similar functions; the discontinuity of related functions; and incoherence when different functions are pursued without relationship to each other (Rein 1970:105).

Uncoordinated responses to such problems have resulted in various felt inadequacies and difficulties. These include duplication of cash benefits, duplication of other services, multiplicity of independent and uncoordinated visiting, duplication of manpower, overuse of services by a small percentage of clients (multiproblem families), and poor access to, and underuse of, services.

Can some order be introduced into the array of possible definitions of integration? Typologies may provide a clue. Baker and Northman (1978) see two meanings in "integration" (coordinating various components of a human service organization; and human service organizations as part of larger community service systems. In system terms, integration is important at both the intrasystem level and the intersystem level (169–170). Integration is commonly understood in the latter sense. Accordingly, a typology is presented in the section below as a typology of interorganizational linkages.

DHEW presents services integration in terms of several factors that are important concerns from a policy point of view but that are not intrinsic to the definitions of integration. These factors are: effectiveness (or quality) of service delivery; efficiency (or economy) of service delivery; and accountability of service delivery (Gans and Horton 1975).

Although these factors are logically distinct from integration, distinctions are not usually drawn. Effectiveness and efficiency are viewed by DHEW as goals and/or assumed consequences of services integration. Effectiveness includes being responsive to consumer needs and generating results that may be evaluated. However, these factors are only assumed to be consequences of integration and are not seen as validated through empirical evaluation (Redburn 1977). Aside from impressionistic observations, few studies or analyses lend credence to such assertions.

An illustration in the criminal justice subsystem of human services is provided in the patrolman: He engages in fewer boundary activities—referral to other community resources or interaction with other professionals—than any other member of the criminal justice segment. Ironically, citizens ask him to make many decisions involving these very activities (Johnson 1977). As one result, "clients" have poor access to services outside the patrolman's awareness.

DHEW's use of the term "accountability of service delivery" applies primarily to the local level of general purpose government. The various rationales for integration can be incorporated into accountability in two ways. The first is that the availability of services to clients who need the services of more than one service provider is greater if delivery is integrated rather than fragmented. The second is that efficiency in the delivery of services to clients who need help from more than one service provider is greater if delivery is integrated rather than fragmented.

In service integration terms, "effectiveness of service delivery" refers to the availability of service rather than to its quality. Thus the issue of availability of service (health services, for example), rather than the quality of the service (whether the health service is competent, sensitive, and so on) is important. In this sense availability has two dimensions: accesibility, which pertains to initial client entry into the system; and continuity, which describes client movement within the system.

The term "efficiency" is the result of the integration of services in three major ways:

1. Reduction of duplication of service delivery.
2. Economies of scale: some things can be done at less cost; and some things can be done that otherwise could not be done (for example, staff training).
3. Impact on problem solution. If the public investment in one service such as job training is to have lasting benefit only if another service, such as job placement service, is also provided, the cost involved in assuring that the client gets the job placement services as well as job training may be justified in terms of protecting the investment in job training. This measure is referred to as *impact on problem solution* (Gans and Horton 1975).

A distinction may be made here between social efficiency and technical-economic efficiency. The former may be described in terms of "a high level of commitment, loyalty, and involvement, as well as a genuine sense of satisfaction on the part of its numerous groups and members" (Georgopoulos 1978:58). While this distinction was applied to an example of intraorganizational integration (a hospital) it is equally applicable to an intersystem situation. The author's assertion that social efficiency is more important may be equally applicable to intersystem problems, although that remains to be tested empirically.

Another generalization becomes possible regarding services integration: the process requires a "holistic" as opposed to a categorical approach to human services needs. The need for a holistic approach has been generally recognized throughout the history of social welfare in the United States. "Holism" became an increasingly urgent need with the passage of new social legislation in the 1960s. The new laws in large part addressed human problems in a specialized, categorical manner. The proliferation of categorical grants resulted in separate procedures for application, funding, budgeting, hiring of personnel, reporting, auditing, and many other administrative processes. The federal response in DHEW and elsewhere has been an attempt to improve and simplify the system. One of the consequences has been presidential directives and initiatives to provide uniformity in administrative procedures and decentralize responsibilities to regions, and, on the other hand, in proposals to simplify funding through block grants and special revenue sharing.

With respect to services, a number of integrative efforts have been made. One of the first organized attempts was through the Office of Economic Opportunity (OEO) Community Action Programs and Neighborhood Service Programs. These were aimed at coordinating service programs through multiservice centers in single geographic locations. Late in 1970 DHEW Secretary Elliot Richardson established a working task force on services integration that made a number of recommendations to the department. One of these recommendations led to the creation of DHEW interagency services integration demonstration program referred to as SITO (Service Integration Target of Opportunity). The new program encouraged and supported the development of various models at different levels of government. DHEW also submitted to Congress the Allied Services Act, which would provide grants to encourage services integration and allow the consolidation of certain funding sources.

Because much of the existing organization of services is by function, the objective of organizing services comprehensively around the needs of the person, family, or community requires the crossing of existing program and agency lines.

The problem may be summarized in the presidential message accompanying the proposed Allied Services Act of 1972 to Congress: "For the uninformed citizen in need, the present fragmented system can become a nightmare of confusion, inconvenience, and red tape" (p. 2).

Redburn (1977) has also noted the paucity of operational definitions of integration. He first distinguishes between administrative or structural integration and integration of service delivery. Within the former category, he distinguishes centralized from noncentralized integration. Where there is centralization of authority, any of the following operational meanings may apply:

> centralization of outreach, intake, diagnosis, referral, and followup operations; creation of a joint planning mechanism; joint training; establishment of a joint planning-programming-budgeting-evaluation system for several agencies; centralization of budgetary authority; consolidation into regional planning districts; designation or clarification of services jurisdictions; joint purchasing, accounting or other sharing of administrative support functions; clarifying roles and lines of authority; sharing of authority by two or more coordinate agencies; purchase of services contracting; legal consolidation of previously separate agencies; creation of "super agencies" with responsibility for coordinating the delivery of services by subordinate agencies. (p. 265).

Where there is no centralization of authority, the following operational terms may apply:

> colocation of services; improved or expanded information and referral services; creation of new treatment roles; such as "case manager" or "client advocate"; client-oriented information systems that facilitate diagnosis of clients' needs, generate appropriate programs of services, facilitate information sharing among the professional providers, and ensure that clients do not get "lost" in the system. (p. 265)

The first list stresses "scientific management," while the latter stresses increases in the flow of information laterally (among professionals) and downward (to clients).

With regard to service delivery, the Allied Services Act of 1975 included these objectives: "facilitate accessibility to all services needed; facilitate utilization of all services needed; improve effectiveness of services; use available resources as efficiently as possible and minimize duplication" (p. 265). Other terms denoting services integration include: "to reduce competition among service agencies; reduce isolation and fragmentation and provide a 'holistic approach' to service delivery; 'humanize' treatment" (p. 265).

Redburn stresses the importance of noting "that maximizing one of these objectives may not maximize others. For instance, increasing access to services may overload the system—reducing efficiency or effectiveness" (p. 265). By using these operational meanings of integration. It is hoped that observing how each aspect varies independently will contribute to an understanding of how they may conflict or compete with one another or reinforce one another. A goal of integration tempered with considerations such as trade-offs is a more realistic situation than an unfettered ideal.

**Linkages**   In practice, services integration is difficult to achieve, as well as to measure, because of problems inherent in any fundamental change. The integration of diverse programs involves coping with interprofessional relationships, with scattered locations of offices, different sources of funding, and changing power and authority relationships among legislators and affected employees. These complicated variables and their interactive effects are difficult to describe as well as to measure successful implementation of a different approach to service delivery as exemplified by the term "linkage."

There are two distinct types of linkages: direct service linkages and administrative linkages (Redburn 1977). Direct service linkages—consisting of core services (outreach, intake, diagnosis, referral, and follow-up) and modes of case coordination (case conference, case coordinator, case team)—tie together the provision of services to specific clients. These linkages have immediate, direct results and focus on a client and his specific needs.

Administrative linkages bring together or consolidate the management of service providers. The linkages are described by Gans and Horton are as follows:

1. *Fiscal*

*Joint budgeting:* a process in which the integrator meets with all service providers, together or individually, to develop a budget.

*Joint funding:* a process by which two or more service providers give funds to support service.

*Fund transfer:* instances in which funds originally targeted for use in one service are shifted for use in another service.

*Purchase of service:* formal agreements that may or may not involve a written contract between the integrator and autonomous service providers to obtain service.

2. *Personnel Practices*

*Consolidated personnel administration:* the centralized provision of some or all of the following: hiring, firing, promoting, placing, classifying, training, and so on.

*Joint use of staff:* the case in which two different agencies deliver service by using the same staff.

*Staff transfer:* the case in which an employee is on the payroll of one agency but is under the administrative control of another.

*Staff outstationing:* the placement of a service provider in the facility of another service provider.

*Colocation:* the stationing of staff by autonomous service providers in a common facility.

3. *Planning and Programming*

*Joint planning:* the joint determination of total service delivery system needs and priorities through a structured planning process.

*Joint development of operating policies:* a structured process in which the policies, procedures, regulations, and guidelines governing the administration of a project are jointly established.

*Joint programming:* the joint development of programmatic solutions to defined problems in relation to existing resources.

*Information sharing:* an exchange of information regarding resources, procedures, and legal requirements (but not individual clients) between the project integrator and various service providers.

*Joint evaluation:* the joint determination of effectiveness of service in meeting client needs.

4. *Administrative Support Services*

*Record keeping:* the gathering, storing, and disseminating of information about clients, including standardized and/or centralized case information; and procedures for flow of information.

*Grants management:* the servicing of grants.

*Central support services:* the consolidated or centralized provision of service such as auditing, purchasing, exchange of material and equipment, and consultative services.

Direct service linkages are equally important, they include:

1. *Core Services*

*Outreach:* the systematic recruitment of clients.

*Intake:* the process (including determination of eligibility) resulting in the admission of a client to direct service.

*Diagnosis:* the assessment of a client's overall service needs.

*Referral:* the process by which a client is directed to another provider for services.

*Followup:* the process used to determine that clients receive the services to which they have been referred and, in general, help them negotiate the service delivery system.

2. *Modes of Case Coordination*

*Case conference:* a meeting between the integrator's staff and staff of agencies who provide service to a given family, for the purpose of discussing that family in general or a specific problem—possibly determining a course of action and assigning responsibility among the agencies for implementing the solution.

*Case coordinator:* the designated staff member responsible for assuring provision of service by multiple autonomous providers in a given client.

*Case team:* the arrangement in which a number of staff members, either representing different disciplines or working with different members of a given family, work together to relate a range of services of autonomous providers to a given client. (The primary difference between case conferences and case teams is that the former may be ad hoc, whereas the latter involves continuous and systematic interaction between the members of the team.) (1975:37–38)

**State Reorganization**  In the past three years, officials in some states have begun to utilize state organizational structures to foster services integration. One of the factors that have aided them is the movement toward the reorganization of executive branch agencies, a movement whose start in 1917 long predated interest in service integration. The movement has achieved unprecedented momentum during the past fifteen years. Starting with Michigan in 1965, eighteen states have undertaken substantial executive reorganizations, and many have reorganized several major functions.

Reorganizations have resulted in the establishment of departments that include several programs in the human resources area. Many such programs can be considered as "human services." These include:

| public assistance | social services |
| public health | adult corrections |
| mental health | probation services |
| mental retardation | parole services |
| medical care | youth institutions and services |
| alcoholism programs | employment service |
| developmental disabilities | manpower programs |
| crippled childrens service | office of economic opportunity |
| maternal and child health | veterans services |
| public education | aging |
| special education | drug abuse programs |
| adult education | vocational rehabilitation |

Some of these services are subsumed under other programs. Medical care (Medicaid), for instance, is usually administered by the department administering public assistance, and alcoholism programs fall into the category of mental health. Major human services that have widespread applicability among all states and that typically have discrete organizational arrangements are as follows:

| public assistance-social service | corrections |
| public health | youth institutions |
| mental health | employment services |
| mental retardation | vocational rehabilitation |

The major programs listed above are not always grouped under a "human services" function. For instance, corrections and youth institutions are often considered part of the criminal justice or law enforcement function. Employment security and vocational rehabilitation can be classified as employment or manpower development, and health-related programs may be kept separate from welfare-related programs. Thus program groupings may vary considerably among states depending in part on their concepts of major functional groupings and in part on politics and personalities at the time the structure is established.

Education may not be listed as a human resource function. Education is universally offered separately from other state activities. State expenditures for education—aid to elementary and secondary education and the direct operation of colleges and universities—amount to 35 percent of total state expenditures, double that of its nearest competitor, welfare. This fact, plus the separation of educational administration under the control of boards and elected heads, reinforced by the strength of education interest groups, has combined to discourage serious thought about establishing little DHEWs in the states. However, with the new federal Department of Education, future changes remain to be seen.

Any grouping of two or more human service functions into one department could be considered the start of a human resource agency. From the point of view of services integration, however, a human resource agency can still be further refined. The focal point of integration appears usually to be the public assistance–social welfare programs. This is attributed to a number of variables such as the large clientele served by these programs: the multiservice needs of many of the clients and their families; the extensive network of service delivery centers already in operation; and Title IV-A of the Social Security Act, which provides federal matching assistance for social services such as day care and family planning. The grants for Title IV-A are made available through the state agency administering public assistance–social services and have frequently provided an incentive for mental health, corrections, and other programs to cooperate in order to contract for the use of these funds.

The reorganization movement has resulted in the establishment of human resources agencies that encompass several major programs. The more programs housed under the same structural "umbrella" or "roof," the more an organizational impetus is presumed to exist for the integration of services. Comprehensive coverage of human service programs does not necessarily mean that services integration is being attempted; only one of the eight states whose human resource agency contains seven or eight major programs has attempted such integration.

**Program Organization**   Organizational design, program inclusion, the statutory authority of the agency head, and other factors contribute to each state's unique human services system.

The organizational arrangements for a state human resource system can be described on three levels: (1) the state central agency structure; (2) the regional (or substate district) administrative and/or delivery structure; and (3) the point of service delivery, usually at the county or municipal level. For the purpose of this study, the state central agency and regional structures are classified as follows:

*State Central Agency*
1. integrated comprehensive human resource agencies
2. consolidated comprehensive human resource agencies

3. confederated comprehensive human resource agencies
4. no comprehensive human resource agency

*Regional Organization*
1. integrated regional organization
2. coordinative regional organization
3. no agencywide regions

*Integrated CHRA*. The statutes that create an integrated comprehensive human resource agency transfer most or all of the administrative and program authority of previously autonomous programs to the new agency. The unique aspect of an integrated CHRA is that program development and program delivery are found in discrete organizational units. This permits an intermeshing of traditionally separate service delivery patterns into one program delivery unit.

The Arizona model became operational in 1973. It has a job-related focus; it operates programs of public assistance–social services, vocational rehabilitation, employment services and unemployment compensation, and mental retardation. It is functionally organized (for example, combining both welfare and unemployment insurance payments into one bureau) and has established a field services division to administer delivery of departmental services through district offices. A pilot integrated service center has been established in one area in each of the six districts. The Department of Health Services (1974) administers health and mental health programs, giving Arizona a dual human services organizational structure.

*Consolidated CHRA*. Like the integrated CHRA, the statutes that create a consolidated CHRA transfer most or all administrative and program authority of previously autonomous programs to the new agency. A consolidated CHRA, however, is organized along traditional program lines, with an agency management and an administrative unit that assist the agency head in establishing agency policy and goals.

*Confederated CHRA*. The statutes that create a confederated comprehensive human resource agency allow the autonomous program units to retain most of their administrative and program authority. But the statutes also establish an agency to coordinate human services activities among programs. A confederated CHRA is organized along traditional, autonomous program lines, with an agency management and administrative unit that assists the agency head in establishing agency policy and goals.

There is little difference between the statutory authority of the integrated and consolidated agencies; the difference is found mainly in their respective organizational designs. Likewise, there is little difference between the organizational design of the consolidated and confederated agencies; the discriminating factor between them is the agency's degree of statutory authority over human resource programs.

The organizational pattern of the CHRA is designed to maximize the possibility of developing a comprehensive, noncategorical approach to a client's needs at the service delivery point of challenging traditional program lines. Program functions are divided between program development and program delivery. Program development units are responsible for the establishment of basic priorities and for the units responsible for design, monitoring, and evaluation of service programs. The program delivery unit is responsible for all direct service functions through an agencywide regional delivery system.

Within such systems there is frequent opportunity for role confusion and/or conflict between program development and program delivery personnel. Program professionals, who have traditionally followed program development through the program implementation stage, find it difficult to divorce themselves from the delivery point. There may also be an additional gray area of responsibility between the monitoring responsibilities of program development and the implementation responsibilities of program delivery. Agencies with an integrated structure, therefore, require clear definitions of the roles to be played by their program development staff and regional personnel as well as operating guidelines that clarify the authority and responsibility of each section.

**Regional Organization**   A CHRA may have a regional organization that divides the state into geographic units (regions or substate districts) for purposes of administration and/or service delivery. Most human service programs use a regional structure for service delivery or for the supervision of field staff in their departments of employment security, vocational rehabilitation, mental health, (catchment areas), public assistance, and social services. A CHRA regional organization provides common boundaries for these programs and usually groups the staff under a CHRA regional director or coordinator, who reports to the state central CHRA. CHRA regional organizations are of two types: one for integrated service delivery, and another for coordinated administration. The majority of states have no agencywide regional network.

In a regional organization intended to integrate service delivery, the CHRA regional director has direct authority over regional program staff and responsibility for service activities. The regional offices have authority for the implementation of programs; the separate CHRA state program development staff is responsible for program development, guidelines and monitoring, and policy interpretations. Arizona, Georgia, and Washington have such regional organizations: the basic reason for these is to maximize services integration opportunities. Therefore, an integrated regional organization is designed to provide the direction that can facilitate local-level integration (CSG 1974).

An integrated regional system is a component of an integrated state central agency. The integrated central agency is, in turn, structured to provide support for a regional organization.

In a regional organization intended to coordinate administration further, a regional representative is responsible to the central office. The representative may or may not have the administrative responsibilities and does not have authority over program delivery. Three states have such a coordinated regional organization: Arkansas, Florida, and North Carolina. Figure 9.1 shows an example of this type of regional organization—the Arkansas Department of Social and Rehabilitation Services.

The regional coordinator in Arkansas has no administrative authority. He uses his influence and power derived from his colleague relationships and has access to the agency head for these purposes: to convene meetings of regional program directors, to introduce issues, to negotiate resolution of problems among programs when possible, and to refer unresolvable issues to the central agency level. Similar functions are performed in Florida and North Carolina by coordinating councils composed of divisional representatives.

Some of the factors that maximize the opportunity for effective regionalization resemble those utilized in the CHRA at the state level. The key determining factor are the persons and their qualifications to assume the positions of regional directors or staff assistants. A number of states have determined their number of regions by examining their budgets for adequate staffing, as opposed to using geographical factors as criteria.

Regionalization is often perceived as a threatening change by program staff, since it modifies traditional channels of communications and, in some employees minds, establishes another level of red tape. Georgia and Arizona have attempted to minimize this reaction among their staff by instituting orientation programs for state central agency and regional CHRA staff.

Human services must be delivered to people at some accessible point. This means that, except for large institutions, services are made available at local levels—the neighborhood, the city, or the country, depending on the population. Programs at the local level, however, may be operated by the

**Figure 9.1**

A REGIONAL COORDINATION NETWORK: THE ARKANSAS DEPARTMENT OF SOCIAL AND
REHABILITATION SERVICES

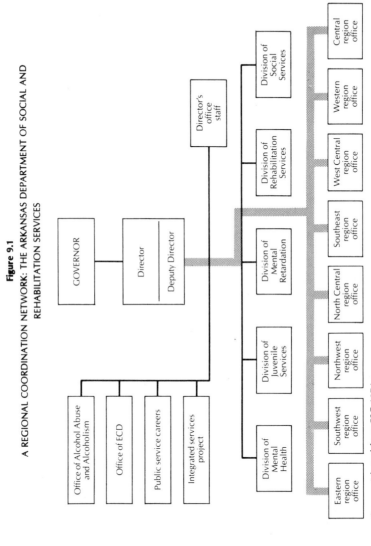

Source: Adapted from CSG 1974.

state, by the local government, or by quasi-public community organizations. The responsibility for program operation varies among states and among various program operations within a state.

The variation among programs within a state with respect to their control over service delivery makes more difficult the coordination or integration of programs. For instance, vocational rehabilitation and employment security are state-operated services in all states. On the other hand, the delivery of social services and public health may be state-controlled or county-controlled, and the extent of such control may vary among counties within the same state—because of population or other political factors. To add to the confusion, mental health programs are often delivered directly by the state through institutions but increasingly by local or quasi-public community mental health programs.

Thus delivery level is characterized by a multiplicity of organizational arrangements and patterns of influence. Service delivery methods are not necessarily linked to particular central agencies or regional structures. Also, for example, a county-administered welfare system does not preclude regionalizing the CHRA, as in Georgia, where a regional network has been established.

Other important factors include prevailing practices of appointment powers, funding arrangements, state civil service coverage and procedures, rule setting, and the interpretation of guidelines.

It is necessary to examine local delivery patterns when evaluating the ability of a state to implement human services integration. The greater the control at the county level, the more difficult it may be for the state to mandate program coordination or integration.

One factor, however, that may assist state efforts toward integration is the recent trend for states to increase their share of county welfare costs. Some states, including Massachusetts, have lifted the entire financial burden from local government, while others, such as Minnesota, New York, and Wisconsin, are significantly increasing the state share.

## COORDINATION

Adequate service delivery is based upon effective coordination. There have been various interpretations and definitions of the word "coordination." March and Simon (1958) refer to coordination as the problem of arranging a delivery system for interdependence—where there is independence but also through planning and feedback, dependence upon one another.

The important factor in coordination is the number of program elements that can be combined into some functional set of interrelationships so that the objectives can be mutually achieved. Moreover, a central factor determining the nature of those linkages is the degree to which the activity is standardized. For example, the more standardized the program linkages, the greater the degree to which coordination can be achieved through a plan or set of program linkages among program elements; the less standardized these linkages, the greater is the degree to which coordination must be achieved through feedback, which involves the transmission of new information (Hage 1974). Health and mental health coordination is a prime example widely used and very successful (Broskowski 1982).

Aiken et al. (1975) defined coordination as the articulation of elements in a service delivery system as to maximize comprehensiveness of, compatibility among, and cooperation among elements. Comprehensiveness refers to the extensiveness and fullness of the components that should logically be a part of a delivery system, given a statement of its goals. Unless a sufficient number of elements needed to attain some desired state exists, coordination will be impossible to achieve. Compatibility refers to the degree to which components are linked together in some coherent manner. There should be a fit between need and service, and services should be provided to clients in an understandable, sensibile, and efficient manner.

Cooperation, finally, indicates the degree to which collaboration and integration exist among the elements in a system. In the context of service delivery systems, this means that collaboration among a collection of agencies, professions, client groups, and resource controllers should take place, guaranteeing that the human services reach the clients in need.

**Elements Requiring Coordination**   At least four key elements must be coordinated in a fully integrated service delivery system: (1) programs, (2) resources, (3) clients, and (4) information. These elements are described in table 9.1.

Each variable represents an important and essential ingredient in any fully integrated service delivery system; the coordination of any one of these components does not necessarily imply the coordination of another. The absence of a given element may, moreover, place serious constraints on the attainment of one of the others. All systems should take into account these four elements in their coordinated efforts to achieve a fully integrated service delivery system.

**TABLE 9.1.**
ELEMENTS REQUIRING COORDINATION

| System Element | Comprehensiveness | Aspect of Coordination | |
| --- | --- | --- | --- |
| | | Compatibility | Cooperation |
| Programs | all needed services; a continuum of care | all needed sequences; all needed joint programs | professionals work together and with other parties |
| Resources | all needed funds and autonomy | correct allocation on basis of client need and caseload | resource controllers work together and with other parties |
| Clients | all eligible clients are treated and in all areas in which they have needs | services are received in correct sequence consistent with individual needs | client representatives work together and with other parties |

Information
central record keeping (clients),
directory of services (programs),
knowledge about available resources,
and continuous feedback relative to the operation
of the system at all three levels.

*Source:* Adapted from Aiken at al. 1975:11.

*Programs and Services.* Five or six different family agencies might be involved in the provision of counseling services, each with some complementarity in terms of different populations of people categorized by geographical location, ethnic or socioeconomic groups, scope and severity of problems, and particular kinds of services offered. These agencies are not necessarily in direct competition and may in fact benefit from program coordination. Cooperation implies that the professionals operating the program have consistent operating philosophies and good working relationships with professionals in related programs. Cooperation at the program level is often aided by informal relationships among professionals, such as membership in the same professional associations or simply meeting for lunch.

Comprehensiveness of a service entails a full array of related programs. That is, there is a continuum of care, in the sense that the service delivery system contains all the programs and services necessary for a given type of client (see March 1968). Compatibility means that services are linked together so that transitions from one stage of a service modality to another are smooth and uninterrupted, the sequencing of services within the modality is coherent, and overlap and duplication are minimized.

*Resources.* The coordination of resources usually signifies the integration of funding but may include other resources, such as the sharing of a facility.

Comprehensiveness of resources means that adequate resources exist to provide information, programs and services, and client management in a fully integrated service delivery system. Lack of funds, preventing comprehensiveness, is probably the greatest deficiency of most delivery systems (such as those with multiply handicapped clients).

With compatibility, resources are provided and administered to reach the appropriate targets and to avoid, or at least minimize, duplication, waste, and needless overlap.

Cooperation implies a consistent set of values that controls the use of resources. This coordination involves the integration of resource controllers—that is, various government agencies and private agencies that control funding and thus have power over organizations in the service delivery system.

*Client Access.* Any service delivery system must make sure that a client receives proper services in the proper sequence. Others have referred to this concept as "case management," "case integration," "case accountability," and "case monitoring" (Kahn 1972).

Comprehensiveness in this context refers to the degree to which all potential clients are identified and treated. Case coordinators periodically monitor the situations of the clients, especially those highly dependent of incapable, such as the mentally retarded.

Compatibility is here concerned with the sequencing of services. Is the system organized so that clients obtain services when they need them? There is some correct order of treatment, presumably different for different clients at different ages, and with different combinations of handicaps or needs. However, since there is usually not much monitoring, a client may move from agency to agency, somewhat at random and in no particular sequence—if he moves at all. Typically, clients with multiple problems receive only part of the services they need.

Cooperation refers to the ability of different client, professional, and other interest groups to reach workable compromises that do not subvert the interests of any one group.

Accountability, or more often the lack of it, has been identified as a central problem in service delivery. A basic aspect of accountability is whether the system is responsive to the needs of clients (Gilbert 1972). The accountability problem is in part addressed through case monitoring and coordination. One possibility here is that case managers play the roles of ombudsmen who intervene in the system on the part of their clients.

*Information.* The coordination of this element has both internal and external aspects. The external component addresses itself to the degree to which information about service opportunities is available to those who are not yet in the system but who seek to make use of it. Information should be made available at some specific site, such as an advice and referral center (March 1968), a neighborhood information center (Kahn 1972), or a council of community service organization (Broskowski and Baker 1972). In a fully integrated service delivery system, the availability of information would be comprehensive, in the sense that service inventories (of service-rendering agencies, their programs and services, and the availability of the services) would exist (Kronick, Perlmutter, and Gummer 1973). Compatibility in this context suggests the existence of a central or fixed point of referral. Cooperation means that this information is available and accessible to everyone.

The other aspect of information coordination is an internal one that involves the operation of service delivery systems themselves including questions of evaluation and feedback. These kinds of questions must be addressed: Are programs accomplishing the goals they were designed to achieve? Are adequate services available to all clients? Do case managers report that their clients are receiving all the services they need, when they need them, and in the correct sequence? Are there adequate feedback mechanisms and consequent authority to take corrective actions when system deficiencies are identified?

Coordination of such information would be comprehensive if there were information channels from all parts of the service delivery system, establishing a flow and exchange of interdependence among the various program and service components and assessing their impact on each other. Cooperation would exist to the extent that communication channels were open, assuring the free flow of information to and from the control center and various system parts (Aiken 1975).

These elements may be understood according to the identified levels of service delivery: that is, resources are best coordinated at the institutional level, programs at the organizational level, clients at the individual caseworker level, and information at each of these levels.

Different problems of coordination exist for each level. At the institutional level, the problem is primarily one of gaining sufficient resources from the environment of the service delivery system, for example, funding from federal, state, and local governments as well as private sources. At the organizational level, programs and service components are invariably conceived, developed, and delivered by service delivery organizations, whether a county welfare department, a private rehabilitation organization like Goodwill Industries, or a local mental health clinic. Whether these programs and services are concentrated in a single superagency or scattered among a number of autonomous agencies that may offer competing and overlapping programs, the central problem is linking these diverse program elements into a coherent "system" of service delivery.

At the level of the recipient, or consumer, the service delivery system is best coordinated by the individual caseworker. The critical problem here is to ensure that the client have the services needed in the proper sequence and at the proper time. Finally, information needs to be coordinated at all levels of the service delivery system—that is, information about obtaining resources from the environment, transforming these resources into programs and services, and delivering them effectively to clients.

**Linkages and Coordination**   Generally speaking, a correlation may be found between the types of linkages used and the mode of coordination used in a program.

Three general categories of coordination may be noted. The three have varying degrees of impact upon programs (Gans and Horton 1975).

*In voluntary coordination,* the integrator is responsible for administering the provision of direct service as well as for developing linkages between autonomous service providers. For example, Head Start central staff are responsible for activities such as child development and nutrition and can involve such other service providers as health practitioners and social service agencies in the implementation of a comprehensive Head Start program.

*In mediated coordination,* the primary mission of the integrator is the development of linkages between autonomous service providers rather than the provision of direct service. For example, the staff of a 4-C Committee does not provide day care services; rather, it relates the services of health provider, early childhood education specialists, and social agencies to the activities of day care centers in order to establish a network with the capability to plan, program, budget, implement, and evaluate comprehensive child development programs.

*In directed coordination,* the integrator has the authority to mandate the development of linkages between legally subordinate service providers, for example, the office of the administrator of a human resource agency has the authority to compel the division heads to participate in joint planning, budgeting, evaluation, and so on.

The impact of the project on accessibility, continuity, and efficiency appeared to vary according to the mode of coordination being employed.

Particularly noteworthy are the relationships between the use of direct service linkages and voluntary projects and between the use of administrative linkages and mediated and directed programs. In the former, the integrator in responsible for providing direct service to a specific client group while developing linkages with service providers. With little available time and no authority over service providers, emphasis is placed on establishing linkages that have immediate rewards in terms of delivering services to clients. In contrast, attempted integration in both mediated and directed programs results in the development of cooperative relationships between service providers, rather than the provision of direct services. Thus, emphasis is placed on the establishment of administrative linkages (Gans and Horton 1975).

The application of general systems theory to organizational analysis (as described in chapter 2) is a fairly recent, rapidly expanding development. A human service agency is a system, and thus its commitment is to the maintenance of its autonomy and continued survival according to: (1) acquiring and maintaining sufficient levels of necessary resources; (2) accomplishing primary tasks that involve establishing a hierarchy of tasks and development of subtasks to be accomplished by its subparts such as departments and roles; (3) achieving integration in the face of differentiating environmental influences in such a way as to facilitate relationships that allow the efforts of individuals and organizational subunits to be effectively coordinated; and (4) adapting to both the environment and its own internal requirements, and to some degree trying to control or adapt the environment itself.

Although the focus of this discussion will be on the third point, each of these elements should be considered part of a systems approach. The term ''system'' includes both independence and interdependence. Human service organizations vary in the degree to which their boundaries are permeable: some agency boundaries are easily penetrated while others tend to maintain stricter boundary controls. This applies to people, information, and ideology; and the relative permeability of an agency's boundaries affects the degree to which the organization can be influenced by various community factors.

Unfortunately, many human service facilities seem surprisingly unaware of, and uninterested in, the activities of other agencies with which it would appear they should have a close functional relationship. Those relationships that do exist often involve strong distrust, prejudice, and a lack of awareness of the behaviors, goals, and plans of the other community organizations. For example, comprehensive health planning emphasizes the importance of increasing interaction and interdependence among the agency, the community, and other caregiving organizations, with an increasing interpenetration of traditional boundary conditions. Since one of the primary aims of a community mental health center or health maintenence organization is continuity of care, permeability is required—not only between the various subparts of the facility, but also between it and other agencies in the larger caregiving network. Human service organizations, in the role of delivery systems, differ in the degree and type of independence they display to the systems that make up the supersystem. Any form of interorganizational relations involves transactions of some kind across organizational boundaries.

Agencies need also to develop differentiated subsystems and draw specialized boundary roles to handle the interrelations among organizations. The human services organization needs to have a representative—such as the case coordinator—who interacts with representatives of other agencies. The attitudes and skills of persons in boundary roles are an important consideration, and agencies would do well to develop adequate training and recruitment programs for boundary spanners. For example, those staff members of a CMHC who have frequent commerce with other health and welfare agencies through their selective filtering of information can exercise a great deal of power and affect the reception of inputs needed by the organization. Community resources are directly and indirectly related in a causal network so that one component of the complex affecting the action capabilities of other parts may be conceptualized as comprising a community system of great importance.

Larger and more differentiated interorganizational systems are likely to be marked by more complicated, diverse, and conflicting roles and relationships than are found within a single organizational system (Gross 1966). The significance of interorganizational relationships and environmental influences in the conceptualization of a caregiving network (i.e., coordination and integration) has received increasing attention from organizational theorists and researchers. Each organization must be viewed as a component of a larger macrosocial system. Component interdependence is a primary attribute of such a system since any system exists only to the extent that its components or parts are linked in some network of internal relations. When the activities and decisions of one human service facility do not affect what other agencies do or decide, their component interdependence is low. Component interdependence will be high when two or more service facilities in a given community have competing needs for scarce resources, when there is intervention by supraorganizational processes (such as the governor or state commissioner of a department), or when individuals or groups cross organizational boundaries to form intersystem bonds.

Thompson and McEwan (1958) have outlined three types of cooperative strategies that organizations may employ in dealing with other human service centers in their environment: bargaining, cooptation, and coalition. In bargaining, negotiations are entered into by a formal organization because support is necessary to develop and maintain agreement for an exchange of goods or services between the two facilities. To the extent that the other agency's support is necessary to maintain the agreement, that agency is in a position to exercise control over the organizational decision processes of the first organization.

Cooptation makes even further inroads in terms of the goal-setting processes: not only must the final choice be acceptable to the coopted party or organization, but to the extent that cooptation is effective, it places the representative of an "outsider" in a position to determine the occasion for a goal decision—to participate in analyzing the existing situation, to suggest alternatives, and to take part in the deliberation of consequences (Thompson and McEwan 1958). From the standpoint of the health system, by providing overlapping memberships, cooptation aids the integration of the diverse parts of such a complex social network.

Coalition refers to a combination of two or more organizations for a common goal. Commitment toward joint action in a coalition may range from a very limited commitment for a short time to a complete commitment for an indefinite time: but it is distinguished from a merger in that the organizations do not lose their separate boundaries and each member can withdraw from the relationship.

**Barriers to Coordination**   A number of factors may act as barriers to coordination in the human service field.

*Complexity of agencies.* A major deterrent to the development of a coordinated system of service delivery is the great diversity of organizations providing specialized human services. This is not only an urban phenomenon but also has been documented in rural areas. Gans and Horton (1975) described that, in 1952, a county now called "Appalachia," where there were more than 600 agencies involved in providing organized health services within the county; and of these, 155 were locally based health-related organizations.

Four main types of health organizations have been identified within the health system: official or public agencies; voluntary or nonprofit agencies; hospitals and nursing homes; and health-related organizations such as welfare and social agencies (Levine and White 1961). Another category that might be added to their inventory consists of the mutual help groups and associations concerned with health problems. Considering the multiplicity of agencies in any given community, and within a particular system such as mental health or criminal justice, it is not surprising that interagency coordination is often poor.

*Mixed authority.* Intraorganizational patterns often have well-defined structures for authority—a direct contrast to an interorganizational analysis, which cannot assume a single well-defined form of authority for any delivery plan.

*Specialization.* Specialization in medicine, social welfare, and more recently in criminal justice has worked against the coordination of both professional persons and human service facilities. The public has become increasingly disturbed, for example, about the number of physicians with whom a family must maintain contact for treatment of varying types and degrees of illness. Although there is concern about cost and inconvenience, the desire of the public for "the best" in professional skill has supported specialization. In contrast, planning mental health services for the poor has led to increasing recognition of the problems of multiple uncoordinated speciality services, and the reemergence of trends toward generalist roles has resulted.

*Deficient communication.* This barrier applies at the organizational and individual level. Individuals frequently receive services from several different agencies or several different professional workers within the same organization, without the individual agent or organization being aware of, or even displaying an interest in, the involvement of others. Cursory and nonsystematized communication seems to be the norm among professional workers; this is particularly true of the gap between health and welfare agencies.

Fromer (1979) notes, for example, that the community health nurse "is in an extremely important and valuable position to advise on the kinds of programs and services needed" (p. 159). But because she is close to the client, there is no assurance that the nurse's competence as an advice giver is exploited.

A mental health worker may be helping a family in crisis cope with the stress and frustration of being parents to acting-out children, while the welfare worker is making a case for child neglect and possible abuse by requesting the court to take action to remove the children from the home and placing them with foster parents.

*Stereotyped beliefs and attitudes.* There are false beliefs and irrational assumptions about how negative attitudes and competition between professional groups will affect cooperation and how these will even work against interdisciplinary coordination for the effective collaboration of service delivery.

*Difficulty in defining "the primary task."* Multiple goals are not necessarily compatible, and they may produce competition for scarce resources among the subparts of an organization in which one component is more committed to one goal than is another. Further, ambiguities usually arise in defining the primary mission because certain goals are denied, while goals the organization claims publicly to pursue will not be realized simply because they were never really intended to be pursued.

In addition to providing the essential client-oriented elements of a comprehensive program, systems also engage in other activities such as research, educational programs for various disciplines, social action services, provision of employment for professional personnel, and self-preservation. Because there are few established priorities for goal setting within the human service system, any particular goals may assume primacy at a given time according to the balance of forces then operating. Priorities are modified as a result of factors such as personnel changes, a gain or loss of federal grants, or changing techniques, ideologies, and government pluralism. Thus any given primary task may only have a limited viability.

**Facilitators and Inhibitors to Integration**   Service integration is an evolutionary process. It takes time—time for organization and implementation of a program; time for a program to attain legitimacy and visibility in terms of the service providers; and time for participating agencies to develop a comfortable working relationship, often a necessary prerequisite to the coordination or consolidation of agencies' functions. Once linkages have been made, they need attention and support so that gains may be protected and further progress made.

There is a wide range of important facilitators and inhibitors that Gans and Horton (1975) have identified for service integration:

*The environment.* Support from government, community, and public and private funding sources, in terms of need for service delivery changes in general and by means of a program in particular, often enhances integrated efforts, while opposition exerts a significant negative influence. The local environment is more susceptible to change if national leaders emphasize the need to overcome problems, if sectors of the community are interested and express a commitment in improving the service delivery system, if adequate resources are available and community consensus and support can be developed, and if there is united effort with local general purpose governments and influential citizens acting through health and welfare planning councils and similar groups.

In Florida, where human services have undergone reorganization, a number of problems in administrative services have arisen. This has aroused the state legislature, which could conceivably set integration back. In Arizona, Washington, and Georgia, integration has "been thwarted by opposition from federal officials, local officials, professional groups, or the legislature" (Lynn 1977:97).

*Program objectives and priorities.* Distinct emphasis in program guidelines as well as technical assistance on the desirability of coordination can affect priorities and legitimize coordination efforts.

*Program director.* The "great man" theory is still of value in that the personality of the executive and his charisma and ability are one of the most important factors in the success of service integration.

Leadership, persuasiveness, commitment, and personal contacts with political sources, the staff of service provider, and the community appear to be the attributes which have had the greatest effect. Professional credentials are less essential where recognition and respect already exist.

*Program staff.* It is essential for staff to have skills, not only in service delivery, but also in the coordination of service providers. Expertise in this area includes that of programming, training, grantsmanship, meeting federal requirements, and interagency cooperation.

*Service provider objectives and attitudes.* Where providers want to obtain absolute control of funds, functions, and internal procedures, and where they vie for control of the delivery system (which is probably normal organizational behavior), service integration is critically impeded.

*Grant administration policies and procedures.* Service integration is facilitated to the extent that the program integrator has control over other service-provider access to funds. In this situation, single-point funding becomes a powerful tool for integration. Also, open-ended funding and the availability of flexible funds is very enticing, and in-kind contributions for federal funds have acted as an incentive to the integrator to seek out and involve provider agencies in service integration efforts. Such service integration results in improved accessibility, continuity, and efficiency.

a) *Accessibility.* Integration has brought services to clients' neighborhoods and has improved the attitudes of traditional service-provider staffs, thus enhancing their ability and willingness to serve new client groups. Integration has also increased the number and effectiveness of outreach personnel who find and admit clients for service and has led to a systematic review of service requirements and resources, resulting in the development of needed services.

b) *Continuity.* Some programs have emphasized the core services of intake, diagnosis, referral, and followup, supplemented by various modes of case coordination (such as the case conference and the use of a case coordinator). These approaches have ensured that client acceptance into one service will result in help from other providers, thereby minimizing red tape and delay. The initial assessment of overall service need and the delivery of specific services in a complimentary, orderly, and timely manner also have been facilitated. Furthermore, programs have achieved greater continuity through concentration on administrative linkages in order to identify service gaps and augment the resources of the delivery system and to ensure that the range of client needs can be met. These administrative linkages, such as joint planning or programming, purchase of service, and joint funding, enable programs to make the necessary commitments with agencies to plan and provide specific services in a manner that is well received among other service providers agencies.

c) *Efficiency.* Integration marks a definite advance in terms of coordinated staff utilization, funding, planning, programming, and evaluation. It has not, however, been justifiable only on the basis of dollar saving alone. From the viewpoint of efficiency, moreover, there is no single "best" services integration model. Services integration can occur at various governmental levels with diverse sponsors, contacts, and activities.

The potential for services integration exists on all levels of DHEW funding. However, to implement service integration, DHEW must make a significantly greater effort. A number of possible alternatives may be cited: first, the creation of an environment receptive to service integration; second,

**TABLE 9.2.**
SUMMARY OF FACILITATORS

| Rank Order | Category | Critical | Major | Minor | Total |
|---|---|---|---|---|---|
| 1 | Environmental influences | 27 | 27 | 17 | 71 |
| 2 | Role of director or board | 26 | 15 | 8 | 49 |
| 3 | Service provider objectives | 15 | 18 | 8 | 41 |
| 4 | Technical and logistical factors | 15 | 15 | 7 | 37 |
| 5 | Project structure and operations | 12 | 9 | 14 | 35 |
| 6 | Grant administration policies and procedures | 13 | 9 | 14 | 35 |
| 7 | Project staff | 6 | 11 | 9 | 26 |
| 8 | Incentives for project participation | 11 | 10 | 3 | 26 |

Source: Adapted from Gans and Horton 1975:70.

the review of support services conducive to service integration projects, such as advocacy, technical assistance, and monitoring support services in order to facilitate implementation of a service integration policy; third, elimination of internal DHEW constraints on service integration—including procedures, policies, and the organization of DHEW, or the appointment of staff within the department whose sole responsibility is coordination of service integration efforts. This activity would be replicated in regional offices. Building services integration into the DHEW grant system through development of guidelines for DHEW funding policy would also facilitate service integration.

Among the major objectives of the research conducted by Gans and Horton (1975) was the identification and analysis of factors that affect the development and implementation of service integration projects. The aim of their discussion was to outline the facilitators and inhibitors that affected particular integrating linkages and to summarize the various substudies of the overall research project. The facilitators and inhibitors were rated "critical," "major," or "minor" to indicate the intensity of their impact on the development of the project under scrutiny. Table 9.2 illustrates by category the facilitators that influence the projects under investigation.

Any effort to foster the facilitators of service integration must embrace a wide spectrum of activity. However, in this study the most important facilitating factors appear to have been: support from the external sociopolitical environment in which the project functioned; the cooperative environment created when the actors in the project—the integrator and the other service providers—share the project's objective; and the cooperative environment created when the service providers did not fear loss of control of their services or internal operations. Almost half of the facilitators fell into these categories. It is interesting to note that federal grant and administrative policies and procedures (less than 10 percent of the facilitators) were not nearly as important as the local influences.

Table 9.3 summarizes eight major categories of project inhibitors of service integration. Assessments of the impact of individual inhibitors are presented in the order of frequency. None of the inhibitors included in these categories was of critical significance in more than 20 percent of the projects in the sample. Therefore, as with the facilitators, it is difficult to conclude that any single factor was a primary impediment to services integration for all or any one of the project types. The research indicates conditions that were generally hostile to service integration efforts and shows that the integrator's objectives and priorities have a high potential for detrimental impact. The most important inhibitor was the project's focus on internal operations or direct service delivery, rather than on the development of integrating linkages.

The next most important inhibitor in this category was the intention of the integrator *not* to develop certain integrating linkages that could contribute to overall project coherence and efficacy. Another associated inhibitor was the integrator's placement of high priority on other objectives. Although service integration may have been a formal objective of the integrator, in fact the

**TABLE 9.3.**
SUMMARY OF INHIBITORS

| Rank Order | Category | Critical | Major | Minor | Total |
|---|---|---|---|---|---|
| 1 | Integrator's objectives and attitudes | 16 | 4 | 8 | 28 |
| 2 | Service provider objectives and attitudes | 9 | 11 | 5 | 25 |
| 3 | Grant administration policies and procedures | 6 | 8 | 11 | 25 |
| 4 | Project structure and operations | 8 | 5 | 5 | 18 |
| 5 | Environmental influences | 7 | 6 | 1 | 14 |
| 6 | Project staff | 2 | 4 | 6 | 12 |
| 7 | Technical and logistical factors | 4 | 5 | 2 | 11 |
| 8 | Service providers policies and procedures | 3 | 4 | 4 | 11 |

*Source:* Adapted from Gans and Horton 1975:82.

objective was not aggressively pursued because the integrator had more pressing service needs to meet or because the funding source dictated that other objectives be given higher priority. The most detrimental attitude was found in the service provider's desire to retain agency prerogatives with respect to control of service delivery. The failure of the integrator to involve service commitments from service providers were among the important impediments to integration. Factors of poor administration included inadequate role definition, unclear lines of authority, insufficient supervision, assignment of incompatible work tasks to staff, permitting contracts to lapse, and poor delineation of reciprocal responsibilities of the integrator and the service providers.

**Summary**  The integration of services has become increasingly important to the U.S. Department of Health, Education, and Welfare over the last decade. In the mid-1960s, DHEW had limited involvement in the Office of Economic Opportunity's attempts, under the Community Action Program, to link together programs serving the poor. Later, DHEW played a coordinative role in the thirteen Neighborhood Services Programs and in the Model Cities Program. In 1971, then-Secretary Elliot Richardson, recognizing the need for improved coordination of HEW's own programs at the state and local level, proposed a new legislative initiative aimed at the integration of services, the Allied Services Act. Simultaneously, the department began a series of demonstration projects—the Services Integration Targets of Opportunity (SITO) grants—to test various services integration techniques, primarily at the delivery level. Under the grants, numerous techniques were developed and demonstrated, including new information and referral systems, client-tracking systems, one-stop service centers, and new case management procedures. SITO projects were funded for up to three years, with the final grants being made in June 1975.

In 1974, the department also initiated a new series of demonstration activities, called Partnership Grants. These grants, expanding on the SITO concept, aimed at building the capacity of state and local governments to carry out comprehensive planning, management, and delivery of human services. In 1975, then-Secretary Caspar W. Weinberger issued a policy statement setting forth the department's intention "actively [to] assist chief executives of state and local general purpose governments [to] improve their capacities to plan and manage human service programs." This Capacity-Building Policy Statement has served to focus attention on governors, mayors, and county executives as critical links in the promotion of services integration (Morrill 1976).

Not surprisingly, the evaluation of services integration projects has proved to be exceedingly difficult. Services integration evaluations of high quality require the assessment of complex institutional processes and organizational arrangements, which are almost always linked inextricably to an active political process. Frequently, the essential baseline data are unavailable, and standard reporting and monitoring are often underdeveloped.

For such reasons, and despite the attention paid to the evaluation of services integration initiatives, the data and analyses that would fully support administrators at the state and local level in their services integration efforts are not yet available. But based on the findings of completed evaluations, as well as extensive dialogue with DHEW regional offices, state and local officials, and leaders of services integration, HEW has developed a basic set of working principles:

First, services integration is a slow, evolutionary process of developing linkages among service providers. In part, this is due to the categorical nature of service delivery, but, more importantly, it is attributable to the pluralistic nature of our federal system and the society at large (Lynn 1977; Redburn 1977). Services integration is primarily a consensus-building process. This consensus building is best complemented but not supplanted by systems development (Baker and Northman 1978).

Second, organizational changes do not necessarily lead to, or even encourage, services integration. Reorganization of the human resources functions of state or local governments may, when coupled with an active consensus-building process, increase the viability of services integration efforts.

Third, services integration seldom reduces costs over the short term. Increased program effectiveness is likely to be seen much earlier than a decrease in delivery system costs.

Fourth, the perception by service providers that they will benefit from a local integration initiative is crucial to their continued involvement in developmental efforts.

Fifth, in large measure, successful services integration depends upon the leadership and talents of elected officials and of those persons responsible for developing consensus and effecting linkages.

Sixth, services integration at the delivery level most often requires shared information systems that are often expensive and always require enormous cooperation between public and private agencies.

Seventh, services integration works best where state and local governments, in tandem, develop a common services strategy.

Eighth, because of the large number of competitive service providers and the complexity of delivery systems in large cities, integrative linkages are much less likely to be adopted in major urban areas than in small cities and rural areas.

Services integration is neither a transient issue nor a problem that will ever be completely solved. As long as the public sector is involved in delivering complex services, it will be imperative that policy makers and administrators focus attention on the coordination of separate human services organizations and programs. If we do not, we are seriously shortchanging the consumers and clients, for whom the entire system exists.

## COMMUNITY ORGANIZATION

**Councils of Community Services**   The contemporary search for more effective methods of organizing and planning and for more comprehensive approaches to human needs and services resembles, in many ways, efforts made sixty and seventy years ago. At the turn of the century, reformers and philanthropists with a mixture of motivations were developing new institutions and techniques.

In Massachusetts, state boards of charities had been formed in 1863 to administer correctional institutions and hospitals and to supervise private institutions receiving public funds. Gradually, these boards developed standards for voluntary hospitals, orphanages, homes for the aged, nursing homes, and other agencies. Planning at the state level for a wide range of institutional and noninstitutional services is the outgrowth of those early efforts at supervision and standard setting.

Reformers and philanthropists also founded a number of voluntary agencies dedicated to serving individuals and families in need of help. Of particular interest was the charity organization society (COS) which, by 1892, had led to the establishment of similar agencies in ninety-two cities in North America (Perlman and Gurin 1972). Later the COS maintained a central registration bureau of charitable agencies in order to avoid duplication of services to individuals. An effort was made to organize assistance for their clients and their relatives, churches, employers, and other private sources in the community. COS agencies established patterns for bringing groups together into a framework that called for joint consideration of needs and for the coordination of activities. The agencies thus laid the foundation for the planning of social programs that is reflected in the work of their successor organizations: the councils of social agencies, and the health and welfare councils.

In the field of social welfare, planning and community organization developed along several different lines. The early charity organization society had a double function. One was to render direct assistance to families. That function became professionalized by social casework and then carried forward by family service agencies that eventually shed most of their relief-giving functions in favor of more intensive counseling of individuals and families. The other aspect of the COS is reflected in the "organization" part of its title. Its purpose was to bring order to the various activities of the many independent relief societies of that period, to eliminate the duplication of relief grants, and to coordinate separate efforts. This line of activity led, over a period of time, to the establishment of a new type of organization that was composed of representatives of "social agencies that want to unite in a common project of establishing and approving standards" (Lubove 1965). Councils of social agencies, welfare councils, and community chests developed as organizational forms. The concept of a community planning function in relation to social services began to emerge, paralleling the physical planning functions that were being articulated in the field of city planning.

Community organization, practiced since the 1920s, and councils of social agencies (composed mainly of socioeconomic elites) have, however, had no appreciable impact on major social problems. The limited scope of the health and welfare councils, which focused on the coordination of services among voluntary agencies, hobbled their effectiveness. Community organization among middle-class–dominated agencies, like community action among the poor, stressed the process of bringing people together for joint activity but also lacked a policy foundation for meaningful social change.

The practices of the community welfare councils were the principal sources for the conceptualization of "community organization," which by the 1960s was being taught in schools of social work across the country. More recently, however, increased interest in analyzing and formulating policies had led to direct action. Value is now being placed on social planning and social policy analysis, not only on the community level but at the state and national levels, and it is moreover concerned with the flow of authority and resources among these levels.

**United Fund**   Today the most prevalent form of intersector coordination at the local community level is the united fund council complex, found in more that 2,000 U.S. communities and represented nationally by the United Way. These organizations are direct descendants of the earlier community chests and the councils of social agencies.

After World War II, the community chest expanded into the united fund, incorporating the fund-raising campaigns of national agencies, as well as local health and welfare services. The fund-raising effort has necessarily involved the United Way in the allocation of funds and therefore, to some degree, in concerted decision making and the setting of priorities. A planning function is at least implicit in these organizations.

Since the early days of chests and councils, it has been recognized—at least in theory—that a close logical and practical relationship exists between the allocation of resources and the planning of programs. Fund allocation and program planning have sometimes been combined, with chest and welfare councils united in a single organization. More frequently, especially in larger cities, the community chest or united fund works as a separate organization to raise philanthropic funds for voluntary agencies. The welfare council or federation functions separately as an organization committed to broader planning responsibilities—including both voluntary and governmental agencies.

The following is a list of the different levels of planning that may be found in the course of the development of a United Fund Council structure (Perlman and Gurin 1972):

1. *Setting minimum standards for affiliated agencies.* A central organization, responsible for joint fund raising, will establish minimum standards as requirements for agency inclusion and participation.
2. *Providing informational and other services.* A central organization may render joint services to affiliated agencies, contributors, and citizens on an informational level. As an adjunct of fund raising efforts, information will deal with "programs and needs of the included agencies. Education programs for board members can be addressed more broadly to community-wide issues.
3. *Reviewing budgets and programs.* Either separate from, of complying with, budgetary review, a first-level approach to joint planning is to bring programs and services that have some relationship with one another into ongoing contact.
5. *Organization of new services.* Such services may be established either as a result of the activities of an independent group, or through the mechanisms of a planning council. In recent years, new programs have been organized as a result of initiative of welfare councils in

fields such as the services to the aged, where a more integrated program was needed than had been previously available through the activities of separate agencies. Sometimes, new agencies are established through the merger of several organizations on the basis of studies and recommendations developed in the planning councils.

6. *Determination of priorities.* A limited amount of progress has been achieved in establishing criteria within a particular field—where the importance of programs has been weighed on the basis of such factors as the number of people reached, the severity of the condition being treated, or the effectiveness of the services rendered. It is particularly difficult, however, to establish quantitative criteria for choosing priorities across fields (for example, health services as against youth services) because of the vague judgments and partisan interests involved.

7. *Long-range planning.* Long-range planning, extending over a five- or a ten-year period, usually becomes most meaningful and substantive at the point when councils and funds are involved in decisions about capital expenditures. Decisions as to whether or not to construct facilities represent critical choices about the future scope and character of various service programs—not to mention investment and upkeep costs. Long-range planning exercises, while not always resulting in concrete plans that actually are implemented, serve at times as ways of clarifying agreements in differences over basic objectives.

**Community Councils**  The community health and welfare planning council is an overlay on the human service organizations supported by the United Way network. The council was described by Demone and Schulberg (1974) as one organizational strategy for generating stability and strength in interorganizational functioning. The responsibilities, problems, and perspectives for such a policy-making body were examined, and some consequences for the future were projected. In recent years, the focus of councils has shifted from the earlier goals of coordination and efficiency to planning activities that are directed toward the resolution of massive social problems. The further evolution of the council's planning thrust has led to a principal concern with social policy, both public and private: the council is now viewed as one of the many local and regional planning instruments. Traditional concern with agency efficiency and coordination has been integrated into a more comprehensive framework for providing human services. Needs and resources are highlighted, and existing agency programs are viewed as one of many alternatives or intervention possibilities.

The council's constituency, because of its close links to the united fund, may be third in size only to the government and organized religions. As a consequence, some action alternatives are limited, if not actually impossible. Nevertheless, the council's individual volunteers are likely to have an active social conscience and are usually influential within the community, so that other advantages are gained.

The council's flexibility is furthered because it does not operate programs, and patronage is unnecessary. The council as an action group can deal differently, not necessarily weighted with the irrational issues and controversy that many governmental agencies experience. In considering alternative options, councils frequently have had experience with many other techniques of social change, such as research, budgeting and cost analysis, general systems theory, committees, consensus, coordination, information systems, forums, conferences, seminars, community organization, consultation, and participation. Not all intervention strategies are equally available to all organizations, nor are they equally appropriate in all situations, but in many councils such experiences have extraordinary value where optimal strategies must be developed.

Another significant factor affecting the council's role in developing human services is the trend toward closer relations between the executive branch of government and the voluntary planning council. A link similiar to legislative bodies is at the testing stage. As the council's problem-solving capacity improves, the council will play an expanded role in policy formation. If, for example, the problem is a lack of low-cost housing for the aged, it may be necessary to seek changes in the construction and financing policies of federal, state, and local governments in order to increase both the number of available units and their quality. Similiarly, attempts may be made to modify building restrictions to accommodate the special needs of the physically handicapped or aged.

The reorganization of our existing human services system to contemporary relevance is a key responsibility and concern of the community council. The welfare nonsystem and problems of malnutrition, family planning, and housing are instances of pressing social concerns that are within the functional competency of council planners. They can, for instance, assume a dual approach to public welfare, maximizing the present system's effectiveness and aiming toward major national health insurance and a guaranteed annual income. The issues that affect the residents of our inner cities— economic viability, adequate jobs and housing, decent education, effective public transportation, a general administration of justice, credit reform, and drug and alcohol abuse—are but some of the additional challenges to, and opportunities for, the community council.

As they begin to assert a major role in the planning of human services, community councils now confront a series of major problems. These troublesome issues pertain to the ambiguous nature of the planning function in the field of human services, the transitory character of the council's constituency, and sanction in its scope of functions. Each council must make its own determination of how national trends will uniquely manifest themselves in their particular communities and then evolve an appropriate format for the future. For example, in the last few years, metropolitan councils operating independently and autonomously have been reduced by half, so that there are now perhaps ten independent councils in existence in such cities as Philadelphia, Baltimore, and New York. In contrast, the formerly independent metropolitan councils, among them those in Chicago and Boston, have become part of the United Way; the council itself is merely a dependent subdivision within a larger bureaucratic structure of the United Way.

In 1970, in the fifty-four Metro I and II cities—who raised $4 million or more in their annual United Way campaigns—there were forty-five independent planning organizations known variously as councils of social agencies, health and welfare associations, social planning councils, and the like. In 1977, there were only nineteen, and five of these nineteen "independents" were undergoing study to consider whether or not, in the next year or two, they too might be merged with the United Way fund-raising organization.

In 1970, in the twenty-five biggest cities—the Metro I's that raise $9 million or more—there were only three combined fund-raising and planning United Ways (Cincinnati, Milwaukee, and Seattle). All the rest—twenty-two of them—had viable, large, well-financed, independent planning organizations. In 1977, there were only ten independents in Metro I cities, and four of these were under study (Akana 1977). As the role of public philanthropy decreases and increasing reliance is placed on public resources, there will be a further shift among independent councils toward becoming subsystems of United Way organizations and toward assuming primary role in citizen monitoring as "the public conscience" or in the task of convening and monitoring, in contrast to previous functions of coordinating or service-oriented packages.

The council's ability to continue its advance as a major force in the planning of human services is, to some extent, impeded by the internal transitions through which it is still passing. The council is struggling to clarify both the explicit and subtle implications of the change in its constituency as it shifts from the previous role as a body of agencies to its current function as a citizen's spokesman. Among the issues to be resolved are the relationship between the community council, with its increased planning orientation, and the United Fund with its money-raising perspective. Although the concerns of the two groups are largely congruent, they also diverge in significant instances. The community council's credibility as a spokesman for human service interests would in many ways be enhanced by its assuming an advocacy position on controversial issues. However, such a stance may also antagonize key contributors to the United Way. The result of this dilemma is that councils are now reassessing traditional funding patterns and turning toward a mixture of voluntary, public, and private funds instead of relying heavily on voluntary funds alone. These new sources of fiscal support provide the council with greater flexibility and permit it to venture into areas that previously had been beyond its scope.

**A Model of a Metropolitan Council**   Shroder and Shiffman (1974) of the Community Council of Greater New York have proposed a model of a metropolitan council that has eight distinct program components: monitoring, research utilization, neighborhood coalitions, information center for citizens, consumers, community service agencies, and legislators on social policy data collection and office of planning for "trends and forecasts."

Between 500 and 600 community councils operate across the country. Aside from the emphasis on allocating increased resources to planning efforts, there is no prevailing pattern among them. The three community councils and organizations outlined in table 9.4 are designed with one common purpose: to aid, each in its own way, in the efficient and effective planning of resources allocation while recognizing and dealing with the many interrelated influences affecting and constraining program planning in human service development. Two of the councils are working to clarify the explicit and subtle implications of changing constituencies as they shift from their previous roles as bodies of agencies to their current structure as citizen's spokesmen. Table 9.4 is a comparative outline of the Rhode Island Council of Community Services (a state council), the Woonsocket County Council of Community Services (a small county council), and the United Community Planning Corporation of Boston (a large metropolitan council). The table includes major variables in any council—support, origin, structure, functions, direct services, catchment area, the relationship to United Way, and deficiencies.

These examples may give the reader some idea of the variations among councils and their approaches and of the elements that currently influence their programs and activities. Although there are now significant differences among councils, it is clear that the issues facing all councils do have a common denominator; it is merely a matter of time before some of these differences become more apparent. The straightforward reason for this is the economics of human services delivery and the role of voluntary agencies, particularly councils of community services in the United Way. The former independence and autonomy of voluntary agencies is no longer present; and the checks and balances to government that have been provided by private nonprofit organizations in the human service fields are now threatened. Accordingly, the determination of human service needs and priorities is increasingly becoming a political process. This trend is already decried in some voluntary quarters by those who feel that well-organized constituencies, such as the elderly and recipients of day care services, are receiving disproportionate shares of public expenditures.

Many changes are taking place in the councils of community services. Many of their employees admit to the insecurity of their employment in these organizations. It is impossible to estimate the impact of the process of economic and political change on the allocation policies of the United Way without reference to a framework of United Way goals and objectives for the years ahead. The question is critical, because it would be a serious error to assume that financial problems are the concern only of those agencies that receive public monies. Government funding policy and social service programming is only a reflection of these financial worries. The economics of human services affect everyone, and virtually all nonprofit human service institutions find themselves in increasingly perilous financial situations.

Leading thinkers on these problems include Paul Akana, senior vice president for research development in program evaluation of the United Way of America, and Frank W. Harris, associate executive director of the United Community Services of Metropolitan Detroit. They describe their assessment of the role of planning in the United Way in an issue of *Community Focus*. Akana and Harris (1977) proposed that the voluntary planning organization of the future be nongeographic in the sense that it should not be a part of a particular community. It should, however, serve specified individuals and agencies such as local United Way organizations, municipal and state governments, and local and regional voluntary agencies with respect to specific issues and problems. They see its primary functions as including data-base maintainence, management consultation, program development, and program evaluation. The operating budget would probably be a minimum of

**TABLE 9.4.**
THE COMMUNITY COUNCILS

| Variable | Rhode Island Council of Community Services | Woonsocket Council of Community Services | United Community Corporation of Boston |
|---|---|---|---|
| Support | Public: $300,000<br>Private: $200,000 (UW) | Administrative budget: $160,000 (city) | Public: $122,000<br>Private: $650,000 (UW) |
| Origin | Originally established 1923 Reorganized 1973 to present status (split from UW). | Began in 1972, outgrowth of local community action agency. | Originally established 1920. Reorganized 1974, outgrowth of United Community Services of Metropolitan Boston. |
| Structure | Originally an organization of agencies. Changed in 1973 to an organization of citizens headed by delegate body: Citizens Congress with committee structure: 100 members, 3 planning directors; staff: 25. | Executive board of 10 members from service agencies: at least ⅓ from groups representing consumer and/or low-income concerns.<br>Committee structure: 1 planning director; staff: 2. | Planning partner of UW of Mass. Board of Directors: 33; Community Trustees: 50 members representing voluntary agencies, govt. agencies, and volunteers. Committee structure; staff: 23. |
| Functions | Voluntary planning agency. Purchase of services relationship with govt. and other agencies. Contracts for services. | Planning and coordination of 45 member agencies and organizations.<br>Allocation and distribution of funds to agencies.<br>Research and investigation of funding sources.<br>Contracts for services. | Independent planning agency with three main tasks:<br>1. research and evaluation<br>2. program development<br>3. policy development<br>Contracts for services with 350 public and private agencies. |
| Direct Services | Information and referral coordination of Tele-Med services (secondary services). | 9 service categories: child care; youth; elderly; health care; mental health; minority groups; housing; volunteerism; outreach and transportation (primary services) | Information and Referral Voluntary action center (secondary services) |

| | | | |
|---|---|---|---|
| Catchment Area | Entire state and surrounding communities in Mass. & Conn. served by agencies in R.I. | Deals with regional agencies which serve Woonsocket and surrounding communities. | Works with agencies in metropolitan Boston area serving entire state of Mass. |
| Relationship to United Way | Ongoing fiscal support from UW. Consultation to budget and allocation panels. Special allocations committee to review requests for resources from nonmember agencies. Study and evaluation of UW agencies. | Active involvement: many member agencies obtain funds from UW. Policy recommendations and joint program implementation. | Planning partner of UW of Mass. Bay: 1. primary fiscal support of core organizational activities 2. joint ties to voluntary aspects of service delivery 3. UW enables entree to citizens troups determining allocation of UW monies. Linked at 3 levels: 1. cross-representation of board memberships 2. committee memberships 3. staff relationships. |
| Deficiencies | Subject to much pressure to do immediate things at expense of long-range planning. More money might enhance capacity to do more. | Lack of funding due to small staff. Doesn't get involved enough with program funding. Unable to assist member agencies in program development to a large extent. | Lack of fiscal provisions for welfare programs. Structural reorganization to date has affected efficiency of resource commitment to ongoing projects. |

*Note:* UW = United Way.

$4 million a year, and local United Way support would constitute not more than 25 percent of this figure. The remainder would be generated from fees for services rendered. The policy-setting role and the role of creating credibility within the voluntary sector would come from a highly influential board of governors. Its new focus would be different from the traditional practices of coordination, consensus making, and advocacy. It also would not be an instrument of any particular United Way. It would be, in effect, "an inside outsider" with respect to any given community issue, interest, or problem: "insider" in the sense that it would have a body of knowledge and experience in the business of human service delivery systems; and "outsider" in the sense that it would not be a part of any particular operation, interest, or local community.

Objections to this proposal referred to its nongeographic concept of regionalization and, thus, its noncommunity aspects. Moreover, it would have limited functions, omitting advocacy, social action, coordination, and mobilization—which are considered necessary components of any voluntary planning organization's services.

What will happen to community-oriented planning? The question is a major issue, since community-oriented planning is a more problem-focused process than operational planning, which tends to be more programmatic. Operational planning in the United Way context usually describes the voluntary sector, and particularly the agencies supported by the United Way. It includes program reviews, special agency studies, and resource and program development. Community-oriented planning begins with the identification of a problem that the planning agency (United Way) believes is important: it is recognized as a problem of the community and is potentially amenable to corrective action. Community-oriented planning relates strongly to the public sector, since more than 90 percent of the funds for human services programs are from public sources.

Frank Harris sets priorities for the local United Way accordingly: to raise the maximum amount of contributed dollars; to allocate funds well, with appropriate fiscal and program accountability; and to plan. He also raises the question: Does the United Way movement have a responsibility to support the community-oriented planning of which it is capable? His answer is affirmative: United Way planning is able to point to a voluntary citizen base for establishing policy and legitimizing recommended action; it has the capacity for objectivity and planning, since the agency is not a direct service provider; it has the capacity for interfacing the needs of various age groups and functional human services areas, rather than being a single-minded advocate for the aging or youth, health or recreation; and it possesses the staff expertise in working with volunteers in the human services planning approach (Akana and Harris 1977).

Although it may be difficult to sense the overall nature of this change, there are many important questions that require answers now. The following are some examples:

Which member agencies and program areas have been most affected by unit-cost problems?

Which member agencies and program areas are likely to be most vulnerable in the future?

Should the United Way accelerate the shift in the framework of its allocations policies, from support for member agencies to support for specific programs and services?

Should the United Way subsidize agencies and services that cannot function within governmental funding policies?

Should the United Way attempt to effect economies of scale in the services it supports, by promoting expanded client volume, centralized administration, and agency mergers?

To what extent should the United Way incorporate unit-cost considerations in its own allocation policies?

Should the United Way withdraw its support in program areas where government responsibility has been confirmed?

Which of the United Way member agencies and program areas are most likely to be "left out" as government sets new directions in social service programming?

Should the United Way participate more actively in determining "need" and defining "quality" in social service programming?

Should the United Way attempt to protect and strengthen the vitality of the voluntary sector as a counterforce to government?

What, in short, is the appropriate "presence" of the United Way in public–private agency relationships?

These are, to be sure, difficult questions. While different relationships between councils and agencies have emerged, the role of the United Fund in relation to community health and welfare councils has remained critically important in the total attempt to meet changing human needs in an increasingly complex environment. The system concept, as elaborated in chapter 2 and applied to the health and welfare council, must focus on the interrelatedness of the organization and the environment and on the internal interdependency and adaptive processes that enable this type of organization to cope and survive.

Continual interaction with the environment permits the community council to receive feedback from it and, by acting on that feedback, to become selectively related to this environment as it changes and becomes more intricate. Viewing a community fund or council as an open system does not imply that it can adapt to all environmental circumstances; nor does it imply that all funds or councils should even attempt to do so. However, an open system is viewed as being capable of changing its form and processes to deal with its environment—as being capable of proaction, or of a response. The council's or fund's ability to adapt effectively to its community—whether the environment is defined by its local, regional, state, or federal boundaries—is limited by external constraints beyond its control, lack of resources, and the inadequate organization of available internal resources to receive, process, and act on community feedback.

The relationship between complex organizations, such as councils of community services, and their environments has been the subject of a growing body of research and theory. Most of this research, however, has been carried out in the profit-making sector rather than in the public or voluntary quarters. The results consistently show that, as the environment changes, the patterns of organizational action required for effective adaptation must likewise change. Every council and fund must deal with the five system dilemmas described by Baker, Broskowski, and Brandwein (1976), who outlined the basic concepts and theoretical perspectives related to the study of community health and welfare planning councils: boundary control versus boundary permeability; variety versus homogeneity; integration versus differentiation; input versus output constituencies; and pro-activity versus re-activity.

**Future of Planning Councils**   The future of the councils of community services, and their relationship to the United Fund in particular, is somewhat uncertain. It is most helpful today to understand the system variables in theoretical perspective in order to deal with the transition. By exercising boundary controls, the council can screen out the differentiating effects of various parts of the community. However, the council must maintain open linkages with the primary community constituencies in order to ensure itself an adequate input flow of money, information, staff, and legitimization. In order to maintain a sufficient variety of internal resources to allow adaptive change in the face of a stressful environment, a planning council needs to incorporate diverse elements, as in a large heterogeneous board of directors. Increased differentiation results from attempting to incorporate the skills and preferences of a wide variety of people into the system, and this incorporation of variety in turn produces concomitant problems of functional integration.

It is easy to demonstrate the highly interactive nature of these five dilemmas by focusing on any one as a starting point and considering its implications for the total system; the other four quickly become salient. For example, the exercise of boundary control to maintain organizational integrity will raise questions of how proactive or reactive the council should be on any specific issue. Increased boundary control will affect the council's relationship with its input and output constituencies. Any decision to be proactive, in turn, will rest on the presumption that there are adequate skills and resources within the council to carry out the chosen task (i.e., the possession of adequate organizational variety). The variety factor then affects the differentiation of subsystems and the organizational mechanisms necessary for integration.

**Conclusion**    In view of recent efforts to effect administrative and services integration, one may well ask, "What results have been observed?" Few conclusive data can be adduced. One observer has noted that "some gains have been made, both at administrative and service delivery levels" (Yession 1978:104). But these gains are marginal, partly because of "the complexity of services integration, but in ever greater part because of the constraints that impede even small, tentative reform efforts in this area" (p. 104). The major obstacle is attitudes and beliefs. Thus, as Chenault (1978) noted, DHEW must contend with powerful public service constituencies with vested interests as well as with those receiving categorical assistance.

Integration is multifaceted. Thus various tradeoffs may need to be acknowledged and effected. In particular, community councils face system dilemmas—themselves interrelated—that are encountered in whatever direction such bodies choose to move. To any reader who sees integration as an unmixed blessing, the following passage should serve as a corrective influence:

> Various authors have suggested correlations between the consolidation of authority over human services delivery and such results as "the whittling away of the *context* of authority, a loss of program identity, client alienation, increased administrative costs, greater difficulty in planning and coordinating, and lower service effectiveness."

Myron Weiner argues that the principles and techniques of "scientific management" are in part responsible for the present inadequacies of the service delivery system. Among the products of this approach are organizations that "give primacy to things rather than people," the use of staff as "automatons," "boundary calcification," "fragmentation of services," "segmentation of the whole man," and difficulty in "focusing on total programs or problems." This sounds very much like a list of the service delivery problems that advocates of the DHEW approach have suggested would be relieved by further rationalization of the delivery system's administrative structure. (Redburn 1977:267)

This may overstate the drawbacks of integration, partly because it assumes the operation solely of centralized authority within administrative integration. Within a pluralistic society, too many constraints may work against systematic centralization. One can still operate in less sweeping ways. Since integration is inexorably linked to political processes, for example, agency executives should be well versed in interorganizational behavior and relationships (Baker and Northman 1978:170). As another possibility, universities might train a new breed of generalists who can blend and transform the work of specialists (Yession 1978:104).

# REFERENCES

Aiken, M., R. Dewar, N. DiTomaso, J. Hage, and G. Zeitz. 1975. *Coordinating Human Services*. San Francisco: Jossey-Bass.

Aiken, M. and J. Hage. 1968. Organizational independence and intraorganizational structure. *American Sociological Review* 33:912–930.

Akana, P. 1977. *Some Thoughts on Planning*. Alexandria, Va.: United Way of America.

Akana, P., and F. W. Harris. 1977. Planning, the United Way. *Community Focus* (December):23–29.

Allen, S. A. 1971. A comparative analysis of corporate-divisional relationships in multi-unit organizations. Paper prepared for the Institute of Managements Sciences, College on Organization, Washington, D.C., March 22–24.

ASPA. 1974. Introduction to *Human Services Integration*. Special publication, March. Washington, D.C.: American Society of Public Administration.

Baker, F., A. Broskowski, and R. Brandwein. 1973. System dilemmas of a community health and welfare council. *Social Service Review*. 47(1):63–80.

Baker, F. and J. E. Northman. 1978. The ideology and education of the future human service executive. In J. Chenault and F. Burnford, eds., *Human Services Professional Education: Future Directions*. New York: McGraw-Hill.

Banfield, E. C. 1962. Ends and means in planning. In S. Malikin and E. H. Van Ness, eds., *Concepts and Issues in Administrative Behavior*. Englewood Cliffs, N.J.: Prentice-Hall.

Broskowski, A. 1982. Linking mental health and health care systems. In H. C. Schulberg and M. Killilea, eds., *The Modern Practice of Community Mental Health*. San Francisco: Jossey-Bass.

Broskowski, A. and F. Baker. 1972. The functions of an information and referral subsystem in a community planning council. Mimeo. Laboratory of Community Psychiatry, Harvard Medical School.

Chenault, J. 1978. Future directions for human services. In J. Chenault and F. Burnford, eds., *Human Services Professional Education: Future Directions*. New York: McGraw-Hill.

CSG. 1974. *Human Services Integration: State Functions in Implementation*. Lexington, Ky.: Council of State Governments.

Demone, H. W. and H. C. Schulberg. 1974. Planning for human services: The role of the community council. In H. W. Demone and D. Harshbarger, eds., *A Handbook of Human Service Organizations*. New York: Behavioral.

Fromer, M. J. 1979. *Community Health Care and the Nursing Process*. St. Louis: C. V. Mosby.

Gabarro, J. 1973. Organizational adaptation to environmental change. In F. Baker, ed., *Organization Systems: General Systems Approaches to Complex Organizations*. Homewood, Ill.: Richard D. Irwin.

Gans, S. P. and G. T. Horton. 1975. *Integration of Human Services: State and Municipal Levels*. New York: Praeger.

Gardner, S., et al. 1971. Service integration in HEW: An initial report. Washington, D.C.: Department of Health, Education, and Welfare.

Georgopoulos, B. S. 1978. Distinguishing organizational feature of hospitals. In A. R. Kovner and D. Neuhauser, eds., *Health Services Management: Readings and Commentary*. Ann Arbor, Mich.: Health Administration Press.

Gilbert, N. 1972. Assessing service delivery methods: Some unsettled questions. *Welfare and Review* 10:25–33.

Gross, B. M. 1966. State of the nation: Social systems accounting. In R. A. Bauer, ed., *Social Indicators*. Cambridge: MIT Press.

Hage, J. 1974. *Communication and Organizational Control: Cybernetics in Health and Welfare Settings*. New York: Wiley.

Johnson, K. W. 1977. *Police Interagency Relations: Some Research Findings*. Beverly Hills: Sage.

Kahn, F. J. 1972. Public social services: The next phase—policy and delivery strategies. *Public Welfare* 30:15–24.

Kronick, J. C., F. D. Perlmutter, and B. Gummer. 1973. The APWA model social service delivery system: A preliminary assessment. *Public Welfare* 31:47–53.

Levine, S. and P. E. White. 1961. Exchange as a conceptual framework for the study of interorganizational relationships. *Administrative Science Quarterly* 5:583–601.

Long, B. B. 1979. Report from the President's Commission on Mental Health. *The Social Welfare Forum, 1978*. New York: Columbia University Press for the National Conference on Social Welfare.

Lubove, R. 1965. *The Professional Altruist*. Cambridge: Harvard University Press.

Lynn, L. E., Jr. 1977. A services integration update. *Evaluation* 4:96–98.

March, J. and H. Simon. 1958. *Organizations.* New York: Wiley.

March, M. S. 1968. The neighborhood concept. *Public Welfare* 26:97–111.

McKenzie, R. H. 1978. The fragmented search for the whole in human services. In J. Chenault and F. Burnford, eds., *Human Services Professional Education: Future Directions.* New York: McGraw-Hill.

Morrill, W. A. 1976. Services integration and the Department of Health, Education, and Welfare. *Evaluation* 3:53–55.

Perlman, R. and A. Gurin. 1972. *Community Organization and Social Planning.* New York: Wiley.

Redburn, F. S. 1977. On "human services integration." *Public Administration Review* 37:265–268.

Rein, M. 1970. *A Social Policy.* New York: Random House.

Richardson, E. 1971. Service integration: Next steps. Secretarial memorandum. Washington, D.C. Department of Health, Education, and Welfare.

Shroder, J. A. and B. Shiffman. 1974. *A Metropolitan City Council Model.* New York: Community Council of Greater New York.

Thompson, J. D. and W. J. McEwan. 1958. Organizational goals and environment: Goal setting as an interaction process. *American Sociological Review* 23:23–31.

U.S. Congress. 1972. *Presidential Message for the Allied Services Act of 1972 to the Congress.* House Document no. 92-296.

Warren, R. L. 1967. The interaction of community decision organizations: Some basic concepts and needed research. *Social Service Review* 41:261–270.

Will, W. H. 1977. United Way allocation policies: New impact of government support for human service programs. *Community Focus* (October):22–25.

Yession, M. R. 1978. Commentary. In J. Chenault and F. Burnford, eds., *Human Services Professional Education: Future Directions.* New York: McGraw-Hill.

# 10

## SERVICE DESIGN, DELIVERY, AND EVALUATION

### SERVICE DESIGN

An open-systems formulation of service organizations views planning and programming as a bounded interacting set of components. Engaging in an input–output commerce with the external environment, such an organization processes material objects, information, and people. Application of the term "system" to an organization implies interdependence in the sense of necessary input and output linkages—but also independence in the sense of maintaining the integrity of system elements through boundary control processes. Human service organizations find themselves entering into relationships and decisions that are aimed at multilevel outcomes. These transactions and resource exchanges must be approached in terms of their relevance to community needs, interorganizational relationships, and intraorganizational requirements for system survival.

**Planning Approaches** The mental health literature includes, increasingly; discussions of ways in which to conceptualize and apply planning techniques, among them methods of program evaluation. Three distinct and specific types of approaches to human services planning (Horton and Miller 1974) may be described as follows:

1. *Project or Operations Planning:* The design of individual and specific projects for the delivery of services and the preparation of an operations plan, including a staffing pattern and line item budget for these projects. The planning may include the establishment of operational standards by which to measure the extent of effectiveness of the actual delivery of services. This planning focuses on service delivery.

2. *Program Planning:* The development of program activity information and measures of impact upon individuals, from the delivery of services and the preparation of supporting human services budgets to finance required service levels to achieve desired impact. Rather than focus on a single service, program planning deals with program areas such as health—and how various health projects relate to one another. It is also concerned with the relationship of program areas such as health to other program areas such as social services.

3. *Policy Planning:* The application of the planning process to relate human services to physical and economic development plans and implementation actions in the community. The allocation of resources between human services and other public activities is a major policy planning activity for the achievement of comprehensive community goals and objectives.

Another way to describe each type of human services planning is by its dominant characteristics. This is attempted in table 10.1.

**The Organization of Planning Functions**   An array of human services has been chosen, and a type or types of planning selected. The next question that arises is: How should the planning function be organized? What administrative structure should be constructed for the planning process? This issue has two aspects. The first concerns the kind of organizational unit that should be used for the administrative location of the function. Once that is decided, then the second aspect, the internal organization of that unit, must be determined.

Three alternative functions were identified for the administrative location of planning: independent agency; staff agency; or line operation.

The term ''independent agency'' refers to a situation in which the human services planning function is administratively placed in an organization or

**TABLE 10.1.**

CHARACTERISTICS OF APPROACHES TOWARD HUMAN SERVICES PLANNING

| | Planning Approach | | |
| --- | --- | --- | --- |
| | *Project or Operations* | *Program* | *Policy* |
| Time frame for plan document | one year or less | three to five years | indefinite |
| Time frame of implementation | one year or less | as function of current budget and updated annually | immediate and ongoing |
| Scope and subject matter | utilization of budgeted resources to deliver intended services | human services as means to improve status of functions of individual | human services as means to achieve comprehensive ends including changing status of individual |
| Evaluation methodology | did or did not projects achieve intended level of service delivery within budget? | change in measurable status of individual; or has individual's status improved? | change in measurable status of society; or has society improved, and if so, what aspects of the quality of life are better or worse? |

*Source:* Horton and Miller 1974:13.

agency other than the one responsible for the conduct of programs and delivery of services. A ''staff agency'' location of the planning function might be described as an agency within an organization such as a state department of human services. That department would have service delivery responsibilities in its line departments. The agency doing the planning would *not* have such operational duties, but would report directly to the head of the department. In a ''line operation,'' the planning function is located in the same organizational unit that is responsible for the delivery of services.

A 1974 study on human services by the American Society for Public Administration concluded than an integrated approach to human services planning would include the following activities:

A. Developing patterns of existing services, facilities, programs, and equipment, including behavioral patterns of use by the typical client in navigating his way through the service systems.
B. Identifying gaps between services where problems or demands are likely to occur or may have occurred and the responsive service was not there to meet it.

C. Developing an understanding and general awareness of where the services and programs of one or more agencies overlap with other agencies, or duplicate each other's efforts in some inefficient way.
D. Charting the potential utilization of patterns by client citizens of present and future services, using wherever possible alternative models and simulation of client and agency-management behavior to determine alternate policy choices.
E. Ascertaining potential formal and informal linkages and relationships that might be developed among and between agencies that are most capable of complementing each other's activities.
F. Exploring and investigating new methods and techniques of service delivery.

**Community Analysis** Program evaluation is an activity undertaken to determine the impact and value of those service elements comprising a human service organization. Evaluation activities make it possible for reasonable judgments to be made about the efforts, effectiveness, adequacy, and efficiency of various program elements such as accessibility to residents of the catchment area, comprehensiveness of services, continuity of care, and relevance of the services provided to shifting needs and demands in the community. Community needs assessment is an integral and inseparable part of the planning and evaluation process. Both needs assessment and program evaluation activities are concerned with the same kinds of analyses, namely, studies of patterns of use of human services, impact studies, studies related to the accessibility and continuity of services, and consumer and citizen evaluation of agency services.

Needs assessment occurs within an ongoing programmatic context of continuing program development and improvement. The purpose is to enhance the relevance and adequacy of a program in its response to community needs. Human service organizations are enjoined to monitor the match of their existing services, through utilization patterns, to community needs. Within this context, needs assessment activities connect with program evaluation activities. Both are parts of the program planning, implementation, and development cycle. Planning is the vital process that links needs to solutions. The role of planning is primarily a long-range one: looking backward at trends and looking around at current developments, but primarily looking forward to problems, issues, and their positive resolution in the future (Sauber 1976).

Community analysis involves assessment of the community according to the classification system or operational definition of "community." A conceptual model of community can be quantitative or qualitative:

Quantitative:
  Geographical Area
  Majority
  Local Minority
  Society-At-Large
Qualitative:
  Common Body
  Feelings of Belongingness
  Elitist
  System of Mutual Interactions                    (Regester 1974

The methodology is original in its community orientation, but the process contains basic similarities to any kind of analysis. The task goes beyond collecting information related to service utilization; it includes an understanding of the structure and dynamics of a community as a living entity and its purpose akin to the issue of identity for the individual. For instance, historically there have been many broad conceptions of mental illness and mental health practice, each approach having a unique and basic unit of study, as illustrated in table 10.2.

A community purpose implies a certain meaning of community: a self-image, if you will. This conception, in turn, is or should be related to what the community does and how it functions. The service organization should be structured to meet and facilitate community goals and purposes. It also

**TABLE 10.2.**
BROAD CONCEPTIONS OF MENTAL ILLNESS AND MENTAL HEALTH PRACTICE

| System | Pathology | Diagnosis | Treament |
|---|---|---|---|
| 1. Personality system | Psychopathology | Intrapsychic | Psychotherapy |
| 2. Physical system | General pathology | Organic | Somatotherapy |
| 3. Psychosocial system | Psychopathology | Intrapersonal | Sociotherapy (e.g., group and activity therapy) |
| 4. Family system | Family pathology | Intrafamilial | Family therapy (e.g., children, parental, marital, family network) |
| 5. Social system | Social pathology | Ecological/community | Intraventions (e.g., populations, environment, organizations) |

Source: Sauber 1976:

should be directed to the future denoted by any conception of purpose. The leadership of a community is the central factor in its adaptation, and the style of community processes and its interorganizational field says much about how the community will adapt.

Community analysis as a method requires a full description of a community's objectives, plans, leadership patterns, and view of itself as well as its relationships with supra- and subsystem elements. The process must enable the community analyst to understand the multiplicity of systems of communication (vertical and horizontal), the formal structure of functioning (community organization and sanction), the mapping of the community (interdependency, boundaries, forces, key points of leverage), service linkages (community leaders and agencies in terms of liaison functions and networks), and working relationships (availability—physical and psychological—and establishing contact in terms of reliability and usefulness). It must help the analyst delineate relevant behaviors in varying settings in the environment and clarify for the rationale of a community—explaining its activities and critically evaluating a community's adaptability and adding a reasoned series of recommendations.

Examples of the kinds of general questions related to the concept of "community" that may be asked in an interview as part of a community analysis (Sauber 1976) are as follows:

1. Tell us about your community.
2. What sort of place is this to live, to work? Why?
3. Tell us about the people here.
4. How are they to live with, to work with?
5. What kind of person is likely to move to your community?
6. What is done here to help a person adjust once he moves to your community?
7. What happens when community problems arise? What happens when a person really needs help?
8. Who are the real leaders in town? Power? Why?
9. In what kinds of things are most people interested?
10. For what does your community say it stands? How does the message get across (e.g., media)?
11. Make believe your community is a person. Think about that person for a minute. Describe that person to us so we can get a better idea of the picture you have in mind. Think of a person doing something. What is he doing? What other pictures come to mind?
12. How much do the people here really know about the community, and to what extent do they participate in local affairs?

13. What would you change in the community? What are some other changes?
14. What are the long-term plans you might make, future changes?
15. What are the major groups in town? Explore. Who are the leaders?
16. Would others view things similarly to you? In what way?

**Methods of Needs Assessment**   Various specific methods of needs assessment are parts of the process of community analysis. A brief description of these methods follows:

1. The community forum approach offers wide citizen participation for information exchange, similar to a town meeting.
2. The key informant approach utilizes mailed questionnaires, individual interviews, and/or group discussions with a selected number of community leaders to estimate needs and services required.
3. The nominal group approach is a structured workshop designed to identify and set priorities for the widest possible range of neighborhood needs, service barriers, and alternative program plans, with a minimum of face-to-face interaction among the participants.
4. The rates-under-treatment approach estimates community needs on the basis of type and duration of services provided.
5. The social indicators approach is based upon need inferences drawn from descriptive statistical findings in public records such as census tracts and health and welfare data. See table 10.3 for a detailed analysis of social indicators.
6. Human services surveys are comprehensive approaches to assessment of citizens at large, population subgroups with special needs, and specific social areas.

Table 10.4 provides a summation of the benefits and limitations of each of these methods.

Ideologically, there are two basic methods of planning strategies to assess needs: the intraorganizational approach to community analysis (the inside-out method), and the extraorganizational approach to community analysis (the outside-in method). In the intraorganizational approach, a director of a juvenile detention center initially assesses the staff's desires and abilities, distribution of resources, and the juvenile delinquent population (e.g., those found by a juvenile court to have committed a crime or to be incorrigible or in need of supervision by the state) in terms of the sociodemographic characteristics of its potential and actual clients and diagnostic descriptions. He then surveys the community's opportunities to utilize the special strengths

**TABLE 10.3.**

ANALYSIS OF SOCIAL INDICATORS

Demographic
Population
Households
Population acre
Persons in household
Persons in dwelling unit
Mobility rates
% of 1 person households
% of 5- or more person households

Income and Employment
Employment by industry
Occupation of head of household
% Production, technical, manager
% Sales, clerical, craftsmen
% Services, operator, unskilled
% Retired
% Military and students
% Unemployed
Median Income
% of families below poverty
% of families $15,000
% of female heads unemployed

Criminal Justice
Types of juvenile offenses
Juvenile probation rate
Violent crimes per 1,000
Property crimes per 1,000
Ranking by planning districts of crime incidence for 10 categories of crime

Environmental Quality
Air quality
Noise level
Safety hazards
Rubbish
Conditions of rights-of-way
Residential fires per 100
Dwelling units

Recreation and Enrichment
Branch library stock utilization
Location of public open space
Acres of open space per 1,000
Open space needs score

Transportation
% of households locking autos
Means of transportation to work
Bus or rail
Walk
Automobile
Place of work
City
Outside city
Remaining county
Location of bus routes

Education
School enrollment
Location of schools
Drop-out rate by school
Young adult drop-out rate
Retention rate by grade level
Adult educational attainment
No schooling
8th grade or less
Some college
4 years of college or more
Vocational training
Achievement scores by grade level

Human Services
Financial Assistance Caseload
Food Stamp Caseload
Medicaid. SLH Caseload
Levels of Immunization
Types of Dental Care
Causes of Mortality
Mortality Rates
Infant Mortality Rates
Incidence of Communicable Disease
New Active cases of Tuberculosis
Lead Poisoning
Location of Food Stamp distribution centers
Location of Public Health Clinics
Financial Assistance Service Rates
Food Stamp Service Rates

Housing
   % of units owned
      % of owned units—black
      % of owned units—female
         heads
   % of units rented
      % of rental units—female
         head
   % of units built before 1939
   % of units built 1940–1959
   % of units built 1960–1970
   Value of owned units up to
      $9,999
      $10,000 to $19,999
      $20,000 to $34,999
      $35,000 or more

Rental Value per Month
   Up to $59
   $60 to $99
   $100 to $149
   $150 or more
Dwelling units net. res acre
   % of units lacking plumbing
   % of black-occupied units
      lacking plumbing

Vacant Rental Units
Long-term sales vacancy
   % of owned units over-
      crowded
   % of black-owned units over-
      crowded
   % of rental units over-
      crowded
   % of black rental units over-
      crowded
   % of units with 1–3 rooms
   % of units with 4–5 rooms
   % of units with 6 or more
      rooms
Structural quality
New residential construction

Real Estate Turnover
   % of households paying 25%
      or more for rent
   Income less than $5,000
   Income $5,000 ro $9,999

Quality of Life Index

*Source:* HSICF 1974:126.

**TABLE 10.4.**

BENEFITS AND LIMITATIONS OF METHODS OF NEEDS ASSESSMENT FOR CONDUCTING A
COMMUNITY ANALYSIS

|  | Methods | | |
|---|---|---|---|
|  | *Community Forum* | *Key Informant* | *Nominal Group* |
| Benefits | Broadened citizen participation, | Input by community leaders, | Identification of diverse areas of need, |
|  | Information exchange, | Establish and strengthen community relations and intraorganizational plans, | Rank order of priorities, |
|  | Recruit citizens for special interest projects, |  | Focused involvement on prescribed issues, |
|  | Increased community support and visibility, | Introduce new services, | Utilized input from diverse groups, |
|  | Stimulate community action, | Specific input, | Extensive problem identification and outlining of problem dimensions, |
|  | Involvement of professional staff in nonclinical functions, | Immediate feedback, | |
|  |  | Preselected goals and parameters of needs assessed, | Highly differentiated solutions, |
|  | Generating new expressions of community needs, | Solicit views of "unknown" informants, | Group decision making. |
|  | Problem identification, | Small group discussion, | |
|  | Positive public relations pre- and post-forum. | Feedback meeting. | |
| Limitations | Large group, | Biased output, | Minimum group interaction, |
|  | Surface discussion of issues, | Selection criteria limited to providers and gate keepers, | Individual work, |
|  | Limited "air time," |  | Imprecise, |
|  | Inadequate for problem solving, | Randomness and representativeness lacking in sample, | Problem redundancy, |
|  | Incomplete and impressionistic data collection, | Noncomprehensive, | Lack of followup, |
|  | Leads to unrealistic community expectations, | Survey methods of mailed questionnaires and individual interviews, | Raises unrealistic expectations for service delivery. |
|  | Very general focus, | Time consuming. | |
|  | No followup, | | |
|  | Nonrepresentative attendance, | | |
|  | Time consuming. | | |

*Source:* Sauber 1976.

**Table 10.4.** (continued)

| Methods | | |
| --- | --- | --- |
| *Rates-Under-Treatment* | *Social Indicators* | *Mental Health Surveys* |
| Availability of existing data, | Availability of existing data, | Comprehensiveness, |
| | | Citizen opinions, |
| Service utilization, | Comparisons of mental health with other human service needs, | Citizen perceptions and attitudes toward services, |
| Minimal time demands. | | |
| | False conclusions easily reached, | Identification of citizens to become involved in special projects, |
| | Rough "pointers" to areas for examination, | Problem identification and service priorities, |
| | Sudden and sharp changes as signals. | Increased citizen participation. |
| Misleading data on needs vs. demands, | Community needs not equal to socioeconomic characteristics, | Expensive, |
| Goal setting, | | Complex, |
| | Inaccurate statistics, | Sampling procedure and size $(n > 1000)$ |
| Lacks community input. | No causal relationship between data and need, | Well-trained interviewers. |
| | Lacks information about community opinions and attitudes. | |

of the department of corrections for satisfying its particular needs and achieving its organizational goals—as reflected in the department's charter and legal mandate and in the community's expectations.

The development of a neighborhood-based youth diversionary program serves as an illustration of this method. Here there is a need to divert juvenile offenders from official processing to less formal, less adversary, and noninstitutionalized community settings. Other examples include specific deterrence (i.e., a preventive effect of actual punishment on the offender so that he does not repeat his crime); release on own recognizance (i.e., pretrial release of an arrested person, usually as an alternative to monetary bail for an indigent defendent likely to appear for trial at a later date); restitution; and training school (i.e., a state institution housing juvenile delinquents on court order to offer educational and vocational training programs).

These avenues require a systemic approach to criminal justice. "Systemic" identifies a system for the enforcement of traditional penal laws.

Analysis of this system involves describing the structural interrelationships of legislatures, appellate courts, and enforcement and administrative agencies as well as their corresponding processes of decision making, from arrest of suspects through charging, adjudication, sentencing, imprisonment, and release on parole. Criminal justice is mostly concerned with the decisions of the various crime control agencies. Within this system, creative attempts have been planned so that the young may receive maximum benefits such as social and rehabilitation services rather than an indictment and incarceration.

The extraorganizational approach begins with a survey, forecast, and analysis of the external environment—including immediate, intermediate, and future conditions. This action is followed by an examination of the organization's resources to serve the population and adapt to external environmental demands. One example is to study a neighborhood with a relatively small population and to learn from the town's citizens and service providers that the adolescent population is at high risk for emotional disturbance or law violations. Youth service utilization rates for this neighborhood were not concordant with adolescent service needs. Children from this bounded area grew up and remained in the same town, with minimal interaction from the surrounding communities. Upon completion of the eighth grade, students attended the nearest high school located in a large city, beyond the residential human services catchment area. Each year, predictable crises would occur in maladjustments to transitions; outreach and consultative interventions needed to be provided. It is likely that this special group would never have come to the attention of the mental health or juvenile justice officials; nor would any preventive attempts have been made on the part of local town leaders if a community analysis had not been conducted to identify the problem and plan a solution. The analysis revealed a sudden increase in absenteeism from school accompanied by high rates of misdemeanors for first offenders. Either the adolescent would socially withdraw and parents and/or teachers being aware of the immediate deterioration in school performance would refer the youth to a mental health center, or the bored, disinterested youth would act out by not attending school and getting arrested for drugs or for larceny or theft.

Setting priorities and allocating resources involves determination of a starting point—that is to say, the intra- versus extraorganizational method of open-systems study. The ideology of the service providers and the resources of the facilities of the organization itself—as well as an understanding of the various sectors and components of the environment—must always be taken into consideration in any community analysis (Sauber 1976).

**Illustrations**   Approaches to community analyses and methods of needs assessment generally have a preventive thrust and objective. Standard public health terms—primary, secondary, tertiary prevention—may be applied to aspects of mental health prevention. Tertiary prevention refers to reduction of the duration of additional side effects or other impairments following treatment. Secondary prevention is aimed at decreasing the prevalence of existing cases in the population which primary prevention is focused on, reducing the incidence of new cases of mental disorder in the community.

An example of an intraorganizational approach to community analysis is the planning and establishment of a community psychiatric after-care service according to the principles of tertiary prevention. Within the service organization, in this case a community mental health center, a systematic study utilizing the needs assessment methodology of the "rates-under treatment" approach identified: (1) the increasingly large and continuous flow of inpatients and day hospital patients who required followup: (2) the service demand for discharged state hospital patients returning to the community with a history of high readmission rates; and (3) the need to develop a viable alternative to psychiatric hospitalization.

The location for developing a community-based social rehabilitation and psychiatric after-care program was selected by analyzing the residential area with the highest service utilization rates and choosing a facility. This turned out to be a church with a minister who is a mental health advocate and that offered these features: a local image of social welfarism, easy access to public transportation, physical space for activities, people and material resources, and a rent-free building. The program design included the following considerations: ideology of social pathology and etiology of "problems-in-living"; an organizational structure in which the service was an extension of the CMHC rather than an independent, autonomous program; staffing by nonprofessionals (volunteers and students with supervision by a paraprofessional); program startup at a three-half-days-a-week schedule for ten "participants," with a growing capacity for a seven-day program for as many as one hundred "participants"; financial management with an annual budget of $2,000; and programmed activities of outreach, counseling (vocational, group, and/or family), educational courses (arts and crafts, dancing, nutrition and diet, cooking, field trips), recreation, medication clinic, social services, and so on.

Most often, the "inside-out" method rather than the "outside-in" approach is utilized by human service administrators and evaluators. This is because of their training, experience, and familiarity with a community from a service provider's point of view. Both administrators and evaluators rely heavily on the caseload data for making decisions about their agency's mission. Whatever conceptual or classification model of "community"—leading as it may to keener appreciation of and sensitivity to the complexity of elements in every community—the most common and popular method of analyzing one's catchment area and making service delivery plans and decisions is based on internal factors and make use of such methods as "rates-under-treatment." Many of the data are collected for purposes of federal and state statistical reporting.

The five other previously described approaches to needs assessment are instances of extraorganizational community analysis. As such, they are more complicated to understand, difficult to conduct, time consuming, and expensive to implement. However, the importance, relevance, and usefulness of this approach are paramount, especially in planning primary prevention activities. For example, community mental health program leaders were aware of low utilization rates for all services by residents in a number of the towns in the catchment area. Speculations have explained this with such factors as travel distance; paucity of public information about the CMHC (e.g., newspapers for these towns did not report mental health events worthy of press coverage that are covered by other community newspapers); and the psychological and geographical "attachment" of several of the towns to another state where goods are purchased and services are sought.

The decision was therefore made to conduct an extraorganizational analysis of the community. A number of the needs assessment methods were used (social indicators, key informant, and nominal group approach). Such an analysis was predicated on having the necessary organizational flexibility to be able to assign or reassign staff and to appropriate or reappropriate funds according to the results of the community analysis. It is noted that there are always constraints and limiting factors on any program planning effort that attempts to respond to environmental demands and opportunities.

One community, classified as the "majority"—the total populace within a specifically designated geographic region—was identified and isolated for study. Through the efforts of one staff member these steps were then taken: first, a social indicators study was undertaken; second, a key informant approach was completed; and third, a nominal group study was carried out with the members of the mental health board. The last approach utilized the data collected from the first two methods. Board members were trained in how to research the informal and formal organizational structure of their community—social, religious, and recreational clubs, neighborhood groupings, and business and governmental associations. Staff and board members made decisions about which community groups to approach, carefully avoiding membership overlap. Although community analysis and program planning were the purposes, the process was directed toward mental health information exchange and education as a preventive objective. The content was aimed at the human services as a system (health, social welfare and rehabilitation, criminal justice, education, and mental health) in terms of human needs and service delivery. Some findings that serve to define the results of the community analysis are as follows:

1. The previously established mental health outpost for direct services did not meet community needs and consequently terminated service delivery due to underutilization of the facility;
2. Consistently, recreation was identified as the major problem, particularly for the adolescent population. Citizens requested the service of a community organizer to develop several recreation programs, such as a boy's club, in contrast with the CMHC assumption that a youth counseling service should be provided;
3. The community was described as a place "where there is nowhere to go and nothing to do," and the typical person, "adult as well as child," was characterized as "apathetic, self-serving, conservative, retiring and withdrawn, insecure, with a negative attitude toward local government, independent, does his own thing, a good worker on the job but a nondoer in town, lacking pride in community affairs." Assistance in community development was needed (Sauber 1976).

Many positive outcomes resulted from the community analysis. Because of citizen interest, community pressure, and local demands, the CMHC had to alter its priorities to respond to the expressed needs. Had these needs not been identified, meager services would have continued to be provided. A major commitment of center resources was extended to the development of an organized network of community services and of an ongoing consultation and education program to local human services workers (Allegra and Sauber 1976).

It is difficult to find a human service system that is being planned and evaluated so systematically that the delivery system that results from a comprehensive planning analysis also predetermines the program evaluation criteria. The global nature of the human services field, as well as its unclear definitions, hinders the development of methods to assess universal needs. Nevertheless, examining the complex array of health, mental health, and social welfare organizations as an intersystem field may provide new guidelines for research on the problems of delivering services. Given that the field of human services constitutes what Emery and Trist (1965) have described as a "turbulent environment" with conditions of increasingly rapid change, there should be an increased openness to change on the part of human service organizations. The movement in the field toward comprehensiveness of planning should find greater receptivity in organizations sensitive to the changes in the environment.

An open system is defined as one that receives a continuous flow of resources from the environment and also sends a continuous outflow of products of its action back into the environment. The environment of a human service agency includes the community it serves, but also the other organizational systems that serve as sources of legal, political, financial, technical, and professional support. Consequently, the continuous process of assessing community needs, planning programs, and evaluating the services delivered is necessary for the organization to function as an open system. In a receptive way it must depend for its growth and vitality, as well as its maintenance and survival, upon the exchanges with the community.

## SERVICE DELIVERY

The delivery of human services depends on the strategies used to design and provide resources and actions to reach people in need. Strategic campaigns to help people through programs involving organized delivery systems to target populations are based on prior issues, issues rooted in assumptions that may or may not be realistic. It is necessary to develop an understanding of the complex array of political, social, economic, and other forces that are operative. These forces shape the assumptions that form the bases for certain kinds of services.

The second fundamental task is to specify the problem, the probable reasons for the problem, and probable solutions. Further assumptions are made regarding such matters as sanctions of the agency, funding sources, and professional ideologies. Assumptions must be made explicit, for it is sometimes difficult even to discover the basis on which many programs evolve, as well as how the planning is actually done. Human services and its related events are not subject to random factors: society created the policy and developed the plans that brought those services into existence.

**Social Policy** Social policy, or domestic policy, is really a blueprint of society's priorities. These, in turn, are based on society's dominant values and beliefs—a central force in the manner of society's functioning. Through social policy, a society defines which areas of human needs the society itself is responsible for and which needs shall be left to the individual to meet for himself. For example, social policy determines that free public school education must be provided for every youngster, whereas college education is not interpreted by social policy as society's responsibility:

Social Values ⟶ Social Policy ⟶ Social Programs
Social Problems ⟶ Societal Support ⟶ Human Services

In every community, social policy mirrors the local values in interaction with other societal forces, such as central religious traditions, available resources, the level of technology, the political system, and the state of the economy. Social policy is probably most closely related to economic policy. Community leaders know the community cannot afford the social costs that result from ignoring people and widespread social problems.

The philosophy of human services entails a commitment to enhance the lives of each such member of the community. That commitment endeavors to assure equal opportunity to everyone for adequate income, nutrition, education, housing, health, and mental health services, as well as other life-supporting services that will enable people to lead satisfying lives together in a just society. Historically, American social policy has been remedial and reactive. That is, policy has been developed to deal with the social problem only after the problem already exists. The consequences of such a policy have grown to sufficient proportions to gain attention and cause alarm. More recently, therefore, increased emphasis has been placed on prevention as a social goal. For example, in the health field, in going beyond merely treating a child for lead poisoning, efforts may be made to prevent an epidemic of lead poisoning by attacking underlying environmental conditions. In another example, child welfare youngsters are not to be moved into foster care until every possible effort has been made to prevent family breakdown.

The values inherent in the human services philosophy provide the framework for human service policy (William and Johnson 1979), which is designed (1) to build a just society in which every member has an opportunity and a right to meet his human needs; (2) to create services that are adequately responsive to meeting people's needs and functionally able to provide for those needs; (3) to prevent conditions in society that threaten or interfere with meeting people's needs or with enabling them to live satisfying lives; (4) to develop an integrated network of human services that can meet the needs of the whole person through the optimal use of society's resources; (5) to maintain services that are accountable to the consumer and relevant to solving people's problems. If delivery of human services is to provide maximum benefit, it must be coordinated and integrated, accessible and comprehensive, effective and efficient.

**Program Strategies**   The planning process is a sequence of events: identifying the problem, setting goals and establishing priorities, gathering data and assessing alternatives, and developing and evaluating the program. Once these stages have taken place, it is time to implement service delivery. The real impetus for service delivery, however, can only come when there is a felt need for such service in the community. That felt need comes from individuals defining a situation as a problem because it has an adverse effect upon them, their reference group, or their community. The definition of the situation as problematic implies a need to change.

The definers are almost always those "without the problem," however. Thus, the "problem of illiteracy" is defined by literate people; the "problem of poverty," by people who are not poor; the "problem of illigetimacy," by people who have children through wedlock. The social distance between those who define "the problem" and those whom the problem "fits" probably affects the qualities of strategies adopted by social work, education, and community mental health professionals.

The difficulty with defining a problem is also strongly affected by the view of problem causation in operation. For example, one theory of causation holds that the minority child, from the moment he enters school, is so poorly prepared to perform in school that failure is almost inevitable. At home, the child receives poor training in verbal skills and auditory and visual discrimination, with little intellectual stimulation. An educator who subscribes to this theory may use compensatory education programs in which the minority child receives extra training in utilizing verbal skills and in sensory discrimination.

Another theory of the etiology of this problem, however, holds that most teachers are from the white middle class and do not understand the minority child; they are frequently intolerant of the child's way of life and have difficulty communicating with him. A believer in this theory is likely to emphasize programs that train minority people for school positions, or that train existing school personnel to understand better the cultures of minority groups and the culture of poverty.

To carry this a step further, program planners or deliverers of service may have similar definitions of a problem and its theory of causation while subscribing to completely different assumptions about how to solve the problem. For instance, a juvenile offender may, after repeated offenses, be placed in a state training school. He is removed from his local environment and given an "opportunity" to receive rehabilitative services in the nature of residential vocational educational training. Another professional may wish to develop a service to avoid institutionalization; accordingly, he may place the juvenile in a job at which he can earn money on a regular basis and learn responsibility.

It is not easy to determine which, if any, of these various assumptions are based on reality. Relatively little research has been done to verify them. A notable exception in education is the research by Coleman et al. (1966), which indicates that the input of compensatory programs for minority children is likely to have little effect on their educational achievement. Thus, for the most part, deliverers of service will have to proceed cautiously from limited knowledge in developing their assumptions and depend instead on professional ideologies and social values.

Whatever strategies the deliverer of services might like to choose, he faces certain constraints: the mandates of the institution, the sources of funding, the community, and the needs and expectations of the consumer. A community action center may have a desire for a particular mode of operation or program of outreach, but the "establishment," which pays the bill, has little interest in developing it. Gottesfeld et al. (1975) identify the following elements considered in strategies adopted for delivering human services: the population, and the services. (What services and how many? How and where to deliver the services? Who will provide and what level of skill is needed? How will the program be monitored and evaluation set up to determine what degree various goals have been reached?)

Despite careful planning and the adoption of well-thought-out strategies, complexities, problems, and program dilemmas inevitably follow because the problem the program tackles is often complex, with roots and ramifications throughout the institutional structure of our culture. Programs are limited by funds, time, staff, and mandates; vested interests battle against the aims of the program; knowledge about program implications is inadequate. Some of the strategies dilemmas have been outlined by Gottesfeld et al. (1973) as follows:

1. Social problems are complex and interrelated with the capacity of the program to deal with that complexity by necessarily limiting the extent. Researchers in the social sciences have indicated that social pathology indices are often highly interrelated. For example, high correlations are favored among deteriorated housing rates, percentage of population unemployed, and percentage of high school dropouts. These indices are part of a

"poverty" cluster, one that goes beyond statistical association to an imputed relationship.

This suggests that a program in education, health, or political action, by itself, is unlikely to have much effect on a given phase of social pathology. For example, a program offering remedial reading to high school dropouts, in an effort to have them return to high school, does not contend with such problems as the fact that the dropouts need to contribute to the support of their poor families. Economic conditions may make jobs more pressing than schooling; crowded and poor living conditions at home make it difficult to study at home; poor health may interfere with schoolwork; and the existence of racial and ethnic prejudices may compromise the value of obtaining a high school diploma and consequently weaken motivation. These problems may be so numerous, confounding, and massive that they override the positive values of the remedial program.

2. Innovative programs will threaten vested interests.

3. Coordination of agencies or programs can impede freedom. For instance, larger agencies and institutions tend to be in a domineering role; under the banner of coordination they tend to constrain smaller agencies that often differ in philosophies and mandates. The question is, Who is to be the coordinator and who is to be coordinated? This dilemma has led to internecine power struggles and to widespread frustration and anger.

4. A knowledge base is absent for the planning of programs.

5. Implementation of programs may depend on qualities and number of staff that may not be available. For example, high turnover of some positions result in discontinuities of program operations.

6. Differing strategies used in a program may tend to negate each other. For instance, setting up an outpost in the community may fulfill a strategy of making services more accessible but may make it difficult to fulfill efficient, coordinating strategies involving other services located within the institution.

7. Mandates and sanctions may severely limit the program. Institutions may be reimbursed according to the number of "client visits" rather than other variables; consequently, the institution's function in consultative or social action efforts will be sacrificed because these services are not reimbursable. Thus the economic pressures to offer more conventional, direct services will predominate.

8. Changes resulting from a program may set in motion forces creating new problems. For example, a successful program to set up a group home for emotionally disturbed adolescents in a local setting can create problems once the referrals increase: with more and more adolescents residing within

a specified neighborhood, the residents feel resentful about their presence and raise community pressure to remove the program from their neighborhood.

Outlines of the assumptions, strategies, and strategy problems for six different service organizations are presented here while a more complete description is available from its source, Gottesfeld et al. 1973.

## Outline A. Assumptions, Strategies, and Problems of Helping Police Cope with Family Violence: A Training Model in Community Intervention

Problem definition
    To help police more effectively intervene in violent family crises
Causation
    Police are not trained in preventive mental health
    Mental health professionals do not reach families at the time of crisis
    Most families do not know how to reach mental health professionals
Necessary inputs
    Police training program
    Supportive social services
    Structural change in police procedures
Mandates and sanctions
    College and faculty support
    Police department cooperation
    Justice department funds
Strategies
  Target populations
    Harlem families who have violent crises—prevention
  Service programs
    Help police with more effective intervention
    Expose clinical psychology students to community work
    Develop special police family crises units
  Monitoring and evaluation
    Formalized—built into program
Strategy problems
    Inability to extend program
    Isolation within sponsoring agency
    Lack of lasting impact on clinical psychology students
    Poor follow-through by local agencies

## Outline B. Assumptions, Strategies, and Problems of the Goals for Girls Project of the Foothill Family Service

Problem definition
    Lack of motivation for treatment of girls on probation
Causation
    Lack of motivation of treatment agencies
Necessary inputs
    Changes in availability of service
    Interagency cooperation
Mandates and sanctions
    Financial limitations
    Mandate of foundation
    Agency function
Strategies
  Target population
    Girls on probation—a passive role as recipients of casework treatment
  Service programs
    Casework treatment
    Outreach
    Interagency communication and cooperation
    Testing and evaluatory procedures
    Additional staff—research consultation
  Monitoring and evaluation
    Formalized evaluation procedures
  Strategy problems
    Case problems in terms of outreach
    Loss of subjects because of rearrest
    Staff turnover in probation department
    Staff morale
    Delays in processing data and making it available for use

## Outline C. Assumptions, Strategies, and Problems of a Community Service Agency and Changing Programs

Problem definition
    The continued existence and growth of undesirable social situations and large numbers of socially disadvantaged people
Causation
    Breakdown in democratic process
    System operates to advantage of those in power

The disadvantaged have no influence
The disadvantaged feel powerless
Necessary inputs
Changes in nature and delivery of professional services
Opening of service delivery system to the disadvantaged
Mandates and sanctions
Board of trustees report
Agency purpose and goal
Time limit for changes
Financial limit—revenues of agency
Strategies
Target population
NYC's socially disadvantaged population—active role but dependent on agency
Service programs
Identification of population through agency's data bank
Opening of system to above group
Services to groups and communities—consultation, mediation, training, fund-raising
Administrative reorganization
Personnel changes and staff training
Monitoring and evaluation
Formalized: linkage of program with evaluation, research, and forecasting
Strategy problems
Staff morale
Staff development
Lack of knowledge about new skills—what and how

## Outline D. Assumptions, Strategies, and Problems of Inner City

Problem definition
Low achievement level of public school pupils
Causation
Overcrowded, chaotic school lacking staff, facilities, and services
Teachers poorly prepared to teach
Poverty conditions and crime rampant in neighborhood
Necessary inputs
Program has broad support and involvement of local community, teaching staff, and educational officials
Teachers need training in how to teach basic skills
School is run in an orderly way

Mandates and sanctions
    Community and teacher expectations
    Board of education regulations
    Teachers' union rules
Strategies
  Target population
    Pupils (passive role in services)
    Teachers (active and passive role in services)
  Service programs
    Saturation program in one grade

## Outline E. Assumptions, Strategies, and Problems of Half-Way House

---

Problem definition
    Drug addiction
Causation
    Emotional immaturity due to faulty familial experiences
Necessary inputs
    Structured residence in which addict can relive a new, therapy
      family experience
Mandates and sanctions
    Community fears of addicts
    City regulations regarding staffing and expenditures of monies
Strategies
  Targeted population
    Drug addicts or experimenters who are motivated to change (move
      from passive to active role in services)
  Service programs
    Residential structured environment
    Therapeutic work program
    Encounter groups
    Educational program
  Monitoring or evaluation
    Records of progress of residents; statistical reports
Strategy problems
    Separation from their families brings hardships to some residents
      at Half-Way House (particularly women with children)
    Difficulty of ex-addict leaving Half-Way House
    Only small fraction of addicts can be helped by Half-Way House
      under present funding arrangements

## Outline F. Assumptions, Strategies, and Problems of Kissena Apartments: An Experience in Housing for Older People

Problem definition
  Decent housing for older people
Causation
  Changing neighborhoods
  Deterioration of housing
  Physical problems of aging and changing needs
Necessary inputs
  Housing project
  Senior center
  Supportive social services
Mandates and sanctions
  Agency mandate for client population
  Income, residence restriction from New York State law and mortgage
Strategies
 Target population
  Aged victims of Nazi persecution—primarily a passive role in relatives to receipt of agency services
 Service programs
  Physically manageable, equipped apartments at reasonable rentals
  Older adult center plus a community center—interagency cooperative
  Cafeteria
  Social services—counseling, homemaker services, and staffing an information service—and staffing
  Housing staff—managing agent, manager, and maintenance staff
 Monitoring and evaluation
  No formal evaluation—some monitoring provided by elected citizen council
Strategy problems
  Initial community opposition
  Cafeteria financial deficit
  Weakness in selection process—problem tenants

**Consumer Advocacy**  Increasing concern focuses on the protection and advancement of consumer interests within the human services delivery system. In evidence is a proliferation of a variety of and mechanisms: action and lobbying organizations composed of consumers; research on their behalf; the use of the law and the courts to defend and expand consumer's rights; the establishment of public bodies with that responsibility; and the resort to grievance procedures and ombudsmen. An important component of human services delivery is advocacy for the consumer dealing with the complexities and frustrations of large bureaucracies.

This raises questions: Who is to perform the advocate role, and what strategies are most effective when the consumer needs an advocate in his relationship with the social service providers? Can a human service agency have its own "refund and complaint" department similar to that in a retail store? These decisions are usually left to the administrators of local and state service organizations; thus, a member or several members of the staff have primary tasks involving consumer rights. For example, the Rhode Island Department of Mental Health has as an employee a mental health advocate. As an attorney, his principal job is to review all cases in the state institutions to determine whether or not the patient's right to treatment has been met and whether their individual rights are upheld.

There are two basic approaches to advocacy. One focuses at the case level in terms of interventions for the benefit of a particular person; the other focuses on institutional change, which entails an analysis of needs, planning, the use of influence, and mobilization of pressure to achieve change on a policy level.

In an interesting example of the use of advocacy, a team was established by the executive secretary of human services and the commissioner of public welfare for the state of Massachusetts in 1972. A two-year demonstration grant was funded to establish a human services advocacy team composed of community people and front-line service workers, each familiar with services at the delivery point. The team acted as a change agent at a systems level to modify ways services do injustice to those for whom they were created. Their goal was to bring about a more humanized social services system in which services are organized and delivered in ways convenient to the people who use them, not necessarily to those who provide them; a flexible, responsive interaction of state and private services that refuses to let people fall between the cracks of inconsistent eligibility guidelines, application procedures, and conflicting policies.

Specific functions of the team included reviews of cases to determine whether advocacy was needed to assist a consumer or group of consumers. The criterion for accepting cases would generally be the need to influence a system organization related in some way to the delivery of human services; the problem would involve one or more components of the state or local human services agencies. The key determinant would be the need for institutional advocacy—notably, when the consumer or caseworker could not normally obtain the needed action or services through action as an individual or without possible detriment to himself or herself (e.g., inordinantly long waiting lists, later repercussions for the consumer or his family). The emphasis would be on correcting problems in the system, working from the assumption that, when things go wrong, it can often be the fault of the system and not of the consumer. Examples of solutions include settling jurisdictional problems between two agencies; encouraging an agency to develop more Spanish-language materials, and helping citizens to identify sources of funding for low-income housing.

In order for this project to be successful, there needed to be external, interagency linkages. This indicates a need for multilevel structure of providers that can relate to the tasks of the team, give the team support and guidance, and help the team to effect change when needed. This was achieved through cosponsorship; state human service organizations were mandated to serve in this capacity. Specifically, the chief administrator of each agency served as a specific cosponsor and attended cosponsor meetings. The regional council on human services coordinated meetings of the different local human service organizations. There it monitored the progress of the advocacy team, whose activity cut across the jurisdiction of each of the agencies. Involvement of personnel inside the human services system was also instrumental in promoting the integration of services by way of interagency linkages. Private and voluntary organizations were also included, and the emphasis was directed toward the public sector.

Other approaches to bring about change are those of community organization social activism, and advocacy. Each of these approaches embodies a different set of goals and behaviors for the human service worker. Traditionally the community organizer primarily facilitates a process by which those with whom he works—community leaders—can select their own goals and take action. He operates primarily through a formal structure and enables committees, who purport to be broadly representative of a community, to arrive at consensually accepted procedures and goals. Community problems and goals are apt to be defined very broadly in order to help achieve consensus. Generally, these priorities deal with adapating, rationalizing, or producing new organizational structures. Details of allocating resources, employing personnel, and setting specific policy are usually left to the professionals, who seek committee approval after the fact.

In the role of social activist, the community professional is engaged in cause-oriented activities of a political nature, each geared to solve specific problems in the community. The community professional, or small group of persons under his leadership, selects and pursues a specific solution. This pursuit is single-minded and sometimes uncompromising. Resources for change are usually sought with the expectation that other causes will make an equal bid for the resources. The community professional's role as social activist requires that he be a strong and effective leader. The cause is stalemated if his leadership breaks down or if his followers lose enthusiasm for the cause.

In the role of advocate, the human services leader is committed to a group of people—often a group of individuals who share some common needs and a group consciousness and who are on the receiving end of community services. The goal of the advocate is to produce a redistribution of benefits and a greater control over these benefits by the consumers or service users. In this role, the human services leader places his skills, time, and knowledge at the disposal of the people. In the purest form of this approach, his actions are in the direction of the consumers. In his capacity as an advocate or as a social activist, the strategies used to deal with community structures are often those of confrontation and political pressure.

Of the many important and diverse kinds of roles for human service professionals, advocacy is one that is essential. Although the concept of advocate might be attached to any kind of cause, it has come to connote primarily working with disadvantaged low-income populations, improving their conditions and increasing their power in local communities or in wider political arenas.

**Manpower Development**   Human services manpower development can be viewed from the perspective of the complexity and change of the larger environment or system in which manpower programs operate and adjust. Population, policy, and programs are each interrelated. Singly or in combination, each will certainly influence the future of human services manpower development, including factors of supply and demand. A system constitutes a way to organize knowledge and resources in order to achieve goals within a specified timeframe. Manpower is a major subsystem of any large service delivery system and has its own components, such as the training subsystem. This is in keeping with current trends in management theory.

Manpower is generally an organization's most costly, yet most valuable, resource. It is a factor critical to the service facility's achievement of its goals. In the process of analyzing and defining activities necessary for the attainment of an agency's service goals, many personal values, prejudices, and needs emerge. Training units themselves are frequently without their own clearly defined goals; moreover, they are often required to function in areas considered peripheral to the central organizational issues. For example, training units have been called upon to perform in crisis situations that do not allow sufficient time for the planning and implementation of training tasks. Because of their key role in the total organization, and because of the large investment in manpower, training subsystems are increasingly being forced to develop a goal-oriented approach. Plans, budgets, and measurable goal criteria are rapidly replacing hip-pocket and crisis-oriented training activities.

The elements that affect manpower training subsystems are complex and must, of necessity, remain uncertain. On the other hand, definite segments can be identified along with a number of services than can be delivered by an agency. The tasks can be identified, catalogued, and combined in a large but clearly specifiable number of ways. Usually such service tasks have been grouped into job descriptions on the basis of tradition and professional guild authority.

Several examples illustrate the relationships between population changes and service supply and demand factors. While, for instance, associated with child rearing and education may be reduced—particularly not those directly related to child care of the very young—demand for availability of day care services will, in turn, increase the number of women in the labor market. Demands for human services for the elderly will also increase. With anticipated shifts in the relative sizes of the elementary, secondary, and college populations for the remainder of this century, today's surplus of elementary school teachers may become tomorrow's undersupply of teachers for colleges or special vocational schools. The increasing mean and model ages of the population will create changes in the *type* of medical care being demanded.

As citizens and local and state governments gain increasing control over the flow of funds, they will have greater influence over manpower training, allocation, and distribution decisions than ever before. This will contrast sharply with the past, when decision makers were influenced by federal bureaucracies, categorical constituencies, professional associations, and other special interest groups.

A major trend in the delivery of human services has been a shift toward the integration of existing resources and away from the new programs and agencies of the 1960s. The thrust of an integrated services strategy has been to increase the accessibility, comprehensiveness, continuity, and accountability of the total delivery system. The attitudes and training of service personnel are factors that are critical to achieving an integrated service system. Integrated service networks will demand a greater degree of interdisciplinary work, including the maximum utilization of professions that were previously excluded as critical to the human service arena. Architects, land planners, engineers, lawyers, information specialists, and economists are just a few of the many professionals whose contributions are needed. This will be necessitated by problems created by new treatment technologies, new joint service locations, and new financial models and administrative structures.

Major intraorganizational and interorganizational changes include the greater use of new management planning tools. Examples of these would be information systems, shared management services, cost-accounting systems, and complex organizational network structures such as multiservice centers and service consortiums. In general, it is expected that there will be a greater concern for the economics of human services delivery and manpower development, including a consideration of cost–benefit ratios. For example, one econometric analysis for the evaluation of manpower programs points out a frequently forgotten fact: one of the greatest costs of training programs is the foregone earnings lost to the participants during the program and post-program period.

A trend in manpower development resulting from deinstitutionalization has been deprofessionalization in the proliferating community-based programs. The movement toward institutional reform is evident in the closing of state mental hospitals, decreasing reliance on nursing homes for the aged, and a turning away from large correctional facilities. Institutionalized service programs will become smaller, more refined, and more differentiated.

Another noteworthy shift in program delivery systems has been the rapid emergence of a self-help philosophy of treatment, as outlined in Chapter 8. More and more people—many of whom were formerly ignored by professionals or socially stigmatized—are organizing their own groups to help one another. The self-help movement is really an aspect of a larger trend toward using naturally existing support systems for preventive (Broskowski and Baker 1974) and ameliorative purposes (Kaplan 1973).

Support systems will inevitably recast the role of professionals and paraprofessionals in the service delivery mix. Trained specialists in particular services such as health, corrections, welfare, rehabilitation, mental health, and education will be asked to contribute to these new groups and support systems by helping them to initiate and organize new ones. In addition, professionals can offer consultation and education to the organizers and members of these support systems.

A related trend is the increased use of volunteers as part of organized delivery systems. Federal regulations and federal support are further accelerating the trend to volunteerism. The emphasis on integrated and community-based services, together with trends in self-help, volunteerism, and natural support systems, will have profound impacts on the professional manpower pattern. The role of professionals as direct service providers may become more constrained as people find out that they can get help from each other while spending their discretionary funds on other types of services or goods.

These program trends will also intensify the generalist–specialist dilemma. While lower-level personnel will increasingly be trained as specialists at highly technical tasks, they will also seek ways to further generalize their experiences, in an attempt to adapt to obsolescence and changing demands. Higher-level personnel will need sufficient expertise to train and supervise the complex variety of lower-level personnel. Furthermore, the traditional professions must find new roles as some of their own activities are taken over by persons with task-specific training. Professionals must seek and solve new challenges to justify their status, authority, and salary levels. As more treatment activities are carried out by personnel with lower salaries and less training, higher-level personnel must assume more demanding roles in the areas of policy formulation, planning, and administration (Demone 1973), research and development (Broskowski and Schulberg 1974), and program evaluation (Suchman 1967; Weiss, ed. 1972). Such changes are now appearing in the formal curricula and field placements of professional training programs (Broskowski and Smith 1974).

Manpower training programs have to adapt to a number of dimensions according to population, policy, and program changes. For example, they must be designed for diversity, flexibility, and a greater degree of integration with multiple operating human service systems. There must be a shift from the concept of closed and isolated classroom teaching to a variety of open-field settings, many of which will be sponsored by human service agencies that use apprenticeship and work–study models. Continuing education will become a predominant trend, increased by the need to keep up with the rapid changes in service technology and service demands. In-service training and on-the-job training units will become regular organizational features of large-scale planning, research, and service delivery systems.

The volume of training will broaden at the academic entry levels, with increasing growth for community colleges and the number of associate of arts degrees in human services. All types of new career training programs will continue to increase (McPheters 1971), regardless of the multiple barriers to adequate job status and career development that presently exist. A good sampling of the multiple levels of innovative mental health training programs—both academic and nonacademic, for the roles of service, teaching, research, and prevention—are provided by the National Institute of Mental Health (NIMH 1971).

The concept of career ladders is being expanded further to become the concept of "career lattices" (Vidaver and Carson 1973). Each level of personnel will assume greater change in career interests as it is exposed to, and moves about in, an increasingly integrated service system. New careers and second careers are already a familiar occurrence among middle- and upper-income business men and women returning to the job market. Increased diversity will heighten concerns within traditional service and educational systems regarding regulation and standardization of credentials. Well accepted and entrenched professions will resist the development of new professions. If this resistance fails, the intense professions are likely to attempt cooptation of direct control of new professionals. Established programs will demand that newer roles and practices be evaluated while resisting any attempts to examine their own outcomes.

The installation and development of new service systems require a massive local and statewide training effort. New policies, will need to be explained, new tasks and skills taught, and different staff attitudes developed. Because the use of many of the services by citizens is voluntary, service personnel must begin with the skills that would aid potential clients in the use of the new approach. As new service tasks are identified, new positions are created that do not necessarily require professional degrees. Work experience and formal credentials have equal validity as criteria for promotion and position. The skills of planning, management, and evaluation have been taught to existing staff acquired through recruitment from outside the system. Maine, for example, developing a manpower planning capability through a contract with the University of Maine. This planning capability should allow the state to forecast manpower needs and then design its support for specific training programs to meet these needs (Davis, 1973).

Probably the most significant change in manpower development has been the enhanced and integrated position of manpower policy in the overall service organizational structure: job description, classification, restructuring, and personnel selection, promotion, and training have been integral management tasks to the overall context of services delivery. An illustration of systematic statewide approach to manpower training is that of the State of Utah's Division of Family Services, which is pioneering a unique and powerful technology for manpower planning called functional job analysis (HSICF 1974). Functional job analysis provides a model for linking staff development and personnel considerations with program service goals; it also provides a way of developing the basic work information essential for job design, job mobility, and an ability to change as the needs of clients shift. Each worker is evaluated on the ability to perform a set of tasks in a manner which meets clear by criteria. The skills necessary to accomplish these tasks may come from any combination of college education, life experience, inservice training, or continuing education as Broskowski and Smith (1974) point out.

Another systematic approach to manpower training and development is modular education, which brings together the service delivery system with the established education system in a joint effort characterized by flexibility and responsiveness. At the Human Resource Institute at the University of Maine, several hundred such modules have been developed in close collaboration with the state agencies for health, mental health, welfare, rehabilitation, aging, and corrections. The outcome is a training program for human service occupations ranging from the level of an associate of arts degree to beyond the master's degree. The general categories covered by the training include counseling, community development, and human services management. Specialization in a particular discipline with any one category is possible at any level. Any one or a combination of modules can be built into an agency's inservice training program to meet particular needs of the individual learner as well as those of the agency. The design of modules is keyed to functional task analyses at the local service delivery level. The modular education plan is further integrated into the state's broader plans for service delivery (Davis 1973).

In much the opposite way, a course was developed in human services, a component of the Health and Society Program at Brown University, that brought the educational component into the local and state service systems. The curriculum integrated the various systems of human service delivery through lectures, discussion groups, and field work placements (Sauber 1975).

Another trend worthy of attention is that given to adult education—or andragogy, which describes the philosophy of how adults learn—in distinction to pedagogy, or child learning (Knowles 1970). The educational profession in particular has been noting these assumptions as programs in adult and community education have grown to meet the developmental needs of a society characterized by rapid job changes, second careers, and leisure interests.

Manpower development must be broadly conceived, and its classifications system equally understood. The definition of a professional—which is presumably a rubric signifying confidence and high standards—is only one particular element in the manpower development field. The other levels of individuals in human service manpower classifications include community caretakers, volunteers, self-help nonprofessionals, paraprofessionals, urban agents, and natural nonprofessionals.

Of particular note here is the role of community caretakers, those key individuals providing essential community services. Such individuals would include the police, clergy, lawyers, physicians, nurses, teachers, and mental health workers. In this context a particular aspect or presenting problem of human services is being addressed by an individual outside of that area of expertise. For example, these people are considered professional within their given fields but are viewed here as nonprofessional only insofar as they are not formally trained in a particular aspect. For instance, a policeman within the mental health field may be engaged in resolving many kinds of family crises and thus may be conceptualized as a community caretaker rather than a mental health professional. A law enforcement officer would be considered a professional within the criminal justice field, whereas a teacher offering assistance would be considered a community caretaker if the problem were involved with juvenile delinquency. A teacher within the educational system would be considered the professional, whereas a policeman called upon to assist in resolving school attendance problems is the role of community caretaker. The principal point is that there are professionally trained individuals in the community that participate in all aspects of human services; the distinction lies in whether they are formally designated as the professional according to expertise and training or as the nonprofessional, in terms of being a resourceful individual who nonetheless has the respect and trust of the members of the community.

Volunteers comprise the largest group of nonprofessional personnel. They include a variety of people, such as interested homemakers, college students, and high school students. These individuals provide a tremendous work force resource for such settings as psychiatric hospitals, community mental health centers, programs and institutions for the retarded, nursing homes, and crisis intervention facilities. Often these programs are set up as peer helper systems like those that work in school districts. A community

organization called Fish is an example: Volunteers created their own organization to provide telephone information and voluntary transportation to
individuals in need and in crises. These volunteers work within a professionalized institution, and their roles are defined by other paid staff.

Self-help nonprofessionals may be paraprofessionals or volunteers. However, they also often consist of lay members of various groups who are
striving to create a mutual support system for one another so as to meet their
particular needs and problems—which the professional community has either
ignored, underserviced, or inappropriately handled. Included in this category
are members of Alcoholics Anonymous, consciousness-raising groups, and
the long list of associations described in Chapter 8.

Paraprofessionals make up another major and growing category of workers. They are paid for middle-level tasks and are either formally or informally trained in newly emerging nontraditional training programs. Service
agencies and institutions of all kinds, as well as community colleges, offer
programs of certification such as the associate of arts program in human
services technology. Exotic types of community leaders, such as witch doctors and faith healers, may also be frequently found in urban and rural settings and are quite esteemed and often sought out for assistance with physical and emotional ailments. Increasing use is being made these natural healers
by their professional counterparts.

Urban agents are included as nonprofessionals who are involved in less
formal helping relationships than those for caretakers. However, their roles
within a community put them in key positions to offer direct help to troubled
persons and to serve at least in liaison functions to appropriate professional
agencies. Examples of potential urban agents are such people as shopkeepers, taxi drivers, foremen, bartenders, and beauticians. This group consists of what may be called "natural neighbors"—the types of people to
whom others turn for aid during both mild and severe crises: industrial labor
personnel, bartenders, barbers and others. Many persons tend to talk to such
individuals about their problems. As noted, Dumont (1967), in studying
tavern culture, observed that bartenders are providing for the needs of numerous homeless and disturbed individuals untouched by available health
and welfare agencies. Taking this one step further, a program sponsored by
the Milwaukee County Mental Health Association trains bartenders in referring and handling customers' difficulties and problems. Bartenders acquire
these skills and knowledge: identification of deviant behavior, methods of
handling drunken patrons, techniques for reflective listening, handling suicide and depression, mutual-help techniques, and facts about alcohol abuse

and treatment. Malcolm (1974) and Snyder (1971), having surveyed the influence of both nonpsychiatric professionals and nonprofessional caregivers in the urban community, found that more people turned to family, friends, and natural neighbors than to physicians, lawyers, and clergymen. One overriding commonality appears to be the strong perception of such people as friendly and sensitive individuals with whom others can share and talk about their problems. Reiff and Riessman (1965) described a number of generic jobs for indigenous nonprofessionals in a community setting:

*Home Service Aide:* to help in the home by counseling on various aspects of homemaking such as buying and preparing food, raising children, sewing, and decorating; to organize groups of mothers for educational programs in these areas.

*Child Service Aide:* to work with groups of children in formal and informal settings (homes, backyards, playgrounds) under professional supervision; to promote more significant recreational activities and positive adult relationships; to free mothers to keep appointments or participate in rehabilitation programs.

*Casework Aide:* to help the social worker in interviewing clients and families; to do administrative work such as maintenance of files and clinic records; to collect record materials from other agencies; to identify needs of families in the neighborhood; and to share knowledge of family with the caseworker.

*Research Aide:* to work in any agency with a research program, including agency self-evaluation; to interview, record observations, collect data, and help in technical and interpretive aspects of data analysis; to secure and interpret information from low-income people (Reiff and Riessman 1965).

For the future, human services promises increased diversification and broader manpower options. Thus, the range of models must go beyond the traditionally specialized and credentialed training given in formal academic settings. New human services careers at all levels will emerge as program changes promote a greater integration of policy, planning, and service delivery. Training will be more closely integrated with service delivery and less buffered by the exigencies of the marketplace economy. An understanding of the multiple forces that influence manpower subsystems requires a total perspective on the "human services system" that transcends the limited content of what the trainers may like to teach or what is currently fundable by the federal government (Broskowski and Smith 1974).

## SERVICE EVALUATION

This book has emphasized presentation of human services in a systems perspective. The present chapter has discussed thus far the design and delivery of services. Evaluation performs a system function; with evaluation, these processes come full circle, and evaluative feedback provides an information loop to guide the design and delivery of present and future projects, programs, and policies. In another sense evaluation can be viewed as an aspect of systems; this process is itself a way of assessing the multifaceted and interdependent consequences of implementing a program. Thus, evaluation is both an aspect and a tool of systems.

There are common confusions between the terms evaluation, research, and accountability. Some fundamental definitions are provided by Burck (1975) according to popular conceptions.

*Evaluation*
—is the systematic process of judging the worth, desirability, effectiveness, or adequacy of something according to definite criteria and purposes. In a broad sense, evaluation can be defined as the process of deciding the value of something or as the science of providing information for decision-making (Sauber 1973).

—generally includes the tasks of: establishing desired objectives; collecting and organizing information to assess the accomplishment of objectives, judging the adequacy of accomplishments; and making decisions for improving programs (Wysong 1972).

—is a judgment of merit, sometimes based solely on measurements such as those provided to test scores but more frequently involving the synthesis of various measurements, critical incidents, subjective impressions, and other kinds of evidence (Ebel 1965).

—is the process of delineating, obtaining, and providing useful information for judging decision alternatives (Stufflebeam et al. 1971).

*Research*
—to advance knowledge, i.e., to depict, correlate, conceptualize and test. "These criteria do not include practical considerations—they do not require findings to be relevant to current operating problems, useful to practitioners, or translate into new products" (Stufflebeam et al. 1971).

—science is concerned with the study of process or the interdependence of events or phenomena . . . it usually involves the test of some hypothesis concerning the relationship between an independent or 'causal' variable and a dependent or 'effect' variable: i.e., the more a, the more b (Suchman 1967).

—as commonly practiced is theoretical in emphasis . . . concerned with furthering the individual disciplines . . . deals with problems generated and solved within the disciplines themselves . . . has to do with the search for theoretical models that explain and predict phenomena of some definable kind and with the means for measuring and codifying the phenomena (Dyer 1972).

—is aimed at the advancement of scientific knowledge. There is no need for research to be immediately useful or practical, and there can be great concern for making sure that the exact relationship between independent and dependent variables is known (Oetting and Hawkes 1974).

*Accountability*

—(system) . . . a set of procedures that collates information about accomplishments and costs to facilitate decision making (Krumboltz 1974).

—means that the providers of services have a responsibility of being accountable to the users and inquirers for service, as well as to the public at large . . . (Sauber 1973).

—has come to mean a focus on results—on the learning to be achieved as stipulated before the process begins . . . the degree to which a system succeeds in delivering on its promises for the resources provided (Lessinger 1972).

—is the process by which professional workers at all levels interact to bring about the successful achievement of pre-determined and mutually agreed-upon goals and objectives (Nikolas 1972).

## DIFFERENCES BETWEEN EVALUATION AND RESEARCH

Similarities and overlaps exist between evaluation and research with respect to accountability. Both evaluation and research can be accountability activities. Yet, there are some variations, at least in degree, which allow us to speak of evaluation and research as separate kinds of activities. Table 10.5 is an attempt to highlight and illustrate some of these differences, the emphasis being that human services programs might better be evaluated than researched (Burck 1975).

**Significance of Evaluation**   The only way to substantiate one's efforts is through evaluation and research, and in recent years, there has been extensive discussion of what has been coined "social accuracy." Flaherty and Morrell (1978) attribute this phenomenon to the greater requirements for accountability in publicly funded programs, increasing interest among social

CHARACTERISTICS OF EVALUATION AND RESEARCH

| Dimension | Differences | |
| --- | --- | --- |
| | *Evaluation* | *Research* |
| Purpose | —collect information for decision making<br>—to explain<br>—mission-oriented | —provide knowledge more generally valid<br>—to explain and predict<br>—theory-oriented |
| Process | —systems approach models (e.g., CIPP, PERT)<br><br>—treatment intervention usually more implicit<br>—concerned with relationship between outcomes and established goals | —traditional experimental designs (randomness, hypothesis testing, rigorous controls, sophisticated statistical analyses, operational definition, etc.)<br>—treatment intervention more explicit<br>—concerned with relationship between independent and dependent variables |
| Level of specificity/controls | —process more general—minimal amount of control<br>—use of nonequivalent control Ss often used | —order of events quite specific—great control<br>—use of equivalent control Ss |
| Setting | —in the work or delivery-system situation, *in vivo* | —controlled setting, *in vitro* |
| Personnel | —all personnel (intervenors & evaluators) must endorse and cooperate for maximum impact<br>—program usually cannot be started over again | —cooperation important but not as crucial because of greater control over situation<br>—research study can usually be restarted |
| Instrumentation | —constructed for specific program (homemade); high content validity | —standardized measures used; reliability and validity already established |
| Measurement/data | —less precise<br>—use of available data permitted | —more precise<br>—decided beforehand (pre-designed and carefully selected) |
| Objectivity | —judgmental—evaluator's values are explicit and usually respected | —less judgmental—researcher's values show more implicitly |
| Cost effectiveness/benefit | —specific to program/intervention<br>—great concern | —more generalizable<br>—less concern |
| Use of outcomes | —to effect immediate change—to assist decision makers<br>—immediately applicable; practical | —advance scientific knowledge<br>—theory building and reconceptualization |

*Source:* Burck 1975.

scientists in social relevance, an increasing scarcity of resources for the traditional social sciences, and an expansion of social science methodologies appropriate to research in applied settings. While early evaluation studies were generally more limited in their outlook, the present context of evaluation is broader, including as it does these elements: the goal of improvement of impact; multiple perspectives, including the neglected one of the client; attempts to rectify deficiencies in development, particularly their unplanned, categorical, specialized, fragmented, discontinuous, costly, and inefficient aspects; emphases on the service concept, with its program commonalities and linkages especially suited to the multiproblem client; multilevel linkages requiring constant evaluation; and the human service concept that has primary meaning for policy makers, planners, administrators, and program evaluators—all of whom must maintain a generic and systemic perspective on service funding, delivery, and impact (Attkisson and Broskowski 1978:21).

Program evaluation seeks primarily to improve the impact of ongoing projects and services. Thus a wide range of evaluative functions and activities must necessarily take place so that program impact can be viewed from multiple perspectives. These varying points of view include those of service providers, administrators, regulators, funders, and legislators. The criteria for program impact will usually include many measures: program efforts by staff, service outcomes for individuals or groups, efficiency in terms of costs, and effectiveness and adequacy in meeting the estimated levels of program severity and community needs. Further, a desirable service must also be readily available when needed and operate in a way that does not create undue burdens or expenses for the consumer. Thus it should be accessible geographically, temporally, and financially.

The criteria of program impact must include systematic comprehensiveness. As evidenced by studies of the prevalence of the multiproblem client, between 86 percent (DHEW Study) and 95 percent (Lancaster Study) of all DHEW clients have multiple problems; single services provided independently of one another do not result in changes in clients' dependency status or life changes (DHEW 1973:3). If a client's multiple problems are to be treated in a simultaneous or sequential fashion, the client's perspective of good services must include the degree to which one service is coordinated with another—or at least the degree to which the client can be referred from one program to another. Thus evaluation criteria should also include a measure of program continuity.

Currently, it appears that in many programs the rate of effective referrals between separate programs is very low. Consequently, the impact of single programs on multiproblem clients is severely limited. Program evaluation must be viewed as an integral component of organizational design and development. That is, evaluation is a function that takes place within an organizational context, and therefore the program evaluators must understand the dynamics of organizational structures and interactions—including the multiple types of transactions within and between organizations that must be carried out in the process of service delivery. More to the point, program evaluation is primarily a process employed in the service of organizational management, decision making, and planning; it is only secondarily a research enterprise designed to make new scientific discoveries. The products of evaluative efforts must meet external as well as internal management and planning needs.

An example of dual perspective is provided by the criminal justice subsystem. The intrinsic goals include rehabilitation of offenders, isolation of offenders who pose a threat to community safety, deterrence, expression of the community's condemnation of the offender's conduct, and reinforcement of the values of law-abiding citizens. Extrinsic goals, on the other hand, include the maintenance or enhancement of the organizational welfare of components of the criminal justice system and maintenance or enhancement of personal or career welfare of system members. These are the external and internal requirements, respectively, to which evaluation can respond.

Program evaluation must meet the organization's responsibility to its external environment; evaluative information must be available to meet administrative needs of other government or private agencies. Evaluators at a program or system level cannot supply all of the evaluative information needed by the level's own external environment. Within that limitation, evaluation at a given level of program can provide a variety of information. It can supply information for that program's internal management planning purposes; it can comply with external reporting requirements; it can collaborate with other organizational levels; and it can receive and provide consultation. External agencies always have to supplement the information received from other program levels with additional information obtained through their own independent efforts. Program evaluation capabilities must include knowledge and skills in management information systems, cost accounting, and program outcome management.

Because evaluation must be considered in the context of complex organizations and their shifting environments, the interface between these elements depends on multiple sources of data. Such data will vary as regards level of detail, source, cost, and ease of collection, validity of interpretation, and scientific merit. The methods by which these data are collected, processed, and blended into useful information will vary considerably, but should in all cases be systematic. The evaluator must accept tradeoffs between precision and timeliness. In the balance, one can only expect reasonable judgments and not scientifically verified facts (Attkisson and Broskowski 1978).

Among the many definitions of program evaluation, one that is gaining increased acceptance is offered by Attkisson and Broskowski (1978). The definition emphasizes the systematic role of evaluation in that it focuses on the utility and efficiency of the human services network in terms both of specific client needs and of the entire range of human service needs within a community. Thus, program evaluation is defined as a process of making reasonable judgments about program effort, effectiveness, efficiency, and adequacy, based on systematic data collection and analysis and designed for use in program management, external accountability, and future planning; it focuses especially on accessibility and acceptability, awareness, availability, comprehensiveness, continuity, integration, and cost of services (p. 24).

**Methods of Evaluation**   Three distinct general approaches to evaluation have evolved. The first stresses the role of the scientific method; the second, the goal-attainment approach versus the systems model; the third, the use of evaluation information.

Each approach has its own set of concepts, strategies, technologies, and purposes. The scientific approach entails the use of evaluation research methods that adhere as closely as possible to accepted standards of research methodology. Weiss (1972) has made several important criticisms of this approach: it requires that the program be constant, rather than facilitate its continual improvement; it has utility for making decisions only after a project has run its full cycle and not during its planning and implementation; and it attempts to control too many conditions, making the program aseptic, that is, ungeneralizable to the real world.

Another approach to evaluation, which is an offspring of this earlier approach, rests on questions concerning the kinds and timing of information that evaluations should provide; namely, the goal-attainment approach and summative evaluation in contrast to the systems model, which uses formative evaluation. The former defines the primary function of evaluation as the measurement of the achievement of a program's predetermined goals. This corresponds to what Hoole (1978) calls ''impact evaluation,'' as opposed to ''process evaluation.'' This approach in operation refers to the information that is provided only after program termination, when the attainment of final objectives has been measured. Implicit in this approach is the belief that all program goals can be outlined and specified before the program is actually implemented.

This approach contrasts to Schulberg and Baker's (1969) systems approach or Weiss's (1972) formative evaluation, which refers to process evaluation and implementation. The latter approaches are predicated on the assumption that the uses of information are best served by a comprehensive description of how the program actually functions with ongoing feedback about the attainment of program objectives. Here one requires data on unexpected results and program efforts and about the relationship between program functions and the attainment of objectives at continuous points during the program's course—rather than after program termination. The proponents of the systems approach share the belief that the goals of a program cannot be fully specified before a program begins (Schulberg and Baker 1979). A basic feature of formative evaluation is ongoing management in intervention and decision making—which is internal to the program—rather than summarizing its external impact (see figure 10.1).

The third basic approach that differs in practice from earlier methods is that of evaluation information. Recognition of the impact that evaluators can have on utilization of the data produced is gaining increasing attention. Edwards, Guttentag, and Snapper (1975) consider information utilization an integral characteristic of evaluation: "Evaluations . . . exist (or perhaps should only exist) to facilitate intelligent decision making. . . . If [evaluation] does not improve the basis for decisions about the program, it loses its distinctive character as evaluation research and becomes simply research" (p. 140). Thus, information utilization based upon methods of data collection and analysis are essential to this approach.

A number of basic concepts and techniques of evaluation can be applied to all areas of human services, including levels of evaluation criteria, need assessment, goal-attainment scaling, the method of utilizing evaluation findings referred to as the VICTORY technique, the decision-theoretic approaches, and process and outcome evaluation. Kiresuk and Sherman (1968) wrote the classic article on goal-attainment scaling, which has been extended from its original application—the measurement of progress of individual patients and therapy—to comparison of program effectiveness and the achievement of program and administrative goals. Initially used in mental health settings, this methodology has been accepted in drug abuse programs, rehabilitation services, and programs for the retarded. VICTORY is an acronym for the seven factors that one should consider in planning for the utili-

**Figure 10.1**
A GENERAL FLOWCHART OF GOAL EVALUATION

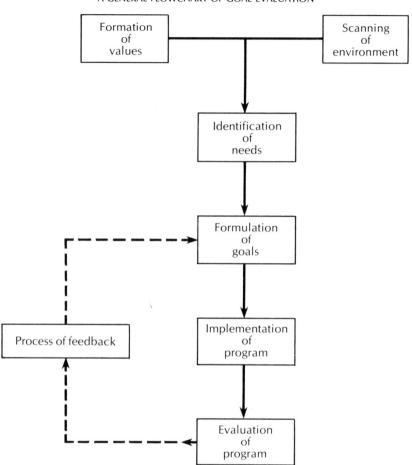

zation of evaluation research: values, idea, circumstances, timing, obligation, resistances, and yield. This technique has been applied in numerous evaluation projects and is reported to be successful in increasing utilization (Davis and Slasin 1975).

Another concept by Edwards, Guttentag, and Snapper (1975) was developed to facilitate the role of evaluation in decision making. This provides a framework for the total process of decision making that has consequences for the dissemination or utilization of evaluation research results. The last concept is based upon the distinction between process and outcome: process variables are generally assumed to be those variables that make up the delivery of program service as it is actually carried out, not as it was intended to be carried out. Weiss (1972) suggests that the "process approach directs attention to the essentials, . . . allows a test of the theoretical linkages and enables the evaluator to say useful things about the stage where things go awry and adjustment is needed" (p. 324). Suchman (1967) recommended that the criteria of evaluation be considered according to the levels of program effort (input), performance (output), adequacy (goal-related), efficiency (output divided by input), and process (a study of the means whereby a program produces its results) See table 10.5. This fourfold classification of evaluative criteria has been employed, for example, in the health care subsystem (Stamps 1978:6–7).

A multiple-criterion approach to evaluation can be adapted to a particular subsystem or situation. For example, Bellin, Kavaler, and Schwarz (1978) used twelve different criteria to evaluate advisory committees for ambulatory services in New York City. These included structure (membership), process (attendance, activeness, and change over time), motivations (of hospitals, consumers, and the health department), styles of discourse (for these three groups), interaction among the three parties, and attributions of outcome.

Examination of the general category of adequacy may be instructive because it integrates the process of needs assessment discussed earlier in the chapter. Needs assessment is the effort to determine the appropriate mix of human services for a community and to detect the important gaps in those services, thus forming a basis for comparison with actual service mix. As noted in the service design section, there are numerous methods of needs assessment available, such as social and health indicator analyses, social area surveys, and community group approaches. There is an emerging consensus that needs assessment and planning should be coordinated within geographic regions for all health and other human services—rather than expecting narrowly defined categorical programs, with their vested interests—to plan to fill gaps or avoid excessive duplication.

Table 10.6 lists specific evaluation activities for four different levels of evaluation: systems resource management, client utilization, outcome of intervention, and community impact. Also shown are management tasks that would be subject to evaluation at these four levels. Thus the organizational significance of evaluation is shown operationally, along with the possible specificity of criteria.

**TABLE 10.6.**

EVALUATIVE DOMAINS: TYPICAL CRITERIA AND MEASUREMENT TOOLS

| Evaluative Domains | Typical Criteria and Informational Requirements | Typical Methodological Tools, Procedures, and Indices |
|---|---|---|
| Effort measurement | (information about the amount and distribution of resources put into the program): | Management information systems |
| Input | Sources of income and expenditures | Explicit structural and process standards mandated by law, regulations, and accreditation bodies |
| | Allocation of staff time | Quality assurance procedures such as utilization review and peer review |
| | Numbers and types of clients | Capacity for effort as reflected by indices of service availability, accessibility, comprehensiveness, and integration |
| | How dollars, staff, and clients are interrelated | |
| Performance measurement | (information about the outcomes and effectiveness of program effort): | Scales measuring client functioning and status |
| Output | Clients' acceptance of services offered | Scales assessing client satisfaction |
| | Improvement in clients' status | Goal-oriented idiosyncratic scales developed for specific clients |
| | Changes in incidence or prevalence of problems addressed by programs | Rates of successful referrals for multiproblem clients |
| | Acceptability of services to clients | Range of services available that are known to be necessary for specific communities |
| | Effective linkage of clients to other necessary and appropriate service resources | Enumeration of cultural, linguistic, psychological, geographic, and organizational barriers to service accessibility. Measurement of reduction in barriers to accessibility over time. |
| | Level of service availability and accessibility achieved over time | |
| Adequate measurement | (information about effort and performance relative to measures of community need or demand): | Review and analysis of mandated services or documented needs |
| | Match between efforts and needs | Undertake needs–resources assessment methods |

| | | |
|---|---|---|
| *Output* / Need | Adequacy of performance effectiveness relative to level of need | Review and analyze management information system and outcome assessment data to assess client utilization rates relative to known service needs, mandated target populations, and high risk groups |
| | Appropriateness of clients being served relative to high risk groups or mandated target populations | |
| | Awareness of services among citizenry | Survey citizens' awareness of available services |
| Efficiency measurement | (information about how effort is organized so as to get greatest *performance* and adequacy): | Calculation of cost per unit of service |
| *Output* / Input | Cost of providing effective services | Cost–outcome and cost–effectiveness comparisons using management information system data and outcome assessment data |
| | Comparisons of the efficiency and efficacy of different programs or methods of service | Cost–effort–outcome–effectiveness comparisons for different target groups |
| | | Efficiency studies to compare different organizational methods in costs and effectiveness |
| Process measurement | (information about the underlying processes by which effort is translated into outcome): | Descriptive, correlational, and experimental methodologies that vary type or amount of independent variables and measures immediate and long range dependent variables |
| Outcome = *f*(Effort) | Specification of salient attributes, recipient characteristics, contextual conditions, and the potency and range of effects associated with the program | |
| | Identification of causal relations between effort and outcome | Alternative quasi-experimental research designs |
| | | Replication of studies demonstrating causal relationships |
| | Establish maximal generalizability of effects to other environments | Studies designed to establish and enhance data reliability and validity |
| | Control or explain other factors, independent of program effort, that could possibly account for program outcomes | Decision-theoretic approaches to maximizing the quality of administrative decisions and thereby program efforts and outcomes |
| | | Operation research methodologies |
| | | Multisite, collaborative randomized clinical trials |

*Source:* Suchman 1967:7.

Both general and more specific kinds of criteria have been illustrated above. The generalized nature of human services, and of evaluation research itself, has raised the question whether there is some general model that can subsume all evaluative criteria. Stamps (1978) sees two models: the goal model; and the goal-free model. The first is concerned with issues such as effectiveness; the latter with the intrinsic worth of a project. The goal-free model may not really obtain, however, since it may be asserted that goals always exist, even implicitly. One ultimate goal posited as an overall evaluative criterion is social justice—a "minimum-of-regret standard" for those who participate in a system (Keeley 1978). At present, however, no single model serves as a consistent guide for evaluation activities.

**Accountability**  Professional accountability for service delivery has become an increasingly pressing responsibility in the area of human services. This responsibility encompasses not only policy makers and program designers but all levels of program personnel. In competing for scarce resources, it is imperative that each service organization clearly delineate the scope of its charge, clearly define its mission, and optimally organize its present resources to achieve goals and objectives consistent with the organization's mission. Stretch (1978) asserts that every human service worker must participate in providing valid documentation that their efforts were well managed and that the effects of their efforts were defensible. Unless human service professionals are careful to delineate what they expect to accomplish and, in turn, to produce evidence of results, those who control available resources will impose their own special criteria by which services will be judged. These criteria may well not correspond to what professionals in the human service field consider feasible or desirable. Service accountability requires that the development, deployment, and delivery of human services be managed so as to satisfy the three criteria of relevancy, effectiveness, and efficiency.

The roles required include planning, program design, allocation of resources, evaluation, and resource development. Accountability must be documented according to its relevance to a specific need, which can and should be met through a human service organization's professional activities, as well as fiscal accountability, which verifies that budgeted funds were allocated appropriately and were expended in accordance with acceptable financial accounting principles. There is also the exercise of performance and efficiency accountability: the former documents the reality that relevant resources were well targeted and brought about the program activities that were intended; the latter documents the fact that the intended outcomes were achieved with the least possible expenditure of resources.

In carrying out the simultaneous levels of accountability, the human service manager must be conscious of, and address himself to, the legitimate interests of a number of constituencies and audiences, which include: the community and its sociopolitical structures; the client-consumer; the professional audiences; the internal organizational staff; and the system as an integrated whole.

First, services are designed and justified as an institutional mechanism to further the overall goals of a given community, communities have varying commitments and levels of objectives to be served by human services. The human service manager and evaluator must make himself aware of his community's priorities and his community's value structure, in which he must operate if he is to carry out the mandates of the community he is serving. At a minimum, diversified community representatives should serve on the board of directors of the agency, in order to provide constantly the interests and objectives of the community as a whole.

Second, the human services manager and evaluator must be sensitive to the changing needs and rising expectations of the client-consumer group his agency serves. Recent class action suits have shown the need to be directly accountable to client needs and community interests. Here, evaluation research may provide some useful baselines. For example, Campbell (1979) found for two districts of New York State that, of 139 consumers of day care, homemaker, and counseling services, only 24 were aware of opportunities to participate in the planning of social service programs.

Third, continuing changes and developments in professional ideas and technologies acquire new staffing and service delivery patterns. For example, human service workers are currently being called upon to develop better interdisciplinary approaches that engage new solutions to redress persistent and insistent social problems.

Fourth, staff members need a climate of continual renewal. Management must provide both job incentives and professional inducements to upgrade constantly the milieu for growth and development in an agency. Functions of staff must be periodically reassessed to determine relevance and appropriateness. If necessary, new structures or realignments of existing structures must be developed to carry out essential functions responsive to changes in the organizational mission and to the full range of objectives that flow from the central mission.

Fifth, critical to increased service integration and coordination is the provision of network of services relevant to meeting changing needs and rising expectations. Relatedness is a central managerial concept within a general systems orientation period. Thus, professional managers should see the full complement of his services as part of a larger community response to the needs to be served. Such conceptualizations open doors for closer collaboration and creative interfacings between public and private sectors, for servicing of commonly held objectives (Stretch 1978). The most distinctive contribution of program evaluation is the introduction of information about program effects and the relative cost-effectiveness of program management decisions.

Several emerging external and internal forces are compelling most human service organizations to become accountable for the services they provide to society. Hospitals, for example, in response to the mandate for comprehensive care, now need to institute community records (Sigmond 1978). As a starting point, the emerging external forces of social accountability may be traced to dissatisfaction with macroeconomic statistics. Olson (1969) makes this point clearly, when he states:

> "For all their virtues, the national income statistics don't tell us what we really need to know about the condition of American society. They leave out most of the things that make life worth living. They leave out the learning of our children, the quality of our culture, the advance of science, the compatibility of our families, the liberties and democratic processes we cherish. They neglect the pollution of the environment, the deprivations of crime, and the toll of illness." (p. 86)

Because many significant aspects of the services needed and received by citizens are ignored in national income data, new and different indicators of service performance are emerging to provide better information for decision making. Sorensen and Grove (1968) point out that an indication of pressure for service accountability is in the activities of auditors who serve legislative bodies such as the General Accounting Office, which is the primary auditing force of the Congress, recently establishing performance or operational auditing standards.

> The key feature of the standards is the pronouncement that an audit of a governmental entity should encompass not only an examination of financial transactions but also a review of efficiency and economy in the use of resources and, more significantly, an evaluation as to whether desired results are being effectively achieved. (Granof 1973:1079).

Accountability is now being required at every level of legislation—federal, state, county, and municipal. Community mental health centers, for example, possess two major accountability objectives: (1) evaluating the effectiveness of the center's programs in servicing the needs of the residents of its area; and (2) monitoring the quality of the center's services. With greater frequency, external agencies are asking for evidence of program outcome or impact as it stands in the relationship of the benefits to expenditures—especially when public monies are involved (Zussman and Wurster 1975). Internally, the program manager is often faced with limited or decreasing resources to meet varied needs and requires evaluation to aid in the planning and controlling of program operations.

Managerial decisions about levels of funding require performance information that is often remarkably similar to the information sought by external agencies. The emerging forces of accountability, as exemplified by external GAO evaluation standards and internal program evaluation needs, pose problems for human service management information and decision systems.

Sorenson and Phipps (1975) discuss three methods for accountability in program management: the social indicators approach; the program planning and budgeting system approach (PPBS); and cost–benefit analysis. Only the last method will be described here. Among ways of measuring accountability in evaluation of human service programs, three general types of evaluation emerge from the literature: monitoring techniques; social research techniques; and cost-analytic techniques (Tripodi, Fellin, and Epstein 1971). Monitoring techniques include accountability or administrative audits and time–motion studies. Heavy emphasis is usually given to resource input and process activities. Process statistics on the process of service delivery, including measures of efficiency, currently exist and have been applied (Smith and Sorenson 1974). Process measures have included audits of records—for instance, case-by-case evaluation, direct observation of staff and program activities, examination of client and patient conditions, testing of professional staff, and comparison of actual and desired profiles or ratios. Social research techniques include experiments or quasi-experiments, surveys (including client satisfaction), and case studies.

Cost-analytic techniques include approaches where resource consumption is a common element of the analysis. There is a range of techniques from which to choose: from cost accounting to cost finding for programs, units of services, and from episodes to techniques that link resource consumption to outcome or benefits, such as cost–outcome and cost–benefit analysis.

As measures of human service accountability and program management, cost-outcome and cost-effectiveness analyses are interrelated. Cost-outcome analysis ascertains programmatic resources consumed to achieve a change to a measure of client functioning (e.g., symptoms, social performance). Cost-effectiveness analysis relies upon the comparison of cost outcomes to identify the most effective programs in terms of beneficial outcome to the cost of programs, modalities, or treatment techniques.

This service accountability measure must be broken down into manageable measurement problem areas. The cost-effectiveness approach is advocated as a viable solution to problems of service accountability and program management because it properly attempts to divide the complex service measures in causal networks into manageable units.

Another aspect of program evaluation is quality assurance, which is also required by recent federal health legislation. These are the two primary mechanisms by which human service programs must evaluate their own activities to ensure accountability to regulatory agencies, funding sources, and consumers of services. Recent legislative emphasis on dual purchase to self-evaluation signals the need for clarification of the differences between quality assurance and program evaluation. In contrast to program evaluation, quality assurance activities have more extensive legislative mandates; rely more extensively on peer review and substantially less on administrative review; is client and service-provider specific; is organized to assure adequacy and appropriateness of care and to control cost by preventing overutilization; and relies on methods that focus on specific service plans and service transactions—and hence that involve minimal data aggregation, focus on service records, and do not rely on computer applications for data processing (Woy, Lund, and Attkisson 1978).

Accountability has changed the relationship of community programs to funding and regulatory agencies. Organizations do not now define the services they offer primarily by their service process but by reference to a standard lexicon of problem definitions and service step objectives. Objectives include not only outcome, productivity, and cost of individual services, but also the impact objectives that are defined in relation to overall estimated community needs.

## CONCLUSION

The increasing importance of evaluation, integration, and systems concepts in the human services has not come about by coincidence. Evaluation—in its formative aspect—will provide increasing guidance in the development of a project or policy; evaluation—in its summative aspect—will provide more wide-ranging information on the processes and impacts of a project, thus giving more guidance for future projects in the planning and implementation phases.

In the meantime, there are many gaps to fill within the evaluation phase. Human services in particular are difficult to evaluate. Rossi (1978) offers two reasons for this: the theories underlying delivery are often deficient; and delivery is highly operator-dependent—and thus highly transformed in delivery in ways that tend to negate the intended treatment effects. The second factor may not be as readily remediable as the first.

# REFERENCES

Allegra, M. and S. R. Sauber. 1976. Local Community analysis and program development. Manuscript, Providence, R.I.: Brown University.

Attkisson, C. C. and A. Broskowski. 1978. Evaluation and the emerging human service concept. In C. C. Attkisson, A. Hargreaves, and J. Horowitz, eds., *Evaluation of Human Service Programs*. New York: Academic Press.

Attkisson, C. C., T. R. Brown, and W. A. Hargreaves. 1978. Roles and functions of evaluation in human service programs. In C. C. Attkisson et al., eds. *Evaluation of Human Service Programs*. New York: Academic Press.

Bellin, E., R. Kavaler, and A. Schwartz. 1978. Phase one of consumer participation in policies of 22 voluntary hospitals in New York City. In R. Kovner and P. Neuhauser, eds., *Health Services Management: Readings and Commentary*. Ann Arbor, Mich.: Health Administration Press

Broskowski, A. and F. Baker. 1974. Professional, organizational, and social barriers to primary prevention. *American Journal of Orthopsychiatry,* 44:707–719.

Broskowski, A. and J. Driscoll. 1978. The organizational context of program evaluation. In C. C. Attkisson, W. A. Hargreaves, and M. J. Horowitz, eds., *Evaluation of Human Service Programs*.

Broskowski, A. and H. C. Schulberg. 1974. A model training program for clinical research and development. *Professional Psychology,* 5:133–39.

Broskowski, A. and T. Smith. 1974. Manpower development for human service systems. In D. Harshberger and R. Maley, eds., *Behavior Analysis and Systems Analysis: An Integrative Approach to Mental Health Programs*. Kalamazoo, Mich.: Behaviordelia.

Burck, H. D. 1974. Needed: More evaluation, not research. *Personnel and Guidance Journal* (April).

Campbell, A. 1979. Consumer participation in planning social service programs. *Social Work,* 24(2):159–162.

Coleman, J. S. et al. 1966. Equality of Educational Opportunity. Superintendent of Documents, Catalog No. FS 5.238,38001. Washington, D.C.: GPO.

CSG. 1974. *Human Services Integration: State Functions in Implementation*. Lexington, Ky.: Council on State Governments.

Davis, H. R. 1973. Change in innovation. In S. Feldman, ed., *Administration in Mental Health Services*. Springfield, Ill.: Charles C. Thomas.

Davis, H. R. and S. E. Slasin. 1975. The utilization of evaluation. In E. L. Struening and M. Guttentag, eds., *Handbook of Evaluation Research*, vol. 1. Beverly Hills, Calif.: Sage.

Demone, H. N., Jr. 1973. Human services at state and local levels and the integration of mental health. In G. Caplan, ed., *The American Handbook of Psychology*, vol. 11. New York: Basic Books.

DHEW. 1972. *Integration of Human Services in HEW: An Evaluation of Services Integration Projects*, vol. 1. Publications no. Srs 73-02102. Washington, D.C.: DHEW.

Dumbaugh, A. 1978. The evaluation of performance in the management of health care organizations. In D. R. Kovner and P. Neuhauser, eds., *Health Services Management: Readings and Commentary*. Ann Arbor, Mich.: Health Administration Press.

Dumont, M. P. 1967. Tavern culture. The sustenance of homeless men. *American Journal of Orthopsychiatry*, 37:938–945.

Dyer, H. S. 1972. Vice-President of Educational Testing Service, Princeton, N.J. Speech.

Ebel, R. 1965. *Measuring Educational Achievement*. Englewood Cliffs, N.J.: Prentice-Hall.

Edwards, W., M. Guttentag, and K. Snapper. 1975. A decision theoretic approach to evaluation research. In E. L. Struening and M. Guttentag, *Handbook of Evaluation Research*, vol. 1. Beverly Hills, Calif.: Sage Publications.

Emery, F. and E. Trist. 1965. The causal texture of organizational environments. *Human Relations*, 18:21–32.

Flaherty, E. W. and J. A. Morell. 1978. Evaluation: Manifestations of a new field. *Evaluation in Program Planning*.

Garwick, G. and S. Lampman. 1972. Typical problems bring patients to a community mental health center. *Community Mental Health Journal*, 8:271–280.

Goldstein, S., C. Marcus, and M. Perkins. 1978. The nonutilization of evaluation research. *Pacific Sociological Review*, 21(1):21–44.

Gottesfeld, H. et al. 1973. *Strategies in Innovative Human Services Programs* New York: Behavior Publications.

Gruber, M. 1974. Total administration. *Social Work*, 19(5):625–637.

Hoole, W. 1978. *Evaluation Research and Development Activities*. Beverly Hills, Calif.: Sage.

Horton, G. T. and J. H. Miller. 1974. *Alternative Approaches to Human Services Planning*. Arlington, Va.: Human Services Institute for Children and Families.

HSICF. 1974. Approaches to human services planning. Arlington, Va.: Human Services Institute for Children and Families.

Hunt, W. J. 1972. Training program for bartenders as mental health referral agents: The preliminary report. Milwaukee, Wisc.: Milwaukee County Health Association.

Kaplan, H. 1973. Institutions and community mental health: A paradox in Wyatt V. Stickney. *Community Mental Health Journal*, 9:34–37.

Keeley, L. 1978. A social-justice approach to organizational evaluation. *Administrative Science Quarterly*, 23(2):272–292.

Kiresuk, T. and R. Sherman. 1968. Goal attainment scaling: A general method of evaluating comprehensive community mental health programs. *Community Mental Health Journal*, 4:443–453.

Knowles, M. 1970. *The Modern Practice of Adult Education*. New York: Association Press.

Krumboltz, J. D. 1974. An accountability model for counselors. *Personnel and Guidance Journal*, 52:639–646.

Lessinger, L. M. 1972. Toward a humanistic accountability. *Impact*, 2(3):4–11.

Malcolm, A. H. 1974. Bartenders being trained to provide counseling as well as drinks. *New York Times* (October 13).

NIMH. 1971. *Planning for Creative Change in Mental Health Services: Information Sources and How to Use Them*. Publication no. (HSM) 71-9058. Washington, D.C.: National Institute of Mental Health.

Nikolas, N. A. 1972. The pros and cons of accountability. *Impact*, 2(3):24–25.

Register, D. C. 1974. Community mental health: For whose community? *American Journal of Public Health*, 64(9):886–893.

Reiff, R. and F. Riessman. 1965. The indigenous nonprofessional: A strategy of change in community action and community mental health program. *Community Mental Health*, monograph no. 1.

Rossi, H. 1978. Issues in the evaluation of human services delivery. *Evaluation Quarterly*, 2(4):573–599.

Sauber, S. R. 1974. *Preventive Educational Intervention for Mental Health*. Cambridge, Mass.: Ballinger.

Sauber, S. R. 1975. Human services: An interdisciplinary-interorganizational course. Providence, R.I.: Brown University. Manuscript.

Sauber, S. R. 1976. Community analysis and program planning. Paper presented at New England Conference on mental health treatment evaluation. Brown University, Providence, R.I.

Schulberg, H. C. and F. Baker. 1969. Program evaluation models and the implementation of research findings. In H. C. Schulberg, A. Sheldon, and F. Baker, eds., *Program Evaluation in the Health Fields*. New York: Behavioral.

Schulberg, H. C. and F. Baker. 1979. *Program Evaluator in the Health Fields*, vol. 2. New York: Human Sciences Press.

Sigmond, M. 1978. Changing hospital goals. In D. R. Kovner and P. Neuhauser, eds., *Health Services Management: Reading and Commentary*. Ann Arbor, Mich.: Health Administrative Press.

Smith, T. S. and J. E. Sorensen. 1974. *Integrated Management Information Systems for Community Mental Health Centers*. DHEW Publication no. ADM 75-165. Rockville, Md.: National Institute of Mental Health.

Snyder, J. A. 1971. The use of gatekeepers in crisis management. *Bulletin of Suicidology*, 8:39–44.

Sorensen, J. E. and D. W. Phipps. 1975. Cost finding and rate setting for community mental health centers. DHEW Publication no. ADM 76-291. Washington, D.C.: GPO.

Stamps, L. 1978. *Ambulatory Care Systems,* vol. 3: *Evaluation of Out-Patient Facilities.* Lexington, Mass.: Lexington Books.

Stretch, J. J. 1978. Increasing accountability for human services administrators. *Social Casework,* 59(6):323–329.

Stufflebeam, D. I. et al. 1971. *Educational Evaluation and Decision Making.* Itasca, Ill.: F. E. Peacock.

Suchman, E. A. 1967. *Evaluation research: Principles and Practices in Public Service and Social Action Programs.* New York: Russell Sage Foundation.

*Team Development Manual for the Human Service Advocacy Project.* 1972. Regional Office of Human Services. Lyn, Mass. Publication No. 1M-2-73-075—460.

Tripodi, T., P. Fellin, and I. Epstein. 1971. *Social Program Evaluation: Guidelines for Health, Education, and Welfare Administrators.* Itasca, Ill.: Peacock.

Vidaver, R. M. and J. E. Carlson. 1973. A new framework for baccalaureate careers in human services. *American Journal of Psychiatry,* 130:474–478.

Weiss, C. H. 1972. *Evaluation Research.* Englewood Cliffs, N.J.: Prentice-Hall.

Weiss, C. H. 1978. The usefulness of social research for decision-makers in mental health. Doctoral dissertation, Columbia University, 1977. *Dissertation Abstracts International* 38: 5730A. University Microfilms No. 78-02, 349.

Weiss, C. H., ed. 1972. *Evaluating Action Programs.* Boston, Mass.: Allyn & Bacon.

Wilkinson, G. L. 1972. Needed: information on cost analysis. *Education Technology,* 12:33–38.

Williams, T. A. and J. H. Johnson. 1979. *Mental Health in the Twenty-First Century.* Lexington, Mass.: Lexington Books.

Woy, J. R., D. A. Lund, and C. C. Attkisson. 1978. Quality assistance in human service program evaluation. In C. C. Attkisson, W. A. Hargreaves, and M. J. Horowitz, *Evaluation of Human Services Programs.* New York: Academic Press.

Wysong, H. E. 1972. Accountability: Foibled fable or solution? *Impact,* 2(3):32–37.

Zussman, J. and C. R. Wurster eds. 1975. *Program Evaluation: Alcohol, Drug Abuse, and Mental Health Services.* Lexington, Mass.: Lexington Books.

# AUTHOR INDEX

# SUBJECT INDEX

## DATE DUE

PRINTED IN U.S.A.